# CIVIL RIGHTS MOVEMENT

**Selected titles in ABC-CLIO's Perspectives in American Social History series**

American Revolution: People and Perspectives

British Colonial America: People and Perspectives

Civil War: People and Perspectives

Early Republic: People and Perspectives

Industrial Revolution: People and Perspectives

Jacksonian and Antebellum Age: People and Perspectives

Making of the American West: People and Perspectives

Reconstruction: People and Perspectives

PERSPECTIVES IN
**AMERICAN SOCIAL HISTORY**

# Civil Rights Movement

## People and Perspectives

Michael Ezra, Editor
Peter C. Mancall, Series Editor

A B C • C L I O

Santa Barbara, California • Denver, Colorado • Oxford, England

Copyright 2009 by ABC-CLIO, Inc.

**Library of Congress Cataloging-in-Publication Data**

Civil rights movement : people and perspectives / Michael Ezra, editor.
p. cm.—(Perspectives in American social history)
Includes bibliographical references and index.
ISBN 978-1-59884-037-7 (hardcover : alk. paper) — ISBN 978-1-59884-038-4 (ebook)
1. African Americans—Civil rights—History—20th century.   2. Civil rights movements—United States—History—20th century.   3. African American civil rights workers—Biography.   4. Civil rights workers—United States—Biography.   5. United States—Race relations.   I. Ezra, Michael, 1972—

E185.61.C 6167 2009
323.1196073—dc22

2008045738

12  11  10  09    1  2  3  4  5

This book is also available on the World Wide Web as an ebook.
Visit www.abc-clio.com for details.

ABC-CLIO, Inc.
130 Cremona Drive, P.O. Box 1911
Santa Barbara, California 93116–1911

This book is printed on acid-free paper ∞

Manufactured in the United States of America

# Contents

# Series Introduction

Social history is, simply put, the study of past societies. More specifically, social historians attempt to describe societies in their totality, and hence often eschew analysis of politics and ideas. Though many social historians argue that it is impossible to understand how societies functioned without some consideration of the ways that politics works on a daily basis or what ideas could be found circulating at any given time, they tend to pay little attention to the formal arenas of electoral politics or intellectual currents. In the United States, social historians have been engaged in describing components of the population that had earlier often escaped formal analysis, notably women, members of ethnic or cultural minorities, or those who had fewer economic opportunities than the elite.

Social history became a vibrant discipline in the United States after it had already gained enormous influence in Western Europe. In France, social history in its modern form emerged with the rising prominence of a group of scholars associated with the journal *Annales Économies, Sociétés, Civilisations* (or *Annales ESC,* as it is known). In its pages and in a series of books from historians affiliated with the École des hautes études en sciences sociales in Paris, brilliant historians such as Marc Bloch, Jacques Le Goff, and Emmanuel Le Roy Ladurie described seemingly every aspect of French society. Among the masterpieces of this historical reconstruction was Fernand Braudel's monumental study, *The Mediterranean and the Mediterranean World in the Age of Philip II,* published first in Paris in 1946 and in a revised edition in English in 1972. In this work Braudel argued that the only way to understand a place in its totality was to describe its environment, its social and economic structures, and its political systems. In Britain the emphasis of social historians has been less on questions of environment, per se, than in a description of human communities in all their complexities. For example, social historians there have taken advantage of that nation's remarkable local archives to reconstruct the history of the family and details of its rural past. Works such as Peter Laslett's *The World We Have Lost,* first printed in 1966, and the multiauthored *Agrarian History of England and Wales,* which began to appear in print in 1967, showed that painstaking work could reveal the lives and habits of individuals who never previously attracted the interest of biographers, demographers, or most historians.

Social history in the United States gained a large following in the second half of the 20th century, especially during the 1960s and 1970s. Its development sprang from political, technical, and intellectual impulses deeply embedded in the culture of the modern university. The politics of civil rights and social reform fueled the passions of historians who strove to tell the stories of the underclass. They benefited from the adoption by historians of statistical analysis, which allowed scholars to trace where individuals lived; how often they moved; what kinds of jobs they took; and whether their economic status declined, stagnated, or improved over time. As history departments expanded, many who emerged from graduate schools focused their attention on groups previously ignored or marginalized. Women's history became a central concern among American historians, as did the history of African Americans, Native Americans, Latinos, and others. These historians pushed historical study in the United States farther away from the study of formal politics and intellectual trends. Though few Americanists could achieve the technical brilliance of some social historians in Europe, collectively they have been engaged in a vast act of description, with the goal of describing seemingly every facet of life from 1492 to the present.

The 16 volumes in this series together represent the continuing efforts of historians to describe American society. Most of the volumes focus on chronological areas, from the broad sweep of the colonial era to the more narrowly defined collections of essays on the eras of the Cold War, the baby boom, and the United States in the age of the Vietnam War. The series also includes entire volumes on the epochs that defined the nation, the American Revolution and the Civil War, as well as volumes dedicated to the process of westward expansion, women's rights, and African American history.

This social history series derives its strength from the talented editors of individual volumes. Each editor is an expert in his or her own field who selected and organized the contents of his or her volume. Editors solicited other experienced historians to write individual essays. Every volume contains first-rate analysis complemented by lively anecdotes designed to reveal the complex contours of specific historical moments. The many illustrations to be found in these volumes testify too to the recognition that any society can be understood not only by the texts that its participants produce but also by the images that they craft. Primary source documents in each volume allow interested readers to pursue some specific topics in greater depth, and each volume contains a chronology to provide guidance to the flow of events over time. These tools—anecdotes, images, texts, and timelines—allow readers to gauge the inner workings of the United States in particular periods and yet also to glimpse connections between eras.

The articles in these volumes testify to the abundant strengths of historical scholarship in the United States in the early years of the 21st century. Despite the occasional academic contest that flares into public notice, or the self-serving cant of politicians who want to manipulate the nation's past for partisan ends—for example, in debates over the Second Amendment to the U.S. Constitution and what it means about potential limits to the rights of gun ownership—the articles here all reveal the vast increase in knowledge of the American past that has taken place over the previous half century.

Social historians do not dominate history faculties in American colleges and universities, but no one could deny them a seat at the intellectual table. Without their efforts, intellectual, cultural, and political historians would be hard pressed to understand why certain ideas circulated when they did, why some religious movements prospered or foundered, how developments in fields such as medicine and engineering reflected larger concerns, and what shaped the world we inhabit.

Fernand Braudel and his colleagues envisioned entire laboratories of historians in which scholars working together would be able to produce *histoire totale*: total history. Historians today seek more humble goals for our collective enterprise. But as the richly textured essays in these volumes reveal, scholarly collaboration has in fact brought us much closer to that dream. These volumes do not and cannot include every aspect of American history. However, every page reveals something interesting or valuable about how American society functioned. Together, these books suggest the crucial necessity of stepping back to view the grand complexities of the past rather than pursuing narrower prospects and lesser goals.

Peter C. Mancall
*Series Editor*

# Introduction

Civil Rights Movement: People and Perspectives explores the history of the struggle by African Americans for freedom, justice, and equality. History textbooks usually define the civil rights movement as taking place from 1954 to 1968, beginning with the U.S. Supreme Court's landmark *Brown v. Board of Education* decision, culminating with the assassination of Martin Luther King Jr., and existing predominantly as a southern struggle against segregation and state-supported racial inequalities that prevented blacks from realizing first-class citizenship. With its focus on heroic figures like Rosa Parks and large-scale protests like the March on Washington, the standard civil rights narrative has become an important part of how individuals learn U.S. history. Recently, however, historians have challenged the traditional version of events in an effort to reintroduce lost aspects of the movement into U.S. memory. This book balances the traditional civil rights model with these attempts to expand the definition of the movement.

The civil rights movement accounts for only a small portion of the centuries-long black freedom struggle—the historical battle by African Americans for self-determination. The origins of the black freedom struggle can be traced as far back as the Middle Passage of the 1500s, when Africans were transported to the New World as part of the Atlantic slave trade. Some captives, rather than accept a future as chattel, abandoned ship midvoyage and drowned. In the New World, blacks resisted enslavement and cultivated their humanity in myriad ways. Slaves never abandoned their African heritage. They invented new cultural forms, created societies, developed skills, and started families. They also resisted slavery directly. Slaves would feign illness, break tools, aid runaways, plot rebellions, and even murder their captors. As long as there has been antiblack discrimination in North America, there has been an accompanying black freedom struggle. At no time did African Americans simply accept their oppression, and in every succeeding historical era they raised the level of their struggle for equality. Although blacks have constituted the overwhelming force behind their own liberation, nonblack allies, including whites, have also lent support.

There is good reason why the era called the King Years (1954–1968) has become the one most prominently associated with the civil rights movement:

the period was characterized by five conditions that created an unprecedented moment in the history of the black freedom struggle and led to lasting gains in the fight for equality.

First, massive grassroots activism marked the era. An unparalleled black insurgency, bolstered by thousands of first-time protesters and freedom fighters of all ages and backgrounds, created a groundswell of participation in the freedom struggle. These numbers gave the movement vitality and momentum, ensuring its survival after setbacks, despite ferocious opposition by recalcitrant whites.

Second, during the King Years the black freedom struggle received unmatched support from nonblack allies, particularly whites. While blacks primarily drove the civil rights movement, whites were more willing to help than at any time before or since. They donated money, lent their skills, and even gave their lives in an effort to aid the cause. The period was also distinguished by widespread white sympathy for the black freedom struggle. In a country dominated numerically, politically, and economically by whites, this peculiar climate had a positive impact on the movement's chances to make gains.

Third, during the years 1954–1968, the black freedom struggle enjoyed significant backing from all three branches of government. Supreme Court decisions like *Brown* gave freedom fighters the legal backing necessary to successfully demand equality. Congress passed a series of civil rights laws that closed constitutional loopholes and gave the federal government the ability to enforce antidiscrimination statutes. In King's final years, during the presidency of Lyndon Johnson, the White House supported the movement through speeches, with executive orders, and by mobilizing federal resources.

Fourth, the African American freedom struggle received extensive international support. Less than a decade before *Brown*, the United Nations adopted the Universal Declaration of Human Rights, and many of its member countries questioned the moral authority of the United States on the basis of its treatment of blacks. During the Cold War, as the United States vied with the Soviet Union to win the loyalty and confidence of Third World nations, this issue held particular significance, since the federal government could highlight civil rights gains to address international misgivings about a country that appeared to be torn apart by racism.

Fifth, the King Years were influenced by a sympathetic mass media that kept the black freedom struggle in the news and portrayed its participants as protagonists. On a daily basis, in newspapers and on television, Americans were faced with positive images of the civil rights movement being positioned as the nation's moral conscience.

Unique philosophical and tactical elements also characterized the black freedom struggle during the era. The movement's dominant ideology was integration, creating patriotic overtones that positioned its primary goals as first-class citizenship and full access to American society for blacks. Churches were paramount to the civil rights struggle, serving as both spiritual guides and gathering places, giving the movement overt moral authority. Combining righteous indignation, Christian faith, and mass protest, nonviolent freedom fighters took to the streets a campaign that had already been launched within the courts.

People have come to understand the civil rights movement as one whose primary actors were clergy and their organizational structures. According to this perspective, because the South was where the majority of black Americans lived, and because it was where legalized segregation existed, it became the site of mass-action protests designed to test gains that had been made in the courts. *Civil Rights Movement: People and Perspectives* is faithful to this account, exploring the people, places, and events that have come to typify traditional narratives about the black freedom struggle during the King Years.

*Civil Rights Movement: People and Perspectives,* however, also recognizes that traditional civil rights narratives have not always adequately chronicled the story. These narratives have not tied the movement to its pre-King roots. They have overlooked the significance of black nationalism to the movement. Traditional accounts also spotlight a few charismatic leaders at the expense of the everyday people who made the movement happen. They obscure the importance of freedom fights outside the South and the economic campaigns that occurred in the shadow of mass political protest.

These deficiencies have driven a number of scholars to reject the King Years model and turn to the idea of a long civil rights movement that began well before the *Brown* case and continues into the present. This long civil rights movement model was most clearly articulated in a 2005 article entitled "The Long Civil Rights Movement and the Political Uses of the Past," by historian Jacquelyn Dowd Hall. The long civil rights paradigm stretches the boundaries and definition of the movement and frames the King Years as the classical phase of a much larger struggle. The long civil rights movement is not just a temporal description but also one that points to an expanded philosophical and tactical scope. It shifts the time period of the movement backward to its roots in the 1930s and 1940s. The long civil rights movement model takes into account black nationalism and understands that self-determination was as important a goal as integration. This new model shifts the limelight away from charismatic leaders and their organizational structures and perceives everyday people as primary actors. The long civil rights movement also explores how the black freedom struggle was fought on multiple fronts, including the labor movement. It recognizes that there was a cultural aspect to the black freedom struggle, an explosion of appreciation for and investment in black culture that continues today to have great effect on our society. The long civil rights movement expands our geographical understanding of the movement, taking into consideration how the South was tied to the Northeast, Midwest, and West Coast. It also explores relationships between the civil rights movement and anticolonial struggles for self-determination by people in Latin America, Africa, and Asia and shows how the African American freedom struggle inspired countless other movements in the United States—by disabled people, women, Native Americans, Chicanos and Latinos, gays and lesbians, and Asian Americans.

The long civil rights movement theory has fostered a reinvigorated campaign to defend a third way of understanding the black freedom struggle of the mid- to late 20th century, one that divides the King Years and the decade that followed into two overlapping parts: a civil rights movement from 1955 to 1968 and a black power movement from 1965 to 1975. The driving force behind the renewal of this perspective, which for a long time dominated civil rights scholarship, was a 2007 article by historians Sundiata Keita Cha-Jua and Clarence Lang entitled "The 'Long Movement' as Vampire: Temporal and Spatial Fallacies in Recent Black Freedom Studies."

Scholars who defend this civil rights/black power perspective believe that proponents of the long civil rights movement theory define the black freedom struggle and its phases too loosely. In particular, defenders of the civil rights/black power model challenge four suppositions that the long civil rights movement theory commonly takes for granted. First, the black freedom struggle was a national social movement, not a series of local struggles. Second, the civil rights/black power era transcended the period 1955–1975. Third, the civil rights movement and black power movement should not be distinguished from one another. Fourth, southern racial oppression was not distinct from that of other regions, and the southern freedom struggle was not much different from those that sprung up outside the South. Those who stress the dichotomous civil rights/black power model reject all four of these propositions.

Instead, supporters of the civil rights/black power dichotomy believe that the civil rights movement and black power movement were distinctive campaigns that operated within specific time periods and took on radically different regional characteristics. These scholars, led by black power movement historian Peniel Joseph, argue that the black power movement was distinctive from the civil rights movement in four major ways. First, the primary focus of the black power movement was black self-determination rather than access to American institutions. Second, the black power movement consciously connected local struggles to global ones. Third, the black power movement advocated a revolutionary remaking of American society rather than its reform. Fourth, black power activists were willing to use self-defense proactively or engage in revolutionary violence. They were neither nonviolent nor merely reactive in their use of self-defense. Supporters of this perspective also insist that the black power movement fundamentally transformed and redefined American democracy by legitimizing the black presence in American cultural, educational, and political institutions. *Civil Rights Movement: People and Perspectives* incorporates these important ideas into its historical analysis of the black freedom struggle.

By taking seriously the traditional model that focuses on the black freedom struggle during the King Years as well as the theory of the long civil rights movement and the idea of a civil rights movement/black power movement dichotomy, *Civil Rights Movement: People and Perspectives* provides readers with new ways of understanding this critical aspect of American history. Each of the eight chapters and four reference sections of this book takes into account all three methods of defining the civil rights movement.

In Chapter 1, Marsha Darling examines the early pioneers who laid the groundwork for the civil rights revolution of the 1950s and 1960s. She discusses the philosophical roots of the movement, accounting for the roles played by early black nationalists, black clubwomen, and integrationists. The chapter pays particular attention to the legal campaign for equal rights led by the National Association for the Advancement of Colored People (NAACP), investigating how lawyers like Charles Hamilton Houston fought for precedents that would eventually lead the Supreme Court to its *Brown* decision. The chapter gives readers an expanded history of the civil rights struggle that considers how issues like labor rights, school funding, and city services informed the early movement.

Darling also recognizes that it is impossible to discuss the civil rights movement without considering the importance of World War II. Federal military desegregation acknowledged the citizenship rights of African Americans who had fought and died to preserve American liberty. Ideologically, the war marginalized those who would try to legitimize racism, since it contradicted the American stance against Hitler. Tactically, the war created a black leadership class that returned home ready to lead the civil rights revolution. Military service gave some veterans experience as officers. They gained organizational skills, experience with arms, and confidence not only in their right to first-class status but also in their ability to lead struggles for it. The horrors of war prepared veterans for the terror and repression visited upon them by racists who battled ferociously to maintain white supremacy. The political, ideological, and social impact of the war invigorated the black freedom struggle.

In Chapter 2, Francis Shor's work on student activism highlights the centrality of social issues to the civil rights movement, exploring how gender and generational differences led to philosophical and tactical debates within the struggle. The importance of this work comes from its treatment of movement ideology, particularly the debates that took place around the concepts of interracialism and black nationalism. Turning a spotlight on leaders like James Lawson and Ella Baker, Shor shows how white-dominated groups like Students for a Democratic Society interacted with black-led organizations like the Student Nonviolent Coordinating Committee. The chapter makes clear that the King Years stimulated belief that white people could become allies to the black freedom struggle, but it also reveals the limits of interracial cooperation. Although student activism during the civil rights movement was biracial, it had to be black-led in order to work. Blacks, not whites, made the fundamental decisions concerning the direction of the freedom struggle, and only when whites refused to accept this reality were they marginalized by black nationalists within the movement.

In Chapter 3, Jill Gill explores the fundamental role that clergy played during the movement. While a study of African American churches is at the heart of the chapter, Gill looks closely at how whites of all major U.S. religions—Protestants, Jews, Catholics—responded to the movement as both allies and foes. Paying attention to both clergy and their congregations, Gill encourages a bottom-up view of religion, reinforcing the idea that church leaders sometimes directed their congregations and other times altered their views in response to them. This important dynamic can be applied to other phases of the movement. While the historical record pays heed to the lawyers, politicians, and activists said to have led the movement, Gill's study reminds us that the rank and file often drove the agendas of those supposedly in charge.

Lauren Chambers, Aggie Ebrahimi, and Barbara McCaskill use Chapter 4 to take a traditional perspective that addresses the roles played by southern organizations and leaders. They focus on the most celebrated movement participants, synthesizing their most important works into a cohesive narrative. Included among the organizational structures the authors explore are the Montgomery Improvement Association, Women's Political Council, Student Nonviolent Coordinating Committee, Albany Movement, Southern Christian Leadership Conference, NAACP, Voter Education Project, Southern Regional Council, Alabama Christian Movement for Human Rights, Urban League, Nashville Student Movement, Congress of Racial Equality (CORE), Council of Federated Organizations, Mississippi Freedom Democratic Party, Deacons for Defense and Justice, and Poor People's Campaign. This comprehensive examination of the South is critical to any understanding of the classical phase of the civil rights movement.

In Chapter 5, Michael Ezra explores the civil rights movement beyond the South and focuses on how the NAACP and CORE carried the movement nationwide. Ezra's work illustrates how issues such as fair housing, labor rights, educational inequalities, and hiring practices were at the heart of the struggle. The chapter calls for reconsideration of the NAACP during the King Years, rejecting portrayals of the organization as retrograde and a hindrance to the progressive movement vanguard. Instead of judging the NAACP solely in terms of its conservative national office, Ezra views it as a loosely connected group of local branches that were in tune with the movement's cutting edge. Highlighting local militancy, Ezra repositions the NAACP as a vital part of the movement's classical phase.

Yusuf Nuruddin's work in Chapter 6 emphasizes the centrality of black nationalism to the long civil rights movement and counters the historical declension model, which positions the integrationist black freedom struggle during the King Years as triumphant and heroic and the black power movement that followed as its death knell. Resisting the tendency to characterize black nationalism as something that occurred apart from the movement, Nuruddin illustrates how it revitalized the civil rights struggle in the years following King's assassination. Rather than leading the movement up a violent and immoral road, black nationalists brought forth new perspectives that gave direction to a struggle looking for leadership in the wake of rapid change. Nuruddin argues that integrationists like Martin Luther King operated not only in opposition to black nationalists like Malcolm X but often drew from the same ideological repertoire, even as media concentrated on their differences.

Arica Coleman's Chapter 7, on the Black Panther Party, which she calls "the most demonized and romanticized of the radical protest groups to emerge during the period commonly referred to as the black power movement," expands our understanding of the relationships between black nationalists and integrationists. Coleman explores the Black Panther Party's complex political philosophies, community organizing programs, and international sensibilities to challenge common beliefs that the group operated violently and lawlessly in opposition to an otherwise wholesome movement. Illustrating how the organization drew strength and inspiration from Martin Luther King, Coleman's work blurs the all-too-easy distinctions between black nationalism and integration. It also highlights the influence that the black freedom struggle had on outside communities by identifying how Chicanos, Chinese Americans, and Puerto Ricans incorporated Black Panther Party ideals into their own campaigns. Coleman also explores the leadership roles women played in the organization.

The book's eighth chapter is Jennifer Lemak's account of the crucial contributions to the classical phase of the movement made by women who served as leaders and organizers. Focusing on key actors, including Rosa Parks, Ella Baker, Septima Clark, Fannie Lou Hamer, Anne Moody, Daisy Bates, Gloria Richardson, Mary Fair Burks, and Jo Ann Robinson, Lemak shows that despite facing opposition to their participation, women informed all of the movement's vital functions.

In addition to these eight topical chapters, *Civil Rights Movement: People and Perspectives* contains a four-part section that includes a reference chapter in the form of an A-to-Z glossary, a 20-year movement chronology, a series of primary source documents, and a bibliography. These chapters, like their topical counterparts, balance the King Years perspective with the notion of a long civil rights movement. The reference chapter consists of short, definitive sketches that identify more than 200 key civil rights activists, events, and terms. The chronology provides a timeline charting more than 200 important developments during the movement's classical phase. The primary sources include Supreme Court documents, the founding statements by the Student Nonviolent Coordinating Committee and Black Panther Party, and a speech by Malcolm X. The bibliography contains nearly 1,000 entries that address all aspects of the civil rights movement. In short, *Civil Rights Movement: People and Perspectives* is a comprehensive work that employs both traditional and cutting-edge scholarship to explore the black freedom struggle, its antecedents, and its legacy.

Michael Ezra

# About the Editor and Contributors

**Arica L. Coleman** is assistant professor of black American studies at the University of Delaware. She teaches courses in African American–Native American relations and African American history. Her research focuses on racial identity formation within mixed-race communities. Her latest work explores early encounters between Africans and the Powhatan Indians of Virginia.

**Marsha Darling** is professor of history and the director of the Center for African American and Ethnic Studies Programs at Adelphi University. She edited three volumes in the series Race, Voting, Redistricting and the Constitution: Sources and Explorations on the Fifteenth Amendment (Routledge, 2001). Her current work explores the intersections of race and gender in the eugenics movement.

**Michael Ezra** is associate professor of American multicultural studies at Sonoma State University. He is the author of *Muhammad Ali: The Making of an Icon* (Temple University Press, 2009). His current work addresses the historiography of the civil rights movement.

**Jill K. Gill** is associate professor in the Department of History at Boise State University. Her research focus and publications have centered on the response of mainline Protestantism to social justice and peace issues in the 1960s. She is completing a book manuscript on the National Council of Churches and the Vietnam War to be published by Northern Illinois University Press.

**Jennifer A. Lemak** is senior historian and curator of African American history at the New York State Museum. She is the author of *Southern Life, Northern City: The History of Albany's Rapp Road Community* (State University of New York Press, 2008), which chronicles an African American chain migration between Shubuta, Mississippi, and Albany, New York.

**Barbara McCaskill** is associate professor of English, General Sandy Beaver Teaching Professor, and codirector of the Civil Rights Digital Library Initiative at the University of Georgia. She directs the construction and content

production for Freedom on Film: Civil Rights in Georgia (www.civilrights
.uga.edu), a Web site featuring news footage housed in the special collections of the Walter J. Brown Media Archives. Aghigh Ebrahimi (MA English)
and Lauren Chambers (PhD English) served as research assistants during the
first year of this project.

**Yusuf Nuruddin** is an independent scholar and veteran activist who has
taught in the African American studies departments at the University of
Toledo; Seton Hall University; and John Jay College, City University of New
York. He is a member of the editorial board of the journal *Socialism and
Democracy* (www.sdonline.org) and managing editor of the forthcoming
journal *Timbuktu Review* (www.timbuktureview.org).

**Francis Shor** is professor in the Department of History at Wayne State University in Detroit and teaches courses in 20th-century U.S. social and cultural
history. He is the author of *Utopianism and Radicalism in a Reforming America,
1888–1918* (Greenwood Press, 1997). His present research is focused on white
student activists in the black freedom struggle. He is a veteran activist and
longtime board member of the Michigan Coalition for Human Rights.

# Chronology

## 1954

**January** African Americans in Memphis, in response to being mistreated on the city's streetcars, demand that the Memphis Street Railway Company force its drivers to treat black passengers respectfully, end its segregated seating practices, and hire blacks as drivers. Organizers threaten a boycott unless the company incorporates these changes.

**February** Judy Johnson, the former Negro League player, becomes the first African American to become a Major League Baseball coach when the Philadelphia Athletics hire him as an assistant coach.

**April** Archbishop Robert E. Lucey of San Antonio orders the desegregation of the area's Catholic schools, becoming the first such leader to do so in the Deep South.

**May** The U.S. Supreme Court delivers its landmark decision in the *Brown v. Board of Education* case, which declares that "separate but equal" public accommodations for blacks and whites are unconstitutional, paving the way for their desegregation. The decision destroys the legal basis upon which the Jim Crow South is supported and becomes the foundation upon which the civil rights revolution of the next 15 years is built.

**June** The National Association for the Advancement of Colored People (NAACP) announces that it will organize a series of voter registration drives in 13 southern states in an effort to bring 1 million new black voters to the polls.

**September** Violent white mobs in Milford, Delaware, surround the local high school on the first day of school, preventing black students from entering and forcing the closure of the town's entire public school system for 10 days. Similar resistance occurs in West Virginia, Mississippi, Texas, Louisiana, and Ohio. In some places, including towns in Arkansas and Maryland, desegregation takes place without incident.

**November** Charles Diggs Jr. of Detroit becomes the third African American elected to the U.S. Congress in the 20th century.

**December** In an effort to maintain segregated education, Mississippi voters endorse a constitutional amendment authorizing the state legislature to abolish public schools and fund private schools.

## 1955

**January** Washington, D.C., transit officials announce that they will allow African Americans to become city bus drivers.

**February** Dorothy Dandridge becomes the first African American to be nominated for a best actor or best actress Academy Award for her work in the motion picture *Carmen Jones*.

**March** In Montgomery, Alabama, 15-year-old Claudette Colvin is arrested for disorderly conduct after she refuses to move to the rear of a city bus. She is later convicted and placed on probation. In North Dakota, an 1861 law banning interracial marriages is struck down by the state legislature. In Louisiana, eight interracial couples are indicted by a grand jury for violating the state's antimiscegenation laws.

**April** Roy Wilkins becomes executive secretary of the NAACP.

**May** NAACP organizer George Lee is murdered in Belzoni, Mississippi.

**June** Responding to the slow pace of school desegregation in the South, the U.S. Supreme Court requests that its ruling in the *Brown* decision be carried out "with all deliberate speed." Because it does not order a specific desegregation date, however, the court leaves the measure vulnerable to further delay by recalcitrant school districts.

**August** Fourteen-year-old Emmett Till is lynched in Money, Mississippi, for allegedly propositioning a white woman. His brutal murder heightens nationwide awareness of southern racism and leads to protests around the country.

**September** Two college professors become the first African Americans to serve on a grand jury in New Orleans since Reconstruction.

**November** The Interstate Commerce Commission rules that racial segregation of interstate passengers on buses and trains and in stations and waiting rooms is illegal.

**December** Rosa Parks is arrested in Montgomery, Alabama, after she refuses to give up her seat to a white man on a city bus. Following her arrest, local organizers form the Montgomery Improvement Association (MIA) in an effort to address widespread racial inequalities in the city, announcing that blacks will boycott the city's public transportation until they are treated fairly. Local pastor Martin Luther King Jr. is elected MIA president, and the ensuing yearlong protest springboards him to national prominence. The Montgomery action inspires similar campaigns around the country and is given widespread credit as the beginning of what is now known as the civil rights movement.

## 1956

**January**  The states of Mississippi, Alabama, and Louisiana resist the Interstate Commerce Commission's November 1955 ban on segregation by installing new signs for "white" and "colored" people in railway stations and bus terminals. In Illinois, officials accept the ban and begin working with railroads and bus companies to integrate all of the state's relevant facilities.

**February**  City officials in Oklahoma City open all municipal facilities to African Americans.

**March**  Martin Luther King Jr. is convicted of conspiracy to boycott city buses in Montgomery, Alabama, and sentenced to more than a year of hard labor. He is released on bail pending an appeal.

**June**  Violence grips a park in Knoxville, Tennessee, when 1,500 blacks and whites fight over its occupancy.

**September**  The home of Gerald Harris, patriarch of the first black family to move into an all-white neighborhood in Placentia, California, is bombed.

**November**  *The Nat King Cole Show* becomes the first network television show starring an African American entertainer. The U.S. Army bans segregation in schools and classes offered on army bases.

**December**  Baltimore's fire chief bans segregation in city firehouses. Oklahoma City hires its first African American city bus driver. Bus service in Tallahassee, Florida, is halted when violence erupts after blacks try to ride on a desegregated basis.

## 1957

**January**  Ministers in Atlanta, Georgia, are arrested when they refuse to move from the white section of a public bus.

**February**  Black residents of Memphis; Birmingham, Alabama; and New Orleans file suits in federal district courts against transit companies that refuse to desegregate local lines. Arkansas governor Orval Faubus signs a bill into law giving parents the right to refuse to send their children to an integrated school.

**April**  Racial violence escalates in Chicago when three white teenagers are accused of murdering a black resident. New York governor W. Averell Harriman signs into law a bill banning racial discrimination in the hiring of apprentices in the state building trades.

**May**  The Alabama Court of Appeals overturns Martin Luther King's conviction for boycotting city buses on a technicality. A federal district court judge in New Orleans rules that state laws requiring segregation on public transportation are unconstitutional and issues injunctions to terminate their enforcement.

**June** Martin Luther King and Ralph Abernathy meet with Vice President Richard Nixon and U.S. Department of Labor secretary James Mitchell to discuss race relations.

**August** State troopers are dispatched to Levittown, Pennsylvania, when mob violence ensues after William J. Meyers and his family purchase a home in the all-white community. The U.S. Senate passes the first civil rights bill in more than 80 years, which later is signed into law as the Civil Rights Act of 1957.

**September** Nine black students attempting to desegregate Central High School in Little Rock, Arkansas, are met by a violent white mob. President Dwight Eisenhower sends in paratroopers and the Arkansas National Guard to maintain order.

**October** The Chicago City Council unanimously passes its first civil rights law, banning discrimination in all public accommodations.

**November** The Tennessee Board of Education calls on state-supported colleges to admit all qualified students without discrimination and also votes to comply with a court order to integrate its public schools.

## 1958

**February** Minnie Jean Brown, one of the nine students that desegregated Central High School in Little Rock, Arkansas, is expelled after she physically retaliates against white students who had repeatedly harassed her. Three white students involved in the incident are also expelled.

**May** Ernest Green becomes the first black student to graduate from Central High School in Little Rock, Arkansas. Officials in New Orleans vow to defy the federal court decision to ban segregation in the city's transit lines.

**June** President Eisenhower meets with civil rights leaders at the White House. The U.S Department of State issues a passport to activist entertainer Paul Robeson after withholding it for several months when Robeson refused to respond to a federal inquiry into whether or not he was a Communist.

**August** Birmingham, Alabama, officials allow African American residents to take the county civil service examination for the first time. Thirty-five members of the NAACP Youth Council in Oklahoma City conduct a sit-in at a local luncheonette and are refused service. President Eisenhower announces his belief that school integration is happening too quickly and urges its proponents to move at a slower pace.

**September** Sit-ins, usually sponsored by local NAACP Youth Councils, take place in cities throughout the Midwest, including Stillwater, Oklahoma, and Wichita, Kansas. Southern states continue their resistance to school integration as black students are turned away from all-white schools in Memphis and Raleigh, North Carolina. Four qualified black students are also turned away from Memphis State University despite passing all of the college's entrance exams, and police eject a group of black residents from a city zoo.

**December** A student exchange program between Oberlin College and American University is canceled when American's president refuses to allow Oberlin's black students to live in dorms housing whites.

## 1959

**January** The New Orleans Board of Commissioners responds to a U.S. Supreme Court order by deciding that all citizens should have the right to use all city parks and recreation facilities.

**February** In Snow Hill, North Carolina, 2,800 black students boycott the segregated elementary schools and high school because of inadequate facilities. Sidney Poitier becomes the first African American nominated in the best actor Academy Award category for his role in *The Defiant Ones*.

**March** *A Raisin in the Sun,* by Lorraine Hansberry, debuts on Broadway, becoming the first such play to be written by an African American woman.

**April** In Washington, D.C., more than 30,000 people attend the Youth March for Public School Desegregation. The Kansas state legislature passes a civil rights bill prohibiting racial discrimination in public accommodations and proposes fines for merchants who fail to comply.

**May** An interracial group of protesters is refused service when it conducts a sit-in at a Miami lunch counter. In Menards, New York, a swimming pool manager becomes the first person jailed for violating the state's antidiscrimination law.

**June** After filing a complaint with the New York State Commission against Discrimination, two New York City blacks become the first nonwhite members of the International Longshoreman's Union.

**August** Police raid the Highlander Folk School, an adult education and citizenship training center in Monteagle, Tennessee, which had been conducting voter registration workshops, arrest Director of Education Septima Clark, and threaten to close down the school. A petition is filed in state court to withdraw Highlander's tax-exempt status.

**September** Bombs explode around Little Rock, Arkansas, as white resistance to school integration intensifies. Arkansas governor Orval Faubus closes the city's public schools.

**October** The city commission in Miami unanimously reverses the city manager's decision to allow blacks unrestricted access to city recreational facilities.

**December** The Minneapolis Lakers of the National Basketball Association announce the cancellation of a game scheduled in Charlestown, West Virginia, because of racial discrimination practiced by local hotels.

## 1960

**January** Delaware's Supreme Court rules that privately owned restaurants are not required by law to serve African Americans.

**February** North Carolina Agricultural and Technical College students sit in at a Greensboro, North Carolina, Woolworth's lunch counter. Other students across the state follow their example, and the sit-in movement quickly spreads throughout the South as thousands of student protesters demand equal access to public accommodations.

**April** Southern student leaders meet in Raleigh, North Carolina, to discuss the sit-in movement and found the Student Nonviolent Coordinating Committee (SNCC) to organize their antidiscrimination efforts. Casinos on the Las Vegas Strip agree to drop their ban against African Americans following threatened protests by the local NAACP chapter.

**May** The 1960 Civil Rights Act passes Congress and is signed into law by President Eisenhower. The new law further protects black voting rights.

**June** A white mob in Pontiac, Michigan, attacks the office of a real estate agent after he sells a home in a previously all-white neighborhood to an African American. The board of education in Houston votes to integrate only 3 of 177 city schools.

**August** Philadelphia ministers call off a proposed boycott against a local baking company after it agrees to abandon its discriminatory employment policies and hire black personnel.

**October** Presidential candidate John F. Kennedy telephones Martin Luther King's wife, Coretta Scott King, and offers assistance to her husband, who was jailed in Georgia on specious charges. The move increases nationwide black support for Kennedy that accounts for his razor-thin margin of victory in the November general election.

**December** Statistics reveal that merchants in Atlanta suffer a major decline in holiday shopping revenues as a result of sit-ins and boycotts at segregated department stores.

## 1961

**January** Massive student violence occurs when Charlayne Hunter and Hamilton Holmes become the first African Americans to attend the University of Georgia. Their successful admission and retention leads to the desegregation of dozens of other southern institutions of higher learning previously closed to blacks. The National Council of Churches passes a resolution urging increased vigilance against discriminatory hiring, especially within churches.

**February** Martin Luther King's Southern Christian Leadership Conference (SCLC) announces that it will join forces with the Highlander Folk School to train civil rights leaders.

**March** President Kennedy issues an executive order ending employment discrimination. The federal government later announces that it will introduce antidiscrimination clauses to virtually every new federal contract.

**April** The NAACP announces "Operation Mississippi," a voting rights, fair hiring, and desegregation drive to take place throughout the state.

**May** Participants in the Congress of Racial Equality (CORE) Freedom Rides have their bus set on fire and are then attacked by a white mob when their protest campaign reaches Anniston, Alabama.

**June** Former Monroe, North Carolina, NAACP head Robert F. Williams appears in Harlem, New York City, to break up an NAACP rally, shouting down NAACP executive secretary Roy Wilkins and encouraging blacks to meet racial violence with violence of their own.

**July** Illinois governor Otto Kerner agrees to sign a bill establishing a statewide fair employment practices commission. New Hampshire's state government passes a law banning discrimination in public accommodations and private housing.

**August** SNCC members led by Bob Moses open a voter education school in McComb, Mississippi, to teach local citizens how to navigate barriers created to stop blacks from voting.

**October** More than 100 high school students in McComb, Mississippi, are arrested after they march on city hall to protest the expulsion of two peers who participated in a sit-in.

**November** Black citizens and organizations in New Orleans launch a registration drive in hope of adding 100,000 new voters to the rolls.

**December** Hink's, a Berkeley, California, department store, hires two African Americans as clerks, marking the end of its 57-year discriminatory hiring policy.

## 1962

**January** Fred Shuttlesworth of SCLC begins serving a 90-day jail sentence in Montgomery, Alabama, for violating a segregation law that had since been declared unconstitutional.

**April** Martin Luther King criticizes the Kennedy administration for providing weak leadership on civil rights issues, particularly the administration's reluctance to enforce civil rights legislation and its refusal to issue a fair housing executive order. An executive order banning housing discrimination soon follows, and eight months later the first formal complaint is filed by a man who was refused the chance to purchase a home.

**May** Black police officers in Atlanta are authorized for the first time to arrest white offenders. Previously, black officers could only patrol black neighborhoods and arrest African American suspects.

**July** Martin Luther King and Ralph Abernathy are arrested in Albany, Georgia, for their part in SCLC's desegregation activities, which had been going on in the city since the previous December.

**September** Catholic schools in New Orleans are desegregated for the first time in 50 years, with 196 black students entering 36 Catholic schools. The transition goes smoothly and without incident.

**October** Amid massive rioting and the dispatch of federal troops to campus, James Meredith becomes to first African American student to attend the University of Mississippi.

**November** Noelle Henry, the wife of Mississippi NAACP president Aaron Henry, is fired from a public school teaching position she held for 11 years. She sues the local school board.

**December** President Kennedy holds a two-hour meeting with black leaders Roy Wilkins, Martin Luther King, A. Philip Randolph, Dorothy Height, James Farmer, Whitney Young, and Theodore Brown. Kennedy pledges to appoint blacks to key diplomatic positions.

## 1963

**January** After a long battle, Harvey Gantt enrolls at Clemson College in Clemson, South Carolina, and becomes the first black person in the state since Reconstruction to go to school with whites at any level.

**February** South Dakota state legislators pass a bill banning discrimination in public accommodations after black servicemen complain about discrimination in area establishments.

**April** Rather than desegregate its public recreational facilities, the city of Albany, Georgia, puts them up for sale. City tennis courts, swimming pools, and recreation centers had been closed since the previous summer. Martin Luther King writes his "Letter from Birmingham Jail."

**May** Protesters in Birmingham, Alabama, many of whom are adolescents and teenagers, are attacked by police dogs and sprayed with high-powered fire hoses. The assault on these nonviolent demonstrators creates nationwide outrage.

**June** Medgar Evers, the NAACP's first-ever field secretary in Mississippi, is murdered in Jackson, Mississippi, by white supremacist Byron De La Beckwith. The Maryland National Guard is called in and martial law is declared in Cambridge, Maryland, after a series of protests and confrontations over desegregation.

**August** More than 250,000 people participate in the March on Washington for Jobs and Freedom organized by A. Philip Randolph and Bayard Rustin, where Martin Luther King delivers his famous "I Have a Dream" speech.

**September** While 4,000 white protesters demonstrate outside city hall, the city council of Chicago passes a fair housing ordinance that bars real estate brokers from discriminating against clients interested in buying, selling, renting, or leasing houses.

**October** Nearly 250,000 black pupils stage a one-day boycott of Chicago public schools to protest discriminatory policies. A corresponding protest march draws 20,000 participants.

**November** President Kennedy is assassinated in Dallas. Vice President Lyndon Johnson declares that, as president, he will pursue the civil rights agenda initiated by the late commander in chief.

**December** President Johnson meets with civil rights leaders in Washington, D.C. The meeting includes Martin Luther King, Roy Wilkins, John Lewis, James Forman, and A. Philip Randolph. Johnson pledges to remain in contact with the civil rights community.

## 1964

**January** President Johnson calls for an end to racial discrimination in his State of the Union address.

**February** One-day public school boycotts in Chicago and Boston draw massive participation, as nearly 300,000 students stay home to protest segregation.

**April** CORE demonstrators picket the World's Fair in Flushing, New York, causing a number of disruptions.

**June** A civil rights rally in Chicago draws 75,000 people. Three CORE field workers—James Chaney, Andrew Goodman, and Michael Schwerner—are murdered in Mississippi after investigating a church bombing.

**July** President Johnson signs the 1964 Civil Rights Act into law, ending legal discrimination in the United States.

**August** Philadelphia is rocked by riots, leading to hundreds of injuries. At the Democratic National Convention, the Mississippi Freedom Democratic Party, a mostly black delegation, demands to be seated in place of the all-white delegation from the state Democratic Party.

**November** Martin Luther King meets with President Johnson in Washington, D.C., to discuss the role of southern federal judges in the civil rights movement.

**December** Martin Luther King receives the Nobel Peace Prize for his nonviolent commitment to civil rights.

## 1965

**February** Malcolm X is assassinated in New York City while delivering a speech for his Organization of Afro-American Unity.

**March** Nonviolent protesters marching for voting rights are brutalized by state troopers in Selma, Alabama, leading to nationwide outrage.

**April** Nevada governor Grant Sawyer signs into law a state civil rights act banning discrimination in public accommodations and employment.

**June** Vivian Malone becomes the first African American student to graduate from the University of Alabama. Harvey Gantt becomes the first African American student to graduate from Clemson University.

**July** Martin Luther King leads a march on city hall in Chicago.

**August** President Johnson signs the Voting Rights Act into law, removing almost all of the legal barriers preventing African Americans from voting in the South. Rioting in the Watts neighborhood of Los Angeles leads to 34 deaths and more than 1,000 injuries. Riots also occur in Chicago.

**September** "Operation Exodus" begins in Boston as several hundred black parents begin transferring their children to predominantly white schools.

**October** CORE leads a four-day school boycott in Milwaukee as black students stay home from segregated public schools and attend "freedom schools" instead. The first civil rights law in the state of Missouri, banning discrimination in all public businesses except neighborhood barbershops and beauty salons, goes into effect.

**November** Robert Henry becomes the first black mayor of any city since the Reconstruction era when he is elected to the post in Springfield, Ohio.

**December** The Oklahoma Supreme Court rules that it will not void the state's ban on interracial marriage unless forced to do so by the U.S. Supreme Court.

## 1966

**January** SNCC becomes the first civil rights organization to formally declare its opposition to the Vietnam War. Robert Weaver becomes the first African American named to a cabinet post when President Johnson appoints him secretary of housing and urban development.

**February** Muhammad Ali is reclassified as draft eligible for the Vietnam War and tells the press that he is opposed to the war.

**March** The U.S. Supreme Court rules poll taxes in state elections to be illegal in its *Harper v. Virginia Board of Elections* decision.

**May** The Lowndes County Freedom Organization, a black-led political party in Alabama, holds a political convention to nominate candidates to challenge the all-white Democratic and Republican parties in the upcoming primaries. Stokely Carmichael replaces John Lewis as SNCC chairman, signaling the organization's turn toward black nationalism.

**June** "Black power" becomes a rallying cry during a protest march in Mississippi.

**July** The Chicago Freedom Movement, a coalition between Martin Luther King and local organizers in Chicago, becomes the first large-scale antidiscrimination campaign in a major northern city. Rioting erupts in Cleveland's Hough neighborhood.

**August** The Chicago Freedom Movement ends after Martin Luther King and Mayor Richard J. Daley sign a 10-point agreement calling for the enforcement of antidiscrimination laws in exchange for a halt to the protests.

**September** Riots occur in the Hunter's Point neighborhood of San Francisco.

**October** The Black Panther Party for Self-Defense is founded in Oakland, California, by Huey P. Newton and Bobby Seale.

**November** Edward Brooke, a Massachusetts Republican, becomes the first African American since Reconstruction to become a U.S. senator.

**December** The U.S. Supreme Court rules that the Georgia House of Representatives' refusal to seat SNCC's Julian Bond because of his political views, despite Bond's being fairly elected, is unconstitutional.

## 1967

**March** Marian Wright, an attorney with the NAACP Legal Defense Fund, testifies before the Senate Labor Committee's poverty subcommittee about conditions in Mississippi.

**April** Martin Luther King delivers a speech in New York City declaring his opposition to the Vietnam War.

**June** The U.S. Supreme Court invalidates state laws against interracial marriage in the *Loving v. Virginia* decision. Muhammad Ali is found guilty of draft evasion and sentenced to five years in prison.

**July** The worst rioting in U.S. history—triggered by long-term causes such as poverty, unemployment, police brutality, and racism—occurs when deadly violence sweeps through Detroit and Newark, New Jersey.

**September** Thurgood Marshall becomes the first African American appointed to the U.S. Supreme Court.

**November** Carl Stokes of Cleveland and Richard Hatcher of Gary, Indiana, are the first African Americans to be elected as mayors of major U.S. cities.

## 1968

**February** Local police fire into a crowd of antisegregation protesters in Orangeburg, South Carolina, killing 3 and injuring 27.

**March** Martin Luther King leads a march in support of striking sanitation workers in Memphis.

**April** Martin Luther King is assassinated in Memphis. Riots ensue in more than 120 American cities in response to King's murder. President Johnson signs into law the 1968 Civil Rights Act banning discrimination in the sale, rental, and financing of housing.

**May** The Poor People's Campaign begins in Washington, D.C.

**June** Robert Kennedy, a presidential candidate and an ally of the civil rights movement, is assassinated in a Los Angeles hotel.

**July** The Selective Buying Campaign begins in Durham, North Carolina, as antidiscrimination advocates demand changes in city welfare, housing, and employment practices.

**October** American track-and-field athletes Tommie Smith and John Carlos raise their fists to symbolize black power while on the medal stand at the Summer Olympics in Mexico City.

**November** The first interracial kiss on American television takes place on the show *Star Trek*.

## 1969

**January** President Richard Nixon postpones a deadline that would have cut off federal funds for five southern school districts that failed to desegregate.

**March** James Earl Ray is sentenced to 99 years in prison for the murder of Martin Luther King.

**April** Ralph Abernathy of SCLC leads a march of more than 700 striking hospital workers in Charleston, South Carolina.

**June** President Nixon requires federal agencies to establish equal opportunity and affirmative action policies.

**July** The hospital strike in Charleston, South Carolina, ends.

**August** The U.S. Department of Justice files suit against the state of Georgia for its failure to desegregate its schools.

**October** The U.S. Supreme Court orders Mississippi school districts to desegregate immediately in its *Alexander v. Holmes Board of Education* decision.

**December** Fred Hampton and Mark Clark, two leaders of the Chicago chapter of the Black Panther Party, are killed by police in a raid.

## 1970

**February** In Denver, antibusing activists dynamite a fleet of school buses that had been used as part of the city's efforts to achieve racial balance in local schools.

**March** The U.S. Supreme Court orders the Memphis public school system to desegregate.

**May** Police kill two student demonstrators at Jackson State College in Jackson, Mississippi.

**July** The Internal Revenue Service announces that it will tax previously exempt private academies that practice racial discrimination in their admissions policies.

**September** The Revolutionary People's Constitutional Convention, a conglomeration of underrepresented groups, meets in Philadelphia.

**October** The NAACP files suit against the U.S. Department of Health, Education, and Welfare, charging it with defaulting its enforcement of desegregation guidelines.

## 1971

**February** Eight black federal employees file suit in federal court claiming that the major civil service qualifying exam for college graduates is culturally and racially discriminatory.

**April** The U.S. Supreme Court upholds the constitutionality of busing to achieve racial balance in public schools in its *Swann v. Charlotte Mecklenburg Board of Education* decision.

**May** Rioting takes place in the Brownsville section of Brooklyn, New York, as a protest against statewide cuts in welfare programs escalates into violence.

**June** The U.S. Supreme Court rules that municipalities can close publicly owned recreational facilities as an alternative to desegregating them. The U.S. Supreme Court overturns Muhammad Ali's conviction for draft evasion.

**July** State troopers are called to Columbus, Georgia, to maintain order following a series of racial disturbances.

**August** George Jackson, an inmate at San Quentin State Prison in California whose writings made him a hero to many black revolutionaries, is gunned down by guards during an alleged escape attempt. Fourteen Chicago lawmen are indicted for their roles in the deaths of Black Panthers Mark Clark and Fred Hampton.

**September** Inmates at Attica State Prison in New York riot in response to poor conditions at the facility.

**December** Jesse Jackson founds Operation PUSH, a Chicago-based organization designed to increase economic opportunities for blacks and to pressure major companies to hire more African Americans.

## 1972

**January** Four people are killed during a clash between police and black militants in Baton Rouge, Louisiana, and the state governor calls in the National Guard to establish order.

**March** Eight thousand blacks, representing a wide range of political views, gather in Gary, Indiana, to attend the first National Black Political Convention.

**June** College professor and revolutionary Angela Davis is acquitted of charges stemming from her alleged role in a 1970 shootout at a San Rafael, California, courthouse.

**August** President Nixon announces his opposition to busing as a way of achieving educational equality.

**November** For the first time since Reconstruction, blacks from the South are elected to Congress, as Andrew Young of Atlanta and Barbara Jordan of Houston win seats in the U.S. House of Representatives.

## 1973

**January** The Nixon administration calls for an end to preferential hiring for racial minorities as a remedy for past injustices.

**April** Bobby Seale, running as a Democrat, finishes second in the Oakland, California, mayoral race and earns a runoff against incumbent John Reading.

**June** Tom Bradley is elected mayor of Los Angeles, the first African American to be elected to the post.

**November** The number of black elected officials in the United States rises from 370 to 2,991, mostly on the municipal and county levels. Examples include Maynard Jackson of Atlanta, who becomes the first black mayor of a major southern city, and Coleman Young, who becomes mayor of Detroit.

## 1974

**January** A group of black leaders meets with Vice President Gerald Ford in Washington, D.C., in an effort to improve relations between the African American community and the Nixon administration.

**March** The U.S. Department of Justice releases documents revealing that the Federal Bureau of Investigation waged a campaign against black nationalist groups during the 1960s and early 1970s.

**April** Henry Aaron of the Atlanta Braves breaks the Major League Baseball home run record previously held by Babe Ruth.

**July** In *Milliken v. Bradley,* the U.S. Supreme Court bars busing across district lines without evidence that the districts had deliberately engaged in a policy of racial segregation.

**December** Antibusing riots and demonstrations grip a number of neighborhoods in Boston, and police are forced to restrain violent protesters.

## 1975

**September** WGPR-TV, the first black-owned and -operated television station in the United States, goes on the air in Detroit.

# Early Pioneers | 1

## Marsha Darling

Despite some progressive efforts to protect and empower black Americans in the South during Reconstruction, the ideology of white supremacy and the practice of racism subsumed all erstwhile efforts to promote black American social equality from the post–Civil War era through the middle of the 20th century. White supremacy meant not only advancement and the exercise of a broad-based cluster of rights for white people but also the deliberate subversion of any measure of social equality for black Americans. White opposition to black American social progress and to political and economic equality also meant that most whites, especially in the South where the majority of black Americans lived, were deliberate and visible about obstructing black progress toward equality and advancement.

## History and Background

In the South, many whites used mob violence, physical intimidation, and social coercion to construct and maintain race-based social inequality. Legislating separation and unequal access to opportunity, whites institutionalized the grossly unequal disparities that characterized Jim Crow segregation. Where de jure segregation and white supremacy in the South were held in place by the ever-present threat of violence and official, state-sanctioned disparate and unequal treatment, de facto segregation in the North was held in place by long-established patterns of discriminatory restrictions on black American access to opportunities, goods and services, and public institutions.

Most importantly, under de facto segregation, racial separation and inequality were both established and maintained as a normative standard that inferred its appropriateness. As the decades passed and whites pushed the many thousands of working-class black southern migrants arriving in the North into residentially segregated areas where blacks of any class could live, the social custom of restricting access and denying opportunity based on race and segregated physical "place" became established and expected social practice.

In terms of African American self-help initiatives, in the decades that followed Reconstruction, a generation of "race uplift" black American leaders emerged, whether integrationist, Pan-African nationalist, back-to-Africa proponents, or Nation of Islam separatist. Black "race advancement" advocates who rose to prominence prior to the collapse of state-sanctioned racial and gender segregation include Booker T. Washington, W. E. B. Du Bois, A. Philip Randolph, Marcus Garvey, Father Major J. Divine, Elijah (Poole) Muhammad, Walter White, Charles Hamilton Houston, Adam Clayton Powell Jr., Bayard Rustin, James Weldon Johnson, and Thurgood Marshall.

## Black Women

In the decades leading up to the mid-20th century, the call to include black women in race uplift work came from early advocates of the clubwomen's movement: Mary McLeod Bethune, Mary Church Terrell, Ida B. Wells-Barnett, Josephine St. Pierre Ruffin, and Anna Julia Cooper. Each of these leaders worked toward a vision of racial/ethnic progress, while some also worked for the advancement of black women. They each had their eye on the prize of community building, equality under the letter and practice of the law, and social advancement, even though they often disagreed on the tactics and protocols to be used for ethnic group and gender advancement. Significantly, few worked separately from communities of black people who helped directly to frame important social justice issues.

## Self-Help Initiatives

It is also important to attest to the compelling significance of a tradition of organized black American self-help, including (a) the creation and growth of mutual aid societies, benevolence associations, independent African American denominational churches, literacy and fellowship societies, and northern-based, semi-independent "free schools" and (b) the growth of black American self-help economic activity—the ownership of personal property and commercial and real estate property; the expansion of wealth-building collective activity within secret societies like the Masons, Elks, Knights of Pythias, Shriners, and Eastern Star; participation in unions and farmer alliances; entrepreneurship in mortuary services, manufacturing, wholesale and retail sales and services, and newspaper and journal publishing; and patent holding for inventors—that had predated the Civil War and continued as an important dimension of black American self-help.

## Education

In the decades following Reconstruction, the creation of historically black colleges and universities and the cultivation of a black American educated elite—

This mobile agricultural school on wheels, an extension program of Booker T. Washington's Tuskegee Institute, was designed by George Washington Carver as a means of educating rural African Americans. (*National Archives*)

the "Talented Tenth," as Du Bois called them—added another dimension to a long-standing black American self-help tradition, namely, black professionals (teachers, doctors and nurses, lawyers, dentists, writers, artists, musicians, scientists, bankers, life insurance professionals, accountants, and institution builders and administrators) and their sororal and fraternal organizations.

It should come as no surprise that black American efforts to promote and advance race uplift emerged as a calling, a goal propagated by both integrationists and those black American nationalists who sought to build race pride and positive self-esteem as important attributes of race consciousness. Here, Du Bois's reflections on the eternal two-ness of being black and being American are instructive, because only by the development of black culture and unity, claimed Du Bois, would African Americans ever overcome second-class citizenship.

## Black Nationalists

Du Bois, who worked in interracial alliance with progressive whites to launch the National Association for the Advancement of Colored People (NAACP) in the opening decade of the 20th century, was very widely read by black Americans. Du Bois later became a Pan-Africanist who cautioned black Americans that if they were to become a part of the worldwide black community, they

W. E. B. Du Bois, a founding member of the National Association for the Advancement of Colored People and an important Pan-Africanist, devoted his life to the struggle for equality by people of color worldwide. (*Library of Congress*)

must develop an original culture that would first and foremost serve their own needs. Du Bois's vision called black Americans to a far-reaching and engaged, messianic, freedom-fighting, transformational role in U.S. society and the world; black Americans were called to fully claim their birthright in the United States, but also to resist being swept up into the worst of the United States by always keeping their eyes on the prize of freedom.

In addition to black American nationalists who sought to empower an ethnic consciousness based on self-pride in one's own people and in their attainments, other black nationalist strands of thought sought to identify one's group as the centerpiece of commitment. This strand of black nationalism had two branches, one buried deep in the 19th-century militancy of antebellum black nationalists Paul Cuffe and Martin Delany, whose embrace of a back-to-Africa movement emerged as a response to the virulent white racism that accompanied U.S. slavery and that so invasively afflicted the free black community's options and choices. The other strand hatched in the 20th century, when Jamaican-born Marcus Garvey mobilized a separatist black nationalist back-to-Africa message and agenda with his leadership of the Universal Negro Improvement Association.

Another strand of black nationalism that has strengthened black communities, particularly in the North, is the racial separatism of the Nation of Islam, whose members are black Muslims who have consistently advocated producing, buying, selling, building, and socially and culturally advancing only black people. The black Muslims have stood for linking race-conscious ideas, ideals, and values with race-uplifting economic activities, including buying and building within the black community.

## Legal Advocates

Dating from the U.S. Supreme Court's decision to affirm racial segregation in public accommodations in *Plessy v. Ferguson* (1896), black American civil rights advocates and their white allies put out the call to resist legalized segregation. The call to resist *Plessy* in the courts was a key aspect of Du Bois's vision to create the NAACP, the nation's oldest civil rights organization, which committed itself to using legalism to fight for and attain key civil rights victories. NAACP lawyers scored their first Supreme Court victory in *Guinn v. U.S.* (1915), a case in which Oklahoma's grandfather clause was declared unconstitutional.

Six pivotal cases argued and won at the Supreme Court level during the 1940s by the lawyers representing the NAACP Legal Defense Fund laid the groundwork for the tumultuous civil rights changes that began occurring in the 1950s around the demise of "separate but equal" public accommodations: *Mitchell v. U.S. Interstate Commerce Act* (1941), *Smith v. Allwright* (1944), *Morgan v. Commonwealth of Virginia* (1946), *Sipuel v. Oklahoma State Board of Regents* (1948), *Shelley v. Kraemer* (1948), and *Sweatt v. Painter* (1950). All involved black American plaintiffs. Other victories also made clear the organization's effectiveness in seeking civil redress.

In considering the importance of the above-mentioned cases, we must identify Charles Hamilton Houston's leadership vision. Houston, a black American attorney, toured the South with a movie camera in hand, documenting the egregious racial disparities in public accommodations that he observed. Often overlooked by historical accounts, Houston was instrumental in the NAACP's decision to carefully litigate segregation cases that were argued and won by demonstrating that segregated public facilities were, as most people knew, grossly unequal. Importantly, the victories won by demonstrating that segregation was separate and unequal, and therefore in violation of the "separate but equal" standard articulated in the majority opinion in *Plessy*, were significant because the Supreme Court ordered the equal provision of a service or an accommodation as a redress at the local, state, or federal level. These cases, therefore, became the foundation for attacking segregation in the provision of education to children, which resulted in the *Brown v. Board of Education* (1954) decision.

In addition to his legal genius in correctly identifying *Plessy*'s Achilles heel, Houston helped assemble the NAACP legal team and was a mentor for a number of its brilliant young legal talents—Thurgood Marshall, William Hastie, Spottswood Robinson, Robert Lee Carter, Oliver Hill, and Constance

## A. Philip Randolph

Asa Philip Randolph was a labor leader who spent most of his career working to create equal employment opportunities and conditions for African Americans. In 1917, Randolph founded the magazine *Messenger*, a radical socialist voice that pushed for civil rights for African Americans. As a result of his writings, namely those urging African Americans to refuse conscription into World War I military service, Randolph was arrested under the Espionage Act and the *Messenger* was temporarily banned from the mails.

The *Messenger* was especially popular with Pullman porters, all of whom were black and many of whom were educated, for its relentless exposure of discriminatory working conditions

A. Philip Randolph organized the Brotherhood of Sleeping Car Porters, the first trade union to be led by African Americans, in 1925. He also helped organize the 1963 March on Washington for Jobs and Freedom. (*Library of Congress*)

Baker Motley. It should be noted that while Houston and his colleagues astutely assessed the contradictions that were evident in juxtaposing the *Plessy* standard against the realities of what segregation looked like on the ground, NAACP lawyers litigated these cases before a particularly liberal Supreme Court. And while advocates for racial justice on behalf of black Americans were encouraged by the important civil rights litigation victories of the 1940s, no one presumed from these victories that overturning *Plessy* entirely would be an easy matter. Indeed, many knew that to venture an all-out legal attack on segregation as unconstitutional would mean taking on the risk of losing such a challenge. Nonetheless, the legal victories of the 1940s raised the hopes and expectations of black Americans and their white allies.

In addition to the optimism that key legal victories provided, the unprecedented changes in labor force participation and military service for large numbers of black American women and men during World War II provided experiences that prompted new perspectives and discourses about social expectations. Two very important transformations occurred. Black American men have fought in all U.S. wars, and World War II was no exception. Although barred from active duty in the Marine Corps and the Army Air Corps, and only allowed to serve in menial positions in the U.S. Navy, that African Americans faced. In 1925, Randolph founded the Brotherhood of Sleeping Car Porters, the first predominantly black labor union, which had approximately 10,000 members. Randolph lobbied the U.S. Congress for years to amend the Railway Labor Act in order to gain federal recognition of porters' labor rights, and in 1934, he gained the desired changes. Pullman conceded its own recognition of the union the following year and negotiated a contract with the union in 1937 that led to employee pay increases, overtime pay, and a shorter workweek.

Dissatisfied with the federal commitment to labor equality, Randolph remained an important civil rights activist over the next few years, joining forces with the National Association for the Advancement of Colored People and National Urban League to lobby President Franklin Roosevelt to desegregate military and defense industries prior to U.S. involvement in World War II. When Roosevelt was slow to respond, Randolph, along with Bayard Rustin and A. J. Muste of the Fellowship of Reconciliation, began planning a Washington, D.C., demonstration in which at least 10,000 African Americans would march to protest discrimination in wartime industries. Only when Roosevelt agreed to issue Executive Order 8002, which outlawed such practices and created the Fair Employment Practices Committee to investigate violations of the new law, did Randolph agree to call off the march.

Throughout the 1950s and 1960s, Randolph continued to push for equal treatment under the law for African Americans, especially in terms of labor. Sensing that the time was again right for a march on Washington, Randolph worked with Rustin and Martin Luther King Jr. to organize the movement's most famous protest on August 28, 1963, featuring King's "I Have a Dream" speech. President Lyndon Johnson awarded Randolph the Presidential Medal of Freedom the following year.

record numbers enlisted. About a million black men entered the armed forces (including 4,000 black women and the Tuskegee Airmen). In addition, record numbers of black American women also entered the labor force during the war years, earning wages in industries in which they would not have been employed but for the absence of male workers pulled away by war service (Jaynes and Williams 1989, 55–112).

Importantly, for this exploration of the factors that contributed to the social justice activism of the 1950s, the "Double V" campaign instigated by African Americans who began to embrace a twofold struggle—the battle against fascism abroad and racism at home—was specifically directed against discrimination in federal hiring, the defense industry, and the armed services. A. Philip Randolph, the head of the Brotherhood of Sleeping Car Porters, was a key figure in attempts to prod President Franklin Roosevelt and then President Harry Truman to use their office to ban discrimination in federal employment and the armed services. And on the ground, the Congress of Racial Equality, an interracial pacifist organization based in Chicago, launched sit-ins on behalf of integrating public accommodations, while female students at Howard University conducted sit-ins at segregated cafeterias in Washington, D.C. Following the 1947 release of the report *To Secure*

## Fellowship of Reconciliation and Congress of Racial Equality

The Fellowship of Reconciliation (FOR) was an international ecumenical organization that was founded in 1914 by a coalition of religious leaders in Europe who were interested in preventing the outbreak of World War I. Its U.S. branch, the FOR-USA, was formed the following year.

During the 1940s, as World War II was escalating, Howard University School of Religion graduate James Farmer became FOR's secretary for race relations, helping the organization develop its policies and public responses to such problems as bigotry, discrimination, and poverty. Living in Chicago, Farmer began connecting people who wanted to apply the FOR's pacifism toward nonviolent resistance campaigns against segregation and racial prejudice.

Along with two other FOR members, Farmer formed the interracial Congress of Racial Equality (CORE) in 1942 to carry out this vision. The organization embarked upon a series of protests that would become models for civil rights demonstrations that would take place over the next two decades. CORE's first actions included sit-ins and boycotts, and in 1947 it organized its first Journey of Reconciliation, a direct-action campaign in which an interracial group of protesters, including future movement strategist Bayard Rustin, traveled throughout the South challenging segregated interstate travel facilities. CORE revisited the tactic by embarking upon a series of Freedom Rides, most famously during the early 1960s. Although participants encountered violent white opposition, their campaign led to the desegregation of southern bus terminals, waiting rooms, and restaurants.

The Freedom Rides generated national attention and sympathy for the civil rights movement and established CORE as a vital organization. As the movement progressed throughout the 1960s, CORE partnered with other groups such as the Student Nonviolent Coordinating Committee on issues like voter registration in the South, and was part of the vanguard that brought the movement to the North by focusing on issues like fair employment and economic development. CORE's turn toward black nationalism during the mid-1960s marked a departure from the organization's integrationist roots and its formal connection to FOR, but both groups have remained operative since the movement's heyday.

*These Rights: The Report of President Harry S. Truman's Committee on Civil Rights,* and under threat of a planned protest march on Washington, President Truman authorized two recommendations from the report; he issued Executive Orders 9980 and 9981, thereby banning racial discrimination in federal employment and the armed forces.

## Tracing the Success of Initiatives

Why were black American civil rights initiatives of the 1950s able to transform the South and ultimately the nation? What were the ingredients of the sustained and effective social justice activism that started in Montgomery, Alabama, and spread across the entire South? Why did the social justice activism that began the movement not start sooner? After all, Irene Morgan's successful Supreme Court victory over segregation in the Commonwealth of Virginia could have arguably launched a more ambitious attack on separate and unequal segregation. And Claudette Colvin refused to give up her bus seat to a white man in Montgomery approximately nine months before Rosa Parks challenged Jim Crow bus policy. What was it about Rosa Parks's case that eventually propelled a social justice movement forward?

In exploring an explanation, no single factor emerges to account for the dramatic changes that engulfed first Montgomery and then the rest of the South. Instead, it is important to consider the intersection of several key factors. First, the racial climate in the nation was ripe for a social justice initiative or movement, as northern and southern segregation, economic exclusion, and political marginalization continued into the 1950s. While the decade brought many whites prosperity and opportunities for building wealth based on home ownership and greatly increased access to education, especially for returning veterans of World War II, black Americans were largely left behind in the huge postwar boom. For example, black GIs faced racial exclusion from opportunities to buy homes in government-built suburbs. Racial discrimination in the management of these suburbs was directly linked to discriminatory federal policy and practice, and not just local politics. The effects of such inequalities continue to the present as whites have been able to sell these suburban homes at enormous profits. Most northern black families, on the other hand, even those of returning black veterans, were confined to racially segregated, urban public housing projects or ill-kept and rundown tenements in inner cities. Even as NAACP lawyers won key Supreme Court victories striking down restrictive real estate covenants and eliminating racial admissions barriers for black Americans to attend professional and graduate schools, most blacks watched angrily as the disparities widened between them and their largely working-class white counterparts (Lipsitz 1998, 1–23).

In the South, most whites imagined that Jim Crow would look the same in the early 1950s as it had in previous decades. But many black southerners envisioned breaking down the discriminatory boundaries imposed by segregation. Navy veteran Harry Briggs and 24 other Clarendon County, South Carolina, residents were the spearhead for *Briggs v. Elliott* (1950), the South's first *Plessy* challenge involving elementary school children. Black plaintiffs in Clarendon County were concerned parents who sought redress for the grossly disparate educational gaps their children endured: dilapidated schoolhouses, lack of school buses (while surplus buses were available for whites), and unequal expenditures for educating black and white children ($179 per white student vs. $43 per black student for the 1949–1950 school year). *Briggs* was one of a cluster of cases eventually subsumed under *Brown* that sought to dismantle segregation.

In the NAACP's 256-page legal brief, attorney and future Supreme Court justice Thurgood Marshall was eloquent and forceful in his arguments against the *Plessy* doctrine before the Court. Marshall referred to *Plessy* as a legal aberration that was a product of an era dominated by provincialism, emotionalism in race relations, and white supremacy. On May 17, 1954, the Supreme Court ruled unanimously that maintaining segregation based on a racial classification violated constitutional protections that afforded equality. The Court concluded that separate but equal had no place in public education and that separate educational facilities were inherently unequal. It destroyed the legal basis for segregation and began a new chapter in the black American battle for equality.

Between the May 1954 *Brown* decision and the December 1955 Montgomery bus boycott, two conditions propelled the exercise of civil rights by black Americans to the fore: rising expectations and decreasing patience. First, black men and women, especially soldiers, were changed by their participation in World War II. World War II was a global war to end fascism and promote democracy. Black men and women took these messages seriously and applied them to their own lives. Promoting democracy meant challenging and tearing down the most visible impediments to first-class citizenship. For many servicemen, the contradiction between having risked life and limb for the United States only to return to confront the discrimination they had left behind loomed large enough to motivate action. Many soldiers were sorely disappointed by their exclusion from the benefits of the GI Bill and with federally sanctioned discrimination in both the North and South. Hence, veterans like Medgar Evers and Amzie Moore of Mississippi, conscientious objectors like Bayard Rustin and Bill Sutherland, newspapers, churches, and other organizations and institutions became increasingly visible and vocal in their dissatisfaction.

At the same time, the Great Migration of working-class blacks from the South meant vastly increased political power in the North. Black Americans elected men like Adam Clayton Powell Jr. to the U.S. Congress, where he advocated for civil rights. Powell understood the global dimensions of the struggles of people of color against European and U.S. colonialism, and he advocated policies that had the best interests of black people in mind. Hence, during the 1950s, an increasing number of black Americans took interest in their political circumstances. At the same time, the United States had entered into the Cold War with the Soviet Union and vied aggressively for the attention and loyalty of newly liberated African nations. White leaders in the United States knew that these countries would be closely watching the nation's racial situation. Black Americans perceived this and used it to their political advantage (Dudziak 2000, 79–114; Blumberg 1984, 83).

Rising black expectations were accompanied by a sense that it was important to challenge a social order that was long overdue for change. Nearly every decade in the 20th century has recorded race riots in northern cities. Lynching had long been a part of U.S. history, and black men returned from World War II to face renewed racial violence, sometimes while still in military uniform. Very importantly, black Americans were raising a generation of children to understand that there was as yet unfinished "racial equality business" to be addressed in the United States. Hence, the preconditions for social justice ferment were set and awaiting a trigger event. Then, in the first half of the 1950s, two key trigger events occurred that served to dramatically accentuate the meanings people ascribed to the ebb and flow of things occurring around them. They were the Montgomery bus boycott and the lynching of Emmett Till.

The early rumblings of an emerging social justice movement were made in a letter by the Women's Political Council (WPC) of Montgomery to the city's mayor only a few days after the *Brown* decision. Jo Ann Robinson, a professor at Alabama State College and president of the WPC, expressed concerns over the city ignoring the demands of black bus riders who were outraged by both their poor treatment on city vehicles and a proposed fare increase. In pressing for concessions in a city where 75 percent of passengers were black, the WPC letter urged the mayor and city commissioners to respond favorably to its concerns, warning that 25 or more local organizations and businesses were considering a citywide bus boycott. The mayor ignored the letter.

Within a decade of its inception in 1946, the WPC, made up of 40 black middle-class women, had shown itself willing and able to challenge white supremacy. The WPC's zeal to challenge the second-class citizenship imposed by white power was accompanied by the personal courage and commitment of E. D. Nixon, who in 1943 had formed the Montgomery Voter's League. In seeking to mobilize the black community, Nixon, a Pullman train porter who was also head of the Alabama chapter of the Brotherhood of Sleeping Car Porters and president of a local chapter of the NAACP, joined forces with the WPC and Montgomery's black attorneys, business leaders, professionals, church representatives, and civic leaders to devise a strategy to challenge and destroy the practice of segregation and discrimination in Montgomery.

Jo Ann Robinson, E. D. Nixon, and others recognized that the *Brown* decision's invalidation of the *Plessy* standard opened a tremendous opportunity to pursue a test case against the constancy with which Montgomery's whites took segregation for granted. Ever watchful for the right opportunity to prompt meaningful political activity in opposition to segregation and discrimination, concerned blacks in Montgomery watched carefully as local law enforcement officials arrested 15-year-old Claudette Colvin for refusing to give up her seat to a white person on a city bus in March 1955. While the WPC was prepared to spur the black community to activism on behalf of the exercise of their civil rights, E. D. Nixon argued that Colvin did not present the kind of public image that would galvanize Montgomery's black community.

The second trigger event was the August 1955 lynching of Emmett Till and the subsequent trial of his murderers, which was unjustly biased in favor of the defendants. While visiting relatives in Mississippi, Till flirted with a white woman in a store. That evening, he was murdered by the woman's husband and brother-in-law, who subsequently boasted of the crime in a story they later sold to *Look* magazine. Till's youth, the gruesome nature of his murder (which Till's mother insisted the public see via an open-casket funeral), and the mockery of any sense of justice for calculated murder pushed many black people and their white allies to the edge of tolerance.

Within months of Till's murder, and with the *Brown* decision on her side, on December 1, 1955, Rosa Parks, a graduate of the laboratory school at Alabama State College, self-employed seamstress, secretary of the Montgomery branch of the NAACP, and mentor for the local NAACP Youth Council, boarded a bus in Montgomery, paid the fare, and refused to give up her seat to a white person when ordered to do so by the bus driver, who had insulted her on an earlier occasion. Parks was arrested, booked at the police station for violating Montgomery's segregation laws, and fined $10 plus court fees.

Immediately, as if the right moment had presented itself, two things happened. First, E. D. Nixon bailed Rosa Parks out of the city jail and asked for her approval to mobilize community residents. Second, the next day, Jo Ann Robinson, along with other WPC members, students, and community activists, printed and circulated 35,000 handbills decrying the discriminatory treatment of Montgomery's black citizens. The flyer, in highlighting the fact that Rosa Parks's case marked the second time a black woman was arrested for refusing to surrender her seat to a white person in Montgomery, asked community residents to participate in a one-day bus boycott to show city officials that Montgomery's black residents were ready to assert their new social expectations.

Rosa Parks's civil disobedience and arrest became the trigger event that instigated the mobilization of Montgomery's black community. By boycotting city buses on December 5, 1955, Montgomery's black community set a movement into motion. E. D. Nixon, a number of ministers, and other community leaders convened a meeting at the Holt Street Baptist Church to discuss whether to continue the boycott. They created an organization, the Montgomery Improvement Association (MIA), to spearhead the protest. As the organization's president they chose Dr. Martin Luther King Jr., the young, educated, articulate new minister of Montgomery's Dexter Avenue Baptist Church. Only 26 years old at the time, King was invited to address an immense audience that filled the church to capacity. Outside, thousands more listened on loudspeakers as King invoked an idea he would return to in many future speeches: the connection between the expectation of equality as a realizable goal in the United States and direct-action social protest. When Reverend King had completed his comments, Rosa Parks stood and was applauded for her tenacity. Then Rev. Ralph Abernathy rose to present the demands advanced by the MIA and to call for those present to express their will. The response from those assembled was a resounding affirmation of the plan to push forward to destroy discrimination on Montgomery's buses.

That momentous evening marked the threshold point at which Montgomery's black community connected the expectation of better treatment with their ability to initiate and sustain direct-action social protest; the bus boycott lasted 13 months and succeeded in changing social policy in Montgomery. Further, that evening marked a recognition of the ability of a small group of visionary activist community leaders and residents to conceive and orchestrate the mobilization of thousands of their neighbors. It established a community's courage and resolve in deciding to articulate and stand behind core values that defined and guided their decisions and choices. That evening revealed a community's wisdom and trust in choosing a very young, energetic, courageous, and visionary spokesman in Martin Luther King Jr. Finally, that evening and King's speech launched his leadership of the MIA and placed him at the forefront of what became the 20th century's Great Awakening.

In the days and weeks that followed the Holt Street Baptist Church meeting, the boycott continued as resourceful community activists organized carpools. Many black women and men simply walked. Although many

Rev. Martin Luther King Jr. speaks at a 1956 meeting of the Montgomery Improvement Association. (*Library of Congress*)

Montgomery blacks feared retaliation and violence, especially by police, the Ku Klux Klan, or the White Citizens' Council, they would not quit. Weekly meetings kept community residents informed, kept the carpooling efforts as sharp as possible, and raised money for the MIA. Frequent speeches by King infused a belief in the power of nonviolence. King's message on the importance of meeting hate with love established a moral pillar that strengthened those involved in the struggle in Montgomery and galvanized compassionate allies who looked from afar. Even after terrorists bombed his home on January 30, 1956, King refused to surrender to hate.

Two days after King's home was firebombed, longtime Montgomery civil rights attorney Fred Gray filed a federal lawsuit on behalf of five plaintiffs challenging Montgomery's bus segregation. The same day, E. D. Nixon's home was bombed. Days later, in an effort to destroy the boycott, Montgomery officials convened a grand jury to indict MIA leaders on a municipal antiboycott law. On February 21, 1956, Dr. King, 24 ministers, and 64 Montgomery residents were indicted for conspiracy to boycott. The press publicized the boycott, particularly King's nonviolent leadership style. As King accepted invitations to speak around the country, his visibility and popularity grew steadily, lending a great deal of support to the boycott. King was becoming a prominent and influential national presence.

Nevertheless, King's arrest indicated that segregationists were not going to back down, even if they no longer had the law on their side. Southern intransigence was indicated by *The Southern Manifesto*, presented by southern governors, members of Congress, and business leaders in March 1956. The document announced their refusal to abide by the *Brown* decision. The visibility of the intransigence of southern segregationists and their total unwillingness to compromise or follow the law appalled many blacks in other parts of the country, as well as a number of moderate whites who looked on in disbelief. As the national media contrasted the nonviolence of civil rights efforts under King's direction with the violence of the Ku Klux Klan and other white individuals and organizations, public opinion began to shift in favor of integration and civil rights protesters.

On November 13, 1956, the Supreme Court affirmed a lower court's ruling that segregation on buses was unconstitutional. Montgomery blacks had scored their biggest victory. In Birmingham; Mobile, Alabama; Tallahassee, Florida; and other cities, black Americans launched bus boycotts. Building upon the success of the MIA, King, Abernathy, and a number of other ministers met in Atlanta in January 1957 to reflect on the boycotts and the future of the movement. The decision was made to form a new organization: the Southern Christian Leadership Conference. Dr. King was elected its president.

While the social justice challenges that drew Rosa Parks, Jo Ann Robinson, E. D. Nixon, the MIA, Martin Luther King Jr., and Ralph Abernathy into a complex set of circumstances were compelling in their own right, elsewhere in the South equally compelling events unfolded. In Little Rock, Arkansas, 1957 proved to be a complicated year in terms of civil rights. Little Rock had made greater progress toward integration than many other southern cities. One-third of black voters in Little Rock were registered. Parks, libraries, and public buses had already been integrated. Black men served on the city's police force. Daisy Bates, president of the Arkansas NAACP, referred to Little Rock as a progressive city in terms of civil rights.

Although the *Brown* Supreme Court decision called for desegregation "with all deliberate speed," Little Rock officials were extremely slow to adopt any official desegregation policy. Segregationists called for a state constitutional amendment to obstruct the Supreme Court's edict. Gov. Orval Faubus announced that he would not promote any change that whites were opposed to. In response, the Arkansas NAACP filed a lawsuit challenging the school board's delay in desegregating Little Rock's schools. To counter this action, the state legislature created the Sovereignty Commission, which made attendance at integrated schools voluntary, required the NAACP to disclose the names of its members and its budget, and made funds available to the segregationist Capital Citizens' Council. Additionally, the Little Rock school board narrowed down the number of black students who would integrate Central High School from 75 to 9. Then, just before their arrival, the school's chancellor received a temporary injunction to delay desegregation. When a federal judge ordered that the ban be superseded, Governor Faubus announced that he was going to surround Central High School with 250 National Guard troops because rioting would occur if integration efforts proceeded.

This defiance of a federal court order compelled President Dwight D. Eisenhower to send more than a thousand troops from the 101st Airborne Division to secure the safety of the nine black students chosen to integrate

Central High School from mobs of segregationists who outnumbered Little Rock's police force and threatened violence. Each student was assigned a bodyguard to protect him or her on the trips to and from Central High School, as well as within the building. As weeks became months, a federalized National Guard was required to stay at Central High School to protect them. Ernest Green was the first to graduate, saying that he knew he was walking for all the others who had braved so much hate. The following year, Governor Faubus closed the city's public schools, choosing to work with other segregationists to privatize Little Rock's schools. Their efforts were finally turned back for good in August 1959, when NAACP and federal efforts led to the reopening of Little Rock's schools.

## Conclusion

Although historians usually identify the civil rights movement as having occurred between 1955 and 1968, it is vital to connect the events of those years to their antecedents and successors. Such relationships establish that the black freedom struggle continues to this day and will remain an important part of the fabric of the United States until all marginalized groups achieve the full equality promised them by the U.S. Constitution. The seeds sown by people like A. Philip Randolph, Marcus Garvey, and W. E. B Du Bois did not die with them, but have taken on myriad forms that have permanently and forever altered our society's cultural, political, economic, and social landscapes.

## References and Further Reading

Aptheker, Herbert, ed. 1993a. *A Documentary History of the Negro People in the United States, 1951–1959: From the Korean War to the Emergence of Martin Luther King, Jr.,* vol. 6. New York: Carroll.

Aptheker, Herbert, ed. 1993b. *A Documentary History of the Negro People in the United States, 1945–1951: From the End of World War II to the Korean War,* vol. 5. New York: Carroll.

Arnesen, Eric, ed. 2003. *Black Protest and the Great Migration: A Brief History with Documents.* Boston: Bedford/St. Martin's.

Badger, Anthony. 1999. "The White Reaction to *Brown*: Arkansas, the Southern Manifesto, and Massive Resistance." In *Understanding the Little Rock Crisis: An Exercise in Remembrance and Reconciliation,* edited by Elizabeth Jacoway and C. Fred Williams. Fayetteville: University of Arkansas Press.

Baldwin, Lewis V., and Aprille V. Woodson. 1992. *Freedom Is Never Free: A Biographical Portrait of Edgar Daniel Nixon.* Atlanta: A. Woodson.

Blaustein, Albert P., and Robert L. Zangrando, eds. 1968. *Civil Rights and the American Negro.* New York: Washington Square Press.

Blumberg, Rhoda Lois. 1984. *Civil Rights: The 1960s Freedom Struggle.* Boston: Twayne.

Carson, Clayborne, David J. Garrow, Gerald Gill, Vincent Harding, and Darlene Clark Hine, eds. 1991. *The Eyes on the Prize Civil Rights Reader: Documents, Speeches and Firsthand Accounts from the Black Freedom Struggle, 1954–1990.* New York: Penguin.

Carson, Clayborne, Emma J. Lapsansky-Werner, and Gary B. Nash, eds. 2005. *African American Lives: The Struggle for Freedom, Volume Two: Since 1865.* New York: Pearson Longman.

Cronon, Edmund. 1955. *Black Moses.* Madison: University of Wisconsin Press.

Darling, Marsha Jean. 1994. "We Have Come This Far by Our Own Hands: A Tradition of African American Self-Help and Philanthropy and the Growth of Corporate Philanthropic Giving to African Americans." In *African Americans and the New Policy Consensus: Retreat of the Liberal State?* edited by Marilyn E. Lashley and Melanie Njeri Jackson. Westport, CT: Greenwood Press.

Du Bois, W. E. B. 1973 [1903]. *The Souls of Black Folk.* Millwood, NY: Kraus-Thomson.

Dudziak, Mary L. 2000. *Cold War Civil Rights: Race and the Image of American Democracy.* Princeton, NJ: Princeton University Press.

Giddings, Paula. 1984. *When and Where I Enter: The Impact of Black Women on Race and Sex in America.* New York: William Morrow.

Gosse, Van, ed. 2005. *The Movements of the New Left, 1950–1975: A Brief History with Documents.* Boston: Bedford/St. Martin's.

Gray, Fred. 1995. *Bus Ride to Justice: Changing the System by the System: The Life and Works of Fred D. Gray, Preacher, Attorney, Politician.* Montgomery, AL: Black Belt Press.

Greenberg, Jack. 1994. *Crusaders in the Courts: How a Dedicated Band of Lawyers Fought for the Civil Rights Revolution.* New York: Basic.

Hamilton, Charles V. 1991. *Adam Clayton Powell, Jr.: The Political Biography of an American Dilemma.* New York: Atheneum.

Hampton, Henry, and Steve Fayer. 1991. *Voices of Freedom: An Oral History of the Civil Rights Movement from the 1950s through the 1980s.* New York: Bantam.

Jaynes, Gerald David, and Robin M. Williams Jr. 1989. *A Common Destiny: Blacks and American Society.* Washington, DC: National Academies Press.

Lawson, Steven F., ed. 2004. *To Secure These Rights: The Report of Harry S. Truman's Committee on Civil Rights.* Boston: Bedford/St. Martin's.

Lincoln, C. Eric. 1961. *The Black Muslims in America.* Boston: Beacon Press.

Lipsitz, George. 1998. *The Possessive Investment in Whiteness: How White People Profit from Identity Politics.* Philadelphia: Temple University Press.

Martin, Waldo E., Jr., ed. 1998. *Brown v. Board of Education: A Brief History with Documents.* Boston: Bedford/St. Martin's.

McNeil, Genna Rae. 1993. *Groundwork: Charles Hamilton Houston and the Struggle for Civil Rights.* Philadelphia: University of Pennsylvania Press.

Moses, Wilson. 1978. *The Golden Age of Black Nationalism, 1850–1925.* New York: Oxford University Press.

Muhammad, Elijah. 1965. *Message to the Blackman in America*. Chicago: Muslim Mosque No. 2.

Nieman, Donald G. 1991. *Promises to Keep: African Americans and the Constitutional Order, 1776 to the Present*. New York: Oxford University Press.

Robinson, Jo Ann Gibson. 1987. *The Montgomery Bus Boycott and the Women Who Started It: The Memoir of Jo Ann Gibson Robinson*. Knoxville: University of Tennessee Press.

Sitkoff, Harvard. 1993. *The Struggle for Black Equality: 1954–1992*. New York: Hill and Wang.

Sterling, Dorothy. 1994. *The Trouble They Seen: The Story of Reconstruction in the Words of African Americans*. New York: Da Capo Press.

Stockley, Grif. 2005. *Daisy Bates: Civil Rights Crusader from Arkansas*. Jackson: University Press of Mississippi.

Washington, James M., ed. 1986. *A Testament of Hope: The Essential Writings and Speeches of Martin Luther King, Jr*. San Francisco: Harper and Row.

Williams, Juan. 1987. *Eyes on the Prize: America's Civil Rights Years, 1954–1965*. New York: Viking.

Woodward, C. Vann. 1974 [1955]. *The Strange Career of Jim Crow*. New York: Oxford University Press.

# Student Activists | 2

## Francis Shor

When four black students from North Carolina Agricultural and Technical College sat down at a "whites only" lunch counter in Greensboro, North Carolina, on February 1, 1960, they posed more than a momentary challenge to the segregated facilities at this particular Woolworth's store. Although this was not the first civil rights protest led by students, the Greensboro sit-in galvanized the imaginations of black and white students throughout the United States. Cleveland Sellers, then a 16-year-old in Denmark, South Carolina, later wrote that the Greensboro sit-in "hit me like a shot of adrenalin" (Sellers 1973, 18). That shot resonated throughout the South, where thousands of students, mostly black, initiated what one study of the civil rights movement called a "decade of disruption" (Morris 1984, 195).

In the furious few months that followed the Greensboro sit-in, black students in the South, particularly at movement centers such as Nashville; Atlanta; and Washington, D.C., and white students on northern campuses from Boston to Berkeley, California, became the shock troops of the civil rights movement. In the process, they formed critical student-based national organizations including the Student Nonviolent Coordinating Committee (SNCC) in April 1960 and offshoots such as the Northern Student Movement (1961) and Friends of SNCC (1962). These civil rights protests and networks also informed the early activities of Students for a Democratic Society (SDS). By contesting segregation at the local, state, and federal levels, student activists underscored their commitment to the expressions of moral politics and participatory democracy that defined the protests of the 1960s.

Although the wave of student sit-ins in the South during early 1960s created the compelling context for student activism throughout the decade, how that activism developed and changed, especially from 1960 to 1966, is the subject of this chapter. By considering the struggles of student activists, this chapter sheds light on their motivations, commitments, and accomplishments.

The sit-in movement began when four North Carolina A&T students sat at a segregated lunch counter at a Greensboro Woolworth's store. Their protest for equal access to public accommodations jumpstarted the civil rights movement throughout the South. (*Library of Congress*)

While their developing radicalization will be a topic of concern, it is nonetheless important to emphasize that "initially most student protestors aspired to middle-class status and did not basically object to American society or its dominant political institutions. They protested against the pace rather than the direction of change" (Carson 1981, 14).

On the other hand, the changes demanded by student activists in the civil rights movement had profound effects not only on the social and political institutions that perpetuated racial oppression but also on the political consciousness of a whole generation of young people. Certainly, the civil rights movement involved more than college students. In fact, the mass mobilizations that swept through the South involved everyone from children to senior citizens. Yet it was college students, frustrated by outmoded authority structures, relatively free from constraining responsibilities, and insistent on the immediacy of change, who, in the words of Charles McDew, the first chairman of SNCC, "seized the initiative . . . instead of sitting idly by" (Sellers 1973, 44). According to Tom Hayden, a founding member of SDS and the key contact between SDS and SNCC in the early period, the "student civil rights movement took the moral leadership, showing how values could be translated into direct action. Students across the country became agents for social change on a larger scale than ever before" (Hayden 2003, 29).

## Motivations

For some of the first student activists in the civil rights movement, preexisting religious beliefs and networks informed their commitments and direct-

## Student Nonviolent Coordinating Committee

The Student Nonviolent Coordinating Committee (SNCC) was formed as a result of a series of meetings that were held by college students involved in the 1960 sit-in campaigns that spread throughout North Carolina and neighboring states. After witnessing several months of student-led sit-ins beginning in February, organizer Ella Baker, the executive director of the Southern Christian Leadership Conference (SCLC), held a conference for student activists at Shaw University in Raleigh, North Carolina, in April.

At the conference, Baker urged these student leaders to form a new organization to not only challenge white racism but also push traditional civil rights groups into more radical action. The group elected a president, Fisk University student Marion Barry, and set up headquarters in Atlanta. In its first year, SNCC expanded its activities from sit-ins at lunch counters to demonstrations at chain stores and restaurants.

SNCC began its voter registration efforts in 1962, combining with organizations like the National Association for the Advancement of Colored People, SCLC, and the Congress of Racial Equality to form the Voter Education Project and concentrating its efforts in Louisiana and Mississippi. SNCC organizers, most notably the former Harvard University student Bob Moses, went from town to town organizing local residents into voting blocs. Because Mississippi's state Democratic Party did not allow blacks to vote in the primary, SNCC set up a freedom vote in 1963, which paralleled the all-white election and allowed 80,000 blacks to participate in an electoral process normally closed to them.

SNCC took this Mississippi campaign for political representation a step further the following year when it helped create the Mississippi Freedom Democratic Party, which demanded to be seated at the Democratic National Convention in place of the all-white state Democratic delegates. Although President Lyndon Johnson failed to seat the group, it brought national attention to the issue of black disenfranchisement and forced the party to reconsider the rules of its state primaries and apportionment of delegates.

During the mid-1960s, the integrated organization reconsidered its core values and began to kick whites out of the organization. It ousted John Lewis, a disciple of Martin Luther King Jr. from the chairmanship and elected Stokely Carmichael as its new leader, thus signaling its turn toward a black power ideology.

action activities. In its inception and early years, SNCC often articulated a self-reflective African American social gospel. This was particularly evident in the movement center of Nashville and the influence of Rev. James Lawson. Lawson, whose radical Christian ideology and militant nonviolence permeated much of the discursive and dramaturgical moments of SNCC's initial direct-action campaigns, including the 1960 sit-ins and the Freedom Rides of 1961, conducted a series of workshops in 1959 for Nashville college students. As David Halberstam noted, the "crucial lesson" was that "[o]rdinary people who acted on conscience and took terrible risks were no longer ordinary people. They were by their very actions transformed" (Halberstam 1998, 62).

When members of the Nashville Student Movement met with other college students from around the South in April 1960 in North Carolina for the founding of SNCC, Lawson was there as one of the keynote speakers to inspire the gathering with his religious vision. "Love," Lawson preached, "is the force by which God binds man to Himself and man to man. Such love goes to the extreme; it remains loving and forgiving even in the midst of hostility. It matches the capacity of evil to inflict suffering with an even more enduring capacity to absorb evil, all the while persisting in love" (Branch 1999, 291). According to historian Milton Viorst, Lawson's role in shaping "a student movement in the South . . . would become more influential than [Martin Luther] King in imparting to it a nonviolent character" (Viorst 1979, 103).

In its founding documents and in articles published during its first years in the SNCC newspaper *The Student Voice*, the organization endorsed not only Lawson's nonviolent orientation but also his transcendent ideals. SNCC's original statement of purpose echoed Lawson: "We affirm the philosophical or religious ideal of nonviolence as the foundation of our purpose, the pre-supposition of our faith, and the manner of our action. . . . Through nonvio-lence, courage displaces fear; love transforms hate . . . hope ends despair. . . . The redemptive community supercedes systems of gross social immorality" (Carson 1981, 23). Commenting on the sit-ins and kneel-ins conducted by SNCC members throughout the South, writers in the October 1960 edition of *The Student Voice* related such actions to evidence of "love by God" (Kneen 1960, 1, 4) and "the calling to American Christians to take a stand on this moral dilemma" (Laue 1960, 1, 4). Among the young black college activists participating in the kneel-ins in Atlanta was Spelman College first-year stu-dent Ruby Doris Smith. Her comments in the August 1960 *Atlanta Ledger* underscored the redemptive orientation of such actions: "I think the kneel-in is an appeal to the consciences of Christians, who are primarily 'good' people" (Fleming 1998, 56).

The religious and spiritual ethos that underscored Lawson's influence on SNCC was given further credence in the reflections of Nashville students who later became important SNCC leaders. Diane Nash, a Fisk University student and organizer of both the Nashville sit-ins and the Freedom Rides, affirmed, "We aspired in the sixties to the redeemed community or, as we frequently called it, the beloved community. A community recovered or ful-filled, a community that could become more of what its potential was" (Greenberg 1998, 18). In his memoirs, John Lewis, one of the Nashville seminary students and SNCC chairman from 1963 to 1966, avowed that "believers in the Beloved Community insist that it is the moral responsibil-ity of men and women with soul force . . . to respond and to struggle non-violently against the forces that stand between a society and the harmony it naturally seeks." For Lewis, the Beloved Community was "nothing less than the Christian concept of the Kingdom of God on earth" (Lewis 1998, 87).

If Lawson was the intellectual mentor for student activists in SNCC, their organizational mentor was Ella Baker, the former organizer for the National Association for the Advancement of Colored People (NAACP) and the Southern Christian Leadership Conference (SCLC). In response to Baker's guidance, SNCC developed a "group-centered leadership" (Ransby 2003, 259) that implicitly critiqued charismatic church leaders such as Dr. Martin Luther King Jr. Baker saw in black student activism the potential for

In 1961, the Congress of Racial Equality sponsored a series of bus trips called Freedom Rides, which consisted of interracial groups of civil rights volunteers traveling throughout the South. One of the buses was attacked in Anniston, Alabama. The passengers were beaten and the bus was firebombed. (*Library of Congress*)

a mass-based freedom movement in the South. She confided to her close comrade and white antiracist activist Anne Braden that such a movement "may only be a dream of mine, but I think it can be made real" (Ransby 2003, 238). Making it real for Baker meant breaking "with the largely middle-class male centered leadership of existing civil rights organizations" and stripping away "the class-based and gender-based notions of who should and could give leadership to the movement and the black community" (Ransby 2003, 245).

Among the early student leaders in SNCC, Diane Nash and John Lewis helped to forge the connections between the Baker-inspired "group-centered leadership" and the Lawson-inspired religious spirit and militant "soul force" into direct action. One of the most dramatic and bloodiest of these campaigns was the Freedom Rides, the integrated effort by the Congress of Racial Equality (CORE) to desegregate interstate bus transportation in the South. After the protesters faced horrible violence in Alabama and were forced to discontinue their campaign, SNCC activists including Nash and Lewis took their place.

However, not all of the student Freedom Riders, like Stokely Carmichael, born in Trinidad and raised in New York City, were motivated or moved by religious convictions. Carmichael nonetheless answered the call to join the Freedom Rides with other student members of Howard University's Nonviolent Action Group (NAG). When the Freedom Riders were arrested and thrown in jail in Mississippi, the "NAG folk," Carmichael recalled, "would generally abstain from the prayer and hymn singing and discuss the politics of our situation quietly off to one side" (Carmichael and Thelwell 2003, 172).

The politics of "NAG folk," as Carmichael explains, "were secular and militantly confrontational within the framework of a nonviolent activism" (Carmichael 2003, 259). Claiming to be "an organization mostly of students but . . . not a student organization" (Carmichael and Thelwell 2003, 146), Carmichael remembers NAG's role as "foot soldiers on the picket lines" (Carmichael and Thelwell 2003, 162). When Cleveland Sellers joined NAG in 1962, the organization already had a formidable local reputation for conducting demonstrations to desegregate facilities throughout Washington, D.C. Eventually, NAG moved beyond the confines of the U.S. capital into the segregated hinterlands of Maryland and Virginia, joining with SNCC in the process but bringing a secular and tentatively tactical commitment to nonviolence (Sellers 1973, 59–80).

Nonetheless, the Nashville religious ethos spread throughout early SNCC endeavors. SNCC field secretary Hollis Watkins testified, "I had the kind of faith and confidence in the Creator that because I was doing part of His work, I would be able to come through it" (Powledge 1991, 467). Charles Sherrod, director of SNCC's Albany Movement, asked his constituents, "If God be for us, who can be against us?" (Greenberg 1998, 58). Picking up on the religious sensibilities of southern blacks, a special edition of *The Student Voice* entreated locals: "We ask for your prayers and a strong conviction to act as a Christian must. We are not supermen. We are only young people with a determination to be FREE and to be FREE NOW!" (*The Student Voice* 1962, 2).

SNCC was a voice not only for black students but also for whites who were drawn to the civil rights movement. Southern white students attracted to SNCC were usually from Christian backgrounds. White SNCC activists Sam Shirah, Bob Zellner, Mary King, and Jane Stembridge had fathers who were ministers. Commenting on the social gospel preached by her father, a Methodist minister, Mary King wrote, "The gospel was to him the radically transforming news that each individual is precious in God's sight, and therefore personal salvation was all but meaningless to my father if it was devoid of concern for fundamental justice for others" (King 1987, 54). Bob Zellner described both his parents as "sincere Christians who believe not only that all men are brothers but that good people should actively work to 'post proof that brotherhood is not so wild a dream as those who profit by postponing it pretend'" (Zellner n.d., 2).

When Bob Zellner, along with four other students from the all-white Methodist school Huntingdon College, acted on these convictions by worshiping at black churches, they were asked to withdraw from school. Other white southern students, especially women, also became involved with SNCC as a result of their associations with Christian networks. Constance Curry, reared in vacation Bible schools and church camps, used her position as the Southern Human Relations project director for the National Student Association to become an early adviser to SNCC. Jane Stembridge, a Christian, became SNCC's first office secretary. Sue Thrasher and Joan Browning were in Nashville in 1961, becoming part of the Lawson workshops and

## Southern Student Organizing Committee

The Southern Student Organizing Committee (SSOC) was a short-lived organization that formed to attract more white support to the civil rights movement. The SSOC was designed not for whites to simply latch onto black freedom struggles, but so that they could take the civil rights movement into white communities in order to convince whites to make the struggle their own.

In April 1964 in Nashville, a handful of white students convened and adopted a statement against poverty, racial discrimination, and segregation called "We'll Take Our Stand," which delineated the following goals: an end to segregation and racism and the rise of full and equal opportunity for all; an end to personal poverty and deprivation; an end to public poverty, which left people without decent schools, housing, parks, medical care, and communities; a democratic society in which politics poses meaningful dialogue and choices that affect people's lives; an end to man's inhumanity to man; and a world working toward erasing the tensions of the Cold War with a positive emphasis on peace, disarmament, and worldwide understanding.

SSOC members were generally white, middle class, and deeply religious and often took their cues from their black predecessors in the civil rights struggle. While its early campaigns, such as its White Folks Project, mirrored contemporary civil rights protests, as the movement turned toward black nationalism and much of its vanguard moved away from interracial coalitions as a means of solving racism, the SSOC shifted its focus to other issues of the day. Most notably, its organizers began to concentrate on antiwar demonstrations, but the SSOC also partnered with labor unions to organize southern workers and challenged *in loco parentis* laws that universities used to clamp down on student protests. While the organization only lasted until the end of the decade, it had an effect on the era by marshaling white support for the black freedom struggle, legitimizing student protest, and raising awareness of the struggles of working-class whites.

SNCC activism. In Texas, Dorothy Dawson Burlage and Sandra "Casey" Cason brought their antiracist activism as members of interracial religious organizations, such as the Young Women's Christian Association and the Christian Faith and Life Community, into early efforts with SNCC.

SNCC also attracted secular leftist northern white students. One such activist was Dorothy Miller. After graduating from college she worked with the Southern Regional Council in Atlanta and as an aid to SNCC's Julian Bond. For Miller, who was married to Bob Zellner, these experiences constituted her "first exposure to Black culture and . . . to ministers and religious people" (Schultz 2001, 6). Another northern student, Penny Patch, became in 1962 the first white woman to participate in an SNCC project in the Deep South.

By 1963, white student activists, spurred by the increasing tempo of civil rights demonstrations, particularly SCLC's campaign in Birmingham and the March on Washington, were coming to the South in larger numbers. A biracial coalition of students also became a major force during a civil rights campaign in Cambridge, Maryland. Beyond lending assistance in projects from fund-raising to clothing drives, student activists also engaged their desire for social change. "We went South," according to one white student activist, "because we could see no way of making our own lives meaningful by working for change in our white world" (Louis 1970, 110). Harvard University student John Perdew traveled to Georgia in 1963 with "only an abstract, intellectual concept of race relations" (Carson 1981, 72–73). After getting arrested in a civil rights march, going to jail, and then getting arrested again after his release, Perdew began to understand the racial injustices encountered daily by southern blacks. As one study of northern, middle-class students asserted, "exposure to the southern judiciary and personal suffering stemming from the limitations of federal as opposed to state power . . . served to teach lifelong lessons to those young people in American democratic reality" (Fager 1967, 95).

## Commitments

SNCC's primary focus was to mobilize the South's indigenous black population. SNCC organizers not only moved students to action but also recruited local people. Among SNCC's most inspiring student activists was Bob Moses, a black northerner and Harvard graduate. With his religious background as a Quaker, his philosophical orientation to prophetic Christianity, and the almost mystical devotion he elicited from many SNCC members and indigenous black folk, Moses convinced many local people to join the movement. As his biographer noted, "Inspired by Moses and the other civil rights workers, by 1963 Delta blacks were more often courageously standing their ground in the county courthouses, more frequently willing to go to jail or to risk their lives; they were becoming psychologically and morally empowered" (Burner 1994, 94).

Organizing throughout Mississippi, especially on voter registration campaigns, Moses drew both students and adults to SNCC-initiated projects. As one local asserted, "I just couldn't understand what Bob Moses was. Sometimes I think he was Moses in the Bible. He pioneered the way for black people in McComb [Mississippi]" (Carson 1981, 78). Black Mississippian and student activist Anne Moody also referred to Moses as a religious figure: "I thought Bob Moses, the director of SNCC in Mississippi, was Jesus Christ in the flesh. A lot of other people thought of him as J.C., too" (Moody 1976, 252).

By turning their attention to voter registration between 1961 and 1964, Moses and SNCC not only provided the impetus for the 1965 Voting Rights Act but also transformed SNCC organizationally. According to historian Allen Matusow, the "decision to mobilize black communities behind efforts to secure political rights decisively changed the character of the organization. It thereafter ceased to be an extracurricular activity of student leaders and became instead the vocation of dedicated young men and women who temporarily abandoned their careers to become full time paid workers (or 'field secretaries') in the movement" (Matusow 1972, 499).

Despite SNCC's transformation, northern students still participated in southern civil rights campaigns. One such campaign was the brainchild of Allard Lowenstein, a former president of the National Student Association

A student worker talks to two southerners during a 1964 voter registration drive. (*National Archives*)

who became immersed in civil rights issues after the murder of Mississippi NAACP activist Medgar Evers. As dean of student affairs at Stanford University, Lowenstein convinced Bob Moses to sponsor a "freedom vote," a mock election intended to empower Mississippi blacks. With the aid of approximately 80 white students from Stanford University and Yale University in the fall of 1963, thousands of black voters turned out in the face of constant harassment and violence.

To draw U.S. attention to the incredible violence faced by civil rights activists, Bob Moses urged SNCC to bring hundreds of white students to Mississippi in the summer of 1964. This project would become known as Freedom Summer. Freedom Summer was probably both the high point and low point of northern student involvement with the southern black freedom struggle. By the end of the campaign a thousand arrests; scores of bombings; beatings; and the murder of six civil rights activists, including white northerners Michael Schwerner and Andrew Goodman and black Mississippian James Chaney, had taken place. As a result of such drama, Freedom Summer mobilized students nationwide to pursue the civil rights agenda in an increasingly radical fashion.

SNCC relied on two mechanisms to recruit students for Freedom Summer: speaking engagements on college campuses by SNCC leaders and the expansion of activities by Friends of SNCC chapters. At an April 1964 appearance at Stanford, Bob Moses addressed 400 students. Calling civil rights the spearhead for the examination of all the nation's ills, Moses reminded potential recruits of the existential dilemmas they would face by joining Freedom Summer. At another such meeting, he told students, "Don't come to Mississippi this summer to save the Mississippi Negro. Only come if you understand, really understand, that his freedom and yours are one" (Burner 1994, 155).

Campus visits by SNCC leaders led to an increased number of Friends of SNCC chapters from a handful in 1962 to more than 50 in 1964. At the University of Wisconsin, a visit by Diane Nash and the efforts of other SNCC activists led to the creation of the Madison Friends of SNCC. Beyond its fund-raising and support efforts, the Madison group became a conduit to directly fund Mississippi projects during and after Freedom Summer. Students like Stuart Ewen, who went to Mississippi during the summer of 1964, returned to campus as transformed activists. Ewen later recalled that the experience was "a political education that changed who I was. . . . I returned to Madison in the spring of 1965 as someone for whom politics and action had become central" (Ewen 1990, 180).

While state universities, such as Wisconsin, the University of Michigan, and the University of California at Berkeley, provided a significant pool of student volunteers, Ivy League schools were even more prominently represented. Although schools like Harvard and Yale had been connected to the civil rights movement prior to the summer of 1964, efforts to attract students from these schools rose for Freedom Summer. According to SNCC executive secretary James Forman, "we made a conscious attempt . . . to recruit from some of the Ivy League schools . . . you know, a lot of us knew . . . what we were up against. So, that we were, in fact, trying to consciously recruit a counter power-elite" (McAdam 1988, 40, 42, 47).

Forman, Moses, and other SNCC leaders knew that the media would follow the high-profile white students to the South, casting a national spotlight on Mississippi in a way that would further arouse the United States to support the civil rights agenda. Beyond the media glare, however, northern student supporters would become the shock troops pushing that agenda and keeping pressure on federal officials during the summer. When Schwerner, Goodman, and Chaney disappeared, Friends of SNCC chapters mobilized. In New York City, hundreds of students demonstrated at the federal building in Manhattan. Friends of SNCC set up a similar effort at the federal building in Boston. Even smaller towns such as Carbondale, Illinois, had such protests, even though the only federal facility for conducting the vigil in Carbondale was a post office.

Beyond the efforts to keep the focus on the dramatic events in Mississippi during the summer of 1964, there were less-publicized changes going on in the lives of Freedom Summer volunteers that would have profound consequences for student activism across the United States. One such volunteer whose experience transformed him from a participant in the civil rights movement to a seminal student leader was Mario Savio. Savio had transferred from Queens College to Berkeley in the fall of 1963 and started interacting with Friends of SNCC and CORE activists. Joining a major demonstration by campus activists against discriminatory hiring practices by the Sheraton Palace Hotel in San Francisco, he was one of the many arrested. He heard about Freedom Summer during his time in jail and decided to volunteer. Reminiscing about what had transpired during his time in Mississippi working on voter registration campaigns, Savio pointed to "a determination on the part of a significant number of young white Americans that racism had to go" (Savio 1985).

When Savio returned to the Berkeley campus in the fall of 1964, he became the new president of the local Friends of SNCC chapter. As such, he, along with other civil rights campus activists, received notification from the university that they could no longer set up recruiting tables for literature distribution on university property. For Savio, with his strong Catholic background and moral commitment to civil rights, to accept the university's restrictions was to betray endangered black Mississippians struggling for racial justice and freedom. Joining with civil rights veterans on campus and student organizations appalled by the curtailment of their free speech, Savio became the impassioned spokesperson for what would become a critical element of student activism, the Berkeley Free Speech Movement (FSM). Without recounting all of the details of the FSM conflict, it is apparent that "for most of the leaders of the Berkeley revolt, the movement was seen as an extension of the civil rights struggle and the Summer Project in particular. The tactical, ideological, and personal imprint of Freedom Summer was everywhere evident in the events at Berkeley" (McAdam 1988, 162).

While the impact of Freedom Summer on white student activists and northern college campuses was instrumental in increasing activism, problems developed within SNCC as a result of the influx of northern white secular students and their unconscious undermining of nascent indigenous black leadership. Nonetheless, SNCC committed itself to the establishment of the Mississippi Freedom Democratic Party (MFDP) to challenge the racist and exclusionary politics of the regular Democratic Party. As an organizational vehicle for empowering marginalized blacks, the MFDP, according to one SNCC field worker, "was the best means of physically organizing the Negroes of Mississippi, of finding indigenous leadership, and building a political structure" (Belfrage 1965, 85). When the liberal establishment undermined the MFDP at the Democratic National Convention in August 1964, Moses observed, "The liberals getting upset at us was inevitable. We are raising fundamental questions about how the poor sharecropper can achieve the Good Life, questions that liberalism is incapable of answering" (Dittmer 1994, 318). In raising these fundamental questions, SNCC also found itself entangled in an organizational and ideological crisis. SNCC's efforts to reshape its outlook and structure in the fall of 1964 reflected not only a break with liberalism but also a turn away from civil rights toward black power. The refusal of the Democratic Party to seat the MFDP convinced many civil rights activists that neither the Democratic Party nor liberals could be counted on for meaningful social change.

Northern white student involvement in the civil rights movement increased during the 1965 Freedom Summer, organized by SCLC. Designated as Summer Community Organizing and Political Education, or SCOPE, this project attracted more students than the 1964 SNCC Freedom Summer, perhaps as a consequence of the national attention devoted to a 1965 voting rights campaign in Selma, Alabama, where state troopers brutally attacked peaceful marchers and killed local activist Jimmie Lee Jackson. In response to these events, demonstrations occurred on many northern campuses. Student outrage intensified when two northerners who had traveled to Alabama for follow-up protests, Rev. James Reeb and Viola Liuzzo, were murdered. These murders unleashed even more campus activity, from vigils to fund-raising to recruiting additional volunteers for a march from Selma to Montgomery. In response to these events, a SCOPE volunteer reflected, "I feel that Civil Rights is the most pressing problem of our time and that working in Civil Rights is the most useful way I can spend my summer, both in terms of duty to humanity and deep personal value" (Rothschild 1982, 39).

Nevertheless, for many students, the 1965 Freedom Summer project created feelings of inadequacy because SNCC was not involved. Some SCOPE volunteers had worked in Mississippi in 1964 as tutors at freedom schools. Others conducted voter registration for the MFDP. A great number idolized Bob Moses. As one study noted, "there was a substantial contingent of SCOPE workers who viewed SCLC as a second-best affiliation. To these people, SNCC represented the soul and the muscle of the movement by virtue of its more militant grassroots credentials when compared to SCLC" (Demerath, Maxwell, and Aiken 1971, 127).

Although most SCOPE volunteers identified themselves as liberals, their liberalism reflected an increasing radicalization. One activist described herself as "a white liberal because I'm white and I'm from the North and I'm working with the Movement" (Alter 1965). Another recognized the need for white northerners to go to the South because it "brings the mass media down here when there are Northern white volunteers getting beat on the head" (Drexel 1965). However, echoing Bob Moses's admonition to the 1964 Freedom Summer volunteers, this student also asserted, "I didn't come down here to help Negroes. I came down here with very selfish intentions to help myself because I live in this social structure and I would help to cure the sickness" (Drexel 1965). The persistence of racism reinforced among student activists that liberalism was at best inadequate and at worst a part of the problem. One student drew the following lesson from the summer: "I could no longer believe in the liberal myth in America" (Demerath, Maxwell, and Aiken 1971, 173). Another SCOPE volunteer acknowledged, "The contradiction between ideology and practice became acutely apparent—apparent to a degree I would not have been aware of if I had remained a 'northern-white liberal.' We're a sick people with a system fabricated on lies" (Demerath, Maxwell, and Aiken 1971, 164).

Another contradiction that became evident to many white students in 1965 was their potential to undermine a movement whose aim was increasingly for black self-determination. Conceding that whites often monopolized leadership to the detriment of the local community, one student hoped for a decrease in white participation. Another SCOPE volunteer and civil rights veteran whose activism included the March on Washington, the freedom vote, and tutoring in a freedom school admitted that "many of us made the mistake of taking over too much . . . instead of training other people to do what we were doing" (Billman 1965).

The flood of white student volunteers created tension within SNCC at the precise moment of its growing estrangement from white liberalism and increasing commitment to black consciousness and empowerment. Additionally, SNCC workers were becoming more alienated from the religious roots of the organization. Already grappling with myriad internal issues, SNCC questioned the religion-inspired hope for a redemptive society at a November 1964 retreat. James Forman contended, "We must continue not necessarily to work for the redemptive society, but to work toward a new spirit of brotherhood, a spirit that transcends both black and white, a spirit that supercedes, a spirit that goes above and a spirit that sees all of us simply as men and women, struggling for a sense of dignity" (King 1987, 449).

Despite such sentiments, Forman's sense of this struggle ignored religion. Throughout his autobiography, for example, Forman manifested a disdain for religion, highlighting the waning influence of Lawson and King and their ideas of redemptive suffering in SNCC. Instead, asserting that "the original religious thrust of the Student Nonviolent Coordinating Committee became a contradiction" (Forman 1985, 238–239), Forman identified the relationship in SNCC between decreasing religionists and increasing revolutionaries. Indeed, from 1963 to 1965, a great number of early SNCC members dedicated to the religious ethos, including James Bevel, Diane Nash, and Charles Sherrod, resigned. In their absence, northern secularists like Cleveland Sellers and Stokely Carmichael claimed leadership roles.

Carmichael's SNCC career particularly represents the coming to power of northern black student activists whose race consciousness and antagonism to religion often pitted them against southern religionist leaders like John Lewis. Lewis felt that people like Carmichael were not interested in the principles of nonviolence or even the Bible. In his autobiography, Carmichael admits that he "never saw my responsibility to be the moral and spiritual reclamation of some racist thug" (Carmichael and Thelwell 2003, 259). During the summer of 1961, this attitude, and the provocative actions that accompanied it, led to Carmichael's being asked to leave the Nashville Student Movement. By the middle of the decade, however, Carmichael's perspective had become predominant within SNCC.

More critically, Carmichael became the most prominent articulator of the "black power" slogan and ideology. Even though its advocates and opponents often invested the phrase with multiple meanings that were sometimes contradictory and confounding, black power galvanized rural blacks in the South and urban blacks in the North. Within SNCC, part of the confusion over black power was attributable to its secular definitions of self-determination, rooted in sources as varied as the speeches of Malcolm X, the anticolonialist writings of Frantz Fanon, and the struggles for Third World liberation. For SNCC, the implications of adopting black power as a primary ideology were crucial not only to the organization but also to a potentially transformed civil rights movement.

Within SNCC, the rifts between separatists and integrationists led many to leave the organization. Even Carmichael found that those in SNCC who

Stokely Carmichael, head of the Student Nonviolent Coordinating Committee, speaks against the draft at the University of California at Berkeley on October 29, 1966. (*AP/Wide World Photos*)

called for black separatism had misunderstood his articulation of black power. One group of SNCC staffers pushed the envelope of black power to a militant nationalist extreme. Denouncing white cultural hegemony in any form, this group, through its actions, reflected a disdain for SNCC's Christian roots. Driving through a black neighborhood, these staffers taunted residents through a loudspeaker: "What has your White Jesus done for you today?" Although this group was marginalized in SNCC, the media seized upon its separatist message, which led to charges that SNCC had become "antiwhite." Carmichael and other advocates of black power denied such misrepresentations (Carson 1981, 229–243).

## Accomplishments

Although SNCC's organizational difficulties were exacerbated by its advocacy of black power, this new direction sustained a number of local efforts, such as the formation of an independent black political party in Lowndes County, Alabama. Black power also invigorated militancy in northern ghettos and college campuses. Although Carmichael contended that SNCC had difficulty responding "nationally to events [because] it carried a southern mentality with it" (Greenberg 1998, 167), Forman argued that "the call for Black Power drew substance from the realities of the lives of black people across the nation. With the equalizing of our problems in North and South, the concept evoked a national response. It had emerged from the Southern experience, but had meaning for black people everywhere" (Forman 1985, 458). Nonetheless, as historian Charles Payne maintains, "The transition

from the Beloved Community to Black Power was accompanied by a jetti-
soning of some of the moral and social anchors that helped regulate relationships among activists when SNCC was in its community-organizing phase"
(Payne 1995, 366).

SNCC's turn to black power came at a time when the attention of white
student activists began to move away from civil rights to other issues, especially those surrounding the Vietnam War. In some instances, white students
who were working among blacks accepted the legitimacy of black power and
returned to their campuses to focus on antiwar activities. According to one
activist, "In the South, the transition from civil rights to the war and campus
issues was continuous and direct. Students who participated in the civil
rights movement were radicalized by their experiences in it" (Michel 2004,
89, 103). By 1966, for most white student activists, the war had become
the defining national issue. Even SNCC felt compelled to issue an antiwar
statement after SNCC volunteer and Navy veteran Sammy Younge Jr. was
murdered when he attempted to use a segregated restroom. Bob Moses crys-
tallized SNCC's philosophy that the Vietnam War was related to the continuing oppression of blacks in the United States. "Our criticism of Vietnam
policy does not come from what we know of Vietnam," argued Moses, "but
from what we know of America" (Hall 2005, 22).

Student activism not only moved the United States toward desegregation but also raised questions about the social construction of race. For
white student activists in the civil rights movement, this confrontation with
the meaning of race challenged their own identities. As the civil rights
movement increasingly adopted black power ideals, both blacks and whites
in the movement came to see the struggle to be as much about white privilege as about black self-determination. Although Carmichael insisted that no
more whites be involved in SNCC, he also clarified that whiteness could be
cast away by those "unusually conscientious and socially aware young people" (Carmichael and Thelwell 2003, 308) who joined the movement and
accepted black leadership. Carmichael also noted that when SNCC's white
student activists "experienced the full force of racist hostility from Southern
white politicians, police, and public opinion, compounded by the indifference or paralysis of the national political establishment, whatever class and
color privileges they might have taken for granted were immediately suspended" (Carmichael and Thelwell 2003, 308).

Taking responsibility for sociopolitical issues and becoming historic
agents of change drew students by the tens of thousands to become activists
in the civil rights movement. During the Berkeley Free Speech Movement,
one campus radical asserted that "students have turned to the civil rights
movement because they have found it to be a front on which they can attack
basic social problems, a front on which they have some real impact" (Martin
2002, 87). Many students gravitated toward SNCC because it offered the
opportunity not only to address continuing racial inequities but also to
engage their own visions of racial justice and human rights. As one historian
contended, "SNCC provided a home for white antiracist activists at a time
when the very notion of white antiracism was all too rare for most Americans" (Schultz 2001, 2).

## Conclusion

Whether going south or staying local, student activists pushed an antiracist agenda that would continue to inform social movements throughout the 1960s. Through a common collective consciousness, historical understanding, and vision of necessary social change, students sought in the civil rights movement an outlet for their insistence on justice and freedom for all Americans. Recalling his involvement in SNCC, Mendy Samstein provided what could stand as a tribute to the legacy of those student activists in the civil rights movement: "I felt, yes, I'm in a black movement, I'm in a civil rights movement, but not just that I'm in a civil rights movement and not just that I'm in a certain struggle at a specific time, but I felt I was joining the human race, and this was what was so moving and continues to move me" (Greenberg 1998, 126).

## References and Further Reading

Belfrage, Sally. 1965. *Freedom Summer*. New York: Viking.

Billman, Bob, Patti Alter, Edith Black, Warren Drexel. 1965. KXSU Interviews. Project South papers, Department of Special Collections, Stanford University Library, Palo Alto, CA.

Branch, Taylor. 1999. *Pillar of Fire: America in the King Years, 1963–1965*. New York: Touchstone.

Branch, Taylor. 2006. *At Canaan's Edge: America in the King Years, 1965–68*. New York: Simon and Schuster.

Burner, Eric. 1994. *And Gently He Shall Lead Them: Robert Parris Moses and Civil Rights in Mississippi*. New York: New York University Press.

Carmichael, Stokely, and Ekwueme Michael Thelwell. 2003. *Ready for Revolution: The Life and Struggles of Stokely Carmichael (Kwame Ture)*. New York: Scribner.

Carson, Clayborne. 1981. *In Struggle: SNCC and the Black Awakening of the 1960s*. Cambridge, MA: Harvard University Press.

Chappell, David. 2004. *A Stone of Hope: Prophetic Religion and the Death of Jim Crow*. Chapel Hill: University of North Carolina Press.

Collier-Thomas, Bettye, and V. P. Franklin, eds. 2001. *Sisters in the Struggle: African American Women in the Civil Rights–Black Power Movement*. New York: New York University Press.

Curry, Constance, Joan C. Browning, Dorothy Dawson Burlage, Penny Patch, Theresa Del Pozzo, Sue Thrasher, Elaine DeLott Baker, Emmie Schrader Adams, and Casey Hayden. 2000. *Deep in Our Hearts: Nine White Women in the Freedom Movement*. Athens: University of Georgia Press.

Demerath, W. J., III, Gerald Maxwell, and Michael T. Aiken. 1971. *Dynamics of Idealism: White Activists in a Black Movement*. San Francisco: Jossey-Bass.

Dittmer, John. 1994. *Local People: The Struggle for Civil Rights in Mississippi*. Urbana: University of Illinois Press.

Ewen, Stuart. 1990. "The Intellectual New Left." In *History and the New Left: Madison, Wisconsin, 1950–1970*, edited by Paul Buhle. Philadelphia: Temple University Press.

Fager, Charles E. 1967. *White Reflections on Black Power*. Grand Rapids, MI: William B. Eerdmans.

Fleming, Cynthia Griggs. 1998. *Soon We Will Not Cry: The Liberation of Ruby Doris Smith Robinson*. Lanham, MD: Rowman and Littlefield.

Forman, James. 1985 [1972]. *The Making of Black Revolutionaries*. Seattle: University of Washington Press.

Gitlin, Todd. 1989. *The Sixties: Years of Hope, Days of Rage*. New York: Bantam.

Greenberg, Cheryl Lynn, ed. 1998. *A Circle of Trust: Remembering SNCC*. New Brunswick, NJ: Rutgers University Press.

Halberstam, David. 1998. *The Children*. New York: Random House.

Hall, Simon. 2005. *Peace and Freedom: The Civil Rights and Antiwar Movements in the 1960s*. Philadelphia: University of Pennsylvania Press.

Hayden, Tom. 2003. *The Rebel: A Personal History of the 1960s*. Los Angeles: Red Hen Press.

Holt, Len. 1965. *The Summer That Didn't End*. New York: William Morrow.

King, Mary. 1987. *Freedom Song: A Personal Story of the 1960s Civil Rights Movement*. New York: William Morrow.

King, Richard H. 1992. *Civil Rights and the Idea of Freedom*. New York: Oxford University Press.

Kneen, Brewster. 1960. "Nonviolence and Vision." *The Student Voice*, October, 1, 4.

Laue, James. 1960. "Sociology, Sin, and Snails?" *The Student Voice*, October, 1, 4.

Levy, Peter B. 2003. *Civil War on Race Street: The Civil Rights Movement in Cambridge, Maryland*. Gainesville: University Press of Florida.

Lewis, John. 1998. *Walking with the Wind: A Memoir of the Movement*. New York: Simon and Schuster.

Louis, Debbie. 1970. *And We Are Not Saved: A History of the Movement as People*. Garden City, NY: Doubleday.

Marsh, Charles. 1997. *God's Long Summer: Stories of Faith and Civil Rights*. Princeton, NJ: Princeton University Press.

Martin, Waldo. 2002. "Holding One Another: Mario Savio and the Freedom Struggle in Mississippi and Berkeley." In *The Free Speech Movement: Reflections on Berkeley in the 1960s,* edited by Robert Cohen and Reginald Zelnik. Berkeley: University of California Press.

Matusow, Allen J. 1972. "From Civil Rights to Black Power: The Case of SNCC, 1960–1966." In *Twentieth Century America: Recent Interpretations,*

2nd ed., edited by Barton J. Bernstein and Allen J. Matusow. New York: Harcourt Brace Jovanovich.

McAdam, Doug. 1988. *Freedom Summer*. New York: Oxford University Press.

Michel, Gregg L. 2004. *Struggle for a Better South: The Southern Student Organizing Committee, 1964–1969*. New York: Palgrave Macmillan.

Miller, James. 1994. *"Democracy is in the Streets": From Port Huron to the Siege of Chicago*. Cambridge, MA: Harvard University Press.

Moody, Anne. 1976 [1968]. *Coming of Age in Mississippi*. New York: Laurel.

Morris, Aldon D. 1984. *The Origins of the Civil Rights Movement*. New York: Free Press.

Payne, Charles M. 1995. *I've Got the Light of Freedom: The Organizing Tradition and the Mississippi Freedom Struggle*. Berkeley: University of California Press.

Polletta, Francesca. 2002. *Freedom Is an Endless Meeting: Democracy in American Social Movements*. Chicago: University of Chicago Press.

Powledge, Fred. 1991. *Free at Last? The Civil Rights Movement and the People Who Made It*. Boston: Little, Brown.

Ransby, Barbara. 2003. *Ella Baker and the Black Freedom Movement*. Chapel Hill: University of North Carolina Press.

Robnett, Belinda. 1997. *How Long? How Long? African-American Women in the Struggle for Civil Rights*. New York: Oxford University Press.

Rogers, Kim L. 1993. *Righteous Lives: Narratives of the New Orleans Civil Rights Movement*. New York: New York University Press.

Rossinow, Doug. 1998. *The Politics of Authenticity: Liberalism, Christianity, and the New Left in America*. New York: Columbia University Press.

Rothschild, Mary Aickin. 1982. *A Case of Black and White: Northern Volunteers and the Southern Freedom Summers, 1964–1965*. Westport, CT: Greenwood Press.

Savio, Mario, interview by Brett Eynon. "Reminiscences of Mario Savio." Interview transcript. 1985. Oral History Collection, Columbia University Library, New York.

Schultz, Debra L. 2001. *Going South: Jewish Women in the Civil Rights Movement*. New York: New York University Press.

Sellers, Cleveland. 1973. *The River of No Return: The Autobiography of a Black Militant and the Life and Death of SNCC*. New York: William Morrow.

Stanton, Mary. 2003. *Freedom Walk: Mississippi or Bust*. Jackson: University Press of Mississippi.

Stoper, Emily. 1989. *The Student Nonviolent Coordinating Committee: The Growth of Radicalism in a Civil Rights Organization*. New York: Carlson.

*Student Voice, The*. 1962 (October): p. 2.

Van Deburg, William L. 1992. *New Day in Babylon: The Black Power Movement and American Culture, 1965–1975*. Chicago: University of Chicago Press.

Viorst, Milton. 1979. *Fire in the Streets: America in the 1960s.* New York: Simon and Schuster.

Zellner, Bob. n.d. "Unpublished Biography." Robert Zellner papers. Tacoma: Washington State Historical Society.

Zinn, Howard. 2002 [1964]. *SNCC: The New Abolitionists.* Cambridge, MA: South End Press.

# Religion and Clergy | 3

## Jill K. Gill

Religious beliefs, cultures, organizations, and clergy were so integral to the civil rights movement that it is difficult to find an aspect of the struggle they did not touch. The contributions of religion and clergy to the movement were so diverse and numerous that it would require volumes to discuss them all. In the first 12 years after the U.S. Supreme Court's *Brown v. Board of Education* decision (1954), which ordered school desegregation, they were indispensable to it, providing much of the needed motivation, energy, resources, education, strategy, organization, and leadership. Clergy and seminarians played key roles, for they were often more able and ready than laity to take personal risks on behalf of social justice. The goal of this chapter is to explain the unique religious contexts that both motivated and mitigated against religious action for civil rights.

## Civil Rights as a Moral Issue

Activist clergy generally saw civil rights as a clear moral issue that compelled religious reflection and response. To them, the issue of race relations called forth divine commands about the treatment of one's neighbors and common humanity before God. Specific issues related to school desegregation evoked biblical dictates about respecting governmental authority while obeying God's higher law. Questions about economic justice stirred up the plethora of biblical injunctions against greed or ignoring the poor. For Jews, the Hebraic tradition's emphasis on ethical behavior and good works, not to mention their own history of enslavement and persecution, strengthened their identification with blacks and fueled their desire to help them gain freedom. For African Americans, Jesus's words about the meek inheriting the earth, the last being first, and divine promises that justice would roll down like a mighty stream made civil rights a religious cause. Conversely, and unlike debates over slavery, those seeking biblical support for racial discrimination found little in Scripture useful to their cause. Segregationists usually leaned more on legal and political arguments than Scripture to defend Jim Crow laws because they were more plentiful and effective.

The televised brutality of racist suppression, in the form of bombings, beatings, murders, and the use of dogs and fire hoses on children, compelled many religious leaders to speak and act on civil rights. However, the voluntary system of religious adherence in the United States, which often ties monetary contributions and attendance to a pleased congregation, meant that clergy had to balance their responses to moral religious questions raised by the movement with the self-interests of their congregants, their neighborhoods, their regions, and themselves.

Although the relationships between clergy and civil rights activism can be traced back centuries, it is prescient to begin with a discussion of the radical pacifism of the 1920s and 1930s that held strong influence among Christians who embraced nonviolence as a way of life, not merely as a tool for social change. Many Christian pacifists also saw racism as a cause of war. Some of them adopted Mohandas Gandhi's nonviolent revolutionary tactics because they were dedicated to changing an unjust system and converting the heart of the oppressor through truth sharing, noncooperation with evil, and a willingness to suffer. Gandhi rooted his methods in spiritual principles that appealed to activists of many faiths. In the United States, students involved in the pacifist Fellowship of Reconciliation created a group called the Congress of Racial Equality (CORE) in 1942 specifically to employ Gandhian nonviolent, direct-action methods to the racial crisis, becoming among the first pioneers to do so. Most of the founders, like James Farmer, were divinity students or were active in the Christian student movement of the 1930s. The group's early focus on interracial cooperation and creating an integrated society reflected Christian values of reconciliation.

Civil rights burst more prevalently into U.S. consciousness as a moral and democratic issue during World War II. Adolf Hitler's extreme racial ideology and genocidal methods helped Americans equate racism with oppression and immorality, two things deemed antithetical to a democratic and Christian America. The Cold War subsequently pitted this supposedly Christian nation against the atheist Soviet Union, thus catapulting the United States onto the world stage in a way that compelled the federal government, and missionizing churches, to protect the national image abroad by seeking greater visible consistency between its words and deeds on racial matters. Modern media gave civil rights activists an effective new tool for exposing the nation's dirty laundry on race to the world in ways that would coerce the government into action.

## Prophetic Clergy

Whereas some clergy retreated from prophetic roles during the repressive and communism-obsessed 1950s, other black and white clergy embraced them through the civil rights movement. Being prophetic was a way for clergy both to seek justice and to revitalize churches and synagogues. These clergy claimed that God was marching in the streets with the oppressed, moving through a wave of liberation activities worldwide, and that persons of religious faith should join them. While clergy often embraced this stance, finding it biblical, laity invested in the status quo did not. Rather, they tended to believe that these social revolutions denoted Communist challenges to legitimate authority. That clergy would seemingly cease being peacemakers to become protesters rankled those who saw this as unchristian and unbecoming for pastors. To different degrees, both black and white clergy had to navigate three sets of challenges when responding to issues raised by the civil rights movement: disagreements over what denoted the sacred and the secular, conflicts between the clergy's priestly and prophetic roles, and the clergy-laity gap that emerged between pastors and parishioners over the first two issues (Friedland 1998, 2–12).

Additionally, economic and political interests weighed against challenging the system. White clergy often found it easier to be prophetic away from their home regions, almost as a missionary activity, rather than in their own neighborhoods. Therefore, many northern white clergy went south to witness against racial injustice where their home congregations had little to lose and could more easily support their leader's work. In conjunction, white clergy without congregations who were paid by an administrative body (e.g., campus ministers, chaplains, seminary professors, members of convents/monasteries, denominational administrators, directors of ecumenical programs) found prophetic work for civil rights far easier because they could afford to be bolder and more active in protests. Conversely, black clergy, who were paid by their congregations, often enjoyed a mandate and freedom to act for civil rights that black laity in the employ of whites lacked. Job security certainly played a role in influencing who participated in the movement and how (Friedland 1998, 7).

Finally, in the 1960s especially, a large gap emerged between clergy and laity in many Protestant, Catholic, and Jewish communities because clergy, and their religious hierarchies, often were more willing to embrace an active prophetic role than laity deemed appropriate or desirable. Polls reveal a direct correlation between regular church attendance and conservatism; the more frequently one attended church, the more likely one was to adhere to conservative theological and political perspectives and to be critical of civil rights activism. On numerous occasions, such laity withheld financial support and attendance to chasten clergy and denominational executives who they felt went too far in advancing social, cultural, political, and economic changes in the name of the Lord. Nevertheless, the power of the civil rights movement, framed as a religious cause and buoyed by spiritual energy, drew a sizable coalition of interfaith clergy and laity together to advocate for it in the face of frightening opposition. This situation occurred at a time when ecumenism and interfaith activity blossomed among Catholics, Protestants, and Jews in new ways. The civil rights movement became a critical means through which to promote such relationships and cooperation (Friedland 1998, 7–8).

Blacks in Albany, Georgia, with the help of civil rights organizations, carried out a local protest movement during 1961 and 1962. In this photo, a group of 500 demonstrators kneel in prayer following their arrest for parading without a permit. (*Bettmann/Corbis*)

## Southern Clergy and Civil Rights

For southerners living in a Bible Belt speckled thickly with churches, religious arguments and leaders carried considerable legitimacy. After the Civil War, segregation among southern churches gave blacks independent organizations through which to mobilize the masses. Religious belief permeated southern black communities. As black activist and sharecropper Fannie Lou Hamer once said, "Only God has kept the Negro sane" (Chappell 2004, 74), and she appealed to visiting northern white activists to respect the deep religious devotion of the black masses. For blacks in the South, the power of their religious beliefs, combined with the ability of their ministers to motivate, inspire, and organize through the churches, made religion indispensable to their fight for freedom.

Changes during and after World War II inspired hope that God might be moving not only in the United States but also around the globe to deliver freedom to the captive. Ministers like Martin Luther King Jr. and Fred Shuttlesworth believed that a revived prophetic faith could both mobilize people into the grassroots force needed to change the white establishment and revitalize black churches by freeing them from local co-optation and complacency. To them, God was at work bringing spiritual powers to bear within their human efforts. King heard the voice of Jesus personally calling him one evening to stand up for righteousness with the promise that God would be with him in the process. After the successful Montgomery bus boycott, the ministers involved created the Southern Christian Leadership Conference (SCLC) to carry civil rights projects into other cities using nonviolent protest to compel legal and political changes. Its leadership structure was rooted in the black southern ministerial community, and it relied upon the authority within ministers' congregations to organize civil rights projects throughout the South and mobilize the laity to make necessary sacrifices to achieve success. It also organized interfaith coalitions of religious leaders to assist with projects like those in Albany, Georgia (1962), Birmingham, Alabama (1963), and Selma, Alabama (1965). Religious books scattered throughout SCLC's Atlanta offices illustrated its strong theological orientation.

Mass meetings held in churches prior to protest marches were often revivalist, drawing out assurances that God was with the people even as they suffered. Some described these meetings as even better than church because they focused on God's plan for the here and now rather than for the afterlife. Many involved, including members of the Student Nonviolent Coordinating Committee (SNCC), saw protest in spiritual terms. Fannie Lou Hamer of SNCC saw herself as working for Jesus through the movement. SNCC leader and future member of the U.S. Congress John Lewis described the student sit-ins as a holy crusade and the dinner prior to the Freedom Rides as a last supper. Like many of SNCC's early leaders, Lewis had been raised in the black church, studied religion in college, and had been drawn into the Nashville student movement under James Lawson's tutelage. Lawson, a seminary student, minister, and Christian pacifist who learned Gandhian methods in India, became a key force for teaching those methods to U.S. activists. Even secular civil rights leaders, such as Bayard Rustin and Bob Moses, recognized the genuine and invaluable commitment that black ministers could generate among a devout black population.

Ardent segregationists discovered quickly that white churches and synagogues would not become the activist bulwarks for segregation that they had hoped for. In fact, when the Supreme Court ordered desegregation of public schools in 1954, the Southern Baptist Convention and the Presbyterian Church in the United States issued statements appealing for obedience to it. These two southern-based Protestant denominations were born out of the slavery debate and had been central to defending slavery. That they refused to fight the Court's desegregation order is significant. In another example, the Catholic archbishop of New Orleans threatened excommunication to segregationist laity who resisted his order to desegregate the city's parochial schools. It is also important that the administrators of religious bodies were usually more supportive of desegregation than the laity. Their pronouncements in favor of obeying the high court received strong condemnations by disappointed white laity whose opposition was stirred by southern politicians promising to defy desegregation by any legal means necessary (Chappell 2004, 123–138; Friedland 1998, 37–43).

White southern clergy who embraced even a gradualist or moderate position on desegregation risked personal attacks by members of their congregations, with some being accused of communism and/or driven from their pulpits by angry parishioners. Often, this anger resulted from a minority of strong segregationists taking action against the minister or rabbi amid

## Martin Luther King Jr.

The rise of Martin Luther King Jr. as the most recognizable leader of the civil rights movement testifies to the importance of religion to the black freedom struggle. King was the eldest son of minister Martin Luther King Sr., who was the pastor of Ebenezer Baptist Church in Atlanta. The younger King was himself ordained as a Baptist minister in 1947 at age 18.

The precocious King graduated from Crozer Theological Seminary in Upland, Pennsylvania, when he was only 22 years of age. He then went on to earn a doctorate in systematic theology from Boston University in 1955. While pursuing his degrees, King studied the teachings of Mohandas Gandhi, the nonviolent Indian leader. He also read antiracist sermons by white Protestant ministers and African American leaders.

In 1954, King accepted his first pastorate at the Dexter Avenue Baptist Church in Montgomery, Alabama. On December 1, 1955, Rosa Parks, a secretary for the local branch of the National Association for the Advancement of Colored People (NAACP), was arrested in Montgomery when she refused to give up her seat to a white man on a bus. City residents, long angered by the shoddy treatment they had received on public transportation, entreated local NAACP official E. D. Nixon for help. Nixon believed that King would be an asset in the antisegregation campaign, and at a meeting at the Dexter Avenue Baptist Church, the minister was elected president of the newly formed Montgomery Improvement Association (MIA). The MIA decided to boycott city buses, and its campaign lasted more than a year, eventually ending segregation on local public transportation and, more importantly, jumpstarting a nationwide series of protests that would eventually come to be known as the civil rights movement. King served as president of the Southern Christian Leadership Conference, which was one of the movement's leading forces.

King's leadership of the civil rights movement was always guided by theology. At the center of his preaching were the Christian ideas of nonviolence and love for one's enemy. In 1959, he visited India and further developed his ideas about Gandhi's philosophy of *satyagraha*. The next year, he left Montgomery to become copastor of Ebenezer alongside his father. From the southern black hub of Atlanta, King became the movement's preeminent spokesperson and most visible figure.

a complacent majority unwilling to fight about it. Laity in numerous congregations also withheld donations from churches, synagogues, and denominational headquarters that supported desegregation. They also often appealed for withdrawal from northern-based ecumenical bodies like the National Council of Churches of Christ in the United States (NCC), which actively supported civil rights. The clergy-laity gap widened (Webb 2001, 169–210; Chappell 2004, 136).

White religious leaders in southern communities frequently criticized their northern compatriots who came to take part in civil rights demonstrations. They accused the northern leaders of stirring up tensions, then returning home to a hero's welcome while ignoring racial tensions and blight in their own neighborhoods. For example, a group of southern Jews confronted northern rabbis who had come to Birmingham in the spring of 1963 to participate in SCLC's civil rights protests. These southern Jews feared that

Martin Luther King Jr. waves to the crowd as he delivers his famous "I Have a Dream" speech during the March on Washington for Jobs and Freedom in Washington, D.C., on August 28, 1963. King was awarded the Nobel Peace Prize in 1964 for his work in the area of human rights. (*Hulton-Deutsch Collection/Corbis*)

their small community would be targeted for heightened anti-Semitism if the rabbis marched with blacks. Particularly, Jewish merchants might be punished economically by customers, investors, and banks if other Jews joined the movement. Some southern Jewish leaders worked individually behind the scenes to facilitate desegregation plans in cities like Dallas, Memphis, and Atlanta. They usually supported gradualist efforts toward racial progress, but they resented the appearance of "rabbinic carpetbaggers" who they felt were grandstanding while putting at risk the quiet goodwill local Jews had tried to nurture with the power structure. In private, however, some southern clergy confessed to their northern brethren that they would participate in such struggles, too, if they did not live in the South and were not answerable to their congregation (Friedland 1998, 37, 49–50, 80).

A few bold southern white clergy, like Methodist Rev. Ed King, worked at the forefront of civil rights activism. As the white chaplain at Mississippi's historically black Tougaloo College, he took part in sit-ins, voter registration drives, the creation of freedom schools, and political organizing. King's most provocative act was his church visits campaign of 1963–1964, when he brought blacks to Jackson's segregated white churches for Sunday worship, forcing uncomfortable confrontations as white congregations wrestled with the hypocrisy of their rhetoric. One historian called King "the most visible white activist in the Mississippi movement" (Dittmer 1994, 202).

## Northern Seminaries and Jewish Involvement

Prior to 1963, white religious organizations outside the South tended to advocate for desegregation through official statements but had done little by way of physical involvement. The NCC, the largest ecumenical religious body in the United States at the time, comprising more than 30 Protestant and Orthodox denominations that represented more than 40 million Americans as members, condemned racism in the 1950s but had maintained a cautious tone that relied on moral appeals and educational approaches. Individual clergy and students of faith often acted on their own or as part of groups not bound by religious organizations. CORE participated in the first interracial Freedom Ride in 1947, called the Journey of Reconciliation, to test the recent Supreme Court decision to desegregate interstate transportation. In the 1940s and 1950s, CORE activists also focused on ending racial discrimination in public accommodations, housing, hospitals, schools, and employment in the urban North, Midwest, and West. But as religious bodies, churches and synagogues did little. The *Brown* decision compelled white churches nationally to address segregation, if only verbally, and a few white ministers went to the South to help directly. Some rabbis also did so, but usually as individuals rather than as representatives of their synagogues. Occasionally, clergy tried to serve as peacemakers in areas where school desegregation was volatile. Whereas a northern clergy presence often attracted the media and sometimes forestalled violence, efforts aimed at religious reconciliation by nonsouthern clergy toward their southern white colleagues instead often bred resentment (Findlay 1993, 11–47; Newman 2004, 1–3, 21–29).

At the same time, northern liberal seminaries were producing a new breed of clergy who saw God acting in the world for justice, were ready to use direct action to aid this divine movement, and emphasized action over theological reflection. When the sit-in movement exploded across the South in 1960 and 1961, official church organizations like the NCC, the General Assembly of the United Presbyterian Church in the U.S.A., and the National Council of the Episcopal Church applauded it. The World Council of Churches also moved rapidly toward greater religious support for social justice in the world, where God's will seemed active and apparent. Similarly, during the Second Vatican Council, called Vatican II (1962–1965), Pope John XXIII initiated a series of landmark reforms in the Catholic Church, which included a new emphasis on social justice and seeing the Church as servant to the world rather than as a retreat from it.

Many Jewish college students and graduates, who were frustrated by the complacency of their suburban parents and fired by moral and democratic values, joined the civil rights movement. Such folk comprised a large percentage of CORE's Freedom Riders who went south in 1961 to test the recent Supreme Court ruling ordering desegregation of interstate bus facilities. As a result, CORE developed a tight relationship with northern Jewish organizations, which donated money for the program and bail. One Mississippi rabbi, even as he criticized the Freedom Rides as endangering the progress of local gradualist efforts, nevertheless visited the jailed riders regularly and provided them with supplies, spiritual support, and means of contacting worried loved ones, in spite of harsh congregational criticism and two efforts to remove him from his pulpit. His actions illustrate the often-complicated feelings of white southern clergy who opposed civil disobedience and northern invasions but supported an end to racial violence and discrimination. Reform Jews created the Religious Action Center in 1961 in Washington, D.C., to facilitate social action on the era's most important moral issues, including racial justice. An interfaith, integrated busload of 40 clergy and laity traveled from Chicago to Albany, Georgia, to aid SCLC's project there. Jews found that collaborating with Christians shielded them from the anti-Semitic charge that the civil rights movement was a Jewish-led Communist conspiracy to overthrow the South. Despite the efforts of a courageous minority, it would take SCLC protests in Birmingham and King's "Letter from Birmingham Jail" to draw religious organizations outside the South into active involvement with the movement (Staub 2004, xvi–xxi, 19–20; Webb 2001, 184–188, 203; Masse 2004, 162).

The shocking news footage from SCLC's 1963 Birmingham campaign, combined with King's letter responding to eight critical white Alabama clergymen, caught the attention of northerners who felt compelled by what they saw. The Rabbinical Assembly, which was meeting during the SCLC campaign, also felt the need to do something in Birmingham. Nineteen rabbis volunteered to travel there immediately, and the rest donated $1,500 out of pocket to fund the trip. The Assembly passed a resolution that empowered these 19 to "speak and act on behalf of human rights and dignity" in Birmingham for the whole Assembly, a group that ministered to more than a million and a half congregants. This effort was a new step beyond individual rabbinical action (Staub 2004, 23–24).

Also inspired by King's appeal and the events in Birmingham, the NCC created a unit called the Commission on Religion and Race (CORR) to organize its 30-plus member denominations for civil rights action. The commission focused its efforts on three areas: Washington, D.C., where elected officials were debating federal civil rights legislation; their home regions, where grassroots pressure on members of Congress might create incentives to help pass such legislation; and in the South, where King and others were appealing for clerical marchers to join SCLC and SNCC projects.

One of CORR's first acts was to mobilize church involvement in the March on Washington of August 1963. It helped assemble a sizable interfaith, ecumenical coalition of white clergy that made this televised march appear less dangerous and more acceptable to white viewers. The Union of American Hebrew Congregations did so as well. CORR also began a campaign to generate political support for the civil rights bill that was being filibustered in Congress. Interfaith groups held rallies and visited members of Congress regularly, appealing for its passage. Seminarians maintained a continuous interfaith vigil at the Lincoln Memorial that stretched from April 19, 1964, to the bill's signing date in late June. Clergy also held daily religious services, with prayers for the bill, at the Lutheran Church of the Reformation until it passed. Meanwhile, outside the South, especially in the Midwest, CORR organized a series of local meetings to ignite discussions about the Christian principles involved in civil rights issues and to rally parishioners to write their congressional representatives in support of the bill. The Midwest proved a strategic choice because it was highly Christian; fairly conservative; and, with a few urban exceptions, predominantly white. Therefore, midwesterners could support civil rights legislation as a moral issue while incurring little practical impact on their own, largely white, home areas. Mail, much of it revealing church influence, poured in to Congress. Vice President Hubert Humphrey credited the "unremitting support" of CORR's efforts, clergy activism, and the deluge of religious-based letters with making the bill's passage possible (Friedland 1998, 85, 91, 100; Findlay 1993, 50–62; Masse 2004, 162).

In 1964, Reform Jews established volunteer programs in New York and Chicago called Mitzvah Corps, which sent college-age Jews to the South to work for civil rights. As a result, many young Jews participated in SNCC's 1964 Freedom Summer. Two of them, Michael Schwerner and Andrew Goodman, were murdered. SNCC also received a fair amount of financial support from northern Jews. Protestant leaders within the NCC's CORR also admired SNCC and helped organize staff to train white student volunteers who went to Mississippi to register black voters and establish freedom schools. Additionally, the NCC paid the bail for activists jailed in Mississippi throughout the summer. It also supported a minister's project to send clergy into Mississippi to help attract media attention that would deter white violence against demonstrators. For a brief period it worked, compelling local officials to call for law and order while clergy and media were present. Approximately 235 clergy and laity participated in Freedom Summer. Such practical direct activities made those involved feel as if formal religion had become more relevant as Christians and Jews put actions behind their principles and practiced a social rather than an individualistic pietistic faith. When SNCC workers created a new political party called the Mississippi Freedom Democratic Party (MFDP) to challenge the seating of the all-white Democratic Party delegation at the 1964 Democratic National Convention in Atlantic City, New Jersey, the NCC backed this effort. Ed King was one of the MFDP's organizers. However, after the MFDP delegation refused to accept an unsatisfactory political compromise designed to appease them at the convention, many SNCC workers grew disillusioned with the fickle, expedient support of northern white liberals who tended to fulfill civil rights promises only when convenient for them (Carson 1984, 118–121; Friedland 1998, 103–107; Newman 2004, 74–75).

## Clergy and Voting Rights

In September 1964, the NCC created an ongoing ministry in the Mississippi Delta to help poor black residents. The so-called Delta Ministry delivered community development, health care clinics, preschool education, direct relief, self-sufficient economic options, citizenship training, and voter registration services. As SNCC's efforts in Mississippi declined after Freedom Summer, the Delta Ministry tried to fill the gap. The World Council of Churches funded 40 percent of it, with the NCC handling the remaining 60 percent. Within the NCC, denominations with mostly northern constituencies, such as the United Church of Christ and the United Presbyterians in the United States, footed much of the bill. Denominations with large southern constituencies, such as the United Methodist Church, the Episcopal Church, and the Disciples of Christ, failed to provide much support due to a backlash from southern laity. The project angered many southern white congregations, who saw its focus on economic and political empowerment of the poor as too radical and its leadership as too northern based. The Delta Ministry operated with mixed levels of success until a loss of funding and divided leadership rendered it ineffective by the late 1970s (Newman 2004, 1–7, 21–30; Findlay 1993, 140–168).

In 1965, the struggle for voting rights became focused in Selma when black marchers were beaten savagely. SCLC appealed to nonsouthern clergy to join the effort, and scores of them did, including numerous bishops, seminary professors and deans, administrators of major denominations, and pastors. Empowered by Vatican II's recent reforms, large numbers of Catholic priests and nuns went with the blessing of their bishops. But local southern leaders and laity often opposed Catholic involvement. Selma's Catholic churches were segregated, and the bishop of Montgomery tried to prevent northern Catholic clergy from joining the marches, urging them to return home to attend to their own flocks. About 16 rabbis also went, and when arriving in Selma's black neighborhood, one noticed how many stores there had Jewish names. This illustrated that in the urban South, just as up North, Jews often comprised a large number of the business owners in black neighborhoods, making them targets of black boycotts and resentments, even as other Jews advocated for racial justice (Staub 2004, 31–34).

When local whites beat to death Rev. James Reeb, a white Unitarian minister from Boston, more clergy of all faiths descended upon Selma. In fact, they helped lead a voting rights march to Montgomery. News of a northern white minister's death captured the nation's emotions and attracted the attention of President Lyndon Johnson, who made Air Force One available to Reeb's widow. Johnson then met with a largely white clergy delegation to discuss voting rights. While local blacks bemoaned the death of Reeb, they noticed that the earlier murder of a black man, Jimmie Lee Jackson, drew considerably less attention from clergy and the White House. Some also grew angry that white clergy met with Johnson about voting rights, with few blacks involved, while drawing considerable self-importance from that experience. Blacks' gratitude for northern white liberal support mixed with rising ambivalence.

Clergy and civil rights volunteers from around the country joined local protesters for a 1965 voting rights march from Selma, Alabama, to Montgomery, Alabama. (*Bettmann/Corbis*)

The march from Selma to Montgomery helped create political pressure for Congress to pass the 1965 Voting Rights Act. But when the Watts ghetto in Los Angeles exploded over long-ignored racial inequalities that year, national attention turned beyond the South. Martin Luther King Jr. and SCLC went to Chicago a year later to lead a nonviolent protest campaign. Some liberal clergy struggled to draw more attention to northern racism and discrimination. However, white northerners, westerners, and midwesterners, including religious laity, who may have given at least nominal verbal support to the movement when it was southern focused, often resisted change in their own localities and were resentful of clergy who pressed for it. The inner-city riots that exploded every summer during the mid- to late 1960s surprised few northern blacks. Neither did the refusal of northern whites to deal with the economic and political injustices stemming from the region's systemic racism. The ideas underlying the "black power" slogan, which gained popularity in 1966, were already familiar to northern blacks who held few illusions about the goodwill of liberals in the supposed promised land.

## Religious Leaders and Northern Racism

While public places in the North were not legally segregated, many areas like beaches, shopping centers, pools, and playgrounds were still treated like racial turf and sometimes were violently defended, as if officially segregated. As in Dixie, northern racism was organized around preserving political and economic privileges for whites. Therefore, black neighborhoods received few resources. Black schools remained far inferior to white schools in funding, physical quality, curriculum materials, and administrative resources. Residential segregation ensured virtual school segregation, and this condition was maintained through a conspiracy of real estate agents (through the practices of redlining—denying loans and other services to residents of low-income areas and blockbusting—selling houses in previously all-white areas to blacks and then capitalizing on white flight), banks and the Federal Housing Authority (through discriminatory loan practices), and restrictive covenants (whereby homeowners agreed not to sell or rent to blacks), all of which preserved unofficial racial turf boundaries and power advantages for whites. Often, ghettos lacked public transportation lines, resulting in blacks being trapped in one area for jobs, housing, and shopping. This lack of transportation allowed shopkeepers and landlords to force residents to pay higher prices for inferior products. Many of these shopkeepers and absentee landlords were Jewish, as black ghettos had often been previously Jewish. As Jews enjoyed a sharp reduction in anti-Semitism and a healthy spike in economic opportunities after World War II, they often relocated to the suburbs while people of color filled the inner cities.

Vatican II gave the pope's blessing to priests and nuns eager to help ameliorate urban suffering. Since most Catholics lived in the urban North and West, nuns and priests often found themselves on the front lines of neighborhood racial tensions, especially as they struggled to integrate white ethnic parish communities. Priests and nuns joined enthusiastically in northern campaigns for residential and school integration, including marching with King in Chicago. Many were shocked to see white lay Catholics aligned against them, throwing rocks and epithets their way. In Catholic neighborhoods in Chicago and Boston, laity often viewed the racial activism of their clergy to desegregate their neighborhoods as treason. Before Vatican II, the churches had helped nurture and defend the close-knit, ethnic identities of Catholic neighborhoods. Now the clergy seemed to be out to destroy what the Church had built and what its parishioners considered theirs. Lay Catholics also often held racist beliefs leading to conclusions that integration would bring declining property values, crime, loose morals, reduced school quality, and intermarriage to their communities. A clergy-laity gap clearly emerged within the Catholic Church over the repercussions of Vatican II's reforms and how they were manifested in the fight for racial justice (McGreevey 2000, 384–393; Theoharis and Woodard 2003, 125–151).

Jewish laity grew similarly incensed by efforts, often supported by their rabbis, to integrate their schools. While denying prejudicial feelings against blacks, Jewish residents in two New York City neighborhoods worked feverishly to block desegregation plans that would blend black and Jewish schools together. The first incident happened in late 1963, shortly after the March on Washington, when New York City sought to pair a school in the black area of Corona with one five blocks away in the Jewish neighborhood of Jackson Heights. Although busing would be needed for only 30 of the more than 1,600 students affected, blacks would make up only 35 percent or less of both schools after the plan, and both schools would receive significant funding increases for staff, renovation, and counseling, Jewish parents killed the plan. Their resistance was based on preserving their self-interest and on

## Nation of Islam

The Nation of Islam (NOI), while never conceived by its members to be a civil rights organization, had a great influence on the black freedom struggle between 1955 and 1975 because of its strong black nationalist message carried by its charismatic national spokesperson, Malcolm X.

The NOI was founded around 1930 in Detroit by Wallace D. Fard, an itinerant salesman who claimed to have been from Mecca, Saudi Arabia. The NOI was not an orthodox Muslim sect; it borrowed from a wide range of philosophies, including traditional Islam, Christianity, and black nationalism. Fard recruited followers who were attracted by his message of black self-determinism and open antipathy toward whites. Under his leadership, the NOI opened schools and formed the paramilitary Fruit of Islam to enforce its laws.

When Fard disappeared in 1933, he was replaced by Elijah Muhammad, who opened a temple in Chicago and relocated the organization to that city. Under Muhammad, the NOI practiced the economic self-determinism proposed by Fard. The organization formed businesses and employed its members. By 1945, the NOI had acquired enough resources to purchase 140 acres of farmland in Michigan, which

it used to feed its members and sell produce. Over the next two decades the NOI built hundreds of bakeries, grocery stores, small businesses, and temples.

National interest in the NOI began to grow during the late 1950s as the organization stood in contrast to the integrationist civil rights movement and as Malcolm X began to garner attention for his fiery brand of speechmaking. With the organization's business interests growing, and with its militant and disciplined members unwavering in their criticism of American racism, whites began to take notice of the NOI. Internal strife within the NOI led to Malcolm X being ostracized, but the organization remained strong even after its most famous member's departure. Following his heavyweight title win against Sonny Liston in February 1964, the boxer Muhammad Ali publicly announced that he was an NOI disciple.

The NOI provided an alternative to the protest-based integrationism of the traditional civil rights movement by preaching that black independence would only be achieved through economic development and separation from whites, thus foreshadowing the black nationalist revival that rippled throughout the civil rights movement during the mid-1960s.

fear of their children mixing with blacks. Rabbis supporting the plan were accused by members of the congregations of being under Communist influence and were told that they must either represent Jewish interests or leave the neighborhood. Six years later, tempers erupted between blacks and Jews in New York's Ocean Hill–Brownsville school district when the local black community was given more control over the district and its board fired several Jewish teachers. Racial and anti-Semitic epithets flew between members of both communities and tensions spilled into the streets (Fenster 1984, 92–98; Carson 1984, 128).

Protestant, Jewish, and Catholic clergy in northern cities created interfaith coalitions to advocate for fair housing laws and against discriminatory hiring practices. Liberal clergy often saw these issues as moral ones embraced by a God who loved all of humanity. Laity, however, tended to view them in legal and economic terms, or as involving the property rights of individuals. They resented the meddling of clergy who they felt had crossed a secular line.

Woman dressed in traditional garb at a gathering of the Nation of Islam. (*National Archives*)

Clergy frequently were harassed by developers, real estate agencies, and laity for their involvement, and their efforts were often stymied by lack of funding and other needed support (Friedland 1998, 74–77).

As a result, white clerical efforts were often seen as too little, too late in the North, where white liberal support for civil rights often seemed predicated on convenience and the assurance that they would experience no loss of privilege. Members of the Nation of Islam (NOI) saw this tendency as illustrative of white people's innate evil and therefore emphasized the need for a self-sufficient black nationalism, which stressed the creation of black-controlled economic, political, and cultural institutions. After leaving the NOI and becoming an orthodox Muslim, Malcolm X continued to preach black nationalism but stressed that liberal white hypocrisy and self-interest were caused by culture, history, and greed rather than innate evil. Nevertheless, white northerners generally lacked personal incentive to remove racial discrimination in their home areas.

After the Six Day War between Israel and its Arab neighbors in 1967, many Jews began to put Jewish interests, issues, and needs ahead of those of other groups. Some scholars say that this new focus marked a more conservative turn within the American Jewish community as a whole, and a lessening of social justice activism in particular. As several black groups, like SNCC, aligned themselves with Arabs and Palestinians in an anticolonial stance, relations between blacks and Jews became further strained. This tension was combined with the fact that, as northern blacks focused their attention on economic injustice in the inner city, they tended to encounter Jews more than any other white people. As a result, Jews became convenient symbols of white exploitation to northern urban blacks who might not have known about Jewish involvement in the southern civil rights movement. Indeed, in many northern cities, even rabbis admitted that Jews were complicit in exploiting blacks for profit. Furthermore, along with other whites, Jews often opposed affirmative action for blacks, arguing that they should achieve success through legally protected equal opportunity and hard work, as many Jews felt they had done (Carson 1984, 120–129; Staub 2004, xx–xxi, 87–89, 105–106).

## Black Theology

Persons of color were also keenly aware of the centuries of complicity by white churches with broader systems of racial oppression in the United States. The philosophy and strategies of black power blossomed in many northern urban areas in the 1960s, including black churches and larger Protestant and ecumenical organizations. Black theology, which theologian James Cone called the religious arm of the black power movement, emerged to provide a Christian exegesis and perspective for it. In 1969, Cone published *Black Theology and Black Power*, which wove together ideas from a variety of sources familiar to white seminarians. Among other things, it stressed that a nonracial God and Jesus had been whitewashed in images to help justify white power. When Jesus and God were viewed as white, whites then easily identified themselves, their leadership, and their power as divine. Conversely, if Jesus and God were viewed as black, whites' treatment of blacks might come under self-judgment. Jesus self-identified with the dispossessed and said that whatsoever one does to the least of these, one does to him. In the United States, Cone said, the dispossessed are black. Therefore, Jesus and God should be seen through the lens of the dispossessed, or as black. He was not arguing that Jesus was black literally, but rather figuratively, and to see that part of him was to identify also with the dispossessed, which true Christians are commanded to do. He also called upon Christians to work for justice and their liberation, thus making black power a Christian objective (Cone 1969; Prothero 2003, 205–218).

Rev. Albert Cleage Jr. of Detroit agreed. As black theology's most visible proponent, in 1967 he renamed his Central Congregational Church the Shrine of the Black Madonna, celebrating this change with the unveiling of a seven-foot painting of a black Madonna holding a black baby Jesus.

Cleage said, "Black people cannot build dignity on their knees worshipping a white Christ" (Cleage 1969, 3). He felt that such symbols kept blacks entwined in a self-destructive love affair with racist white institutions and white definitions of normalcy at the expense of their own communities and culture. He admired Malcolm X and understood the NOI's criticisms of Christianity as a tool promoting black complacency in oppression. But whereas the NOI saw Islam as the black man's natural religion, Cleage felt that Christianity could be unwhitewashed and restored. Unlike Cone, Cleage claimed that Jesus and God literally were black. Like Cone, he stressed the political nature of Jesus's ministry and challenged Christians to make social justice their primary mission. Cleage criticized Martin Luther King Jr. and SCLC for being too idealistic in believing that a moral order could be created through changed hearts, resulting in a beloved community. To Cleage, this was entirely unrealistic, especially in the urban North, where different ethnic power groups competed for turf and resources. He embraced teachings that called for using organized worldly power to coerce justice from a sinful, greedy system. He refused to credit King for using such strategies in the South—seeing him as too much the darling of liberal whites who loved his dream but showed little commitment to addressing the inequalities that prevented it. Cleage thought that the northern black church had failed to apply the gospel to the real dilemmas that the urban poor faced. His goal was to make these churches central to black community empowerment. He also hoped that this would help keep radical black youth, many of whom had already grown disillusioned, within the church. Therefore, he argued for black separatism as a means of empowerment and blended church and secular advocacy to achieve social justice. This strategy called for a communal salvation on Earth for blacks that contrasted with the otherworldly individualistic salvation promoted by whites (Prothero 2003, 200–205).

After 1966, black separatism grew, often forcing whites out of previously integrated civil rights groups like SNCC and CORE. This trend made it far more difficult for white clergy to participate in the movement. Confrontational and sometimes separatist black clerical movements also rose up within northern-based, white-dominated mainline Protestant churches and organizations during the late 1960s and early 1970s, as black clergy responded to inadequate church efforts to address urban issues. Groups like the NCC sometimes attempted to tackle such problems. CORR shifted focus toward urban areas in 1965 and pressed the Johnson administration to invest federal resources there. The NCC also criticized the Moynihan Report, which blamed northern black families for their own plights and ignored the systemic racism that primarily caused black suffering. However, the NCC's rising criticism of Johnson's policies in Vietnam reduced its influence on the White House. In 1967, it created an ambitious two-year program called Crisis in the Nation to target urban issues. Diffusion of resources, however, left it largely ineffectual (Findlay 1993, 178–182).

As blacks grew concerned about the weakness of white liberal efforts, both within and outside the churches, black clergy within the NCC created an organization in 1966 called the National Conference of Black Churchmen (NCBC). It supported black economic and political power from within white

Protestant ecumenical communities. At first, the NCBC's organizers advocated integration. Over time, however, the group became increasingly supportive of black cultural pride and racial separatism, as expressed by Cleage.

Amid this rise in separatism, in 1967, an interracial group of Protestants, Catholics, and Jews created a new organization called the Interreligious Foundation for Community Organization (IFCO) to serve an intermediary role between black power urban groups doing social justice work and white religious denominations seeking to fund civil rights efforts. The IFCO managed, screened, and distributed funds and created a communications link between white churches and black activist urban groups. In April 1969, with the help of the IFCO and the NCBC, the National Black Economic Development Conference (NBEDC) was held in Detroit to address economic urban issues. James Forman of SNCC used the opportunity to present a self-authored document called the "Black Manifesto." It contained a piercing critique of white religious complicity in racism, followed by a demand for $500 million in reparations to be paid by white churches to blacks working on economic and social justice projects in urban areas. The money, he claimed, was their just due for the profits churches made from racism over the centuries, and it would be used to help ameliorate the repercussions of white racism in cities. The NBEDC voted to approve the manifesto and its program (Findlay 1993, 188).

Forman then launched a series of confrontations with white church leaders that included takeovers of pulpits, meetings, and the occupation of both denominational and NCC headquarters. These protests were designed to grab attention and to command rather than ask for white liberal church money. While white church leaders felt sympathy for Forman's objectives and guilt over the accuracy of his critique, they were appalled by his demanding tone and rude methods. White laity reacted angrily, insisting that the NCC and their denominational leaders reject the manifesto's demand for reparations or else suffer a loss of funding. Seeking a way out of this bind, the NCC and several of its member Protestant denominations authorized money to be donated to the IFCO for distribution to organizations working on black urban issues, but not to Forman's group or the NBEDC. Despite this restriction, the NCC saw a $2.5 million reduction in donations the following year, due in part to its apparent buckling to Forman's demands. Within many mainline denominations and the NCC itself, black clergy began forming their own caucuses to advocate for black power within religious organizations and programs. These caucuses, and the processes that white churches engaged in dealing with the "Black Manifesto," inspired administrators to examine church entanglement with racism. However, withdrawal of significant lay funding during the 1970s also caused white church administrators to cut back on advocacy for racial justice at home (Findlay 1993, 200–217).

## Conclusion

Throughout human history, the power of religious belief to inspire people to action, and provide divine justification for it, has been undeniable. At times it has operated to oppress or conquer, and at others to liberate and express compassion. With respect to the civil rights movement, religion was employed most effectively in the latter. Religion and clergy were not merely peripheral to the movement; they were central players in it. Civil rights, framed as a moral issue, was difficult for most clergy to ignore. For the activists, their identity, beliefs, and purpose as clergy compelled their involvement, often as leaders. Hope that the movement simultaneously would revitalize their religious institutions and expand ecumenical and interfaith relationships also inspired their participation. While racism and resistance to change, unsupportive laity, fears about job security, threats of economic and violent retribution, black separatism, and debates over appropriate clergy roles mitigated against overt support by some, religion in general, and clergy in particular, were critical to the movement's advancement.

## References and Further Reading

Carson, Clayborne. 1984. "Blacks and Jews in the Civil Rights Movement." In *Jews in Black Perspectives*, edited by Joseph Washington. Cranbury, NJ: Associated University Presses.

Chappell, David L. 2004. *A Stone of Hope: Prophetic Religion and the Death of Jim Crow*. Chapel Hill: University of North Carolina Press.

Cleage, Albert. 1969. *The Black Messiah*. Trenton, NJ: Africa World Press.

Cone, James. 1969. *Black Theology and Black Power*. New York: Seabury.

Cox, Harvey. 1965. *The Secular City: Secularization and Urbanization in Theological Perspective*. New York: Macmillan.

Dittmer, John. 1994. *Local People: The Struggle for Civil Rights in Mississippi*. Urbana: University of Illinois Press.

Fenster, Myron M. 1984. "The Princeton Plan Comes to Jackson Heights." In *Jews in Black Perspectives*, edited by Joseph Washington. Cranbury, NJ: Associated University Presses.

Findlay, James F., Jr. 1993. *Church People in the Struggle: The National Council of Churches and the Black Freedom Movement, 1950–1970*. New York: Oxford University Press.

Friedland, Michael B. 1998. *Lift Up Your Voice Like a Trumpet: White Clergy and the Civil Rights and Antiwar Movements, 1954–1973*. Chapel Hill: University of North Carolina Press.

Garrow, David J. 2000. "Martin Luther King, Jr.'s Leadership." In *Major Problems in American Religious History*, edited by Patrick Allitt. New York: Houghton Mifflin.

Hadden, Jeffrey K. 1969. *The Gathering Storm in the Churches*. Garden City, NY: Doubleday.

Marsh, Charles. 1997. *God's Long Summer: Stories of Faith and Civil Rights*. Princeton, NJ: Princeton University Press.

Masse, Mark H. 2004. *Inspired to Serve: Today's Faith Activists*. Bloomington: Indiana University Press.

McGreevy, John T. 2000. "Urban Catholics and the Civil Rights Movement." In *Major Problems in American Religious History,* edited by Patrick Allitt. New York: Houghton Mifflin.

Meier, August, and Elliott Rudwick. 1973. *CORE: A Study in the Civil Rights Movement, 1942–1968.* New York: Oxford University Press.

Newman, Mark. 2004. *Divine Agitators: The Delta Ministry and Civil Rights in Mississippi.* Athens: University of Georgia Press.

Prothero, Stephen R. 2003. *American Jesus: How the Son of God Became a National Icon.* New York: Farrar, Straus and Giroux.

Staub, Michael, ed. 2004. *The Jewish 1960s: An American Sourcebook.* Lebanon, NH: University Press of New England.

Theoharis, Jeanne F., and Komozi Woodard, eds. 2003. *Freedom North: Black Freedom Struggles outside of the South, 1940–1980.* New York: Palgrave McMillan.

Webb, Clive. 2001. *Fight against Fear: Southern Jews and Black Civil Rights.* Athens: University of Georgia Press.

# Southern Civil Rights Organizations | 4

## Lauren Chambers, Aggie Ebrahimi, and Barbara McCaskill

The signal characteristic of the civil rights movement, and a significant source of its transformational impact on U.S. society, was the formation of southern civil rights organizations to agitate for equality and justice. Like the youth-driven, anticolonial resistance movements in Africa, the Caribbean, and South Asia that toppled old empires in the 1950s and 1960s and erected new democracies, southern civil rights organizations demonstrated that enduring social change is predicated on the radical involvement of ordinary men and women, of "foot soldiers" doing daily battle with an oppressive system, taking short steps toward long-term change.

## Background

The names of various southern groups indicate how their members assembled to resolve a variety of issues and show that membership varied from specific constituencies (young people, religious denominations, residents of specific cities and towns) to the general public. Nevertheless, the majority of those who comprised them were African American men and women, and they continued a tradition of bold political activism that had been central to the survival of their families and communities since the Reconstruction era.

When federal troops withdrew from the South in 1876, the blacks who remained faced racial and sexual violence, economic oppression, denial of voting rights, and other inequities and humiliations meant to reinstate their status as an underclass, as lowly as the slaves their parents had been. Yet post-Reconstruction African Americans living in the South did not unilaterally bow to this oppression. They funded and constructed schools and churches, where a fledgling professional class of college-educated teachers, ministers, physicians, and lawyers galvanized their people to action from the podium and pulpit. In the late 19th century, Booker T. Washington's Tuskegee Institute

(Alabama), Bishop Henry McNeal Turner's First African Baptist Church (Savannah, Georgia), and Lucy Craft Laney's Institute (Augusta, Georgia) stood among the most well known of such southern institutions. Their leaders engaged in a juggling act to soothe the anxieties of ex-Confederates fearful of the free black presence while at the same time seeking, by increments or with all deliberate speed, the full rights and privileges of citizenship. Very often, the literate, polished men and women at the forefront of these churches and schools acted as crucial mediators between hostile white neighbors and the vulnerable black masses barely making ends meet, largely occupied as tenant farmers, laborers, and live-in domestics.

A century later, southern civil rights organizations stood as the unequivocal descendants of such early institutions. Like their forebears, activists made all-black schools and churches social and political epicenters by gathering there, when permitted and where safe, to strategize, recruit and train members, and listen to the leadership. But more important than the literal buildings was what they symbolized: the combination of religious faith and reason that became the bedrock and edifice of the collective black response to inequality during the civil rights era. As a minister who had earned degrees from Morehouse College and Boston University, Dr. Martin Luther King Jr. epitomized the aspirations of millions of black Americans because he seemingly embodied the highest elements of spirit and mind, even though in reality the movement depended on the unsung contributions of many, rather than those of one man.

Southern civil rights organizations paid homage to earlier African American institutions by returning again and again to an agenda for civic activism based on the democratic principles on which the United States was founded, as well as the moral values preached to their members at churches, synagogues, and mosques. They held a particular magnetism for the most marginal and disenfranchised members of society: rural and urban blacks, high school and college students, and women. In spite of the disagreements and resentments that sometimes divided them, they were models of the adage "there is strength in numbers," demonstrating that people can accomplish more changes together than alone. Those who would have been reluctant to challenge the Jim Crow structure on their own gained the courage to face violence and insults peacefully when massed with other determined citizens.

However, it was not as if southern blacks had been silent and passive during earlier decades of oppression. They had expressed outrage against lynching, land dispossession, subsistence wages, and other racist practices using the media of their day: (1) widely circulating black newspapers such as the *Chicago Defender, Pittsburgh Courier*, New York's *Amsterdam News*, and Baltimore's *Afro-American*, and (2) the camera. Southern civil rights organizations lifted this culture of dissent to a new and more influential level by making savvy use of national and international reportage, transmitted nightly into Americans' living rooms via the brand-new medium of television and the brisk commentary of reporters such as Walter Cronkite, Mike Wallace, and Tom Brokaw. In this manner, they increased the visibility of the faces and the facility of the voices that defined and shaped the movement.

Additionally, southern civil rights organizations united members across divisions of class, race, region, educational attainment, and religious affiliation to serve a cause greater than any individual: that of freedom and equality for all U.S. citizens. Every member could claim a niche, either contributing behind the scenes by making telephone calls, singing and shouting together at mass meetings, offering cots to out-of-towners, and cooking meals or on the front lines, by picketing segregated businesses, driving voters to the polls, negotiating resolutions with commercial and legal elites, and going to jail. Since sacrifices were required of every participant—jeopardizing job security, contributing hard-earned savings, suffering (perhaps for weeks) in jail, relinquishing precious leisure time—the organizations motivated their members to struggle until victorious, if only because in struggling they risked so much: at best, a few years of bombings and beatings, at worst, their lives.

## Montgomery Improvement Association and Women's Political Council

The Montgomery Improvement Association (MIA) is perhaps the most well known of the southern civil rights organizations. A group of ministers in Montgomery, Alabama, consisting of a young Dr. King, Fred Shuttlesworth, and Ralph Abernathy, organized the association after years of blacks defiantly sitting in the front of city buses instead of the back, to which they were restricted. The Women's Political Council (WPC), founded in 1946 and headed by Jo Ann Robinson, had spoken out on behalf of such protesters before the MIA's involvement. Yet it was only after the arrest of seamstress Rosa Parks on December 1, 1955, that the MIA and WPC decided to coordinate a citywide bus boycott in order to demonstrate the black community's ability to mobilize around a common cause, to highlight the relevance of religious doctrine to everyday affairs, and to emphasize the power of nonviolent resistance.

Thirteen months later, the boycott declared a victory when a U.S. Supreme Court decision pronounced the segregation law unconstitutional. During the protest, blacks circumvented public transportation by using carpools sponsored by churches and private individuals, by taking taxis, or by catching rides from the white women who employed them. Many drivers, members of the MIA or WPC, were harassed by police. White city commissioners also fomented internal divisions among the demonstrators, and private homes, including King's, were bombed. In spite of these setbacks, the MIA and WPC established a pattern for other southern civil rights organizations to overturn discriminatory laws through careful planning and collaboration.

## Albany Movement

Differing from the Montgomery groups, those who formed the Albany Movement did so with the goal of integrating every segregated facility in their small Georgia city of mill workers and farmers. The Albany Movement

Police arrest a protester during a 1962 demonstration in Albany, Georgia. (*Bettmann/Corbis*)

has come to define roughly a 19-month period between the summer of 1961 and spring of 1963, when activism in the town gained the national news media's attention. In the fall of 1961, the Student Nonviolent Coordinating Committee (SNCC) delegated two of its members, Charles Sherrod and Cordell Reagon, to register Albany's black voters. They quickly became involved in the desegregation actions that local black citizens had sparked. A decisive moment occurred on November 1, 1961, when Sherrod and Reagon joined seven other students whom they had trained in nonviolence in a sit-in, designed to test a recent decision by the Interstate Commerce Commission banning segregation in transportation terminals. As a consequence, a dream team of civic and business leaders—including Chevene Bowers (C. B.) King, a scion of the black community and the only black attorney practicing in the state south of Macon; Slater Hunter King, a businessman and C. B.'s brother; Rev. Samuel B. Wells; and the physician William G. Anderson—formed the brainchild of what came to be known as the Albany Movement (Carson 1981, 56; Williams 1987, 164–167).

The members of this group sought to do more than any previous organization by integrating all of the city's public facilities that were off-limits to African Americans. The Albany Movement's leadership also seized the spotlight by inviting Dr. King and Reverend Abernathy to spend intermittent weeks in the city. Yet the black community had attempted to desegregate the bus line long before they invited King and Abernathy to participate, along with a legal team anchored by Constance Baker Motley, who had worked toward the successful verdict in the 1954 *Brown v. Board of Education* decision. And the Albany Movement continued well after the Atlanta leaders departed. Its impact was felt into the 1970s, when a black sanitation worker named Johnnie Johnson led more than 200 fellow employees on strike and initiated a federal lawsuit that resulted in the reform of city and county employment practices.

Like the MIA, the Albany Movement sponsored mass meetings as an organizing tactic and as a method of keeping community members informed of goals and accomplishments. Held primarily in the Mt. Zion and Shiloh Baptist Churches located in the black neighborhood of Harlem, the mass meetings literally became intertwined with the picket lines the Albany Movement organized in an attempt to pressure white-owned, segregated businesses downtown to open their front doors to African American customers and employees. At the end of a series of prayers, speeches, and spirituals, as the entire congregation stood singing a freedom song, picketers would line up with their signs and walk out the church doors a few blocks to the business district, where they would begin another ritual that consisted of kneeling in prayer, picketing, and enduring arrest. The Albany Movement thus refined tactics developed in Montgomery by elevating protest to a powerful and moving antiestablishment drama. By their composure and joy, the picketers intended to inspire the empathy of onlookers, maintain calm within their ranks, and demonstrate the transformational power of nonviolence (Davis 1998, 166–169; Williams 1987, 176–177).

The Albany Movement leaders combined a variety of other strategies that had been tested with varying degrees of success throughout the South during the 1950s and early 1960s. Relying largely on student volunteers, they registered people to vote and accompanied them to the polls. Along with the picket lines, to strike a double blow at segregation, they scheduled sit-ins at the city's bus station, restaurants, public library, and other facilities. They were determined to clog the jails with activists, and they were so successful that the authorities began busing protesters out of Albany for incarceration in surrounding communities. Both the local organizers of the Albany Movement and national leaders such as King were arrested and served jail time. The jarring spectacle of respected, pious, peace-loving citizens behind bars was intended to reflect negatively on the ethics of the city's white leadership.

When 1963 saw a dramatic spike in violence and repression in the region, the Albany Movement mobilized. Though its momentum had begun to diminish, local people imported seasoned activists to organize voter registration campaigns, marches, and picket lines in neighboring communities such as Americus and Smithville. Yet even as the cameras captured images of students joyfully carted to jail and jovial backyard news conferences, tensions existed behind the scenes. The Albany Movement struggled to manage the behavior of black youth who had grown impatient and disgruntled with the slow pace of change and questioned whether nonviolence was a manly or persuasive response to physical and psychological brutality.

Matters deteriorated in July 1962, when a pregnant woman was beaten by police while attempting to deliver food to imprisoned activists. A mob of young men retaliated by pelting police with rocks and bottles, precipitating a campaign by King and Abernathy to visit local pool halls and other hangouts to plead for calm. Furthermore, fearing that King, as well as Wyatt Tee Walker, another Atlanta-based activist who served as the executive director of the Southern Christian Leadership Conference (SCLC), would take the movement in directions they resisted, many locals disagreed with the decision to seek the input of outsiders. In addition, the Albany Movement faced a crafty opponent in the local police chief. Laurie Pritchett had learned from watching Birmingham's police chief, Theophilus Eugene "Bull" Connor, that brutality played badly to families at dinner watching the six o'clock news. So he and his men were conspicuously polite to the marchers (Williams 1987, 169–173).

If the Albany Movement is viewed as a flashpoint of activism in the early 1960s, it is tempting to conclude that it did not succeed in its goal of integrating all facilities and businesses. In *Why We Can't Wait,* Dr. King wrote that the grave mistake of Albany was that it scattered its efforts too widely. However, the consensus among those who pounded the pavement during those weeks is that the Albany Movement was a success by activating a chain of events and court cases that ultimately created progressive social change. Moreover, the Albany Movement made clear that the collective mind-set of black southerners had never been that they were innately inferior and unworthy of respect. Like the MIA and WPC during the 1950s, the Albany Movement of the 1960s broadcast to a global stage the dignity and love of those who participated in it and the fact that they did not internalize the racism that surrounded them (King 1964, 34–35, 48).

## National Association for the Advancement of Colored People

An organization that was very important to the southern civil rights struggle, yet is often overlooked in historical studies of the groups that contributed to it, is the National Association for the Advancement of Colored People (NAACP). Conceived in 1909, the multiracial NAACP had pledged to use the courts, the law, politics, and public protests to end lynching; to dismantle the Ku Klux Klan (KKK) and other hate groups; to register black Americans to vote; and to end segregation and discrimination in schools, neighborhoods, the armed forces, and public conveyances, facilities, and places of employment. Its southern activities gained prominence during the civil rights era. In 1955, NAACP member Rosa Parks was arrested in Montgomery, and in 1957, the NAACP spearheaded legal efforts to admit nine black students to all-white Central High School in Little Rock, Arkansas.

In 1955, when a 14-year-old black youth named Emmett Till was lynched in Money, Mississippi, the organization commissioned its first field secretary, Medgar Evers, to investigate the murder. Evers decreased black southerners' suspicions of the NAACP and reversed the group's outsider image through such investigations and through the mass meetings, boycotts, and protests that he organized in his hometown of Jackson, Mississippi. He would not back down from confrontations with white southern officials who used violence and intimidation to maintain Jim Crow. He became one of the era's martyrs when he was shot to death in front of his house on June 12, 1963.

In addition to adults like Evers, the organization enlisted younger southern members through the NAACP Youth Council to march, go to jail, and participate in sit-ins—all nonviolently—in places like Nashville and Albany. Although the organization usually defended individual southern blacks forced to take up arms against violent mobs that terrorized them, it condemned collective armed resistance to racial hostilities. In 1959, Robert F. Williams, who led the NAACP branch in Monroe, North Carolina, organized local black men equipped with rifles and other weapons to defend themselves against KKK violence. He pressured the NAACP leadership, unsuccessfully, to institute an armed self-defense policy, particularly to protect women and children, and he traveled to New York to accept funds from Malcolm X to buy more weapons. By the mid-1960s, expelled from the NAACP, he had rejected the merits of integration entirely and advocated violent mass rebellions and urban guerrilla warfare as a means of black empowerment. To avoid a criminal investigation of his armed organizing, he expatriated to Cuba, where in 1962 he hosted a program, *Radio Free Dixie*, which broadcast his views about an armed black revolution to households in the U.S. South. Williams and other like-minded individuals are examples of how militant opinions about self-protection were the flipside of the movement's calling card of nonviolence. Throughout the movement's decades of agitation, pacifists coexisted with more radical activists who viewed violence not only as an appropriate defense against terrorism but also as a means of undermining stereotypes about passive, deferential, emasculated African American men (Tyson 1999).

## Southern Christian Leadership Conference

SCLC had formed in January 1957, only a month after the official end of Montgomery's bus boycott. A trio of northern civil rights activists—Ella Baker, Stanley Levinson, and Bayard Rustin—originated the idea for the organization, which would replicate the nonviolent, direct-action, and confrontational tactics of the MIA throughout the South. Reconvening in February, the group elected King as their president and adopted the motto, "To Redeem the Soul of America."

Not an organization in the conventional sense of the word, SCLC looked to black Protestant churches for roots, ideologies, and primary membership. Freighted with biblical rhetoric, its meetings were patterned after Sunday services. In fact, SCLC's leaders based their headquarters in Atlanta for religious reasons. They wanted King to maintain his pastoral responsibilities at Ebenezer Baptist Church, even as he devoted substantial time and energy to the civil rights movement. Certain that a flexible organization could most successfully respond to the unpredictable demands of the movement, SCLC also shunned the rigid internal structure and bureaucratic design of the NAACP. Nevertheless, since it was keen to preserve harmonious, noncompetitive relations with the NAACP, it did not allow individual memberships. It was constituted, instead, of southern affiliates reporting to a board of 33 male directors, some of whom also served in the NAACP, and one woman. SCLC also allied with northerners, both white and black, including lawyers, philanthropists, accountants, politicians, actors, and activists (Fairclough 1987, 33–34; Branch 1988, 222–232).

## Southern Christian Leadership Conference

In January 1957, 60 civil rights activists met in Atlanta for a conference on nonviolent integration. They included Bayard Rustin, Ella Baker, Martin Luther King Jr., Ralph Abernathy, and Fred Shuttlesworth. The meeting spawned a group called the Southern Christian Leadership Conference (SCLC), which would serve as an umbrella civil rights organization. King was its first president, and its goal was "to redeem the soul of America" through nonviolent protest.

SCLC's first organized campaign took place in 1962 in Albany, Georgia. It raised awareness but brought little in terms of gains for local residents. The following year, in Birmingham, Alabama, SCLC was far more successful. Amid fierce criticism by white liberals and many blacks that the campaign was too strident, King and SCLC received a big break when Birmingham police got too rough with a group of student demonstrators, spraying them with high-powered fire hoses and unleashing police dogs on them. Nationwide television audiences were stunned by the violence, and the incident received international attention. The result was an outpouring of support for a movement that had been stagnating. The protest campaign in Birmingham was a major blow against segregation and helped lead to the passing of a federal civil rights law in 1964.

Bolstered by its success in Birmingham, SCLC organized a series of events targeting cities for desegregation, including Savannah, Georgia, and St. Augustine, Florida. It was also a major force behind the 1963 March on Washington for Jobs and Freedom, where King delivered his famous "I Have a Dream" speech. In 1965, it cosponsored with the Student Nonviolent Coordinating Committee a voting-rights campaign in Selma, Alabama.

During the late part of the 1960s, SCLC expanded its vision beyond the scope of the traditional civil rights movement. In 1966, King led the first-ever desegregation campaign of a major northern city when he worked with local activists to create change in Chicago. In 1967, SCLC formed Operation Breadbasket. Instead of focusing on political protest and civil rights, Operation Breadbasket concentrated on eco-

Its first official campaign, the Crusade for Citizenship, set out to register 2 million new black voters before the 1960 presidential election. Named the director by a male leadership that was slow to acknowledge women's intellectual abilities and hard work, Ella Baker activated the campaign in 21 southern cities in February 1958. Despite Baker's organizational and public relations skills, increases in the voter rolls were negligible. As many student activists later discovered, registering voters in the Black Belt required consistent, sustained, pull-up-your-pants-and-get-in-the-mud efforts. It necessitated literacy and citizenship education, transportation, training in confronting intimidation or retaliation threats, and legislative battles. Such activities were unfamiliar to SCLC's ministers, who were accustomed to relying on oratory to convert, motivate, and move people and who were convinced of the power of faith to make changes (Brown-Nagin 1999, 83).

To temper the trend toward an agitated and charged society, the John F. Kennedy administration proposed the Voter Education Project (VEP), directed by attorney Wiley Branton and funded in 1961 with grants chan-

Rev. Hosea Williams of the Southern Christian Leadership Conference speaks at a March 1965 voter registration rally in Selma, Alabama. (*Flip Schulke/Corbis*)

nomic development and saw poverty as the main barrier to black power and independence. Although King's assassination in 1968 was a major blow to SCLC, the organization fought on in his absence, leading a protest campaign in Washington, D.C., designed to make anti-poverty a part of the national political agenda.

neled through Atlanta's Southern Regional Council (SRC). The SRC had been founded in 1944 to attain equality for all southerners, and its liberal members believed in gradual change evolving from collaborations between those who wanted to improve the South and those who wielded the power to do so. By 1951, the SRC was sending field workers, such as historian Howard Zinn and reporter Pat Watters, into besieged cities and towns to document the methods, successes, and failures of local movements, white authorities' responses, and the African American community's resilience (McDonough 1993).

SCLC entered the VEP through its citizenship school training program in Dorchester, Georgia, created by educator Septima Clark. At her citizenship school in the Gullah community of Johns Island, South Carolina, Clark had taught blacks to read, write, pass voter registration literacy tests, and understand their fundamental rights as U.S. citizens. Clark, alongside SCLC's Andrew Young and Dorothy Cotton, recruited volunteers and showed them how to establish training programs in their own communities. By combining forces and placing voter registration drives in the hands of local leadership, SCLC and the VEP focused on enforcing the Fourteenth and Fifteenth Amendments and uprooting the unconstitutional system of Jim Crow (Branch 1988, 576; Fairclough 1987, 28).

The successful Birmingham campaign was SCLC's watershed moment. It nationalized the civil rights movement and ended the federal government's hands-off approach. SCLC coordinated its efforts with the Alabama Christian Movement for Human Rights and employed tried-and-true methods: picketing, boycotting, and jamming jails. The organization's detailed planning and incremental escalation of activities, countered by brutal police, contributed to its success. Images of the fire and police departments unleashing dogs and high-pressure water hoses on school-age marchers permeated homes throughout the United States and compelled the federal government to mediate a resolution between city officials and demonstration leaders.

In Birmingham, SCLC had learned that effectively involving the federal government in the movement depended on the steady exertion of public pressure. Guided by activist A. Philip Randolph, who presided over the powerful Brotherhood of Sleeping Car Porters, civil rights organizations throughout the United States (including the NAACP and SCLC) approached the Kennedy administration with an idea for a massive rally for justice and freedom in Washington, D.C. On August 28, 1963, hundreds of thousands of Americans, representing diverse religions, creeds, and colors, convened at the March on Washington. In homage to the United States's founding principles of democracy and equality, they began at the Washington Monument, where artists such as Joan Baez, Bob Dylan, Mahalia Jackson, and the Albany Movement Freedom Singers performed. The crowd marched from there to the Lincoln Memorial, a symbol of national unity, to hear speeches from various civil rights leaders, including SNCC president John Lewis. The day's most legendary moment stands as Dr. King's delivery of his "I Have a Dream" speech, a remarkable presentation of oratory and rhetoric and an inspired expression of American identity. The March on Washington succeeded in regenerating support for the Civil Rights Act of 1964, which had been mired in congressional debate and filibusters.

Yet, in contrast to this triumph, civil rights organizations, such as the Urban League, headed by Whitney Young, seemed merely to chip away at the devastating problem of poverty. In 1964, Young had proposed a domestic Marshall Plan, which President Lyndon Johnson folded into his War on Poverty, calling for federal assistance in rebuilding and eliminating inequities in U.S. inner cities. Following suit, SCLC decided to attack discriminatory public housing, de facto school segregation, and unequal distribution of wealth in Chicago. Its Chicago campaign was largely unsuccessful because segregation there was merely one part of a larger system of economic and political repression. SCLC also realized that more integrated cities were difficult to organize because the black community was divided along class lines, whereas in the South, nearly all African Americans, regardless of economic or social status, were similarly positioned as second-class citizens. One SCLC effort that did blossom in Chicago was Operation Breadbasket, a selective buying campaign headed by Jesse Jackson (Waite 2001, 170–203).

Despite SCLC's lack of structure, its patriarchal views toward women, its struggle to define and specify its goals, and its brief involvement in local movements, it revolutionized the United States. Like the United States's founders, it whittled down political complexities to the moral issue of right versus wrong.

## Youth Organizations and Student Nonviolent Coordinating Committee

Youth played an instrumental role in the civil rights movement, and they brought an unprecedented vitality to the demand for an end to segregation. They actively participated in creating the United States's most aggressive demonstrations of nonviolent resistance. The nonviolent approach to change required an immense level of tolerance and obedience, and students sponsored workshops to teach activists techniques for refraining from hitting the police and for peacefully enduring arrest and jail. Like the adults, they embraced the teachings of Mohandas Gandhi, whose efforts to promote nonviolence had defined India's successful campaign for independence from British colonial rule. Yet they did not as a whole risk being fired from jobs by angry or fearful white bosses, nor did they typically function as breadwinners for hungry families, so they had less to lose than their adult counterparts and could wage confrontations that were all but impossible until that time. Although the organizations they led faced conflict with more seasoned groups, their collective efforts catalyzed a new wave of activism that fixed the issues and concerns of the African American community into the forefront of America's consciousness.

Despite the constant threat of arrest and physical violence plaguing members of the black American community, many southern youth found they could no longer sit by and passively watch their lives unfold within a racist society. Instead of complaining about the gross injustices of the day, students as young as 10 or 11 decided to join adults in publicly demanding their constitutional rights. They led several key southern organizations that moved civil rights forward, such as the Nashville Student Movement and SNCC, and they created coalitions to confront racial discrimination and make space for freedom in a repressive society. They relied on SCLC support during the Albany Movement, the Atlanta sit-ins, and the Freedom Rides.

Students in Nashville came together in 1960 to learn more about a nonviolent approach taught by Jim Lawson as a way to combat segregation. While studying in India, Lawson had embraced the principles of *satyagraha*, a nonviolent approach to resisting oppression espoused by Gandhi. Among the students Lawson trained were John Lewis and Diane Nash, who rose to prominence as SNCC leaders. A tenant farmer's son who later sat in the U.S. Congress, Lewis had come to Nashville from Alabama for seminary studies and then enrolled at Fisk University, where he began participating in sit-ins. From Chicago, Nash had transferred to Fisk from Howard University. Their training in nonviolent direct social action became pivotal when they and fellow students mounted a challenge to segregation in Nashville.

A student protester in Nashville, Tennessee, sits at a lunch counter reserved for white customers. The napkins on the surrounding seats were placed to deter other customers from sitting down. (*Bettmann/Corbis*)

Nash, Lewis, and others formed the Nashville Student Movement, and they tested the segregation laws through sit-ins. On February 13, 1960, more than 100 students participated in nonviolent sit-ins throughout Nashville. The sit-ins became a fixture of civil rights organizing and rapidly caught on in other southern cities and towns, as a steady flow of students were assaulted, arrested, and jailed. By May 10, six different lunch counters in Nashville had been desegregated, demonstrating that when students pooled their abilities in southern civil rights organizations, ending discrimination became a foreseeable reality.

As sit-ins spread across the Southeast, another call for nonviolent direct action was announced by the creation of the SNCC. The student sit-ins had increased national visibility for the civil rights movement, so from April 16 to April 18, 1960, Ella Baker of SCLC convened a meeting in Raleigh, North Carolina, to discuss how to sustain the inroads they had made. The result was SNCC, which merged the Nashville Student Movement, the Congress of Racial Equality (CORE), the National Student Christian Federation, and other student groups. SNCC challenged its members to heal a sick society and mobilize youth to political action without usurping power from larger organizations such as the NAACP and SCLC. It planned voter registration drives, Freedom Rides, and other projects to raise consciousness within the African American community. Battling racism, it planned to dismantle the structures established by Jim Crow that denied blacks equal legal status and limited educational and economic opportunities.

SNCC held its first official meeting in Atlanta May 13–14, 1960. Its capstone strategies were to use legal channels in order to ensure the constitutional rights of blacks who had been victimized by racism and to empower ordinary citizens to participate in social change. Also, in keeping with the philosophies of Lewis and Nash, its members adopted a statement of purpose that declared allegiance to nonviolent direct action. In addition to its tested effectiveness, perhaps another appeal of this policy was to solidify partnerships with communities and organizations such as SCLC that SNCC could approach for financial support. Field workers became the backbone of SNCC's activism. Compensated with a meager salary of $10 a week, these men and women fanned throughout southern black communities to train residents in nonviolent direct action. One early leader, Julian Bond, notes that they came equipped with information on the economic and social disparities of the communities they visited as preparation for the hard work that lay ahead.

SNCC initiated simultaneous projects in different states. In addition to its voter registration drives in Albany, Georgia, it proceeded in the summer of 1961 with the McComb Project, led by Bob Moses, in McComb, Mississippi. Moses instituted a voter registration drive to inform citizens of their electoral rights and to provide assistance to them in passing the registration tests. Despite their preparation and nonviolence training, SNCC field workers encountered intense white opposition and an uphill road in gaining the black community's trust. When Moses was arrested in November 1961 with other SNCC members, the project came to a standstill. From the McComb Project, SNCC learned an invaluable lesson about the fight that lay ahead: those seeking to stop the advancement of the civil rights movement would do anything and use any methods to silence even a single voice against white supremacy, not to mention an entire community's worth.

A critical element of the McComb Project was SNCC's partnership with CORE, which had agitated for social equality since World War II. In 1947 CORE began what famously came to be known as Freedom Rides, bus caravans of civil rights workers who traveled in the Deep South to politicize the people, desegregate public facilities, register voters, and march for freedom. Under the direction of James Farmer, SNCC and CORE workers riding through the South in the spring of 1961 faced the era's bloodiest encounters with outraged mobs.

During 1962, SNCC united with the Council of Federated Organizations (COFO), a coalition of civil rights groups based in Mississippi including SCLC, NAACP, and CORE. COFO gained prominence during the Freedom Summer of 1964, when northern volunteers traveled to the Deep South to help with the Mississippi voter registration drive and establish freedom schools to offer poor students an alternative to the dilapidated public educational system. Freedom Summer also birthed the Mississippi Freedom Democratic Party, which COFO organized in order to elect black delegates to the August 1964 Democratic National Convention in protest of the all-white representatives the state party always sent. One of the delegates, Fannie Lou Hamer, the daughter of sharecroppers, became a star of the convention when she testified to a national audience about the racism of Mississippi's Democratic Party and the beatings she had received for canvassing voters. While the success of Freedom Summer is disputed, COFO again demonstrated that efforts of concerned citizens could create change when unified under a common cause. It would be years before Mississippi and other southern states actually complied with the law, but COFO's accomplishments moved African Americans considerably closer toward secure access to the ballot. Amid a summer characterized by police indifference, unwarranted arrests, and physical violence, Congress passed the Civil Rights Act of 1964, which prohibited discrimination based on religion, race, color, or national origin. Along with local people, SNCC was also responsible for helping found the Lowndes County Freedom Organization, which was a black-led, independent political party formed to challenge the all-white Alabama Democratic Party in the primaries. In 1966, the organization ran candidates for several county offices, including sheriff and school board positions. With the end of Freedom Summer, SNCC began a new chapter, distinguished by separatist ideals that shifted its power structure and turned members against each other. Some black SNCC members became hostile toward their white colleagues. In addition, some in the organization became disillusioned with its nonviolent tactics, and many women complained of second-class, sexist treatment. At a June 1966 march, Stokely Carmichael's use of the slogan "black power" further divided white and black members. SNCC unraveled, and the country lost one of its most successful grassroots southern organizations. Yet SNCC had created a blueprint for social change by giving young people active and influential roles and by illustrating the central position of educational empowerment in a freedom movement.

While Carmichael's direction change at SNCC measured a growing rejection of nonviolence by civil rights veterans, members of one southern organization, the Deacons for Defense and Justice, literally armed themselves against terrorism and lawlessness in Louisiana. This exclusively male group assembled in March 1965 and elected Percy Lee Bradford and Charles Sims to head chapters in Jonesboro and Bogalusa. They began working nonviolently with CORE on desegregation projects, but a series of particularly virulent racial hostilities, including KKK demonstrations and the drive-by shooting and murder of two black men, persuaded them to carry arms for personal protection. Most of them kept their participation secret, and they took the title "Deacons" to stress that they were law-abiding, Christian men who preferred peace and negotiation to violence and were prepared to shoot only when they or their families and neighbors were attacked. Deliberately establishing chapters in KKK strongholds, they carried firearms and bought bulk supplies of ammunition to distribute among members. Though the

## Deacons for Defense and Justice

The Deacons for Defense and Justice was a short-lived group that emerged in Louisiana in 1964 and grew into a nationwide organization whose goal was to protect nonviolent civil rights protesters from racist attackers. Although the Deacons only lasted until about 1968, the organization attracted national attention and put those who would molest civil rights workers on notice that their actions would not go unpunished.

The Deacons for Defense adapted the theologically driven formula of nonviolence to the realities of ever-present southern violence. While nonviolence was morally feasible and gained political sympathy for the movement, it also made civil rights protest an excessively dangerous activity that often intimidated people from participating. The Deacons sought to mitigate this situation by blurring the lines between violence and nonviolence and vowing to protect those who would not protect themselves.

The Deacons deserve at least a measure of responsibility for several successful desegregation campaigns that took place in the heart of Dixie. In 1964, the Congress of Racial Equality (CORE) sent workers into the northern Louisiana town of Jonesboro, which enraged area white supremacists and Ku Klux Klan (KKK) members. Knowing that the volunteers, as well as the local residents they were trying to help, would be in grave danger, a small group of con-

cerned citizens, including Korean War veteran Earnest Thomas, appointed themselves sentinels in charge of protecting CORE's Freedom House headquarters and of staffing an auxiliary black police force. These men drew up a formal structure and began calling their organization the Deacons for Defense and Justice.

The protests in Jonesboro were a success, beginning with the desegregation of the local library. These gains, however, were met with resistance, as the KKK began an intimidation campaign that included the burning of crosses. The Deacons responded by issuing leaflets threatening to kill anyone caught burning crosses in black communities, and distributed them by having domestic workers anonymously leave them at the white homes where they worked. When the following year a group of students picketing the local high school were confronted by police who threatened to spray them with high-powered fire hoses, a carload of Deacons arrived on the scene and began loading their rifles in plain view. The police left the protesters alone.

The Deacons for Defense and Justice were pioneering figures in the civil rights struggle because they found ways to merge self-defense and nonviolence, presaging the later tendency by a number of black activist groups, most notably the Black Panther Party, to meet violent white resistance with force.

Deacons sought the same democratic goals as other southern civil rights organizations, King and SCLC distanced themselves from the group. Nevertheless, the rapid spread of their chapters in the South and Midwest, like SNCC's disintegration, pointed to a growing discontent with the pace of nonviolence (Hill 2004, 10–51).

Yet King had also grown increasingly critical of U.S. capitalism and politics. In 1966, acting against strong warnings from his northern advisers and fellow SCLC board members, he announced his opposition to the Vietnam War, and in 1968 he activated SCLC's last major civil rights initiative: the Poor People's Campaign. Originally, SCLC's plan was to recruit an interracial

Residents of "Resurrection City," the Washington, D.C., base of the Poor People's Campaign, read newspaper reports about the assassination of Martin Luther King Jr. (*Bettmann/Corbis*)

and interethnic group of 3,000 poor Americans to march into Washington, D.C., and build a makeshift residential community on restricted government property. SCLC already had brought segregated southern blacks into America's living rooms. By bringing poor people from across the United States into the capital, it sought to leverage improvements in public policies that affected them. Although King did not live long enough to see this project realized, SCLC directed the construction of Resurrection City on May 12–13, 1968. During their month and a half of civil disobedience in Washington, D.C., the demonstrators suffered unseasonable rain, muddy streets, interpersonal conflicts, bad publicity, and the assassination of Robert Kennedy. The National Guard closed Resurrection City on June 24, 1968.

## Conclusion

The most visible legacy of southern civil rights organizations is that many of them, such as SCLC and SRC, continue their commitment to freedom and justice. They sponsor voter registration campaigns and antiracist legislation, and the moral foundation of their policies is reflected in the pressure brought by local southern communities to remove the Confederate battle flag from state buildings or to reopen the murder cases of such movement martyrs like Till and Evers. Picking up where King left off during the Vietnam era, they have weighed in on international instances of racism, intolerance, and injustice, such as the apartheid system in South Africa and U.S. policies toward illegal immigrants. The organizations' members also take their nonviolent philosophy and training programs to streets and prisons, where they attempt to stem the United States's growing rates of gang violence and juvenile incarceration. Museums and memorials from Virginia to Texas may honor them, but the most lasting reflection of their prominence in the civil rights movement is the love and tolerance they manifested in Americans' hearts.

## References and Further Reading

Berg, Manfred. 2005. *The Ticket to Freedom: The NAACP and the Struggle for Black Political Integration.* Gainesville: University Press of Florida.

Branch, Taylor. 1988. *Parting the Waters: America in the King Years, 1954–63.* New York: Simon and Schuster.

Brown-Nagin, Tomiko. 1999. "The NAACP's and SCLC's Civil Rights Campaign Reconsidered in Light of the Educational Activism of Septima P. Clark." *Women's History Review* 81:83.

Carson, Clayborne. 1981. *In Struggle: SNCC and the Black Awakening of the 1960s.* Cambridge, MA: Harvard University Press.

Davis, Townsend. 1998. *Weary Feet, Rested Souls: A Guided History of the Civil Rights Movement.* New York: W. W. Norton.

Estes, Steve. 2005. *I am a Man! Race, Manhood, and the Civil Rights Movement.* Chapel Hill: University of North Carolina Press.

Fairclough, Adam. 1987. *To Redeem the Soul of America: The Southern Christian Leadership Conference and Martin Luther King, Jr.* Athens: University of Georgia Press.

Garrow, David J. 1988. *Bearing the Cross: Martin Luther King, Jr., and the Southern Christian Leadership Conference.* New York: Vintage.

Greenberg, Cheryl Lynn, ed. 1998. *A Circle of Trust: Remembering SNCC.* New Brunswick, NJ: Rutgers University Press.

Halberstam, David. 1998. *The Children.* New York: Random House.

Hampton, Henry, and Steve Fayer. 1990. *Voices of Freedom: An Oral History of the Civil Rights Movement from the 1950s through the 1980s.* New York: Bantam Books.

Hill, Lance. 2004. *The Deacons for Defense: Armed Resistance and the Civil Rights Movement.* Chapel Hill: University of North Carolina Press.

King, Martin Luther, Jr. 1964. *Why We Can't Wait.* New York: Harper & Row.

Lyon, Danny. 1992. *Memories of the Southern Civil Rights Movement.* Chapel Hill: University of North Carolina Press.

McDonough, Julia Ann. 1993. "Men and Women of Good Will: A History of the Commission on Interracial Cooperation and the Southern Regional Council, 1919–1954." PhD diss., University of Virginia.

Romano, Renee C., and Leigh Raiford, eds. 2006. *The Civil Rights Movement in American Memory.* Athens: University of Georgia Press.

Tyson, Timothy. 1999. *Radio Free Dixie: Robert F. Williams and the Roots of Black Power.* Chapel Hill: University of North Carolina Press.

Waite, Lori G. 2001. "Divided Consciousness: The Impact of Black Elite Consciousness on the 1966 Chicago Freedom Movement." In *Oppositional Consciousness: The Subjective Roots of Social Protest,* edited by Jane Mansbridge and Aldon Morris. Chicago: University of Chicago Press.

Williams, Juan. 1987. *Eyes on the Prize: America's Civil Rights Years, 1954–1965.* New York: Viking.

# Organizations outside the South: NAACP and CORE  5

## Michael Ezra

The dominant images and overwhelming amount of attention dedicated to the civil rights movement situate it within the U.S. South. In fact, the name "civil rights movement" only describes accurately the battle by southern blacks for legal equality under a system of de jure segregation. In other parts of the United States, where racism was practiced covertly and often in defiance of the law, demonstrators were as likely to demand employment opportunity and open housing as civil rights. Referring to the contemporary black freedom struggle as the "civil rights movement" indicates our lack of regard for what was happening outside the South.

Scholars have tried to address this issue by modeling the era's black freedom struggle as two parts: a civil rights movement and a black power movement. According to this paradigm, the movement originated in the South as an interracial, nonviolent campaign for integration and civil rights, beginning in 1955 with the Montgomery bus boycott and lasting for approximately 10 years. Then, so the story goes, the movement changed dramatically. Demonstrations shifted to northern cities. Black nationalism, rather than integration, became the guiding sociopolitical philosophy. Nonviolence gave way to self-defense. The focus went from integrated participation in the U.S. system to the creation of new, black-controlled institutions. This second phase of the struggle would also last about 10 years, from 1966 to 1975.

This two-part model, however dominant it has been in our understanding of the era, is inadequate for three reasons. First, it creates a false dichotomy between two periods that had much in common. Although their most visible demonstrations and most celebrated rhetoric might have taken on competing forms at times, the civil rights movement and black power movement were both phases of a shared, larger, longer battle for black freedom and equality. Concentrating on their similarities is as reasonable as concentrating on their differences. Second, the model fails to recognize the national scope of the black freedom struggle. As this chapter illustrates, demonstrations and organized campaigns took place throughout the United States during this 20-year period. Blacks fought for equality in New York in 1955 as they did in Alabama in 1975. Third, the model ignores the local character of the movement. Although national civil rights organizations had great influence, they never usurped total authority from the local people who had to live with the net results of civil rights activity. Each town, county, and state had its own nuances, leaders, power structures, and institutions. Although certain interstate and regional campaigns grabbed the most attention and remain predominant within our historical memories, perhaps the civil rights movement is best described as a loose confederation of local struggles that occasionally came together and pooled resources but usually operated independently. In this regard, the civil rights movement is better understood as a zeitgeist than as a group of particular events, leaders, organizations, and campaigns.

This chapter on the civil rights movement outside the South builds on the idea that the black freedom struggle from 1955 to 1975 is best understood locally by exploring the work done by various chapters of two major civil rights organizations: the National Association for the Advancement of Colored People (NAACP) and the Congress of Racial Equality (CORE). It also assesses the relationships between these organizations' national offices and their local branches.

## National Association for the Advancement of Colored People

The oldest, largest, and perhaps most significant civil rights organization was the NAACP. Formed in 1909 by an interracial membership determined to challenge racism in the United States, the NAACP grew rapidly and gained renown for its legal battles against segregation. It spent years lobbying politicians for federal antilynching legislation. It also organized protests against racism in radio and film. Whether through the courts, political maneuvering, or direct action, the NAACP played a vital role in bringing increased opportunity to African Americans throughout the first half of the 20th century.

By the onset of the civil rights movement, the NAACP had spawned two affiliates that had become independent organizations. The NAACP created the NAACP Legal Defense and Educational Fund, Inc. (LDF) in 1940 to provide free representation to blacks who suffered legal injustices or were denied educational opportunity by reason of race or color. The NAACP decided to form the LDF because it wanted to create a tax-exempt corporation to handle its nonpolitical duties. Because it engaged in lobbying and propaganda, the national NAACP was not tax exempt (although local branches sometimes were), which caused it to lose donations. Because the LDF was a charitable organization, it would receive tax-exempt status and donations from those who otherwise might not have given to the NAACP. The move also saved the NAACP's legal team money because it no longer had to pay taxes. The NAACP's legal assault on Jim Crow was fought through the LDF, and it was the LDF that handled the landmark 1954 *Brown v. Board of Education* case that sparked the civil rights revolution (Greenberg 1994, xvii, 19).

Lawyers for the National Association for the Advancement of Colored People celebrate outside the Supreme Court after successfully challenging school segregation in *Brown v. Board of Education* (1954). (*Library of Congress*)

The NAACP cofounded the Leadership Conference on Civil Rights (LCCR) in 1950. Because its membership was dispersed around the United States, the NAACP had difficulty concentrating enough power in Washington, D.C., to effectively lobby politicians. The LCCR, which was directed during the civil rights years by NAACP Washington, D.C., branch director Clarence Mitchell, put the NAACP at the head of a powerful coalition of more than 150 organizations. Mitchell's bipartisan influence and support among policy makers were so strong that he was commonly called the "101st senator." Every major civil rights law of the period, and their strengthening provisions, including the 1957 Civil Rights Act, 1960 Civil Rights Act, 1964 Civil Rights Act, 1965 Voting Rights Act, and 1968 Civil Rights Act, bore the mark of the LCCR.

There were also several levels of organizational structure within the NAACP itself. During the civil rights era, the NAACP's national headquarters was located in New York and its highest-ranking official was Executive Secretary Roy Wilkins, who directed the organization from 1955 to 1977. Unlike some civil rights organizations, like Martin Luther King Jr.'s Southern Christian Leadership Conference (SCLC), the NAACP allowed individual memberships. Those who joined the NAACP grouped themselves into local,

## Roy Wilkins

Roy Wilkins was the executive secretary of the National Association for the Advancement of Colored People (NAACP) between 1955 and 1977. Although Wilkins was often criticized by civil rights activists for what they saw as his gradualism, opposition to direct-action protest, and anticommunism, his stalwart leadership during the civil rights years helped the NAACP remain one of the United States's most significant black organizations throughout the era.

Wilkins began his career as a journalist during the 1920s, working for *The Minnesota Daily* before becoming editor of the African American newspapers the *St. Paul Appeal* and the *Kansas City Call*. Over the years, his interest in black community affairs led him to the NAACP, where he served as assistant executive secretary and later as the editor of the organization's press organ the *Crisis*. As executive secretary of the NAACP, he helped found the Leadership Conference on Civil Rights, which became a national leader in coordinating civil rights legislation.

An articulate spokesperson and respected by Washington insiders and politicians, Wilkins became an adviser to several presidents, including John Kennedy, Lyndon Johnson, Richard Nixon, Gerald Ford, and Jimmy Carter. In 1967, Johnson awarded him the Presidential Medal of Freedom for his contributions to civil rights and black equality.

Wilkins was vital to the NAACP's role during the civil rights movement. Although he opposed the direct-action campaigns waged by more militant groups, Wilkins was at the vanguard of voter registration drives, and under his leadership the NAACP registered thousands of new black voters. Wilkins also advised a number of local NAACP chapters that worked to eliminate segregation in public facilities. Although he sometimes was displeased by their methods, Wilkins rarely censured local branches that ran direct-action campaigns. Wilkins's primary leadership role in the civil rights movement earned him the nickname "Mr. Civil Rights."

In 1977, Wilkins retired from the NAACP. He died in 1981. The following year, his memoir *Standing Fast: The Autobiography of Roy Wilkins* was published.

Youth Council, and college chapters. State conferences were responsible for assembling and coordinating these smaller branches on the county and state level. Regional offices coordinated the actions of state conferences. The function of state conferences and regional offices was limited, leaving the national office and local branches with the vast majority of the organization's responsibilities. Already the United States's largest civil rights organization, the NAACP experienced a growth spurt during the 1960s. By 1961, it had nearly 400,000 members and 1,300 chapters. By 1965, it had increased to 500,000 members and 2,500 branches. During this period, about half of the NAACP's chapters were located outside the South (Berg 2005, 240; Jonas 2005, 178, 182, 224, 270–278).

The NAACP must be looked at not only as a national organization but also as local ones whose tactics and philosophies were as variable as their immediate conditions required them to be. The NAACP meant different things in different cities. In some places, the local NAACP chapter could be described as radical or militant, at the cutting edge of civil rights ideology and tactics. Some local chapters were huge. Chicago's NAACP branch had about 5,000 members before the civil rights years, nearly 15,000 by the mid-1950s, and 20,000 by 1959. In Philadelphia, the local chapter had 5,000 members during the first half of the 1950s, nearly 7,000 by 1958, and 17,000 in 1959. Although a strong national office has always characterized the NAACP, and Roy Wilkins tried to exercise control over the activities of local branches and state conferences, he was not always successful. Some chapters enjoyed a good relationship with the moderate national office; others were defiant and willing to take action against the wishes of NAACP leaders in New York (Reed 1997, 165, 196; Ralph 1993, 10; Countryman 2006, 95).

The NAACP, through its national office and local chapters, took on a wide range of projects and had an extraordinary reach throughout the civil rights movement. Its political influence reached the highest levels of government. Roy Wilkins advised U.S. presidents John F. Kennedy and Lyndon B. Johnson. The LDF argued cases in front of the U.S. Supreme Court. Clarence Mitchell influenced the U.S. Senate. Around the United States, usually through its local branches, the NAACP also engaged in direct action. It conducted voter registration campaigns, fought for open housing, challenged school segregation, and battled for equality in public accommodations. The NAACP also fought along the economic front by waging desegregation drives against discriminatory trade unions and launching equal employment campaigns. During the civil rights era, the NAACP took on remarkable importance.

## Protecting Voting Rights

Before federal legislation was passed to protect voting rights for African Americans, NAACP branches had been waging voter registration campaigns throughout the United States. Chapters needed to take three steps to register voters. First, they had to organize registration drives and provide people with the information and guidance necessary to understand how to become voters. Second, they had to educate residents about the candidates and the issues. Third, they had to make sure that potential voters actually voted. In 1964 alone, the organization added 800,000 new registrants to the rolls. Three-quarters of them had been enlisted as part of its campaign against presidential candidate Barry Goldwater. The anti-Goldwater movement illustrated the NAACP's willingness to directly confront politicians with weak civil rights records. When an Ohio member of Congress appeared to be withholding his support of the 1964 Civil Rights Act, Roy Wilkins responded by threatening to register 25,000 black voters in his district who would presumably vote for his opponent in that year's election. Although much of the NAACP's voter registration efforts, especially prior to the passage of the 1965 Voting Rights Act, took place in the South, the NAACP also waged campaigns in the Northeast and Midwest. By 1967, projects in New York, New Jersey, Ohio, and Minnesota had drawn nearly 600,000 new registrants. At times, NAACP chapters used creative methods to achieve their political aims. Because it had to remain nonpartisan or risk losing its tax-exempt status, the Las Vegas NAACP lacked political muscle. To increase his chapter's bargaining power, President James McMillan helped found an association called the

Nevada League of Voters, which ran candidates for the state board of education, city council, and hospital board (Berg 2005, 145, 164–165, 187, 208–210, 213; Jonas 2005, 167, 216; McMillan 1997, 82–83).

### Open Housing Campaigns

The NAACP also organized around specific political issues. In 1958, the San Francisco and Los Angeles locals spearheaded a statewide "Keep Mississippi out of California" project to challenge Proposition 18, which if passed would outlaw union shops. Black voters wound up rejecting the initiative at a six-to-one ratio, and it was defeated. Using the momentum from this program, the NAACP lobbied for a fair employment practices law, which California's state legislature would pass the following year. The NAACP was also at the forefront of the movement to bring fair housing legislation to California. In 1961, the San Francisco chapter led a sit-in at a housing development that refused to show model homes to blacks, and the national office passed a resolution supporting the action. Such pressure paid off when a state fair housing law was passed in 1963. This series of victories illustrated the NAACP's political effectiveness (Self 2003, 87–93; Crowe 2000, 63–64).

The NAACP also battled for open housing in other cities around the United States. Seattle, Washington's 1,500-member NAACP chapter led an open housing campaign during the summer and fall of 1963. Four hundred protestors marched to city hall in July, leading to a sit-in that occupied the mayor's office for 24 hours. Such pressure convinced the city council to establish a human rights commission that would have the power to draft an open housing ordinance. In Chicago, as part of the Coordinating Council of Community Organizations (CCCO), the NAACP was active in a series of open housing demonstrations during the summer of 1966. In Kansas, the Lawrence-Douglas County chapter of the NAACP lobbied for years for a local fair housing ordinance, which was passed in 1967. In Milwaukee, where extreme segregation forced 90 percent of the city's approximately 100,000 blacks into a 72-block area on its north side, the local NAACP Youth Council led a series of demonstrations that were met by violent resistance. The Milwaukee NAACP was also an example of a branch that diverged from the national office. Although Roy Wilkins repudiated black power at the NAACP's 1966 national convention, the Milwaukee NAACP played a significant role in the local development of the black power movement (Taylor 1994, 197–205; Anderson and Pickering 1986, 2; Monhollon 2002, 55–59; Theoharis and Woodard 2005, 261–275).

These open housing campaigns illustrated not only the NAACP's willingness to take direct action but also its ability to form coalitions with other civil rights organizations. In Seattle, it helped build the Central Area Civil Rights Committee, which included CORE. When the city's voters rejected the NAACP-backed human rights commission's draft of an open housing law in a referendum, CORE responded with civil disobedience including sit-ins at area real estate firms. In Lawrence, Kansas, the NAACP and CORE helped found the Lawrence Fair Housing Coordinating Committee, which combined their efforts to get local fair housing legislation passed. Part of the

NAACP's longevity and influence throughout the civil rights era can be attributed to its willingness to form coalitions and work with a wide range of groups (Taylor 1994, 197–205; Monhollon 2002, 55–59).

## Campaigning for School Desegregation

Another long-standing NAACP battleground was school desegregation. Also working behind the scenes via the LDF to undermine the legal basis for seg-regated schools, the organization's locals sometimes took direct action. Dur-ing the early 1950s, under the leadership of Ella Baker, the president of the New York chapter, who would later help found the civil rights group known as the Student Nonviolent Coordinating Committee, the NAACP escalated its already aggressive campaign to desegregate area schools. The New York NAACP took direct action and also organized an umbrella group called Par-ents in Action against Education Discrimination, which included parents, teachers, veterans, and civil rights organizers. Eventually, parents in Harlem sued the school board for $1 million for purposely maintaining segregation in five schools. The New York campaign for quality, integrated education in the early 1950s was significant because Baker called for parent and commu-nity involvement in schools, anticipating widespread demands for it during the 1970s.

The Boston NAACP also waged a bitter struggle to integrate local schools, ultimately filing a federal desegregation suit against the school system. It started when Ruth Batson, an NAACP member who later became the New England regional president of the organization, heard that a white friend's son had science classes in his school. This surprised Batson because her daughter did not. She reported this fact to the NAACP, which asked her to lead a subcommittee to investigate the matter. Through the new Education Committee of the Boston NAACP, Batson urged the Massachusetts Commis-sion against Discrimination (MCAD) to recognize segregation in Boston's schools. When MCAD denied the condition, the NAACP reported the prob-lem to the school board, which also claimed no segregation existed. As a result of these denials, the Boston NAACP took direct action. It organized a series of sit-ins and a one-day school boycott in 1963 that saw about half of the city's black high school students absent. After a second school boycott the following February that saw 20,000 students statewide stay home, the gover-nor organized a committee to investigate school discrimination. In the mean-time, the NAACP set up Operation Exodus, a busing effort that brought children to open spots in white schools. It also created independent, parent-run schools that recognized students' cultural needs in ways that public schools did not.

As part of the CCCO, a Chicago civil rights umbrella group, the NAACP played a role in the school desegregation campaigns that would later evolve into a full-fledged freedom movement in the so-called Windy City. The CCCO represented 36 organizations, including the NAACP. The CCCO emerged from the fight to oust Benjamin Willis from his job as superintend-ent of Chicago's public schools. Despite an enormous number of empty classrooms around the city, Willis insisted that blacks go to overcrowded neighborhood schools. Formed in April 1962, the CCCO launched a series of school boycotts to draw attention to the problem. On October 22, 1963, 224,770 pupils stayed home from Chicago's schools, which the CCCO saw as a mandate to pursue change aggressively. A second boycott on February 25, 1964, produced 175,000 absences. While the CCCO was unsuccessful in its campaign to oust Willis, it would remain a major civil rights force in Chicago over the next several years.

The Brooklyn NAACP, led by Milton Galamison, was at the forefront of a massive school desegregation campaign. Galamison, the pastor of Siloam Presbyterian Church, was elected head of the Brooklyn NAACP's Education Committee in December 1955 and then branch president the following year. Over the next three years, the Brooklyn branch of the NAACP emerged as a militant organization whose stridency often put it at odds with the NAACP's national leadership. The Brooklyn NAACP organized working-class parents to challenge school administrators through the Parents' Workshop, which it hoped would convert residents from observers to activists. In 1956, the local NAACP convinced area principals to establish gifted classes in minority schools for advanced students. It also forced school officials to make repairs to dilapidated schools in black neighborhoods. It distributed newsletters city-wide on discrimination in public schools. In the summer of 1963, the NAACP helped form the New York Citywide Committee for Integrated Schools, consisting of six area NAACP chapters, several CORE chapters, and members of the NAACP Parents' Workshop. Its goal was to plan a series of boycotts that would force school officials to take action. On February 3, 1964, about 45 percent of the total enrollment of more than a million students skipped school, making it the largest act of civil disobedience of the entire 1960s. About 8 percent of teachers, 3,500 in all, also boycotted. One hundred thousand students attended local, black-run freedom schools. A second boycott on March 16 proved less effective, with only about half of the participants as the first. However, the school board was unresponsive to demands, the coalition that Galamison had helped assemble was weakened by internal differences, and the Brooklyn movement to desegregate public schools would remain somewhat dormant until its revitalization during the 1968 Ocean Hill–Brownsville battle for community control (Taylor 1997; Biondi 2003, 278).

In other cities, the NAACP also made its presence felt in school desegregation campaigns. In 1964, NAACP state chairman Lloyd Barbee formed an umbrella organization, the Milwaukee United School Integration Committee, to press school officials for change. That May, about 15,000 students boycotted the city's public schools. Throughout this period, the NAACP's Milwaukee Youth Council organized direct-action campaigns that brought attention to the problem. The Indiana NAACP and the Indianapolis NAACP headed a long battle against segregated education. In 1965, the NAACP's state president requested from the Department of Health, Education, and Welfare a federal investigation of discrimination in teacher assignments. Three years later, the U.S. Department of Justice directed the Indianapolis school board to alleviate Fourteenth Amendment violations including the maintenance of segregated elementary schools and the practice of assigning teachers according to race. Every day for more than six months in 1965, the

Philadelphia NAACP staged demonstrations demanding that the govern-ment desegregate a private boarding school for orphans located on the city's black north side (Theoharis and Woodard 2005, 264–265; Pierce 2005, 51; Countryman 2006, 2).

## Desegregating Public Accommodations

Nationwide, the NAACP challenged segregation in public accommodations. In the late 1950s, the organization was responsible for an important series of victories in the Midwest. When Joyce Glass, a member of the NAACP Youth Council in Wichita, Kansas, was refused service when she stopped for a drink of water at a Dockum's Drug Store in July 1958, the youth group decided to take action. Over the next month, the NAACP-backed youngsters staged protests twice weekly from before lunch through dinner, sitting in at the drug store's counter. Although Roy Wilkins told Wichita NAACP president Chester Lewis Jr. that the national office did not approve of such direct action, the protests continued with great success. In August, Dockum's agreed to end dis-crimination in all nine of its Wichita stores. Additionally, its parent company, Rexall, the largest drug store chain in Kansas, agreed to desegregate all of its stores in the state. The next year, the Wichita NAACP successfully desegre-gated a city golf course. Four years earlier, it had led a long fight to desegre-gate a municipal swimming pool. Buoyed by the accomplishments of the Wichita branch, other area organizations increased their efforts. In August 1958, the NAACP sponsored a youth-led sit-in at a drug store in Oklahoma City. Sit-ins were also held in Tulsa and Enid, Oklahoma, shortly after the Wichita campaign. The next year, the Washington University NAACP used sit-ins to desegregate a St. Louis restaurant. Also in 1959, Southwestern Col-lege students sat in at a barbershop in Winfield, Kansas, after a black profes-sor was refused service. Lewis also sent a series of letters that led to the desegregation of a roller-skating rink and an airport café in McPherson, Kansas. By 1960, regular Saturday picket lines were seen not only at Kress and Woolworth's stores in Wichita but also in Salt Lake City; Las Vegas; Seat-tle; Portland, Oregon; and 13 cities in California (Eick 2001, 1–11, 39–47).

The rise of the NAACP campaign to end segregated accommodations and discriminatory hiring practices at Woolworth's stores indicated the national office's willingness to adapt to local action. In 1960, perhaps influenced by the successes in Wichita, Roy Wilkins sent a letter to every president of an NAACP branch urging him or her to increase efforts to eliminate segregation in public accommodations. In Las Vegas, hotels were segregated. The only place on the Las Vegas Strip that allowed African Americans to dine was a deli that set aside a few booths for blacks. James McMillan responded to Wilkins's call by writing the mayor of Las Vegas a letter giving him 30 days to explain what he would do to help eliminate segregation and discrimination. The media publicized McMillan's demand. The idea of an NAACP-led boycott of the Strip made national headlines. Hotel owners, along with the governor and mayor, agreed to end segregation and discriminatory treatment in all of the Strip's public accommodations. The NAACP sent out testers, who corrob-orated the promised policy changes (McMillan 1997, 74, 91–97).

## Whitney Young

As head of the National Urban League (UL) during the civil rights movement, Whitney Young greatly increased the organization's reputation, power, and effectiveness by improving its fund-raising endeavors, increasing its membership, and cultivating relationships with powerful white politicians.

Young first volunteered for the UL in 1947 in St. Paul, Minnesota, where he had been a master's degree student in social work. After being appointed to a leadership position at the UL, Young became president of the Urban League's branch in Omaha, Nebraska, in 1949. Not only did Young triple the chapter's membership but he also was successful in getting black workers employed in jobs that had previously been reserved for whites. Young left Omaha in 1954 to become dean of the Atlanta University School of Social Work, where he was stationed until 1961, when he was called back by the UL to become its executive director.

Although the UL under Young did not take the same direct-action approach that most contemporary civil rights organizations did, and did not organize protests, marches, boycotts, or voting rights campaigns, it was nonetheless an important part of the movement, often serving as a liaison between civil rights militants and white business owners and politicians.

By any number of measures, Young's tenure as the head of the UL between 1961 and 1971 could be seen as a success. Under his leadership, the organization grew from about 40 employees to more than 1,500. The Urban League's budget similarly expanded under Young's guidance, and this growth gave the UL more flexibility and power to demand increased employment opportunities for its African American constituents.

Young had a close relationship with President Lyndon Johnson, and Young's idea of a domestic Marshall Plan to revitalize U.S. cities resonated with Johnson, who incorporated some of it into his administration's War on Poverty. Young also used his political contacts to lobby large corporations to hire more black workers and executives. The Urban League initiated a number of innovative programs under Young, including Street Academies, which catered to high school dropouts who still wanted to pursue their educations, and New Thrust, which aligned the UL with local leaders to solve problems in inner-city neighborhoods.

Whitney Young accidentally drowned in 1971, but he left a powerful institution in his wake, and to this day, the National Urban League has more than 100 chapters in 35 states, providing services to more than 2 million people.

In Phoenix, the NAACP led more than 100 protestors to a downtown Woolworth's store in January 1962. The action kicked off a series of demonstrations that saw the Maricopa County NAACP working with local CORE and Urban League branches. In an attempt to pressure the city council to pass an ordinance against discrimination in public accommodations, the three groups staged massive protests at the state capitol building. Hundreds of demonstrators entered the building in March 1964 and remained for several days until the governor ordered state troopers to break up the sit-in. The protests continued, however, and after a series of public debates with NAACP officials, the city council agreed to enact a public accommodations ordinance that July (Whitaker 2005, 150, 160–163).

Although the national office was reluctant to support such civil disobedience, it became increasingly prevalent among NAACP locals by the mid-1960s. At a 1964 sit-in at a downtown Cadillac dealership, San Francisco

Whitney Young was director of the National Urban League from 1961 until 1971. Under his leader-ship, the organization expanded rapidly and became an important voice of the civil rights move-ment. (*Bettmann/Corbis*)

NAACP president Thomas Burbridge and 110 others were arrested when they refused to leave. For his nonviolent actions, Burbridge was sentenced to nine months in jail and three years' probation and had to pay a $900 fine. The umbrella organization United San Francisco Freedom Movement, which included the NAACP and CORE, led a series of direct-action protests and sit-ins throughout early 1964: at the Sheraton-Palace Hotel in January, along Auto Row in February, and at the Bank of America in April. Hundreds were arrested (Crowe 2000, 125).

## Fighting for Fair Employment

NAACP chapters, especially in the West, also led campaigns for fair employ-ment. The Hawaii branch of the NAACP was founded when black residents of the island reported to the national office discrimination at local military installations. In 1955, the Oakland, California, NAACP led a two-year Spend Your Money Where You Can Work campaign, which employed boycotts, propaganda, and demonstrations. A few years earlier it had successfully moved to integrate the Oakland Fire Department and consulted with General Motors and the United Auto Workers (UAW) to open more jobs to black workers at a city Chevrolet factory. In addition, the NAACP led a drive that resulted in a state fair employment law being passed in 1959. Also during the late 1950s, the Las Vegas NAACP boycotted two local dairies that did not employ blacks, driving one out of business and forcing the other to hire a black driver on its route that covered black West Las Vegas. It also boycotted gaming clubs in West Las Vegas that refused to pay equal wages to black employees. The St. Louis NAACP's Job Opportunities Council joined CORE to picket an A&P supermarket in January 1958, resulting in an assurance that the company would hire blacks in all capacities. A similar agreement was reached with Kroger grocery stores. The NAACP and CORE also combined for a campaign against the Taystee Bread Company, which had hired blacks only as menial workers, leading to the company hiring black production workers and salespeople in May 1959. Throughout the summer of 1960, the NAACP demonstrated at Phoenix businesses and called for a meeting with the state attorney general to discuss hiring practices. The next year, it sent a delegation to Motorola to challenge the company's poor minority hiring record. During the fall of 1963, the Las Vegas NAACP threatened to carry out a demonstration against employment discrimination at Strip hotels that would coincide with the blockbuster Sonny Liston–Floyd Patterson heavyweight championship bout. The action would make the city look bad in the eyes of millions of people around the world who would read and watch reports about the big boxing match. Casino owners, urged by the governor and mayor, finally agreed to start hiring blacks in nonmenial and management positions (Jackson 2004, 235; Self 2003, 85, 93; McMillan 1997, 80–82, Meier and Rudwick 1973, 92–93; Whitaker 2005, 147–150; Sawyer 1993, 105–106).

## Influencing Trade Unions

Even more important than its fair hiring drives were the NAACP's battles with discriminatory trade unions. The Philadelphia NAACP, led by President Cecil Moore, began a civil disobedience campaign targeting municipal construction sites that used contracting companies and trade unions that excluded black workers. The protests, which involved the on-site interruption of work, triggered a nationwide evaluation of workforce discrimination that resulted in the U.S. Department of Labor's adopting an affirmative action plan in 1967 known as the Philadelphia Plan. However, these confrontational protests, which at times involved vandalism and other direct action, earned Moore the enmity of the national office, which disagreed with his methods (Countryman 2006, 2, 122–126).

## Herbert Hill's Pervasive Influence

More than any other figure in the organization, NAACP labor secretary Herbert Hill was responsible for challenging segregation in trade unions.

Hill's work with a variety of branches of the NAACP illustrated the successful interaction that often occurred between the national office and its local affiliates. Interestingly, although Clarence Mitchell and the LCCR enjoyed a strong relationship with trade unions and relied on them for key support, Hill's aggressive pursuit of organized labor never seems to have been tempered or compromised by Roy Wilkins and the NAACP central office because of it. In 1955, the Grand Rapids, Michigan, NAACP protested against discriminatory employment practices by a UAW local. Hill demonstrated to the UAW regional director that black workers had been denied advancement to higher classifications and pay levels, and the UAW reprimanded the local. The next year, Hill targeted the International Brotherhood of Electrical Workers, where the Cleveland local refused to admit qualified blacks. A similar campaign was also waged against a Milwaukee bricklayers union, which resulted in the state fair employment practices division finding the union guilty of discrimination and ordering it to hire qualified African Americans. Hill also headed a decades-long pursuit of the International Ladies Garment Workers Union (ILGWU). In July 1962, the New York State Commission for Human Rights (NYSCHR) found an ILGWU local guilty of racial discrimination, forcing its desegregation. It was the first of a series of victories for the NAACP against racial discrimination in the ILGWU. Throughout the 1970s and 1980s, through the federal Equal Employment Opportunity Commission, the NAACP challenged ILGWU locals in Kansas City, Missouri; Baltimore; Chicago; San Francisco; Philadelphia; and Cleveland, gaining a number of important reforms (Jonas 2005, 239–278).

Hill also pursued programs that would increase the quality of life for black workers in various industries. In the early 1950s, Hill spearheaded an NAACP effort to help the United States's migratory workers, especially poor black southerners who had moved to the Northeast. As a result of the campaign, New York's state government passed laws that licensed and regulated those who would hire migrant labor. Hill also coordinated a campaign to desegregate the airline and aircraft manufacturing industries, which led the NYSCHR to persuade the 18 airlines housed in New York to sign an agreement opening employment opportunities to African Americans and promising to promote workers on a merit basis. In the building trades, many black contractors had been unable to bid for work because they lacked the experience, union contacts, and resources to gain contracts. Hill formed the National Afro-American Builders, Inc., which pooled resources among African Americans in the building trades and taught them how to earn contracts (Jonas 2005, 247, 260, 291–292).

## NAACP in the Public Consciousness

Although the NAACP was perhaps the most important organization of the era, a trend has been seen within the scholarly literature on the civil rights movement to overlook or even downgrade its contributions. No books have been published that focus exclusively on the NAACP during the civil rights years, and those that do touch on the NAACP's role within the movement portray it as out of touch and retrograde. The *Eyes on the Prize* film series, which is responsible for educating large numbers of Americans about the period, barely mentions the NAACP. This depiction of the NAACP as weak during these years is unfortunate and inaccurate. At its peak, the NAACP had approximately 500,000 members, making it nearly 100 times larger than CORE. It was the only major civil rights organization funded primarily by the black community. Its LDF was essentially the civil rights movement's legal arm; it gave aid to activists from other organizations, provided council to movement leaders, pursued test cases that ensured the enforcement of civil rights legislation, helped exiled heavyweight champion Muhammad Ali regain his boxing license, and represented SCLC during its Poor People's Campaign. Although the national office and Roy Wilkins did not favor the militant direct action that came into vogue during the 1960s, in most cases they chose not to sanction local branches that used such methods, and even when they did, they could not fully control what happened locally. The faulty portrayal of the NAACP as overly conservative makes the mistake of seeing the group's character as predominantly national instead of as a product of both national and local forces. Like the entire civil rights movement, the NAACP must be viewed with an eye toward the local. Some of the most militant elements of the civil rights movement were associated with the NAACP, as were some of the movement's most conservative ones. Although the NAACP often worked in the background, waging long-term campaigns that did not produce immediate or spectacular results, it was a constant force during the movement whose efforts produced undeniable gains that altered the shape of U.S. society.

## Congress of Racial Equality

Another long-standing organization that took on new importance during the civil rights years was CORE. CORE was founded in 1942 in Chicago when members of a pacifist group called the Fellowship of Reconciliation decided to apply the principles of nonviolent resistance that had guided their antiwar efforts to U.S. race relations. Led by James Farmer, a minister and labor organizer who later became CORE's national director, the group desegregated several Chicago restaurants through sit-ins and picketing. Other early CORE campaigns included a desegregation effort at a New Jersey amusement park and a voter registration drive in the South.

Several distinguishing factors marked CORE's membership, methods, and organizational structure. CORE was formed as an interracial organization. In fact, for most of its history, it was predominantly white. During the early 1960s, CORE's membership was split evenly between blacks and whites. By the middle of the decade, it became predominantly black. Compared with the NAACP, CORE was tiny. In 1960, it had fewer than 30 chapters, about 600 active members, and a paid staff of four persons. By 1963 it had 118 chapters; about 6,000 members; 65,000 financial contributors; and a paid staff of 70 persons, 28 of whom were full-time employees. A typical CORE chapter had between 25 and 50 members. CORE was nonviolent and predominantly used direct action to achieve its goals. During the mid-1960s, however, it accepted self-defense as a philosophy and turned increasingly from direct action to community organization in big-city ghettos. Impor-

James Farmer, national director of the Congress of Racial Equality, leads a demonstration at the New York World's Fair, 1964. (*Library of Congress*)

tantly, CORE should be regarded primarily as a local organization in which the national office was weak and local affiliates were somewhat autonomous, although at times the national office would suspend or reprimand local chapters. With the exception of national projects, all CORE initiatives were introduced and carried out locally (Meier and Rudwick 1973, 10, 304, 357; Bell 1968, 11, 15, 20).

At the onset of the civil rights movement, CORE was moribund and its influence outside the South was minimal. In 1957, the organization tried to revive some of its western and midwestern chapters with little success. Most of the activities of CORE's northern chapters were designed to support its southern affiliates rather than to take action locally. It would not be until the 1960s that CORE would design and implement the new tactics and methods necessary to campaign successfully in the North, where the challenges facing civil rights organizations were different than in the South. Near the end of 1962, for example, CORE held workshops to train northern chapters specifically to fight racism in the North. By 1963, only a third of the organization's chapters were located in the South.

## Segregation Battleground

Although the organization had trouble gaining a foothold outside the South, CORE chapters around the country carried on a number of local campaigns against segregation in public accommodations during the early years of the civil rights movement. In 1958, St. Louis CORE conducted daily picket lines with as many as 50 participants at a segregated Howard Johnson's restaurant. In 1960, Berkeley (California) CORE was reactivated when 60 people came to a meeting and decided they wanted to picket Woolworth's. At the same time, Chicago CORE was holding weekly protests at various sites, Los Angeles CORE was picketing Woolworth's and Kress stores, and San Jose (California) CORE was holding biweekly demonstrations. Cincinnati CORE ended discrimination at two swimming pools and several restaurants, while Columbus (Ohio) CORE demonstrated at an exclusionary swimming pool. The CORE chapter in Columbia, Missouri, picketed restaurants. East St. Louis (Missouri) CORE took matters further, picketing the county courthouse to convince the district attorney to force segregated restaurants to desist in compliance with state law. The demonstration led to 22 arrests, but it also forced the mayor to intervene and order the eateries to serve black customers. The next year, CORE chapters in Rochester, New York; Detroit; and Cincinnati, often jointly with NAACP Youth Councils, held a series of protests against segregated roller rinks and swimming pools. The Ann Arbor, Michigan, chapter conducted a sit-in at an all-white beach and filed complaints with the county prosecutor, which led to the beach being opened to all several months later. A CORE sit-in in St. Louis forced a bowling alley to desegregate (Meier and Rudwick 1973).

### Open Housing Battleground

The other battleground CORE chose during this period was open housing. Boston CORE used testers to determine which developers would not sell homes to qualified blacks. If a developer confronted with the evidence remained intransigent, CORE would make its case to MCAD, which would then order the developer to act in compliance with the law. Brooklyn CORE was the first chapter to take direct action in response to the discriminatory housing market. Over the July 4, 1961, weekend, members sat in at a rental office until its management agreed to do business with blacks. In January 1962, University of Chicago CORE led daily demonstrations at the university real estate office. Although arrests were made and students were threatened with suspension, a faculty committee found the university guilty of housing discrimination and ordered a policy change. That summer, Philadelphia CORE sat in at a housing project and obtained an antidiscrimination agreement from the homeowners association. Later in the year, Newark (New Jersey) CORE picketed a suburban housing complex that excluded blacks. Syracuse (New York) CORE held a sit-in that secured an apartment for two African students. Ann Arbor CORE engaged in a lengthy battle against a company that refused to rent to an interracial couple. Los Angeles CORE sat in at a development where a black physicist was prevented from buying a home, a campaign that ended successfully five weeks later (Meier and Rudwick 1973, 125, 184–186).

During the early 1960s, CORE began to devote an increasing amount of energy to combating employment discrimination. St. Louis CORE leaders had a series of discussions with managers of banks, retail outlets, and department stores, obtaining more than 20 white-collar jobs in downtown businesses. Philadelphia CORE's picketing of a restaurant chain led to a fair hiring agreement in April 1961. However, when after six months the only blacks the restaurant had hired were three waitresses and one cashier, CORE picketed the company's executive office. When management claimed that it could not find qualified blacks for jobs, CORE provided applicants. A year later, the restaurant had 32 black waitresses and 5 black cashiers. Seattle CORE launched the first successful job campaign in the West when its demonstrations against the Safeway grocery chain led to five blacks being hired in October 1961. Denver CORE launched a similar campaign against Safeway, leading to 20 new jobs. Los Angeles CORE led picketing and a boycott against a beer company in 1962 that resulted in the hiring of three black driver-salespeople. The chapter also picketed the Greyhound bus terminal for nearly a year, leading to the employment of two black bus drivers. In Berkeley, after months of negotiation, picketing, and boycotts, a department store agreed to hire black salespeople. Boston CORE lobbied Sears and Filene's department stores, gaining increased employment at Sears and a fair hiring agreement from Filene's. CORE's national office sponsored a New York–area boycott of the Sealtest Dairy Company and won a preferential hiring agreement in which the dairy agreed not only to hire blacks immediately but also to give initial exclusive priority to workers of color for all job openings not already under explicit contractual obligations (Meier and Rudwick 1973, 124, 187–193).

## Shift to Militancy

However, CORE still felt it was unable to make significant headway outside the South. As CORE's frustration grew, its tactics became more militant and the scope of its protests increased. CORE also escalated its demands during this period, asking for more jobs and preferential hiring agreements. By the end of 1962, CORE's campaign against retail stores had expanded to include battles against the banking industry, major consumer goods manufacturers, and the construction trades. In August 1963, CORE disrupted business at the Jefferson Bank in St. Louis. It started when CORE, angered by the bank's willingness to have blacks as patrons but not as employees, demanded from management four jobs in 14 days. When the bank refused, protestors began blocking the main entrance, obstructing teller windows, and sitting on the floor. These actions were in violation of a restraining order that the bank had obtained in anticipation of the protests. As a result, more than 100 people were arrested, 15 of whom served from 2 to 12 months in jail. The action paid off, however, because in the months that followed, 84 blacks obtained white-collar jobs in 15 St. Louis banks, including Jefferson. In February 1964, Boston CORE reached agreements with two area banks that brought 150 white-collar jobs to the city's African American community. When First National Bank continued to resist CORE's efforts, the organization increased its picketing. The bank relented after two months, bringing an additional 43 jobs. CORE chapters in California campaigned against Bank of America in 1964, leading to nearly 240 blacks being hired statewide. In April 1963,

Philadelphia CORE became the first chapter to fight against discrimination in the construction trade unions. When the city used segregated unions to erect a municipal building, CORE picketed the mayor's home, leading to a temporary work stoppage. In July 1963, CORE executive director James Farmer and the NAACP's Roy Wilkins jointly led a march and rally of 25,000 people in Cleveland to protest employment discrimination in the building trades. Also that summer, Brooklyn (New York City) CORE disrupted work at a medical center that used discriminatory unions. Seattle CORE helped form the Central Contractors Association (CCA), a group of black construction workers concerned about union exclusion and the difficulties blacks experienced in gaining building contracts. The CCA made national news when it wreaked havoc on construction sites that failed to employ blacks (Meier and Rudwick 1973, 187, 192, 227, 237–238; Lipsitz 1988, 76–80; Self 2003, 188–189; Taylor 1994, 229–230; Taylor 1997, 117).

CORE's increased militancy produced a mixed legacy. On the one hand, it grabbed headlines, produced results, and made CORE a force in the North. On the other hand, it alienated many of CORE's potential allies. As CORE's protests became more radical, groups like the NAACP hesitated to work with the organization. Sometimes onlookers simply could not understand what CORE was up to. When the East River (New York) CORE chapter staged a sit-in during a weekday rush hour on New York's Triborough Bridge, commuters became outraged. However, it was also clear that CORE's ability to create a sense of urgency added to its effectiveness. In Seattle, CORE developed a new tactic: the shop-in. People would fill shopping carts with merchandise and then abandon them once cashiers had rung them up. This method caused chaos in several grocery stores, forcing two chains to reach fair hiring agreements with CORE. Newark CORE developed a tactic it called a phone-in, in which it would jam the switchboards of businesses with nonstop phone calls. The tactic, which could cripple operations, led to a number of employment concessions. Brooklyn CORE came up with Operation Cleansweep to dramatize the inadequate sanitation services delivered to the ghetto. This demonstration featured 40 persons dumping garbage on the steps of Brooklyn's city hall. Kansas City CORE members went limp to protest a segregated amusement park. They had to be carried to paddy wagons. Long Island (New York) CORE members stopped traffic at Jones Beach to protest for more park jobs. Members of New York CORE chained themselves to doorways and climbed girders at construction sites. In St. Louis, CORE led a dual protest. First, its members marched into the street to block rush hour traffic downtown. As police gathered to deal with the problem, a second wave of CORE operatives moved toward the headquarters of a gas company that had a shoddy minority hiring record. With police diverted, CORE members wrapped chains around the door handles of the gas company's exits and padlocked them, causing 500 workers to be trapped inside until police could find bolt cutters. Such tactics led James Farmer to reprimand several locals and suspend the Brooklyn chapter. Furthermore, since white donors financed about 95 percent of CORE's budget, the organization risked alienating those who had become frightened by its turn toward militancy and black nationalism. By the mid-1960s, donations began to slow

Demonstrators chained themselves to a federal courthouse in New York City to protest southern civil rights abuses. (*AP/Wide World Photos*)

dramatically, leaving CORE in debt (Meier and Rudwick 1973; Lipsitz 1988, 82, 89; Farmer 1985, 258; Bell 1968, 39).

In the second half of the decade, as CORE increasingly shifted its operations and offices to ghettos around the United States, forced out most of its white members, and moved away from direct action and toward community organization, it found itself unable to deliver the results it had during the previous few years. Donations dried up. Fighting increased between the national office and local chapters. As federal antipoverty initiatives poured money into hundreds of community organizations, CORE found itself unable to compete. It began to accumulate debt. Although a few local affiliates pressed forward, the organization dwindled to a shadow of its former self as the decade wore on. Nevertheless, for a short period during the late 1950s and early 1960s, CORE was one of the most important civil rights forces in the United States. The legacy of its work is still felt today.

## Conclusion

Highlighting the work of the NAACP and CORE outside the South is important because it encourages an understanding of the full range of issues that civil rights activists were engaging. When accounts of the movement focus primarily on how organizations addressed and successfully overcame legal barriers to equality, it denies today's freedom fighters a comprehensive legacy from which to model future campaigns in the ongoing fight for justice. Looking more closely at the battles undertaken by the NAACP and CORE for educational parity, against employment discrimination, and toward economic fairness reminds us that although the civil rights movement may have torn down many of the remnants of a segregated society, the problems that its participants were contesting are still at hand.

# References and Further Reading

Anderson, Alan, and George Pickering. 1986. *Confronting the Color Line: The Broken Promise of the Civil Rights Movement in Chicago*. Athens: University of Georgia Press.

Bell, Inge Powell. 1968. *CORE and the Strategy of Nonviolence*. New York: Random House.

Berg, Manfred. 2005. *The Ticket to Freedom: The NAACP and the Struggle for Black Political Integration*. Gainesville: University Press of Florida.

Biondi, Martha. 2003. *To Stand and Fight: The Struggle for Civil Rights in Postwar New York City*. Cambridge, MA: Harvard University Press.

Blumberg, Rhoda Lois. 1984. *Civil Rights: The 1960s Freedom Struggle*. Boston: Twayne.

Countryman, Matthew. 2006. *Up South: Civil Rights and Black Power in Philadelphia*. Philadelphia: University of Pennsylvania Press.

Crowe, Daniel. 2000. *Prophets of Rage: The Black Freedom Struggle in San Francisco, 1945–1969*. New York: Garland.

Dittmer, John. *Local People: The Struggle for Civil Rights in Mississippi*. Urbana: University of Illinois Press.

Eick, Gretchen. 2001. *Dissent in Wichita: The Civil Rights Movement in the Midwest, 1954–1972*. Urbana: University of Illinois Press.

Farmer, James. 1985. *Lay Bare the Heart: An Autobiography of the Civil Rights Movement*. New York: Plume.

Garrow, David, ed. 1989. *Chicago 1966: Open Housing Marches, Summit Negotiations, and Operation Breadbasket*. Brooklyn, NY: Carlson.

Greenberg, Jack. 1994. *Crusaders in the Courts: How a Dedicated Band of Lawyers Fought for the Civil Rights Revolution*. New York: Basic.

Hampton, Henry, and Steve Fayer. 1990. *Voices of Freedom: An Oral History of the Civil Rights Movement from the 1950s through the 1980s*. New York: Bantam.

Jackson, Miles. 2004. "Striving towards Community." In *They Followed the Trade Winds: African Americans in Hawai'i*, edited by Miles Jackson. Honolulu: University of Hawaii Sociology Department.

Jonas, Gilbert. 2005. *Freedom's Sword: The NAACP and the Struggle against Racism in America, 1909–1969*. New York: Routledge.

Lipsitz, George. 1988. *A Life in the Struggle: Ivory Perry and the Culture of Opposition*. Philadelphia: Temple University Press.

McMillan, James, with R. T. King and Gary E. Elliott. 1997. *Fighting Back: A Life in the Struggle for Civil Rights*. Reno: University of Nevada Oral History Program.

Meier, August, and John Bracey Jr. 1993. "The NAACP as a Reform Movement, 1909–1965: 'To Reach the Conscience of America.'" *Journal of Southern History* 59:3–30.

Meier, August, and Elliott Rudwick. 1973. *CORE: A Study in the Civil Rights Movement, 1942–1968*. New York: Oxford University Press.

Melcher, Mary. 1991. "Blacks and Whites Together: Interracial Leadership in the Phoenix Civil Rights Movement." *Journal of Arizona History* 32:195–216.

Monhollon, Rusty. 2002. *This Is America? The Sixties in Lawrence, Kansas*. New York: Palgrave.

Pierce, Richard. 2005. *Polite Protest: The Political Economy of Race in Indianapolis*. Bloomington: Indiana University Press.

Ralph, James. 1993. *Northern Protest: Martin Luther King, Jr., Chicago, and the Civil Rights Movement*. Cambridge, MA: Harvard University Press.

Ransby, Barbara. 2003. *Ella Baker and the Black Freedom Movement: A Radical Democratic Vision*. Chapel Hill: University of North Carolina Press.

Reed, Christopher. 1997. *The Chicago NAACP and the Rise of Black Professional Leadership, 1910–1966*. Bloomington: Indiana University Press.

Sawyer, Grant, with R. T. King and Gary Elliott. 1993. *Hang Tough! Grant Sawyer, an Activist in the Governor's Mansion*. Reno: University of Nevada Oral History Program.

Self, Robert. 2003. *American Babylon: Race and the Struggle for Postwar Oakland*. Princeton, NJ: Princeton University Press.

Taylor, Clarence. 1997. *Knocking at Our Own Door: Milton A. Galamison and the Struggle to Integrate New York City Schools*. New York: Columbia University Press.

Taylor, Quintard. 1994. *The Forging of a Black Community: Seattle's Central District, from 1870 through the Civil Rights Era*. Seattle: University of Washington Press.

Theoharis, Jeanne, and Komozi Woodard, eds. 2005. *Groundwork: Local Black Freedom Movements in America*. New York: New York University Press.

Theoharis, Jeanne, Komozi Woodard, and Matthew Countryman, eds. 2003. *Freedom North: Black Freedom Struggles outside the South, 1940–1980*. New York: Palgrave Macmillan.

Tyson, Timothy. 1999. *Radio Free Dixie: Robert F. Williams and the Roots of Black Power*. Chapel Hill: University of North Carolina Press.

Van Deburg, William L. 1992. *New Day in Babylon: The Black Power Movement and American Culture, 1965–1975*. Chicago: University of Chicago Press.

Watson, Denton. 1993. "Assessing the Role of the NAACP in the Civil Rights Movement." *Historian* 55:453–469.

Whitaker, Matthew. 2005. *Race Work: The Rise of Civil Rights in the Urban West*. Lincoln: University of Nebraska Press.

# Black Nationalists $6$

## Yusuf Nuruddin

The term "black nationalist" conjures up a number of media images: Afro hairstyles; dashikis; the militant rhetoric of Stokely Carmichael and H. Rap Brown; student protesters brandishing rifles on Ivy League campuses; "long, hot summers" of civil unrest; Olympic medal winners shocking U.S. sensibilities with defiant black power salutes; and self-described black liberation armies declaring a war on "pigs," or police officers. These media images are unpleasant, disturbing, or frightening to many Americans, black and white. During the 1960s and 1970s, nationalists were arguably white America's greatest nightmare. Labeled as black extremists, they were vilified or demonized by the press as a dangerous mirror image of white extremists such as the Ku Klux Klan, white supremacist skinheads, or the American Nazi Party. The conventional wisdom was that nationalists were consumed by hate. Their black power agenda was portrayed as the reactionary antithesis of the progressive multiracial coalition politics espoused by Dr. Martin Luther King Jr., and the demise of the civil rights movement was often attributed to their firebrand antiwhite rhetoric and militant tactics. Agent provocateurs from the Federal Bureau of Investigation's (FBI) COINTELPRO counterintelligence program infiltrated black nationalist organizations and fomented internecine conflict in an effort to prevent the rise of a "black messiah."

Disparaged, derided, and/or dismissed, nationalists were the most misunderstood segment of the 1960s and 1970s black freedom struggle. Their legacy was far more complex than the simplistic caricatures cited above seem to indicate. Rather than a blotch or a stain on a morally pristine civil rights movement, African American nationalism made several positive, far-reaching, and long-lasting contributions to the African American populace, U.S. society in general, and the global African community. Moreover, as a powerful idea whose time had come, nationalism was not the ideology of a fringe group but a vision that captivated and motivated an entire generation of black baby boomers. In fact, the conventional use of the term "civil rights movement" to describe the contemporary freedom fight, an intense period of black political activism that actually lasted two decades, from the mid-1950s to the mid-1970s, serves to obscure the key role of nationalists during this struggle. Nationalists played a dominant role during the second half of the movement, a period during which the mood, political consciousness, and cultural identity of African Americans shifted dramatically. These psychological, political, and cultural changes were directly related to the ideological shifts brought on in the freedom struggle by black nationalists.

## Factors in the Shift to Black Nationalism

The shift in the freedom struggle from an emphasis on civil rights during its first decade to a focus on black power during the second decade was precipitated by several factors. First, the civil rights movement was focused on the most blatant aspects of American apartheid—the system of legalized, de jure segregation known as Jim Crow that existed in the South. Civil rights activists targeted segregated schools and universities, lunch counters, municipal and interstate bus lines, and voting rights abuses. Meanwhile, intractable problems of de facto segregation—ghettos, entrenched poverty, and institutional racism—existed in the North. These problems, which afflicted millions of inner-city residents, were not being addressed by civil rights activists. When King finally brought his campaign to Chicago, as a test case of applying civil rights tactics to northern urban problems, he was outmaneuvered by the politically astute Mayor Richard J. Daley, who avoided a classic confrontation by seeming to embrace King's campaign while delivering token concessions. These concessions had little impact on the Chicago ghettos; King's strategy for northern intervention was essentially defeated.

Second, the civil rights movement, whose most prominent leader and spokesperson was King, had adopted not only the tactics but also the philosophy of nonviolence. The philosophy and tactics of nonviolence were called into question by both Malcolm X, the charismatic spokesperson for the black nationalist Nation of Islam (NOI), and the masses of black people in the northern inner cities who spontaneously rose up in one urban insurrection after another during the late 1960s in response to oppressive conditions and police brutality.

Third, the civil rights movement was founded on a belief in the efficacy of moral suasion, of taking the moral high ground of nonviolence in order to appeal to the conscience of white America. By shaming the wrongdoers, by exposing the United States to her ugly side via media images of nonviolent demonstrators being attacked by police dogs, water hoses, mace, and police nightsticks, civil rights activists hoped to prick the U.S. conscience and make the nation contrite about its history of racial injustice. Malcolm X, however, reasoned that nonviolent appeals to morality fell on deaf ears: "You can't ever reach a man if you don't speak his language. If a man speaks the language of brute force, you can't come to him with peace" (Malcolm X 1965a). From Malcolm's perspective, white supremacists only understood the language of force and violence; hard-hearted racists would never be moved by appeals to ethics or morality. This was a revelation to those with political naïveté, those who placed their trust in their fellow man, and those who believed in the essential goodness or virtuousness of human nature. For the nationalists, the United States had been stripped bare; beneath a thin veneer of professed ideals of liberty, democracy, and Judeo-Christian values was the reality of naked power wielding, domestically and internationally. Internationally, the two antagonistic superpowers, the United States and the Soviet Union, vied for world dominance, while other nations vied with one another for a ranking place within the global hierarchy. Domestically, white supremacy had been long established: Whites wielded power over blacks, while various ethnic groups vied with one another for position within the socioeconomic hierarchy. Hence, nationalists reasoned, it was not appeals to morality that black people should be concerned with, but the acquisition of power—black power.

Fourth, the ultimate goal of the civil rights movement was integration and assimilation into mainstream United States. What the civil rights movement actually achieved in its heyday was not integration but desegregation—*token* representation of blacks in formerly segregated neighborhoods, schools, and jobs. Second-class citizenship remained the norm for the vast majority of blacks. In the wake of massive white opposition to integration, many blacks began to look toward community control—black control of segregated neighborhood schools and institutions—as the route to freedom. These community activists advanced a pluralist alternative to the goal of integration based on their perception that the United States was not a melting pot but a mosaic of ethnic enclaves—Chinatowns; Little Italys; Irish, Polish, and Jewish neighborhoods. There was nothing inherently undesirable about black people living in ethnic enclaves such as Harlem and Bedford-Stuyvesant in New York City, Watts in Los Angeles, Hough in Cleveland, North Philadelphia, or the south side of Chicago. What those communities lacked, however, was control over the educational, political, and economic institutions in their midst—schools, law enforcement agencies, banks and lending institutions, and small businesses. Black power pluralists were quite willing to work within the confines of the U.S. political system; they only demanded control over their share of the pie. Nation building took the idea of community control or community empowerment from the local or municipal level to its logical long-range conclusion: a semi-autonomous federation of community-controlled inner cities. Territorial obstacles inherent in such a noncontiguous federation of city-states helped to fuel alternate visions of creating a sovereign, independent nation-state with a suitable land base via a remigration to the Black Belt South (a 12-state region—including its heartland area of South Carolina, Georgia, Alabama, Mississippi, and Louisiana—where the African American population has been historically concentrated) or repatriation to Africa. Thus nation building ran the gamut from visions of a semiautonomous, black-controlled territory within the geographic and political confines of the United States to a new nation carved out on North American soil to a Pan-African resettlement.

Although those who advocated sovereignty in North America were labeled separatists and deemed un-American by their critics, their aspirations in fact mirrored those of the Founding Fathers and the patriots of the

American Revolution. Their ideals were those embedded in the most sacred of U.S. documents, the Declaration of Independence: "But when a long Train of Abuses and Usurpations, pursuing invariably the same Object, evinces a Design to reduce them under absolute Despotism, it is their Right, it is their Duty, to throw off such Government and to provide new Guards for their future Security." The great U.S. document resonated with nationalists who perceived 300 years of slavery, legalized segregation, and continued oppression as "a long Train of Abuses." Certainly, King and the civil rights activists had a dream "deeply rooted in the American dream that one day this nation will rise up and live out the true meaning of its creed—we hold these truths to be self-evident, that all men are created equal" (Washington 1986, 217–220). Yet the nationalist dream was embedded in the same American dream. The civil rights activists and the sovereign nationalists were drawing from the same great document but at times interpreted it differently. In the spirit of the American Revolution, the separatists echoed the very first words of the Declaration of Independence, understanding:

> When in the Course of human events it becomes necessary for one people to dissolve the political bands which have connected them with another and to assume among the powers of the earth, the separate and equal station to which the Laws of Nature and of Nature's God entitle them, a decent respect to the opinions of mankind requires that they should declare the causes which impel them to the separation.

Separatism was a right enshrined in the Declaration, and sovereign nationalists chose to exercise it, believing that freedom, justice, and equality for blacks were not attainable through U.S. democracy.

Fifth, a change took place in black cultural consciousness and identity: a mental revolution, a process of decolonization, an awakening, a rebirth, and a metamorphosis. This transformation was often expressed in art, poetry, and song. During the second decade of the contemporary black freedom struggle, specific images of newly transformed, culturally dignified, and politically conscious blacks were captured by artists like Dana Chandler, Ben Jones, and Tom Feelings; visual artist collectives such as AfriCOBRA and OBAC (producers of the first inner-city mural or "Wall of Respect"); and poets and recording artists such as Amiri Baraka, Sonia Sanchez, Gil Scott-Heron, Nikki Giovanni, the Watts Prophets, and the Last Poets. No longer bound and shackled by the internalized racism known as "mental slavery," no longer bowed by low self-esteem, and buoyed by a new sense of racial pride, many blacks during this period had a new vision of the limitless collective potential of their race. Many whites, however, accustomed to black subservience, were unable to comprehend this transformation and therefore criticized it.

## History

The nationalist movement of the 1960s drew on a rich historical legacy. The earliest African American nationalist movements arose near the end of the 18th century against a growing trend toward segregation that had eclipsed the egalitarianism of the American Revolution. They emphasized the development of independent church congregations like the African Methodist Episcopalian Church, fraternities like the Prince Hall Freemasons, mutual-aid societies like the Free African Society, and emigration back to Africa by free blacks. Paul Cuffe, a black New England shipbuilder and leading emigration activist, transported blacks to Sierra Leone at his own expense because he believed opportunities there would be more abundant than in the United States.

Closely allied to the emigration movement was Ethiopianism, the belief that African redemption was divinely ordained (Psalm 68:31, "Princes shall come out of Egypt, Ethiopia stretches forth her hands to God"). Robert Alexander Young's Ethiopian Manifesto (1829) predicted the coming of a black messiah who would lead a violent uprising to liberate the race. In the same year, David Walker published his Appeal to the Colored Citizens of the World (1829), which also advocated slave rebellion. The insurrectionary Appeal was smuggled and circulated around the United States, and slave owners believed that it helped inspire the bloody Nat Turner uprising of 1831. Black nationalists of the 1960s considered the Turner uprising, as well as failed attempts by Gabriel Prosser in 1800 and Denmark Vesey in 1822, as their historical legacy.

The National Negro Convention movement of 1830–1861 became a key site of debate between advocates of abolitionism and assimilation and those who favored emigration, and also became a platform for those who called for armed slave rebellions. Henry Highland Garnet's "Address to the Slaves" at the 1843 National Negro Convention echoed David Walker's Appeal in its call for violent slave uprisings. Garnet was also a proponent of emigration, as were Martin Delany, Edward Wilmot Blyden, and Alexander Crummell. Liberia, on the west coast of Africa, had been founded as a resettlement nation for freed American slaves, and Garnet, Blyden, and Crummell were among those in favor of Liberian resettlement. Blyden and Crummell actually left the United States to take part in the Liberian experiment. Delany, however, was skeptical of Liberia because of its ties to the racist American Colonization Society, which wanted to deport all free blacks. Therefore, he explored other resettlement possibilities in Africa and Latin America.

The emigration movement, led by Garnet, Delany, Blyden, and Crummell, came to a crescendo with the 1916 arrival of Jamaican organizer Marcus Garvey. Garvey's original intent in coming to the United States was to work under Booker T. Washington, so that he could one day replicate Washington's Tuskegee Institute in Jamaica, but Washington had passed away by then. Garvey stayed anyway, making Harlem, New York City, his base of operations. From 1916 to 1923, Garvey organized the largest movement of black people ever, the Universal Negro Improvement Association and African Communities League (UNIA). It is impossible to know the total number of UNIA branches and members; the most conservative estimates claim 300 branches and 500,000 members, and the broadest estimates claim 1,100 branches and 6 million members. Regardless of the exact figures, UNIA was a huge worldwide organization with branches and members not only in the United States but also in Cuba, Panama, Costa Rica, Ecuador,

Liberia, Australia, and a number of other countries. To promote transatlantic shipping and emigration among Africa, the Caribbean, and black America, Garvey purchased a fleet of commercial ships, which he called the Black Star Line. UNIA members bought stock in the company but lost their investments due to mismanagement and poor business decisions by Garvey's hirelings. Garvey's mass popularity had long invoked fear among government officials, and the mismanagement of Black Star gave them their opening to destroy him. The federal government indicted and prosecuted Garvey on mail fraud charges, convicted him, and deported him, destroying UNIA and bringing Garvey's movement to an end. Although organizations such as the African Blood Brotherhood and Carlos Cooks's African Nationalist Pioneer Movement attempted to uphold Garvey's legacy, black nationalism would not flourish again until the 1960s.

## Malcolm X

The figure that came to epitomize the black nationalist phase of the civil rights era was Malcolm X. Malcolm X commanded a respect and inspired a love that no other personality in the nationalist movement before or since could equal. In fact, the only comparable figure in all of black history held in such awe and esteem was his contemporary and erstwhile ideological rival, Martin Luther King. The two men—leaders, symbols, eloquent orators, and martyrs for their cause—stood astride the mid-20th century like giants, men so heroic that, as one commentator put it, "in life they stood as tall as mountains, and in death they lay as long as rivers" (Van Deburg 1992, 1–10). Assassinated during a speaking engagement in New York's Audubon Ballroom on February 21, 1965, Malcolm X was eulogized by actor Ossie Davis as "our own black shining prince who didn't hesitate to die—because he loved us so."

Though canonized in death, Malcolm had been demonized by many in life. Born in 1925 as Malcolm Little, his father, Earl Little, was a preacher who professed the teachings of Marcus Garvey. For his work, Earl Little was harassed and ultimately murdered by white supremacists in 1931. As Malcolm's family descended into poverty following his father's death, his mother succumbed to mental illness and was committed to an institution. Malcolm and his siblings were split up and sent to foster homes and orphanages. By the time of this family tragedy, Malcolm had distinguished himself scholastically as the top student of his junior high school class and had aspirations to become a lawyer. However, a racist quip from his favorite schoolteacher discounting his career ambitions soured Malcolm against pursuing further education. After residing in juvenile and foster homes and working odd jobs, Malcolm moved to Boston to live with his paternal half-sister Ella. In addition to working as a shoeshine boy in Boston, Malcolm augmented his income with petty crime such as selling marijuana. Later, in New York, Malcolm increased his criminal activity, becoming a numbers operator and getting more deeply involved in drug dealing. Eventually, in 1946, Malcolm's participation in a Boston burglary ring led to his arrest, conviction, and prison sentence of 8 to 10 years.

While in prison, Malcolm X reeducated himself. During this process, he was introduced to the teachings of Elijah Muhammad, leader of the heterodox, black supremacist Nation of Islam, a millenarian/messianic cult that preached a doctrine, aimed at the black urban dispossessed, that blacks were righteous and whites were evil. The NOI arose in the Midwest in 1930, the brainchild of a mysterious itinerant salesman from the Middle East known variously as W. D. Fard, Farrad Muhammad, and Fard Muhammad, whom the NOI faithful believed to be God in person. The racial doctrines of the NOI; its ascetic lifestyle of no pork, alcohol, or tobacco; its paramilitary Fruit of Islam regimen for men; and its Muslim Girls Training and General Civilization Classes regimen for women had the power to recruit and reform hardened criminals and appealed to the black underclass. Malcolm Little, like several other members of his family, embraced the teachings of the NOI, leaving behind his "slave name" Little and taking on the surname X, signifying his lost and unknown "Asiatic" tribal name.

Following his 1952 release from prison, Malcolm quickly rose up the ranks of the NOI, first studying under Elijah Muhammad in Chicago before becoming a minister at NOI temples in Detroit, Boston, Pittsburgh, and New York. Elijah Muhammad also assigned him the position of emissary to the Islamic nations of Africa, which led Malcolm to travel to the United Arab Republic, Sudan, Nigeria, Saudi Arabia, Iran, Syria, and Ghana. In the United States, Malcolm reached countless people through his speaking engagements on secular political issues, primarily in Harlem. He also became the NOI's national spokesperson and, by the end of the 1950s, was probably the NOI's most important figure.

Malcolm's fall from grace within the NOI occurred even more quickly than his rise to the top of the organization. Malcolm's loyalty to Elijah Muhammad, who he believed was divinely sent to liberate blacks worldwide, was shattered when it became clear that Muhammad had violated NOI tenets against adultery. Malcolm's own austere and ascetic lifestyle, his sincere dedication to black liberation, and his unbridled ambition for leadership collided with people in the inner circle of power around Elijah Muhammad who deemed it necessary to cover up internal corruption and protect their own wealth, power, and status. Furthermore, many within the NOI were jealous of Malcolm's rapid rise within the organization. Malcolm's status within the NOI deteriorated further when he made a caustic comment about the 1963 assassination of President John F. Kennedy shortly after the fallen leader's demise. Malcolm's enemies in the NOI seized upon his impolitic remarks as an opening. Elijah Muhammad, perhaps pressured by his inner circle of advisers, placed Malcolm under suspension, banning him from public speaking for 90 days.

Although Malcolm went along with the suspension at first, submitting to the will of his beloved leader and teacher, it soon became clear to him that the NOI was no longer the best outlet for his personal ambition or his plans to help liberate black America. When his suspension ended, rather than return to the NOI, Malcolm publicly defected from the organization, establishing himself instead as a secular nationalist leader and a member of the global orthodox Islamic community. Free to pursue political change and

## Elijah Muhammad

Elijah Muhammad became the supreme minister of the Nation of Islam (NOI) during the 1930s and led the organization until his death in 1975.

Born Elijah Poole, he settled in Detroit in 1923, where he was employed in industrial jobs and did factory work. With three children to support, few economic prospects, and the Great Depression brewing, Poole found himself disheartened and turned to alcohol.

Poole's father, who himself was struggling financially, started speaking to his son about the Islamic movement, and in 1931 Elijah attended his first Islamic meeting, where he met local leader Wallace D. Fard. He quickly became a believer and immersed himself in Fard's teaching, becoming one of his top assistants within a year and changing his name to Elijah Muhammad. As the Islamic movement's influence grew

Elijah Muhammad was the leader of the Nation of Islam from the 1930s until his death in 1975. (*Library of Congress*)

unleashed from the doctrine of the Nation of Islam, Malcolm set up two organizations, the political Organization of Afro-American Unity (OAAU) and the Sunni Muslim religious organization Muslim Mosque, Inc. (MMI). Also during the period immediately following his ouster/defection from the NOI, Malcolm made a holy pilgrimage to Mecca, met with several world leaders throughout Africa and the Middle East, and continued speaking around the United States, both to the media and his followers. Importantly, Malcolm's interaction with white Muslims in Mecca forced him to reject the NOI's absolute correlation of whites with evil.

Upon returning to the United States from Mecca, Malcolm's feud with the NOI escalated when he revealed publicly his findings about Elijah Muhammad's marital infidelity. Death threats began to pour in. On February 14, 1965, Malcolm's home was firebombed. Although he and his family were uninjured, Malcolm blamed the NOI for the attack. A week later, during an OAAU speaking engagement in Harlem, assassins gunned down Malcolm X. Although three NOI members were convicted of the murder, many people believe that the crime was a part of a larger conspiracy that may have involved the FBI and the Central Intelligence Agency (Tryman and Williams 2002, 42–45).

Although the organizations were short lived and withered away in the absence of Malcolm X's leadership and the climate of fear that surrounded the groups following their leader's assassination, the OAAU and MMI deserve attention because they provide insight into the directions Malcolm among local blacks, it became the object of government harassment and investigations. Fard, particularly, was targeted, and when he was ordered out of Detroit, he named Muhammad supreme minister and gave him full administrative power over the NOI.

The opposition by police and government officials in Detroit forced Muhammad to relocate the organization to Chicago, where it began to prosper around Muhammad's philosophies of economic independence and self-help. He suffered a setback when he was convicted in 1942 of violating the Selective Service Act and was sent to federal prison for four years. Nevertheless, he remained the leader of the organization and authorized it to purchase farmland in Michigan. Agriculture and food production would become corner-

stones of the NOI's economic self-help initiatives. Shortly after Muhammad left prison, the NOI formed grocery stores, restaurants, and bakeries in Chicago. By the time Elijah Muhammad died in 1975, the NOI had become one of the most powerful black-owned corporations in the United States.

While the NOI was not formally a part of the civil rights movement and refused to get involved in direct-action campaigns or with civil rights organizations and leaders, its focus on black nationalism inspired many civil rights activists to rethink movement goals during the late 1960s. Malcolm X, who was the NOI's national spokesperson, influenced generations of black political thought, largely by articulating the lessons he had learned from Elijah Muhammad.

would have pursued had he lived. The two organizations were very distinct and in some ways were rivals for Malcolm's time and energy. The MMI was a religious organization; the OAAU was secular.

After leaving the NOI, Malcolm was convinced that the best way to organize black people was through a nonreligious, nonsectarian organization. However, some of his advisers also convinced him that much of his international stature and credibility was connected to his Islamic faith and that he would lose some of this stature if he turned to purely secular politics. Furthermore, they felt, Malcolm's influence would rise if he moved away from the questionable beliefs of the NOI toward orthodox Islam. Thus he formed MMI to establish authentic Islamic credentials. The organization was composed mostly of NOI defectors, about 50 of them—those who wanted an organization like the NOI but were beholden to Malcolm and/or disillusioned by the corruption of NOI leaders. The MMI had an organizational culture that was very much like that of the NOI. The members were grassroots activists drawn from the working class and underclass. They believed in hierarchical leadership and were patriarchal and paternalistic toward women (Sales 1994, 146–152).

Although some MMI members joined the OAAU, its membership, which never amounted to more than a hundred people, came primarily from a black middle-class intelligentsia. Among its ranks were journalists, novelist John O. Killens, scholar John Henrik Clarke, college students, and left-leaning civil rights activists who were disgruntled with moderate movement leadership.

A 1964 photo of Malcolm X in Egypt. Malcolm X's relationships with Muslim leaders worldwide made him one of the most potent political forces of his generation. (*Bettmann/Corbis*)

The organizational culture was democratic and egalitarian, and women held significant positions of authority. Hence a cultural clash existed between the MMI members who joined the OAAU and the predominant OAAU rank and file. Centered in Harlem, the OAAU espoused Pan-Africanism and had international chapters composed of African American expatriates in Ghana, Kenya, Egypt, and France. The expatriate community in Ghana facilitated Malcolm's 1964 visit there, where he met with President Kwame Nkrumah. While there, the ambassadors of revolutionary nations like Cuba, China, and Algeria treated him like a dignitary—an official representative of African Americans. During this and other trips abroad, which would lead Malcolm to visit approximately 30 countries, Malcolm expounded upon a human rights rather than civil rights agenda and courted favor with foreign nations to support his intention to bring up charges in the United Nations against the United States for human rights violations against African Americans (Sales 1994, 200–204).

The OAAU sputtered after Malcolm's death. It was difficult to attract people to rallies that did not feature the charismatic leader, and the internal dissent within the organization became unmanageable once Malcolm was gone. Although the OAAU developed a liberation school that featured a curriculum devoted to African and African American history, political and consumer education, and a newsletter called *Blacklash*, without Malcolm it was doomed. However, the legacy of the OAAU was captured by the 1972 formation of the African Liberation Support Committee (ALSC), which advanced the platform and organizational model of the OAAU. Like the OAAU, the ALSC was Pan-Africanist and reached out to a number of

Caribbean and African freedom movements. ALSC also helped put together the first Pan-Africanist congress since 1945, held in Tanzania and featuring a large delegation of African Americans. Other organizations that also carried out the political legacy of Malcolm X included the Revolutionary Action Movement, Black Panther Party, League of Revolutionary Black Workers, and Black Workers Congress (Sales 1994, 200–204; Kelley 2001, 67–90).

## Black Convention Movement

Another important black nationalist force during the late 1960s and early 1970s was the modern black convention movement. This movement featured black power conferences in Washington, D.C.; Newark, New Jersey; Philadelphia; Bermuda; and Atlanta before its culmination in the 1972 National Black Political Assembly, held in Gary, Indiana. Harlem congressman Adam Clayton Powell Jr. convened the first Black Power Planning Conference, held in Washington, D.C., in 1966. Approximately 170 delegates from 18 states attended, representing 64 organizations. Some contemporary black nationalist organizations, many of which were represented by the convention movement, included the All-African People's Revolutionary Party, African People's Action Movement, Black Liberation Army, Black People's Topographical Research Center, Committee for a Unified Newark, Congress of African Peoples, Council of Independent Black Institutions, Deacons for Defense, Dodge Revolutionary Workers Movement, Institute of the Black World, Institute of Positive Education, League of Revolutionary Black Workers, New Afrikan People's Organization, Pan African Congress, Patrice Lumumba Coalition, Republic of New Afrika, Student Organization for Black Unity, Uhuru, US Organization, and Youth Organization for Black Unity (Woodard 1999, 1–3, 85; Marable 1991, 94–99).

## Other Notable Leaders

In the post-Malcolm era, a number of significant black nationalist leaders emerged. One of them was Stokely Carmichael (later known as Kwame Ture), the person given credit for popularizing the "black power" slogan. Born in Trinidad the son of an activist and raised in New York, Carmichael first became involved in the civil rights movement in 1961 as a Howard University student participating in the interracial Freedom Rides, sponsored by the Congress of Racial Equality. He then became a member of the Student Nonviolent Coordinating Committee (SNCC) and was a key principle in pushing the organization away from an integrationist, civil rights focus toward black nationalism and black power. In 1966 he became the organization's chairperson. Shortly thereafter, SNCC issued a position paper, "The Basis of Black Power," and the following year Carmichael, along with political scientist Charles V. Hamilton, wrote the important book *Black Power: The Politics of Liberation*, which became a manifesto for the black power movement (Carmichael and Hamilton 1967).

## Stokely Carmichael

Stokely Carmichael was a major black nationalist civil rights figure who became chair of the Student Nonviolent Coordinating Committee (SNCC) in 1966, and later became one of the black power movement's most important theorists.

Born in Trinidad and Tobago, Carmichael moved to New York City during the early 1950s to rejoin his parents, who had emigrated years earlier. After graduating high school, Carmichael attended Howard University, where he studied under several important scholars and joined the SNCC-affiliated Nonviolent Action Group. Inspired by the growing participation by youth in the civil rights movement, Carmichael participated in the Congress of Racial Equality's 1961 Freedom Rides. Carmichael graduated in 1964 with a degree in philosophy.

Carmichael was a part of the 1964 Freedom Summer campaign, serving as a regional director for SNCC, and he also helped Mississippi blacks to form the Mississippi Freedom Democratic Party (MFDP), which challenged the segregated state Democratic Party for representation at the National Democratic Convention that summer. Carmichael was troubled by the national Democratic Party's refusal to seat the MFDP at the convention and felt that blacks had to form independent political parties to gain representation.

In 1966, Carmichael went to Lowndes County, Alabama, to organize such a party, the Lowndes County Freedom Organization (LCFO). The LCFO was a great success, and the number of registered black voters in the county rose from 70 to 2,600, which allowed blacks to take advantage of their demographic majority and gain political representation.

Carmichael became chairman of SNCC in 1966 and was influential in the organization's turn away from integrationism toward black nationalism. He was also responsible for popularizing the slogan "black power," which he helped introduce during a civil rights march that summer. The following year, he stepped down as SNCC chair and clarified his politics by writing the influential book *Black Power: The Politics of Liberation* with political scientist Charles Hamilton.

Carmichael moved to Africa in 1969, changed his name to Kwame Ture, and began to refine his political views toward socialism and Pan-Africanism. He was diagnosed with prostate cancer in 1996 and succumbed to the disease two years later.

In 1967, H. Rap Brown (born Hubert Gerold Brown) replaced Carmichael as SNCC's leader. Brown's fiery speech earned him an even more radical reputation than his predecessor. In July 1967, Brown appeared at the black power conference in Newark, where he was photographed alongside the important cultural nationalist Maulana Karenga, whose US Organization urged blacks to turn culturally to Africa to gain greater understanding of their identities and heritage. A few days after the convention, Brown was arrested following a Cambridge, Maryland, rally for inciting people to riot.

By 1968, SNCC, which had been at the vanguard of the King-led civil rights movement, dropped the word "nonviolent" from its title and renamed itself the Student National Coordinating Committee. That year, Brown stepped down as SNCC chairman, and both he and Carmichael briefly aligned themselves with the Black Panther Party. In the spring, when a Columbia University student group seized the school's administrative offices, it touched

Hubert Rap Brown, national chairman of the Student Nonviolent Coordinating Committee and a leader in the black power movement, holds a 1967 press conference. (*Library of Congress*)

off a six-week student takeover of the university. Carmichael and Brown appeared together on campus to support the movement, which had been led by an organization of 60 black students. The following year, Charles V. Hamilton, a radical activist in his own right, joined Columbia's faculty as one of its first black professors. Also in 1969, Brown published the influential book *Die, Nigger, Die!* (Marable 1991, 88–113).

Personalizing his Pan-Africanist leanings, Stokely Carmichael changed his name in 1969 to Kwame Ture in honor of the two leading proponents of Pan-Africanism, Ghana's first president, Kwame Nkrumah, and Guinea's president at the time, Ahmed Sekou Toure. He also formed the African American–based organization the All-African People's Revolutionary Party, which advocated the unification of the African continent under a socialist government. He married the famous South African singer and symbol of the anti-apartheid movement Miriam Makeba and settled in Guinea, where he lived until his death in 1998.

H. Rap Brown was arrested in 1970 and sentenced to 15 years in prison for robbery. He was released in 1976. During his incarceration, Brown converted to Sunni Islam, taking the name Jamil Abdullah Al-Amin and the religious clerical title of imam. Based in Atlanta, Al-Amin became head of one of the largest African American Sunni Muslim movements, the Dar'ul-Islam movement, later known as the National Ummah.

He was later arrested on murder charges for shooting and killing an Atlanta sheriff's deputy, charges that he and his followers claim are trumped up. In 2002, he was sentenced to life in prison without the chance of parole. He is thus viewed by many as a political prisoner and an ideological heir to Malcolm X.

Although the above descriptions represent only an abbreviated exploration of the networks of associations that black nationalists had during the late 1960s and early 1970s, by examining the political trajectories of key individuals, their organizations, and their interpersonal affiliations, we get a better understanding of how interconnected the black power movement was. We see that Carmichael's father was an activist in the Caribbean. We learn that SNCC leaders interacted with Black Panther Party leaders. We witness Carmichael's ideological trajectory from nonviolent integrationism to black nationalism to Pan-Africanism and socialism. We see an international political marriage between Carmichael and Makeba. We witness the ideological trajectory of H. Rap Brown from black power advocate to militant Sunni Muslim. We see how an Ivy League black student organization was involved in national politics and that activist scholars collaborated with movement leaders in espousing black power. We note how prominent activists from diverse organizations came together in conventions and umbrella groups. All of these relationships indicate the interdependent nature of black nationalist organizations in the United States. Indeed, this interdependence makes sense because by definition black nationalism involves the unification of seemingly disparate, but in fact interlinked, black interests.

Two key individuals whose biographies reveal these densely connected networks are Audley E. "Queen Mother" Moore and Amiri Baraka. Queen Mother Moore was active in Marcus Garvey's black nationalist movement during the 1920s and in the communist movement during the 1930s. By the 1950s, she had become an early advocate for the reparations movement, which professes that the United States owes African Americans for 400 years of unpaid labor during slavery. She mentored several nationalist and Pan-Africanist organizations during the 1960s and 1970s. Amiri Baraka's presence was felt nearly everywhere in the black power movement. He was a crucial figure in the black arts movement; organized black power conferences, including the famed 1967 convention in his hometown of Newark, New Jersey; convened the Congress of Afrikan Peoples; promoted various cultural nationalist organizations; and eventually founded socialist organizations after publicly rejecting cultural nationalism.

Baraka's politics during his cultural nationalist phase were closely aligned with those of his erstwhile mentor Maulana Karenga, the founder of the US

Essayist/poet/intellectual Amiri Baraka was an important figure in the black arts movement. He is shown here leading a Trenton, New Jersey, protest against racial inequalities in public schools. (*Bettmann/Corbis*)

Organization and the creator of Kwanzaa, celebrated every year from December 26 through January 1. Each of the seven days of Kwanzaa commemorates one of the Nguzo Saba or Seven Principles of Blackness (listed in Swahili and English): Umoja (Unity), Kujichagulia (Self-Determination), Ujima (Collective Work and Responsibility), Ujamaa (Cooperative Economics), Nia (Purpose), Kuumba (Creativity), and Imani (Faith). The Seven Principles constitute the moral value system at the core of Karenga's kawaida theory, which he defines as "an ongoing synthesis of the best of nationalist, Pan-Africanist, and socialist thought and practice" (Jackson and Richardson 2003, 4). Kawaida was the bedrock of the US Organization. US, which means "us" (blacks) as opposed to "them" (whites), was the preeminent cultural nationalist organization of the 1960s, and kawaida, a theory built upon tradition and reason, was the most theoretical and systematic expression of cultural nationalism. The US Organization became enmeshed in controversy when a 1969 clash with the Black Panther Party resulted in the deaths of Panthers John Huggins and Alprentice "Bunchy" Carter. The Panthers accused Karenga of being an agent provocateur. In the decades since that incident, however, Karenga has established himself as a leading force in both the nationalist community, via the national Network of Kawaida Organizations, and the academic field of black studies, where his *Introduction to Black Studies* is a leading textbook. Karenga's influence as both an activist and a scholar emanated from his West Coast base in Los Angeles. During the black power era, there were at least three other regionally based nationalist organizations with widespread influence: Haki Madhubuti's Institute of Positive Education and Third World Books publishing house, located in Chicago; The East organization, based in Brooklyn, headed by educator and community activist Jitu Weusi and cultural director Yusuf Imam; and Spirit House, spawned by Amiri Baraka, one of many organizations in Newark.

## Black Nationalists: An Analysis

The most common method for analytically grasping this vast array of organizations is to explore their diverse ideological tendencies. The most basic distinction to be made within the black power movement was between pluralists and nationalists. Black power pluralists were reform-oriented activists who fundamentally had faith in the efficacy of the existing political system. Pluralists believed that the existing political system could be reformed or amended to include blacks as an ethnic power bloc—and thus as equal citizens. Central to their belief was the idea that the United States was not an indivisible nation made up of patriotic individuals but a pluralist nation made up of different ethnic blocs vying for power, where the allegiance of individuals was to their own ethnic group first and to the United States second. One of the major bases for an ethnic power bloc was the strong ethnic enclave. Thus, black power pluralists believed reform could be achieved by transforming the powerless ghetto into an empowered ethnic enclave. Whereas ethnic enclaves controlled their own community institutions, outsiders controlled the institutions in the ghetto. Hence, pluralists advocated that community control would be a springboard for empowerment at the municipal, state, and national levels. Specifically, pluralists targeted neighborhood public schools, black economic development, independent black political parties, and caucuses of black elected officials as key sites for community control. Black power nationalists, in contrast to pluralists, were fatalistic about the prospects of reforming the system or gaining power within it. They rejected mainstream values; avoided entering into entangling alliances with the establishment; and were advocates of social, cultural, and political autonomy. When experiments such as the community control of neighborhood public schools failed, as they did in 1968 in the Ocean Hill–Brownsville school district in Brooklyn, New York, nationalist teachers pulled out of the public school system and organized private, black-centered academies under a national umbrella, the Council for Independent Black Institutions (Franklin 1991, 6–8; McCartney 1992, 116–119).

In addition to distinguishing the two main tendencies among black power advocates as pluralists and nationalists, we can further subdivide the nationalists into five major types. Territorial nationalists, like the Republic of New Afrika, advocate black separatism and the creation of a black-governed, sovereign nation-state in either North America or Africa. Revolutionary nationalists, like the Black Panther Party, embrace socialism and advocate a worldwide socialist revolution. Cultural nationalists, like the US Organization, advocate an Africa-centered cultural renaissance as pivotal to the black liberation struggle. Religious nationalists are faith-based communities of black nationalists such as the Nation of Islam. Pan-Africanism, according to Stokely Carmichael, is the highest form of nationalism, and Pan-Africanists, who advocate the unity of blacks worldwide, constitute the fifth major nationalist variety; yet there are two camps of Pan-Africanists. Global Pan-Africanists advocate solidarity, mutual aid in political struggles and economic development, and cultural exchange among blacks in all regions of the African diaspora. Continental Pan-Africanists advocate repatriation to Africa and envision an eventual United States of Africa, politically unified and economically independent. Although rivalries existed among various pluralist, nationalist, and Pan-Africanist organizations, it is important to stress that much overlap also existed among them, both in terms of vision and practice (Bracey, Rudwick, and Meier 1970, xxv–lxvii).

Much civil rights history is inaccurately written in a way that characterizes the movement's first 10 years as a period of success and hope while framing the black power era as one of failure and disillusionment. Because the civil rights movement, according to the way many historians have chosen to chronicle it, died on the watch of the black nationalists, they bear the brunt of the responsibility for its demise. This conclusion, however, accepts a faulty premise that the post-1975 shifting of resources, media coverage, public support, and government recognition away from the black freedom struggle was somehow caused by black nationalists. The supposed demise of the civil rights movement is attributable to a number of factors outside the control of black nationalists, most notably COINTELPRO tampering and corresponding police and government repression. Internecine conflict was also seen among black nationalists, some of it provoked by COINTELPRO agents. At times, the movement was co-opted. Leaders were bought out by private foundations that offered them high-salaried positions and lucrative grants. Popular media that had supported integration also turned against black nationalism. Equally important was a depressed inner-city economic climate, which eroded group solidarity by fostering a survivalist mentality as resources previously used to combat poverty dried up. All of these factors, most of which were beyond the control of black nationalist activists, curtailed the movement.

Another disturbing perspective that the dichotomous civil rights/black power model of the black freedom struggle from 1955 to 1975 promotes is the idea that the movement is dead. On the contrary, the legacy of the black power movement persists, and its black nationalist emphases have remained vital through the turn of the 21st century. In the mid-1990s, Minister Louis Farrakhan of the NOI, the leading exponent of religious nationalism, put out a call for a demonstration. On October 16, 1995, more than a million black men of all faiths and from all walks of life answered the call to the Mall of Washington, D.C., in what was the largest national demonstration ever. The Million Man March was followed by a number of other "million black person" demonstrations including the 1997 Million Woman March, the 1998 Million Youth March, the 2000 Million Family March, and the 2005 10th Anniversary Millions More March.

Participants gather in Washington, D.C., for the Million Man March, a 1995 event organized by Nation of Islam leader Louis Farrakhan as a day of atonement and empowerment for African American men. (*James Leynse/Corbis*)

Nationalist organizing during the 1990s and the new millennium has focused on issues of police brutality, the struggle against the death penalty, and the freeing of black political prisoners, especially black radical activists of the 1960s and 1970s who were jailed on pretenses of crime or given unfair trials, because as revolutionaries they were targets of government repression. Geronimo Pratt, who was eventually freed, and Mumia Abu-Jamal, a journalist who is on death row awaiting execution, are two of the most famous political prisoners, though organizers have also concentrated their efforts on freeing less-known warriors of the black liberation struggle.

The struggle for reparations has also been central to the nationalist organizing of the 1990s and the beginning of the 21st century. Three national organizations—the National Coalition of Blacks for Reparations in America, the National Reparations Congress, and the NDABA (named for the word "ndaba," meaning "big sit-down")—as well as myriad local organizations have taken up the battle for compensation for the injuries of slavery, segregation, and continued oppression. These national and local efforts have been coordinated with international or Pan-African efforts for reparations like the African and African Descendents Caucus that was organized at the 2001 World Conference against Racism.

## Black Nationalist Legacy

The most enduring legacy of nationalism has been the establishment of the academic field of black studies. Just as the black arts movement was the aesthetic wing of the black power movement, the black studies movement was the intellectual arm of the movement. Although the roots of black studies (also known as African American studies, Africana studies, and Pan-African studies) are found in a long and rich black intellectual history reaching back to pioneering scholars of the African and African American experience such as W. E. B. Du Bois, Carter G. Woodson, and E. Franklin Frazier, the movement to create black studies as an institutionalized academic field began during the 1960s. During the height of the black power movement, black college students, who by the mid-1960s had begun to desegregate major universities, fomented widespread campus unrest. They demanded a relevant education, one that was not imbued with Eurocentric bias and that directly addressed and confronted white supremacy and racial oppression. Beginning with a struggle at San Francisco State College during the late 1960s and then spreading across the United States, students battled for the creation of a multidisciplinary field of study that would prepare them as activists and intellectuals to engage in community empowerment, nation building, and black liberation. First and foremost, black studies was to be a counterhegemonic enterprise, meaning that it would challenge, correct, and overturn Western-dominated frameworks of scholarship that marginalized or distorted African contributions to civilization and thus perpetuated a colonized mentality or internalized racism among blacks. Second, black studies would bridge the gap between campus and community: its curriculum would emphasize both academic excellence and social responsibility. In spite of external threats such as underfunding and attacks on the academic integrity of the field, black studies has made its enduring presence felt on college and university campuses across the United States and has produced a public intelligentsia who debate in the national arena (Van Deburg 1992, 64–82; Karenga 1993, 1–66; Alkalimat 1986, 1–28; Joseph 2001, 2–19).

Another enduring legacy of 1960s black nationalism has been its effect on people of color in the United States and worldwide. The rhetoric and tactics of black nationalism were especially inspirational to Native Americans and Chicanos, whose demands for change through organized resistance drew strength from the black power movement. Shortly after black power became a key theme of the African American freedom struggle, Native Americans articulated their need for "red power" and Chicanos expressed a desire for "brown power."

## Conclusion

Although much civil rights literature has portrayed black nationalism as responsible for the death of the civil rights movement, it is just as reasonable to consider it the birthplace of a new, global, multicultural phase of the struggle. The Million Man March and its successors, the battles to liberate political prisoners, and the institutionalization of ethnic studies departments not only bring to mind the nonviolent mass meetings, legal challenges, and analytical reflection that characterized the pre–black power phase of the struggle but also ensure that the message of both the civil rights and black power phases of the movement will endure.

## References and Further Reading

Alkalimat, Abdul. 1986. *Introduction to Afro-American Studies: A Peoples College Primer*. Chicago: Twenty-First Century.

Anderson, S. E. 1970. "Revolutionary Black Nationalism and the Pan-African Idea." In *The Black Seventies,* edited by Floyd Barbour. Boston: Porter Sargent.

Bell, Howard Holman. 1969. *A Survey of the Negro Convention Movement 1830–1861*. New York: Arno Press.

Blackstock, Nelson. 1976. *COINTELPRO: The FBI's Secret War on Political Freedom*. New York: Vintage.

Bracey, John, Elliott Rudwick, and August Meier, eds. 1970. *Black Nationalism in America*. Indianapolis: Bobbs-Merrill.

Brown, H. Rap. 1969. *Die, Nigger, Die! A Political Autobiography*. New York: Dial Press.

Brown, Scot. 2003. *Fighting for US: Maulana Karenga, The US Organization, and Black Cultural Nationalism*. New York: New York University Press.

Bush, Rod. 2000. *We Are Not What We Seem: Black Nationalism and Class Struggle in the American Century*. New York: New York University Press.

Carmichael, Stokely, and Charles V. Hamilton. 1967. *Black Power: The Politics of Liberation*. New York: Random House.

Carmichael, Stokely, and Ekwueme Michael Thelwell. 2003. *Ready for Revolution: The Life and Struggles of Stokely Carmichael (Kwame Ture)*. New York: Scribner.

Churchill, Ward, and Jim Vander Wall. 1988. *Agents of Repression: The FBI's Secret Wars against the Black Panther Party and the American Indian Movement*. Boston: South End Press.

Churchill, Ward, and Jim Vander Wall. 1990. *The COINTELPRO Papers: Documents from the FBI's Secret Wars against Domestic Dissent*. Boston: South End Press.

Clarke, Cheryl. 2005. *"After Mecca": Women Poets and the Black Arts Movement*. New Brunswick, NJ: Rutgers University Press.

Clarke, John Henrik, ed. 1974. *Marcus Garvey and the Vision of Africa*. New York: Vintage.

Collins, Lisa Gail, and Margo Natalie Crawford, eds. 2006. *New Thoughts on the Black Arts Movement*. New Brunswick, NJ: Rutgers University Press.

Cronon, E. David. 1960. *Black Moses: The Story of Marcus Garvey and the UNIA*. Madison: University of Wisconsin Press.

Cruse, Harold. 1967. *The Crisis of the Negro Intellectual*. New York: William Morrow.

Franklin, Raymond S. 1991. *Shadows of Race and Class*. Minneapolis: University of Minnesota Press.

Hamilton, Charles V. 1973. *The Black Experience in American Politics*. New York: Putnam.

Harris, Robert, Nyota Harris, and Grandassa Harris. 1992. *Carlos Cooks and Black Nationalism from Garvey to Malcolm*. Fitchburg, MA: Majority Press.

Harris, Sheldon H. 1972. *Paul Cuffe: Black America and the African Return*. New York: Simon and Schuster.

Hill, Robert. 1987. *Marcus Garvey: Life and Lessons*. Berkeley: University of California Press.

Jackson, Ronald, II, and Elaine Richardson. 2003. *Understanding African-American Rhetoric: Classical Origins to Contemporary Innovations*. New York: Routledge.

James, Winston. 1998. *Holding Aloft the Banner of Ethiopia: Caribbean Radicalism in Early Twentieth Century America*. New York: Verso.

Joseph, Peniel E. 2001. "Black Liberation without Apology: Reconceptualizing the Black Power Movement." *Black Scholar* 31:2–19.

Joseph, Peniel E. 2006. *Waiting 'til the Midnight Hour: A Narrative History of Black Power in America*. New York: Henry Holt.

Karenga, Maulana. 1980. *Kawaida Theory: An Introductory Outline*. Inglewood, CA: Kawaida.

Karenga, Maulana. 1993. *Introduction to Black Studies*, 2nd ed. Los Angeles: University of Sankore Press.

Kelley, Robin. 2001. "Stormy Weather: Reconstructing Black (Inter)Nationalism in the Cold War Era." In *Is It Nation Time? Contemporary Essays on Black Power and Black Nationalism*, edited by Eddie S. Glaude Jr. Chicago: University of Chicago Press.

Konadu, Kwasi. 2005. *Truth Crushed to the Earth Will Rise Again: The East Organization and the Principles of Black Nationalist Development*. Trenton, NJ: Africa World Press.

Litwack, Leon, and August Meier, eds. 1988. *Black Leaders of the Nineteenth Century*. Urbana: University of Illinois Press.

Lynch, Hollis. 1967. *Edward W. Blyden: Pan-Negro Patriot, 1832–1912*. New York: Oxford University Press.

Marable, Manning. 1991. *Race, Reform, and Rebellion: The Second Reconstruction in Black America*, 2nd ed. Jackson: University Press of Mississippi.

Martin, Tony. 1976. *Race First: The Ideological and Organizational Struggles of Marcus Garvey and the Universal Negro Improvement Association*. Westport, CT: Greenwood Press.

McCartney, John T. 1992. *Black Power Ideologies: An Essay in African American Political Thought*. Philadelphia: Temple University Press.

Moses, Wilson J. 1978. *The Golden Age of Black Nationalism, 1850–1925*. New York: Archon.

Pinkney, Alphonso. 1979. *Red, Black and Green: Black Nationalism in the United States*. Cambridge, UK: Cambridge University Press.

Ralph, James R. 1993. *Northern Protest: Martin Luther King, Jr., Chicago, and the Civil Rights Movement*. Cambridge, MA: Harvard University Press.

Sales, William W., Jr. 1994. *From Civil Rights to Black Liberation: Malcolm X and the Organization of Afro-American Unity*. Boston: South End Press.

Smethurst, James Edward. 2005. *The Black Arts Movement: Literary Nationalism in the 1960s and 1970s*. Chapel Hill: University of North Carolina Press.

Thelwell, Ekwueme Michael. 2003. *Ready for Revolution: The Life and Struggles of Stokely Carmichael (Kwame Ture)*. New York: Scribner.

Tryman, Mfanya Donald, and Lawrence H. Williams. 2002. "Conspiracy Theories and the Assassination of Malcolm X." In *The Malcolm X Encyclopedia,* edited by Robert L. Jenkins and Mfanya Donald Tryman. Westport, CT: Greenwood Press.

Van Deburg, William. 1992. *New Day in Babylon: The Black Power Movement and American Culture, 1965–1975*. Chicago: University of Chicago Press.

Vincent, Theodore. 1971. *Black Power and the Garvey Movement*. San Francisco: Ramparts Press.

Walker, David. 1830. *David Walker's Appeal, in Four Articles, Together with a Preamble, to the Coloured Citizens of the World, But in Particular, and Very Expressly, to Those of the United States of America*. Boston: David Walker.

Washington, James M., ed. 1986. *A Testament of Hope: The Essential Writings and Speeches of Martin Luther King Jr.* San Francisco: HarperSanFrancisco.

Woodard, Komozi. 1999. *A Nation within A Nation: Amiri Baraka (LeRoi Jones) and Black Power Politics*. Chapel Hill: University of North Carolina Press.

X, Malcolm, as told to Alex Haley. 1965a. *The Autobiography of Malcolm X*. New York: Ballantine.

X, Malcolm. 1965b. "After the Bombing/Speech at Ford Auditorium." Detroit, February 14. [Online transcript; retrieved 12/5/06.] http://www.malcolm-x.org/speeches/spc_021465.htm.

Young, Robert Alexander. 1973. *The Ethiopian Manifesto, Issued in Defence of the Blackman's Rights, in the Scale of Universal Freedom*. Reprinted in Herbert Aptheker, ed., *A Documentary History of the Negro People in the United States*. Secaucus, NJ: Citadel Press.

# The Black Panther Party | 7

## Arica L. Coleman

W hile much of the United States in early 2006 was occupied with ven-
erating the recently departed civil rights icons Rosa Parks and
Coretta Scott King, the minds of Chicago activists were focused on a
battle to rename a small section of a street after Fred Hampton, the leader of
the local Black Panther Party (BPP) chapter who was killed by police in
1969. Although the proposal received the sponsorship of the alderman of
the ward where the change would take place and a city council committee
approved it, it touched off a heated debate between police organizations and
BPP supporters about Hampton's legacy. A spokesperson for the local Fraternal Organization of Police told reporters, "Fred Hampton preached violence
. . . was part of a violent organization. He lived his life violently and he died
violently. I don't care what good the Black Panthers might have done, you
can't erase the violent aspect of his life" (Patterson 2006). U.S. congressman
and former Chicago BPP member Bobby Rush challenged that assertion,
stating that the slain leader advocated violence toward law enforcement
only as a response to the police brutality prevalent in black ghettos. Rush
also contended that Hampton never personally committed any violent acts
but rather was a humanitarian who organized a free breakfast and lunch
program for schoolchildren, the first of its kind in Chicago. Despite such testimony, the city council withdrew its support from the renaming plan. The
recent controversy in the Windy City, sparked by the desire to rename one
city block in honor of the former BPP leader, is representative of the passion-
ate debates that erupt in response to the legacy of the Black Panther Party
(Ayi 2006).

The BPP is arguably the most demonized and romanticized of the radical protest groups to emerge during the period commonly referred to as the
black power movement. The portraiture of stone-hard faces veiled behind
dark glasses, militant bodies clothed in black leather attire accessorized by
bandoliers and rifles, defiant fists raised overhead in a black power salute,

and angry mouths spewing forth anti-American rhetoric are among the most popular images of the BPP in U.S. culture. Lesser known are the numerous community service projects the BPP initiated to uplift African American communities nationwide. Radical representations of the BPP, both pro and con, have obscured the party's complexity and have perpetuated myths rather than facts. The purpose of this chapter is to provide a panoptic view of the Black Panther Party from its inception in 1966 to its disbandment in 1982 by providing a historical context through which to examine the BPP's ideology, activities, membership, demise, and legacy.

## Background

Although other black organizations have used both the name and the symbol of the black panther, the one that became the vanguard party of the black liberation struggle during the late 1960s and early 1970s was founded in October 1966 by Huey P. Newton and Bobby Seale near Oakland, California. Like many of the city's residents, Newton and Seale had come to Oakland as part of a great migration that took place during World War II as blacks sought employment. Newton, born in Louisiana in 1942, was a toddler when his family came westward. Seale, born in Texas in 1936, was an adolescent when his family arrived. Like the kin of many BPP members, the families of Newton and Seale were part of an influx of migrants that saw Oakland's African American population swell from 8,000 to 42,000 between 1940 and 1950. Even before this increase, however, Oakland was a hub of political activism and radical protest and was the site of a 1934 strike by the Brotherhood of Sleeping Car Porters, the United States's first black labor union. The majority of complaints filed by Oakland residents during this era involved discrimination in public accommodations, employment, and housing. Little difference was seen between the segregation in California and the blatant racist activities that went on in the South (Abu-Jamal 2004, 6–7; Self 2003, 46–51, 161).

Despite its support for World War II, Oakland's black community sensed that the democratic ideals being advocated in anti-Nazi propaganda were not being applied toward African Americans, and like their counterparts around the United States, they began to take a more aggressive posture in their attempts to secure full citizenship. The postwar prosperity imagined by power elites to revitalize the Bay Area after the depression was disproportionately allocated toward the growth of suburbs, which left urban areas such as Oakland grossly underdeveloped. By early 1960, Oakland was controlled by corporate and political outsiders who used law enforcement and the threat of violence to quell black resistance. For Newton, Seale, and countless African Americans disillusioned by the broken promise of postwar urban renewal and the failure of the civil rights movement to tackle urban issues, the situation called for a more aggressive campaign in the struggle for equality. This renewed effort, captured by the rhetoric and programs of the BPP, would create a revolutionary discourse in the language of internationalism (Self 2003, 23–60).

## Huey P. Newton

Huey P. Newton was the cofounder of the Black Panther Party for Self-Defense (BPP) who later earned a PhD from the University of California at Santa Cruz.

As an Oakland (California) City College student during the 1960s, Newton became heavily involved in local politics and community activism. Not only did he join several campus organizations but he also was involved in getting black studies integrated into the college's curriculum. Through his political and community involvement, Newton met Bobby Seale, and the two would form the BPP in October 1966, with Seale serving as BPP chair and Newton becoming the organization's minister of defense.

Newton and Seale believed that police brutality against Oakland's black community was a dire problem and focused much of their efforts on battling it. Because Newton had studied law while in college, he was well aware of the right to bear arms, which he felt was key to neutralizing police brutality. He convinced like-minded community members to help him form armed street patrols that would monitor police activity in Oakland's black areas.

In 1967, Newton was stopped by Oakland police, and the confrontation resulted in a shootout that left one officer dead and Newton wounded. He was charged with murder and convicted of involuntary manslaughter in September 1968. In May 1970, however, his conviction was reversed and, following two mistrials, the case against him was dropped.

Although Newton was at the forefront of a number of important BPP community programs such as free breakfasts for children, health care for community residents, and clothing and food drives for the area's poor, he was also suspected of being a part of Oakland's underworld, involved with both prostitution rings and the drug trade. After he was charged in 1974 with murdering a prostitute, Newton jumped bail and escaped to Cuba, where he remained for three years before returning home to face the murder charge. He was acquitted.

Newton enrolled in graduate school in Santa Cruz's History of Consciousness program, earning his PhD in 1980, but then his personal life spiraled downward as he slid heavily into drug use. In 1989, he was convicted of embezzling state and federal funds that were earmarked for community programs, and later that year he was murdered in what many people believe was a drug-related shooting.

When Newton and Seale met on the campus of Oakland City College (now Merritt College) in the early 1960s, the flames of black power, a nationalist concept that called for African American self-determination and community empowerment, were beginning to reignite across the United States. Black power carried a wide range of meanings and adaptability to multiple contexts. In Oakland, the call for black power revived an agenda that dated back to the 1940s: defending the community against outside violence, delivering jobs and services, promoting economic development, and using black solidarity to influence city politics. The adaptation of black power by the BPP went even further. Influenced by the black nationalism of Malcolm X, the revolutionary philosophy of Frantz Fanon, and the Marxist-Leninist theories of Mao Tse-Tung, the BPP merged these divergent theories into a political ideology that transcended race and called for the empowerment of oppressed peoples worldwide, regardless of color.

## Bobby Seale

Bobby Seale is a civil rights activist who cofounded the Black Panther Party for Self-Defense (BPP) in 1966. He also ran for mayor of Oakland, California, in 1973, and throughout the 1980s was involved in a campaign to help underrepresented youth find employment.

Born in Texas, Seale and his family migrated to Oakland during World War II to take advantage of the area's employment opportunities. He dropped out of high school to enter the U.S. Air Force, where he remained for three years before his dishonorable discharge for insubordination and absence without leave. He then returned to Oakland, working various jobs and attending night school to earn his high school diploma.

Seale began attending Merritt College in 1962 and became a member of the Afro-American Association (AAA), an Oakland community group. Through the AAA, he met Huey Newton. Disillusioned by the direction of the AAA, Seale and Newton formed the Soul Students Advisory Committee at Merritt. Inspired by black nationalist Malcolm X and the rising militancy of the era, the two decided to create the BPP in an effort to inspire and lead Oakland's black community and to battle antiblack discrimination.

Seale was arrested in 1968 for his participation in antiwar demonstrations at the Democratic National Convention in Chicago. During his trial, Seale was ordered bound and gagged by the judge and was eventually sentenced to a four-year prison term for contempt of court. He served two years of the sentence. Following his release, Seale was again put on trial for the murder of BPP member Alex Rackley, who was suspected of being an informant for the police. Eventually the charges were dropped.

In 1973, Seale unsuccessfully ran for mayor of Oakland, and the following year he resigned as BPP chair. During the 1980s he started working with an organization called Youth Employment Strategies. In 2002, he began working with Reach!, a group dedicated to youth education programs. He also taught black studies at Temple University. Seale has published two autobiographies and a cookbook.

## Ideology

The political ideology of the Black Panther Party, as developed by its premier theoretician Huey Newton, examined the African American dilemma through the lenses of race and class. Like his intellectual predecessors, Newton encountered difficulties in balancing analytically the relative significance of race and class to black life. Consequently, the Black Panther Party underwent several significant ideological shifts in order to resolve such contradictions and to adapt to an ever-changing social climate. In developing the Panther revolutionary ideology, Newton and Seale embraced the philosophies of Frantz Fanon's revolutionary violence and Malcolm X's ideas about black nationalism. Referring to urban slums as colonized spaces, Fanon's philosophy of decolonization through revolutionary violence, articulated in his 1963 classic *The Wretched of the Earth*, resonated with Newton and Seale. Fanon stated that successful decolonization efforts required not only a complete change of the social order from the bottom up but also violent confrontation because colonialism "is violence in its natural state, and it will only yield when confronted with greater violence" (Fanon 1963, 61). Like

Bobby Seale, the cofounder of the Black Panther Party, holds a press conference in 1968. (*Bettmann/Corbis*)

Malcolm X, Fanon also repudiated the call to nonviolence because it led to compromises that benefited the elite but did nothing to demolish systematic oppression. Although Malcolm X believed that the United States was uniquely equipped to become the first nation in human history to undergo a revolution without violence, so long as it gave blacks their full citizenship rights, he also believed that the United States would never do right by its black citizens, thus dooming itself to be overthrown violently. According to Malcolm, African Americans had to gain their freedom the way colonized nations in Africa, Asia, and Latin America had done, through armed resistance and nationalism (Malcolm X, 1997, 98).

The Panthers also heeded Martin Luther King's analysis of U.S. cities during the mid-1960s. King described the ghetto as a system of internal colonialism, little more than a domestic colony that exploited its inhabitants. A few months before the BPP's formation, King led a civil rights campaign in Chicago, making clear his understanding that the black freedom struggle needed to expand its scope in order to deal with urban issues. Unlike the BPP, however, he maintained that economic justice, just as desegregation, would be achieved through nonviolent civil disobedience.

Although the BPP was moved by King's analysis, at first it rejected his principles of nonviolence.

To articulate this ideological direction, Newton and Seale originally named their organization the Black Panther Party for Self Defense and circulated a 10-point program that became its platform. Titled "What We Want, What We Believe," this platform reflected the paramilitary and nationalist agendas of the party as influenced by Fanon and Malcolm. Among other points, it asserted demands for the freedom of self-determination for black Americans, full employment, adequate housing, educational curricula that reflected the needs of black Americans, exemption from military service for blacks, an end to police brutality, fair treatment within the criminal justice system, and, as its major political objective, a United Nations supervised plebiscite of blacks to help the community determine its national destiny.

While the 10-point program adhered to the tenets of black nationalism, calling for racial solidarity and acknowledging a unique black cultural identity, by 1968 the BPP had rejected black nationalism because it insufficiently addressed the contradictions between race and class analysis and proposed no solution to destroying the structures that perpetuated oppression. Therefore, the party shifted its focus to a revolutionary ideology that combined nationalism and socialism. This revolutionary nationalism, with its socialist underpinnings influenced largely by Mao's *Little Red Book*, drew a line in the sand that separated the BPP, who saw the capitalist class and economic exploitation as the primary antagonists, from its cultural nationalist counterparts, who viewed white people and racist oppression as the main enemies. Thus the BPP felt that only revolutionary nationalism, with its focus on oppressive structures instead of oppressive people, would cause the twin walls of capitalism and racism to crumble (Hayes and Kiene 1998, 157–176).

The BPP's shift from black nationalism to revolutionary nationalism enabled it to form cross-racial alliances with white radicals. These partnerships proved controversial, however, as many blacks feared that such partnerships would only lead to white co-optation. Ironically, however, it was the Panthers who did much of the co-opting, exercising enormous influence over these groups. In 1967, for example, the Peace and Freedom Party (PFP) became the BPP's first cross-racial ally. The next year, several BPP leaders, including Newton, Seale, Kathleen Cleaver, and Eldridge Cleaver, became PFP officer candidates. Other such alliances soon followed. By 1969, the BPP had convened a three-day conference to form the cross-racial National Committee to Combat Fascism. There were 4,000 people in attendance, the bulk of them from white radical groups such as Students for a Democratic Society, the Young Patriots, and the Communist Party. While alliances with white radicals were beneficial to the BPP, particularly in supplying them much-needed financial and material assistance, these partnerships were also problematic. A series of conflicts led to the betrayal of the BPP by some of its white allies. In addition, the BPP's eagerness to align itself with whites caused many blacks to question its loyalty to the black community and its uplift. Consequently, continued conflicts with black nationalists, including Maulana Karenga's US Organization, deepened the BPP's commitment to revolutionary nationalism (Foner 1995).

By the 1970s, in the midst of a shifting domestic social dynamic and an increasing global consciousness, the BPP's revolutionary nationalism yielded to an internationalist perspective. This shift in the BPP's philosophy reflected more an expansion of the organization's focus than a departure from revolutionary nationalism. The BPP still believed that revolutionary nationalism was necessary for coalition building on the domestic front, but it also realized that the forces faced by oppressed people were global rather than national in scope. U.S. actions in Africa, Latin America, and especially Vietnam recast the United States as an empire. In the minds of groups like the BPP, the United States was a modern-day Babylon whose decadence would lead to its demise. The BPP warned that the United States would perish beneath the weight of its corruption and imperialism. But the destruction of the U.S. empire, according to the BPP, would have to come from the bottom up. It would take grassroots efforts to transform it and rescue it from utter ruin. The BPP envisioned that such efforts had to happen not only on the domestic front but internationally as well. This vision reflected the BPP's belief that the United States was not just a nation but also an empire that sought to promote the interests of the capitalist class globally. Because the struggle was both domestic and foreign, the Panthers proposed a coalition among all oppressed peoples of the world to overthrow its international enemy, the United States (Self 2003, 14).

Perhaps the most radical display of the BPP's internationalism was a 1970 letter from Newton to the "courageous revolutionaries of the National Liberation Front and Provisional Revolutionary Government of South Vietnam." While the BPP platform called for black men to be exempted from military service, Newton offered the assistance of black soldiers to Vietnamese insurgents, reasoning that the historical moment had arrived "to take the concept of internationalism to its final conclusion—the destruction of statehood itself." Newton believed such destruction was necessary because African Americans were uniquely positioned as a people without a nation. He felt that it was the BPP's duty to support those resisting U.S. imperialism. Also in 1970, at the Revolutionary People's Constitutional Convention, the BPP articulated its concept of revolutionary communalism in which the oppressed world would become one large community that would respond in unison to defeat capitalism (Hayes and Kiene 1998, 17–172).

## Membership

Although BPP ideology underwent numerous shifts, the party's commitment to grassroots organizing, particularly among those of the lower classes, remained constant. Despite the skepticism of many that the black underclass could be transformed into political agents for change, the BPP embraced Fanon's assertion that the disaffected and dispossessed could be rallied into a revolutionary force. As Newton observed in his autobiography, "The street brothers were important to me, and I could not turn away from the life shared with them" (Newton 1973, 173–174). Seale, in his autobiography, also noted the importance of organizing on the street but reminded readers that BPP membership was not necessarily limited to the lower classes:

Activists gather in anticipation of the second Revolutionary People's Constitutional Convention, a multicultural November 1970 gathering called by the Black Panther Party. (*Library of Congress*)

He [Newton] didn't just pass out the platform in people's hands. He stopped, talked and discussed the points . . . with all the black brothers and sisters on the block and the mother who had been scrubbing Miss Ann's [white women's] kitchens. We talked to brothers and sisters in colleges, in high schools, who were on parole, on probation, who'd been in jail, who'd just gotten out of jail, and brothers and sisters who looked like they were on their way to jail. (Seale 1991, 64–65)

While Seale also placed emphasis on the streets, his inclusion of women departs from Newton's emphasis on an exclusively male membership. Much like other civil rights organizations, male chauvinism was no stranger to the BPP. Yet, when male BPP members came to realize that law enforcement made little distinction between black men and black women, they began to rethink their gender politics and issued a formal statement against sexism. While the BPP's official stand against sexism theoretically made it the most progressive African American organization of the civil rights era, the reality was different. Within the BPP, some males refused to take orders from women. Despite this refusal, women such as Erica Huggins, Kathleen Cleaver, Afeni Shakur, and Elaine Brown, who headed the BPP from 1974 through 1977, made their mark within the organization. Frankye Malika Adams, a former member of the Brooklyn BPP, went even further, stating, "Women ran the BPP pretty much. . . . We actually ran the BPP's program" (Matthews 1998, 291). In this regard, the BPP was no different from the myriad civil rights organizations that drew strength from the activism of black women.

The membership of the BPP Central Committee, formed in 1968 as the organization's decision-making body, further demonstrates the BPP's diverse class membership on both the local and national levels. From the outset, the BPP recruited on the street, as evidenced by the life stories of some of its first recruits. Robert "Li'l Bobby" Hutton, who became the BPP's first treasurer, had just been thrown out of school and in all probability was one of those Seale characterized as a future inmate. Eldridge Cleaver, the BPP's minister of information, had spent most of his adult life in prison and was on parole when he joined the party in 1967. However, the BPP can hardly be called an entirely bottom-up organization. Chairman Seale and Minister of Defense Newton were college educated and had extensive experience working in the community. Kathleen Cleaver, Eldridge's wife and the BPP communications secretary, was the daughter of a U.S. ambassador. She dropped out of college to join the BPP but later returned to school and eventually received a law degree from Yale University. George Mason Murray, BPP minister of education, was an English instructor at San Francisco State University. The class diversity of the BPP membership can also been seen regionally. While the chapters in Southern California may have been dominated by working-class and underclass members, the Boston chapter of the BPP boasted a large student membership. Coast to coast, in fact, a large portion of BPP membership came from student activists who became Panthers while in high school or college. As demonstrated, BPP membership was far from homogenous as the organization was cut from a wide swath of the African American community. Though such heterogeneity was a source of tension within the organization, the BPP's ability to recruit from a broad cross-section of the African American community is representative of its inclusiveness and wide appeal. It was this heterogeneous group that reported daily to numerous storefront headquarters to receive BPP training and to conduct BPP business (Jones 1998, 43–46).

Community service was the mantra of the BPP from its inception, and the salient issue on the BPP agenda was to protect the community from police harassment. Although originally not the highest priority for the BPP, policing the police quickly became its primary concern. Oakland had a police force of 600, of which only 19 were African American. Hence, a majority black community policed by a majority white police force, whose rolls were swelled by southerners who often used excessive force during apprehensions and often harassed the community, made the city of Oakland akin to an occupied territory. In its effort to safeguard the community from police abuse, the BPP set up armed patrols beginning in January 1967. Carloads of Panthers would randomly cruise various neighborhoods. If they came upon police activity, especially the arrest of a black suspect, the Panthers would get out of their cars, stand the legal distance away from the action, and observe the arresting officer's behavior to ensure that he was operating within the bounds of the law. Police were unnerved by BPP scrutiny and by the fact that the observers carried unloaded weapons out in the open for all to see. Both observing police activity and carrying unloaded weapons were legal in the state of California. To exhibit their awareness of their right to do these things, BPP observers carried along law books from which they cited relevant passages attesting to the legality of their behavior. It was important for the BPP to be able to do this, as their actions were initially challenged by law enforcement officials. Two months after the first BPP patrol, a police officer identified only as Badge 206 called for backup to assist him in confiscating the guns held by BPP members during one such patrol. The Panthers had reached an impasse with the cops, and a local district attorney was called to the scene. To the chagrin of the police, the district attorney asserted that the Panthers were within their legal rights and had broken no laws. As a result of this victory, both citizens and law enforcement became increasingly aware of the BPP, its mission, and its power (Boyd 1995, 12–15; Hilliard 2006, 36–50).

One of the BPP's greatest sources of attention, both from its backers and its critics, was its paramilitary image. It was the magnet that drew many people into the organization, but it was also the factor that caused others to repudiate the BPP. As one BPP member recalled, "Their mystique—the black pants, leather jackets, berets, guns, and their talk—aggressive, direct—attracted me and thousands more across America" (Jennings 1998, 257). BPP self-defense advocacy was influenced by contemporary revolutionaries like Fanon and Malcolm X but was also a continuation of a long tradition of African American armed resistance. Despite its willingness to support violence, the BPP declared in 1969, "Let us make one thing crystal clear. We do not claim the right to indiscriminate violence. We seek no bloodbath. We are not out to kill up white people. On the contrary, it is the cops who claim the right to indiscriminate violence and practice it everyday" (Foner 1995, 19). In other words, it was self-defense and not indiscriminate violence that was at the heart of the BPP directive. As such, the BPP believed that it was metaphorically living up to the true spirit of its symbol, the panther, which is not an aggressor but only attacks when attacked. As its membership grew, the BPP was able to more effectively carry out its self-defense doctrine. As a result, the BPP was able to police the police efficiently. For a time, police brutality declined, resulting in growing Bay Area support for the BPP. Although the BPP silenced some of its harshest critics, others in the community still believed that BPP militancy was aberrant to mainstream civil rights nonviolence (Abu-Jamal 2004, 12–19).

While the BPP's reputation grew in the Bay Area, its national prominence came about by accident. On May 2, 1967, the Panthers were thrust into the national spotlight when Seale led a group of 24 men and 6 women who marched across the lawn of California's state capitol dressed in what is now recognized as trademark BPP attire and toting unloaded firearms. As onlookers, including Gov. Ronald Reagan, stared in disbelief at the open display of weaponry, Seale and his followers filed into the State Assembly meeting room where legislators were debating the issue of gun control. Seale, with a 9-millimeter handgun strapped to his waist and a bandolier across his body, began reading BPP Executive Order #1. The order demanded that all U.S. citizens, particularly African Americans, oppose the Mulford Bill, a gun-control measure that would disarm the BPP and leave it at the mercy of the law enforcement agencies that already brutalized black communities with impunity. Media happened to be on the scene, and the drama was captured. By the end of the day, the incident had been broadcast nationwide, and the Black Panther Party became a household name.

Despite negative press coverage of the BPP as an outlaw organization, an overwhelming number of people wanted to get involved with the movement. Some boarded the next flight to Oakland, making their way to Panther headquarters seeking membership. Others decided to begin BPP chapters in their own communities. When the frenzy over the incident had settled, the BPP was a national organization with chapters in 40 U.S. cities. Other ethnic organizations such as the Brown Berets, which organized Chicanos in Southern California; the Red Guard Party, which was made up of people from Oakland's Chinese community; and the Young Lords, which organized Puerto Ricans in New York and Chicago, began to model their organizations after the BPP. White organizations, such as the White Panther Party in Ann Arbor, Michigan, and the Patriot Party in Chicago, emulated the Panthers as well. The BPP also established an international chapter in Algiers, which would become the home of a number of BPP expatriates, and another in London.

The overnight transformation of the BPP from a local organization into a national and international phenomenon made paramount the need for a well-operated communications network. *The Black Panther*, the organization's official newsletter, which had been published intermittently in its first two years of existence, was put on a weekly schedule starting April 1969. Equipped with a full editorial staff led by Minister of Information Eldridge Cleaver, the Black Panther Community News Services (later known as the Black Panther Intercommunal News Service) eventually reached a circulation of 150,000 domestic and foreign subscribers. Hailed as the voice of the vanguard, the newsletter covered a wide range of issues and provided an important alternative to the mainstream press. It gave readers information about BPP ideology, activities, and internal affairs. It covered mainstream news events. It addressed community struggles and international freedom movements. It also featured poetry and artwork that symbolized the BPP struggle (Heath 1976, 1).

BPP iconography, crafted by artist and BPP member Emory Douglass and others, proved vital in underscoring the revolutionary concepts espoused in the newsletter. These visual representations criticized the U.S. government while creating an empowered African American imagery. BPP artwork also became a hot commodity when the BPP offered select pieces as posters, which were widely consumed by the public. The image that received the widest acclaim and generated the most revenue was that of Newton, dressed in standard BPP attire, seated in a wide-backed rattan chair

One of the most famous images of the era was this photograph of Black Panther Party cofounder Huey P. Newton, which was mass-produced as a wall poster. (*Library of Congress*)

with a zebra rug at his feet, bracketed by African shields while gazing stoically into the camera with a spear in his left hand and a shotgun in his right hand. Through this poignant image, Newton became the face of the BPP. In addition, this iconic presentation permanently codified the BPP as a paramilitary operation despite later efforts to refashion the organization's image.

As BPP membership expanded, so did its community service agenda. Newton referred to these operations as "survival programs," not because he believed that they were necessarily a means to an end, but because they provided people a means to survive as the BPP worked to raise their political consciousness. Many of these programs were begun by local chapters. The Free Breakfast for Children Program was first implemented by the Seattle, Washington, chapter in 1968. The following year, Harlem, New York City, affiliates began a housing advocacy program. Also in 1969, the Kansas City, Missouri, BPP chapter began a community drug program. The Richmond, California, chapter created a liberation school, later called the Intercommu-

A teacher and his students at a Black Panther liberation school in San Francisco. Providing services to urban communities was an important aspect of the Black Panther Party program. (*Bettmann/Corbis*)

nal Youth Institution. Additional services offered by the BPP included the People's Free Medical Research Health Clinic (1969); Free Clothing and Free Busing to Prisons programs (1970); Seniors against Fearful Environment Program; Sickle Cell Anemia Research Foundation; Free Housing Cooperative Program; Free Shoe, Free Pest Control, and Free Plumbing and Maintenance programs (1971); Free Food Program for Needy Families (1972); and Free Ambulance Services (1974) (Jones 1998, 29–31; Abu-Jamal 2004, 70).

Not every chapter offered all of the programs implemented by the BPP. Smaller chapters offered the most basic programs such as the free breakfast, free clinic, and free clothing programs, while larger chapters such as New York, Chicago, and Los Angeles provided a wider range of services. These programs helped the BPP gain widespread appeal within various sectors of the black community as churches, lodges, and schools assisted the organization in its various operations. Noteworthy are the physicians who set up offices in BPP clinics in Kansas City, Oakland, and Philadelphia, donating their services to many who would not have otherwise received medical attention (Abu-Jamal 2004, 71).

## Demise

These expanded community programs marked a shift in BPP priorities as the organization sought to remodel itself into a political rather than a paramilitary group. But the change in direction proved detrimental. As early as 1968 the BPP dropped "For Self Defense" from its name and over the years became increasingly involved in electoral politics. In 1973 Elaine Brown and Bobby Seale made formidable but unsuccessful bids in Oakland for city council and mayor, respectively. These failed campaigns further exacerbated intragroup tensions as many believed the organization had grown more reformist and less revolutionary. Such tensions resulted in factionalism between BPP chapters in the East and West, which escalated into violence that resulted in the deaths of two party members. In addition, membership waned as some party members were publicly ostracized as enemies of the people while others became disillusioned and left on their own.

Intragroup tensions notwithstanding, COINTELPRO, a secret Federal Bureau of Investigation (FBI) counterintelligence program designed to investigate and weaken black militant organizations, proved far more instrumental in the downfall of the BPP. COINTELPRO used legal and illegal tactics to bring down organizations and individuals it found politically dangerous. COINTELPRO was marked by disinformation campaigns, levying false charges against its targets, manufacturing evidence in order to obtain convictions, withholding evidence that would exonerate its targets, and even the assassination of key figures, including Chicago BPP leader Fred Hampton. While COINTELPRO operatives were employed against a number of organizations such as the Socialist Workers Party and the American Indian movement, the organization especially attacked those involved in the civil rights movement. The program's most egregious tactics were reserved for the BPP. This special treatment reflected the beliefs of FBI director J. Edgar Hoover, who in 1968 identified the BPP as the greatest threat to internal security in the United States. Thus, Hoover instructed his agents to employ any and all tactics that would create dissent within the ranks of the BPP and cripple the organization.

Working with local law enforcement agencies, the FBI subjected the BPP to constant harassment, which eventually left the organization in shambles. Of the 295 COINTELPRO actions levied against civil rights activists from 1956 to 1971, the BPP was the organization most frequently targeted. BPP headquarters, child care centers, and free health clinics were vandalized. Furthermore, many BPP members were arrested on trumped-up charges and incarcerated for days without knowing why. Consequently, many of the resources that had been allotted for community programs were being diverted toward efforts to free party members who were being held as political prisoners. Charles R. Garry, a white attorney who served as legal counsel for several BPP members, asserted that law enforcement would arrest BPP members, let them smolder in prison for a few weeks, and then drop the charges. Some members, like Geronimo Pratt, suffered crueler fates. Pratt spent 30 years in prison on a false robbery and murder conviction. He was exonerated and released in 1997. Others, like award-winning journalist Mumia Abu-Jamal, who has been on death row since the 1980s, remain caught within the clutches of the legal system. The American Civil Liberties Union (ACLU), after conducting a survey of law enforcement activities against the Panthers, concluded that both local and federal law enforcement agencies violated the Panthers' First Amendment rights and right to due process. Furthermore, the ACLU charged "that the style of law enforcement applied to the Black Panthers has amounted to provocative and even punitive harassment, denying the constitutional rights of the Panthers to make speeches or distribute political literature" (Foner 1995, 263). Garry agreed: "In the over thirty years I have been practicing law, I have never experienced the type of persecution faced by the Black Panthers. The old rules do not apply to the Black Panther Party. There are new sets of rules, new requirements, new methods of harassment" (Foner 1995, 259).

Perhaps the most egregious act committed under CONITELPRO was the assassination of Chicago BPP leader Fred Hampton. Hampton was one of the most effective leaders in the BPP, whose Chicago branch served as an exemplar within the organization. He was a gifted organizer who caught the attention of law enforcement because of his ability to turn street gangs into political collectives. He had successfully reformed the Puerto Rican street gang the Young Lords into the Young Lords Party. They responded by becoming political affiliates of the BPP. Hampton was engaged in a similar endeavor with Jeff Fort, leader of the notorious Blackstone Rangers gang. However, this effort was frustrated when bogus mail sent by FBI agents between Hampton and Fort contained inflammatory statements that each believed to be written by the other party. The two leaders later discovered that neither had written the letters, but the damage was done and any hope for an alliance was crushed. Many BPP members believed that the FBI had intended for the letters to provoke violence between the BPP and the Blackstone Rangers as it had done between the BPP and Maulana Karenga's cultural nationalist US Organization, which led to a 1969 shootout that left two Panthers dead. With its plan to instigate violence between the BPP and Blackstone Rangers foiled, the FBI took matters into its own hands. It sent in an infiltrator, William O'Neill, to become a BPP member. O'Neill eventually provided Chicago police with the floor plan of the local BPP offices. In the early morning hours of December 4, 1969, Chicago police invaded the headquarters, where Hampton and other BPP members slept. They unleashed a fusillade of bullets, killing Hampton and BPP member Mark Clark. The remaining survivors were arrested, charged with conspiracy, and held for $100,000 bail each. Hampton's family spent the next 14 years in a grueling legal battle attempting to prove that the former BPP leader's slaying was a part of a larger conspiracy organized by state and federal law enforcement agencies determined to neutralize dissenters. In 1983, Judge John F. Grady granted the survivors $1.87 million, ruling that the FBI had engaged in a conspiratorial cover-up that obstructed justice and violated the victims' civil rights. Clearly, COINTELPRO served not as a means of law enforcement but as an agent of repression. Even today, former BPP members appear to suffer continued harassment by the federal government. In 2005, the Justice Department declared Assata Shakur a domestic terrorist and issued an unprecedented $1 million bounty for her capture and return to the United States. Shakur, believed by many to have been framed for murder, has been in exile in Cuba since her escape from a maximum-security facility in 1981 (Churchill and Vander Wall 1988, 64–77; Abu-Jamal 2004, 119–122).

## Legacy

The BPP finally disbanded in 1982. Its legacy is perhaps best summed up in a statement by scholar Carol Henderson Belton to the author in September 2003: "If the power struggle in America is a power struggle over memory, then continuing debates about the legacy of the BPP seek to control not only what is remembered but also how it is remembered." The resurgence of interest in the BPP during the mid-1990s is reflected in popular and scholarly publications, a film adaptation, references in commercial rap music, and the emergence of neo-Panther collectives. These remembrances reflect opposing images which both romanticize and vilify the Panthers. While such polarized images are a distortion of fact, they demonstrate that people of diverse backgrounds are grappling with the historic significance, contemporary interpretation, and future relevance of the BPP. African American literary scholar Barbara Smith once asserted that in order for books to be real and remembered they have to be talked about (Smith 1994, 412). If Smith's assertion is correct, then the greatest testament to the BPP legacy is that it continues to be written and talked about, though the physical organization passed into history more than 20 years ago.

## Conclusion

The recent effort to honor Fred Hampton serves as a case in point. While the honorary street sign campaign was unsuccessful, it should not be viewed as a failure because it once again thrust the BPP and its legacy into American consciousness. With additional literary and scholarly works on the Panthers on the horizon, it is certain that the memory of the BPP will remain firm within the American psyche. Indeed, how we remember the Black Panther Party will be debated for years to come as the United States continues to engage in the power struggle over memory. Yet, what should not be debated is our commitment to the principles of democracy, which numerous people throughout American history have given their lives to protect: a government by the people, for the people. Or in the words of the Panthers, "All power to the people!"

## References and Further Reading

Abu-Jamal, Mumia. 2004. *We Want Freedom: A Life in the Black Panther Party*. Cambridge, MA: South End Press.

Ayi, Mema. 2006. "Haithcock Drops Bid For Honorary Hampton Sign." *Chicago Defender*, April 27.

Blackstock, Nelson. 1976. *COINTELPRO: The FBI's Secret War on Political Freedom*. New York: Vintage.

Boyd, Herb. 1995. *The Black Panthers for Beginners*. New York: Writers and Readers Publishing.

Brown, Elaine. 1992. *A Taste of Power: A Black Woman's Story*. New York: Pantheon.

Churchill, Ward, and Jim Vander Wall. 1988. *Agents of Repression: The FBI's Secret War against the Black Panther Party and the American Indian Movement*. Boston: South End Press.

Cleaver, Kathleen, and George Katsiaficas, eds. 2001. *Liberation, Imagination, and the Black Panther Party: A New Look at the Black Panthers and Their Legacy*. New York: Routledge.

Cone, James. 1991. *Martin and Malcolm: A Dream or Nightmare*. Maryknoll, NY: Orbis.

Fanon, Frantz. 1963. *The Wretched of the Earth*. New York: Grove Press.

Foner, Philip, ed. 1995 [1970]. *The Black Panthers Speak*. New York: Da Capo Press.

Freed, Donald. 1973. *Agony in New Haven: The Trial of Bobby Seale, Ericka Huggins & the Black Panther Party*. New York: Simon and Schuster.

Giddings, Paula. 1984. *When and Where I Enter: The Impact of Black Women on Race and Sex in America*. New York: William Morrow.

Hayes, Floyd W., III, and Francis A. Kiene III. 1998. "'All Power to the People': The Political Thought of Huey P. Newton and the Black Panther Party." In *The Black Panther Party [Reconsidered]*, edited by Charles E. Jones. Baltimore: Black Classic Press.

Heath, G. Louis. 1976. *The Black Panther Leaders Speak: Huey P. Newton, Bobby Seale, Eldridge Cleaver, and Company Speak Out through the Black Panther Party's Official Newsletter*. Metuchen, NJ: Scarecrow Press.

Hilliard, David, with Keith Zimmerman and Kent Zimmerman. 2006. *Huey: Spirit of the Panther*. New York: Thunder's Mouth Press.

Jeffries, Judson L. 2002. *Huey P. Newton: The Radical Theorist*. Jackson: University Press of Mississippi.

Jennings, Regina. 1998. "Why I Joined the Party: An Africana Womanist Perspective." In *The Black Panther Party [Reconsidered]*, edited by Charles E. Jones. Baltimore: Black Classic Press.

Jones, Charles E., ed. 1998. *The Black Panther Party [Reconsidered]*. Baltimore: Black Classic Press.

Matthews, Tracye. 1998. "'No One Ever Asks, What a Man's Place in the Revolution Is': Gender and the Politics of the Black Panther Party, 1966–1971." In *The Black Panther Party [Reconsidered]*, edited by Charles E. Jones. Baltimore: Black Classic Press.

Newton, Huey P. 1973. *Revolutionary Suicide*. New York: Harcourt Brace Jovanovich.

Olsen, Jack. 2000. *Last Man Standing: The Tragedy and Triumph of Geronimo Pratt*. New York: Doubleday.

Patterson, Demetrius. 2006. "Blacks, Police at Odds over Naming Street after Black Panther Leader Slain by Chicago Police." *Chicago Defender*, March 1.

Seale, Bobby. 1991. *Seize the Time: The Story of the Black Panther Party and Huey P. Newton*. Baltimore: Black Classic Press.

Self, Robert. 2003. *American Babylon: Race and the Struggle for Post War Oakland*. Princeton, NJ: Princeton University Press.

Shakur, Assata. 1987. *Assata: An Autobiography*. Chicago: Zed.

Smith, Barbara. 1994. "Towards a Black Feminist Criticism." In *Within the Circle: An Anthology of African American Literary Criticism from the Harlem Renaissance to the Present*, edited by Angelyn Mitchell. Durham, NC: Duke University Press.

Smith, Jennifer B. 1999. *An International History of the Black Panther Party*. New York: Garland.

X, Malcolm. 1997. "The Ballot or the Bullet." In *The Norton Anthology of African American Literature*, edited by Henry Louis Gates Jr. and Nellie McKay. New York: Norton.

# Women | 8

### Jennifer A. Lemak

On December 1, 1955, Rosa Parks left the Montgomery, Alabama, department store where she worked as a seamstress, boarded the crowded Cleveland Avenue bus, and took a seat one row behind its whites-only section. As the bus continued on its route, a group of whites boarded, and all but one found seats. Driver J. P. Blake saw the white man standing and called for the four black passengers in Parks's row to move to the back. When they did not move, he got up and repeated his command. At this warning, three stood up and moved to the back of the bus. Parks sat alone. When the driver again asked Parks if she would move, she said she would not. When threatened with arrest, Parks remained unbowed, and within minutes patrolmen escorted her off the bus to the police station, where she was booked for breaking Alabama's segregation laws.

This event sparked the 381-day Montgomery bus boycott, which tested and led to the upholding of a U.S. Supreme Court decision banning segregation on public transportation. More importantly, the event energized a nationwide civil rights struggle to end segregation. The history of the boycott illustrates in microcosm the role that women played in the black freedom struggle. It was the women in Montgomery who made the bus boycott possible.

There is a long-standing tradition of African American women working for racial equality, dating back to antislavery societies and the women's club movement. Within the civil rights movement of the 1950s and 1960s, women exerted enormous influence, holding key positions in national organizations like the Student Nonviolent Coordinating Committee (SNCC), the Southern Christian Leadership Conference (SCLC), the Mississippi Freedom Democratic Party (MFDP), the National Association for the Advancement of Colored People (NAACP), and the Congress of Racial Equality (CORE). Although male leaders like Martin Luther King Jr. and Malcolm X may have received the most press coverage, an increasing amount of recent historical evidence has identified the critical role that their female counterparts played. Women like

## Rosa Parks

Rosa Parks was an activist whose refusal to give up her seat on a segregated bus jumpstarted the civil rights movement. Parks was a long-time organizer who contributed to civil rights causes for decades, and she should not be defined by the singular act for which she is most famous.

Born Rosa McCauley, she married Raymond Parks, a barber in Montgomery, Alabama, in 1932. Her husband was a member of the National Association for the Advancement of Colored People (NAACP) and inspired her to get involved with the organization's local youth chapter, where she became an adviser. She formally joined the organization in 1943, was secretary of the Montgomery branch, and worked with NAACP state president E. D. Nixon to mobilize a voter registration drive in the city.

In 1955, six months before the incident on the bus, Parks attended a workshop on school integration for community leaders at the Highlander Folk School, a Tennessee-based institute that trained civil rights organizers. Inspired by the workshop and determined to resist segregation in her hometown, Parks was arrested in December when she refused to give up her seat to a white man on a segregated public bus.

The Montgomery NAACP used her arrest as a test case to challenge segregation in the courts, while Montgomery's black community quickly mobilized into an organization called the Montgomery Improvement Association (MIA), which, along with the local Women's Political Council, led a boycott of Montgomery's public buses. The boycott lasted more than a year, and Montgomery's white officials eventually yielded. The victory reminded blacks nationwide that protests against civil rights violations could work and helped to jumpstart what would become known as the civil rights movement.

Parks and her husband, beset by tough economic times in Montgomery, relocated to Detroit in 1957. In 1965, Parks became an administrative assistant for Rep. John Conyers. She never stopped her work as an activist. During the 1980s she was a part of the South African antiapartheid movement, and in 1987 she cofounded the Rosa and Raymond Parks Institute for Self-Development, a Detroit youth center. Rosa Parks died in 2005.

Ella Baker, Septima Clark, Fannie Lou Hamer, Anne Moody, and Daisy Bates were fundamental to the organization of crucial civil rights programs. Others like Gloria Richardson, head of the Cambridge Nonviolent Action Committee (CNAC), led major campaigns. Countless more served the movement informally by putting together voter registration drives, participating in demonstrations, and forming the core of grassroots action. Although they had major responsibilities, until recently women's accomplishments have been absent from historical analysis and were ignored by the contemporary press. Yet through their dedication, organizational skills, teaching, and leadership, it was women who served as the backbone of the civil rights movement.

## Rosa Parks

Rosa Parks's civil disobedience on the bus was not entirely spontaneous and took place within a climate of resistance that had been fueled by the careful

Rosa Parks, whose refusal to give up her bus seat to a white passenger sparked the Montgomery Bus Boycott and fueled the civil rights movement. (*Library of Congress*)

planning of a local organization called the Women's Political Council (WPC). The WPC was formed in 1946 when Mary Fair Burks, a professor at Alabama State College, was arrested and jailed following a traffic dispute with a white motorist. Infuriated by the incident, Burks formed the WPC as a means of protesting the mistreatment of Montgomery's black citizens. WPC members predominantly came from the middle class. Early WPC campaigns tackled voter registration and political protest, but by 1950, under the leadership of Jo Ann Robinson, also a professor at Alabama State College, the WPC had turned its focus toward the mistreatment of blacks on city buses.

Working with leading local black activists E. D. Nixon and Rufus Lewis, the WPC kept the pressure on, meeting several times with the city commission about the situation on public transportation. However, they lacked the power to sway elected officials. After five years of trying to effect change, the WPC began to get impatient. Although its members did not know how black Montgomery and the local government would react to their plan to boycott city buses, by 1955 they felt that it was time for it to happen, and Rosa Parks's refusal to be reseated gave their campaign the spark it needed to get going.

The evening Parks was arrested, the WPC agreed to launch its bus boycott, to begin four days later on Monday, December 5, 1955. Jo Ann Robinson wrote a leaflet that served as the boycott's manifesto. In part, it read:

> Another Negro woman has been arrested and thrown into jail because she refused to get up out of her seat on the bus for a white person to sit down. . . . If we do not do something to stop arrests, they will continue. The next time it may be you, or your daughter or mother. This woman's case will come up on Monday. We are, therefore, asking every Negro to stay off the buses on Monday in protest of the arrest and the trial. Don't ride the buses to work, to town, to school, or anywhere on Monday. (Olson 2001, 112)

Robinson mimeographed 35,000 copies of the flyer. WPC members worked feverishly to ready them for distribution to Montgomery's black citizens. When the job was done, they hit the streets, blanketing the city with the document in an attempt to spread word of the boycott.

Montgomery's black activists and church leaders, including Ralph Abernathy and Martin Luther King Jr., were hesitant to back the WPC-led boycott, but figuring that black locals were going to support it regardless of their endorsement, they got on board. On December 5, Montgomery's city buses were empty. The streets were filled with women, mostly maids and cooks, walking to work. Although women clearly were responsible for the boycott, a mass meeting that evening illustrated the lack of regard many people had for their leadership. At the gathering, local ministers and race leaders addressed the huge crowd. But when Rosa Parks asked to speak, she was turned away, despite receiving a standing ovation. It was during this meeting that these ministers and civil rights leaders realized that the city's black community was galvanized by the boycott. On the strength of the support mobilized by Parks and the WPC, the Montgomery bus boycott would last 13 months, cost the city of Montgomery tens of thousands of dollars in lost revenue, and ultimately force the desegregation of its public transportation facilities.

The Montgomery bus boycott was one of the first major victories in the civil rights movement. It motivated large numbers of people to support the black freedom struggle through nonviolent civil disobedience and protest. Women deserve much of the credit for the success of the boycott, and therefore for the success of the civil rights movement. The WPC planned and organized the beginning stages of the boycott, publicized it, supplied its catalyst—Rosa Parks—and supported it over its 13-month duration.

The bus boycott also sparked the formation of SCLC, which sustained and expanded the activism that occurred in Montgomery. SCLC unified and linked local activists and organizations throughout the South. Despite their accomplishments, Parks and Robinson, as well as other women who made the boycott happen, were denied leadership positions in SCLC. But even as they were relegated to the background of movement struggles, women continued to play vital roles (Ransby 2003, 172–177).

## Ella Baker

One of the most important activist leaders of the civil rights movement was Ella Baker. Born in Virginia, Baker grew up on the farm that her grandparents had worked as slaves. After graduating as class valedictorian from Shaw University in 1922, Baker moved to New York City, where she became active in various labor organizations, racial uplift projects, and women's clubs. In 1931 she became the first national director of the Young Negroes Cooperative League. Baker joined the staff of the NAACP around 1940 and soon became an assistant field secretary. The job involved traveling throughout the South to organize local branches, increase membership, register voters, and solicit donations. Baker, being able to identify with rural southern blacks, expanded the NAACP throughout the South and created a network that served as an important basis for the movement during the 1950s and 1960s. As a result of her effectiveness, the NAACP named Baker its national director of branches, a position she held from 1943 to 1946. Baker advocated for an NAACP shift away from legalism toward community-based activism. An outspoken critic of her organization, she believed that the NAACP should focus less on membership size and more on creating opportunities for involvement by low-income members.

In 1946, Baker resigned her director position but continued to work closely with the New York chapter of the NAACP, eventually becoming the branch head. As her first initiative she relocated the office to Harlem, where it would have a stronger presence within the black community. Baker also led the struggle to desegregate city public schools and improve their quality.

By the middle of the 1950s, as the civil rights movement gained momentum in the South, Baker pointed her efforts toward that region. Alongside organizers Bayard Rustin and Stanley Levinson, Baker cofounded the group In Friendship, which raised money for the southern civil rights movement. In 1957, she moved to Atlanta to help create SCLC. SCLC believed that direct action, rather than the legalism endorsed by the NAACP, was the most viable strategy for achieving civil rights. Martin Luther King Jr. was president. Baker served as the interim executive director. Although she oversaw 65 local chapters, as well as the organization's voter registration and citizenship training drives, Baker was never considered for the permanent executive director position. She was well aware that the ministers who ran SCLC were reluctant to allow women into the organization as equals. Baker also clashed with King over the organization's structure. While King felt that SCLC should have a strong central leadership, Baker believed that it should be community run and include the rural poor, women, and students in its executive branch. Ultimately, she left the organization because of these ideological differences with King (Ransby 2003, 183–189).

As Baker observed the series of student-led sit-ins in cities throughout the South during 1960, she realized the important role that young people could play in the civil rights movement. Sit-ins had garnered national media attention and effectively desegregated public accommodations in a number of Jim Crow cities. Baker and other SCLC leaders invited a group of student activists to Shaw University to discuss how best to harness the recent wave of student-led civil rights activity. Several hundred young people attended, and they formed SNCC. Baker strongly advised the students to remain independent of SCLC and NAACP. SNCC members did so, remaining decentralized; prioritizing direct action; and encouraging youth, women, and the rural poor to assume leadership roles. It was exactly the kind of organization that Baker had been trying to create for years. In 1964, Baker helped SNCC establish the MFDP, a black-led political party that represented those who were excluded from participating in Mississippi state politics and challenged the seating of Mississippi's all-white delegation at the 1964 Democratic National Convention (DNC).

Baker returned to New York and continued working as a civil rights activist until her death in 1986. She inspired a wide range of organizations and leaders and was a constant source of support and guidance to people in the black freedom struggle. Baker's philosophy was that locals should lead grassroots campaigns from the bottom up, regardless of their age, sex, education level, or income. Her biggest contribution to the movement was her commitment to the idea that social change could occur through organizing people to act on their own behalf.

## Septima Clark

Septima Clark's strong commitment to education as a vehicle for activism and change helped sustain the movement. A Charleston, South Carolina, native, Clark decided to become a teacher because it was one of the few professions available to black women in the first half of the 20th century. Upset by the inequalities in pay between white and black teachers regardless of credentials, Clark became a longtime advocate for the equalization of teacher salaries. She attended her first NAACP meeting in 1918 and was so inspired by it that she began going door to door asking people to sign petitions for the organization.

Clark moved to Columbia, South Carolina, in 1935 and turned her focus to teaching citizens the skills they needed to become active and informed. Clark believed that citizenship education led to social reform, and throughout the 1940s and early 1950s she started attending desegregation workshops and supporting civil rights efforts. Clark was fired from her teaching job in 1956, despite 40 years of service, when she refused to resign from the NAACP after the South Carolina legislature passed a law banning city and state employees from being affiliated with civil rights organizations.

As a result of the firing, Clark became a full-time social activist and the director of education at the Highlander Folk School. The Highlander Folk School, founded in 1932, was a citizenship education center for adults that focused on the concept that social change is achieved through education. Clark specialized in teaching reading to illiterate black adults and wanted to transform her students into potential voters with knowledge of their rights and the skill to pass that knowledge to others in their own communities.

Civil rights leaders Rosa Parks, Martin Luther King Jr., John Lewis, and James Bevel were all associated with the school.

After her recruitment by King, Clark became SCLC's director of research and teaching in 1961. She traveled throughout the South conducting workshops for rural blacks. Her literacy and citizenship training classes served as the basis for the movement's voter registration efforts across the South. By the time Clark retired from SCLC in 1970, she had trained thousands of blacks how to read, write, and demand their citizenship rights. Her life turned full circle five years later when the Charleston school board elected her as a member. In doing so, they honored someone who believed that teaching and helping others to attain a better status in life would best serve humanity.

## Daisy Bates

Arkansas NAACP president Daisy Bates led the most publicized school integration fight in U.S. history. Alongside her husband, Bates published a newspaper called the *State Press*, in which she shed light on the issues facing Little Rock's black community: racism, police brutality, labor strikes, and government discrimination against black veterans. Bates's newspaper was particularly important because it dealt with common topics that white papers would not explore. In 1932, while attending Shorter College in Little Rock, Bates became president of the Arkansas NAACP (Bates 1962, 8–49).

After the 1954 *Brown v. Board of Education* case, in which the U.S. Supreme Court banned segregation in public education, black citizens in Little Rock became upset when, more than a year later, no attempt had been made to integrate local public schools. Parents appealed to Bates, as president of both the Arkansas NAACP and its Little Rock chapter, to do something about it. The organization filed suit against the school district, demanding immediate integration of all grades. The court ruled in favor of the school board, but NAACP attorneys appealed. Although the appeals court upheld the lower court's decision, it also ordered the school board to integrate. Under court order, the school district planned for nine black students to attend Central High School when it opened in September 1957. Bates and others used the summer to prepare the "Little Rock Nine" for what was sure to be a harrowing experience.

As the first day of school approached, Little Rock became a battlefield and Bates, as an NAACP activist whose work with the *State Press* had forced the desegregation issue to the forefront, became a target of white resistance. Shortly before the schools were to open, a rock was thrown through Bates's living room window with an attached note: "STONE THIS TIME. DYNAMITE NEXT!" Despite this intimidation attempt, Bates continued to fight for school integration. Finally, on the first day of school, National Guard members surrounded Central High. Segregationist Gov. Orval Faubus declared the school off-limits to blacks, threatening that "blood will run in the streets, if Negro pupils should attempt to enter Central High School" (Bates 1962, 4, 52). As a

Civil rights leader and journalist Daisy Bates stands with students involved with the 1957 integration of public schools in Little Rock, Arkansas. (*Time & Life Pictures/Getty Images*)

result, the Little Rock Nine stayed home. When the students again tried to attend school, they were not allowed past the Guard by order of the governor. As their adviser, Bates insisted they appeal to the U.S. Attorney's Office. Eventually, their case went to trial and the court ruled again that Central High had to integrate and that Governor Faubus could not interfere with the process.

But once again the Little Rock Nine, amid increased harassment and threats, tried to attend school and were unable to get past the violent mobs. Eventually, President Dwight Eisenhower federalized the Arkansas National Guard, ordering its 10,000 troops plus an additional 1,000 paratroopers from the 101st Airborne Division to protect the students and quell the mobs. Soldiers accompanied the Little Rock Nine to school in army jeeps, and each student was assigned a full-time bodyguard. Despite bomb threats, verbal abuse, and the forced closing of her family's newspaper (unlike the students, Bates received no federal protection), Bates remained one of the Little Rock Nine's closest advisers (Robnett 1997, 80–83).

## Gloria Richardson

Gloria Richardson organized and led a major civil rights campaign in Cambridge, Maryland. The Cambridge Movement was distinct for several reasons. It was one of the first major campaigns to occur outside the Deep South, and it focused on economic advancement rather than civil rights. It was also significant because it received federal attention. The John F.

Kennedy administration intervened far more in the Cambridge Movement than in other contemporary civil rights campaigns. Furthermore, the Cambridge Movement questioned the philosophy and tactics of nonviolence.

Richardson, born into a privileged family, grew up in the small town of Cambridge, where segregation limited opportunities for blacks. Because of her family's status, however, Richardson was able to attend Howard University. Nevertheless, at age 40, despite her education and background, Richardson was unable to find decent employment in her hometown.

Cambridge was characterized by an established pattern of segregation and discrimination. The majority of Cambridge's black citizens were poor, and African Americans suffered an enormous 50 percent unemployment rate. Although blacks in Cambridge had been voting since 1800, unlike in southern cities and towns where they were effectively barred from the polls, their politicians did little for them. In 1962, a group of SNCC activists established CNAC in an effort to support the local black community. Richardson believed that the biggest challenges facing blacks in Cambridge were economic and caused the deficiencies in housing, employment opportunity, education, and health care. Although CNAC's original demands were to end segregation in public accommodations, Richardson pushed for more. She recruited area college students and organized a series of demonstrations and protests. Over the next several months, Cambridge became a war zone. Police arrested hundreds of demonstrators, and whites retaliated violently against protests. Richardson continued the fight, calling for even more action. She also appealed successfully to U.S. attorney general Robert F. Kennedy for intervention by the National Guard to help keep order and protect civil rights workers (Olson 2001, 279–280).

As a result of the violence, government officials approached Richardson with an offer. In return for her promise to call off the demonstrations, they agreed to the complete desegregation of public accommodations and schools, the creation of equal employment opportunities and public housing for blacks, and an end to police brutality. The peace lasted only a week when 12 students were arrested for picketing the board of education and officials pulled out of negotiations. Richardson's demonstrations expanded when state-level segregationists attempted to block the application of a public accommodations law by attaching city desegregation plans to a referendum, thus postponing change indefinitely. Over the next six weeks, violence by both blacks and whites escalated (Crawford, Rouse, and Woods 1990, 130–134).

Robert Kennedy had a meeting with Richardson in July 1963 in an effort to quell the upheaval, calling for a "Treaty of Cambridge" to overhaul city race relations. Richardson knew it would be ineffective, and her instincts were confirmed when the proposal was defeated in a referendum three months later. Richardson did not encourage Cambridge's black citizens to vote for it because she felt that they should not have to enfranchise rights they were already supposed to possess by law. As a result, she was accused of boycotting the polls to remain the predominant civil rights leader in Cambridge by perpetuating violence. The stalemate continued for more than a year, until the passage of the 1964 Civil Rights Act forced Cambridge to desegregate (Levy 2003, 2, 87–89).

## Fannie Lou Hamer

Fannie Lou Hamer was a Mississippi voting rights activist who gained fame with her testimony about the hardships faced by Mississippi blacks before the Credentials Committee at the 1964 Democratic National Convention.

Born Fannie Lou Townsend, she dropped out of school at age 12 to work alongside her sharecropper parents and 19 siblings in the cotton fields of the Mississippi Delta. She faced debilitating poverty as a child, living without heat or plumbing. She had a lifelong limp as a result of suffering a broken leg as an infant that was never treated. She married Perry Hamer in 1942 and worked on the plantation where he drove a tractor. She began as a field hand before becoming the plantation's timekeeper.

Fannie Lou Hamer, a Mississippi field hand for much of her life, became a prominent civil rights activist during the 1960s and 1970s. (*Library of Congress*)

While Richardson's tangible gains may have been limited, she created an overall climate that paved the way for change once the Civil Rights Act passed. She also fought successfully for the release of demonstrators from jail in October 1963 and created a job-training program for 200 unemployed locals. Even Richardson, however, the undeniable leader of the Cambridge Movement, faced sexism from her peers. At one rally, for example, male members of CORE interrupted her speech, shouting her down and calling her a "castrator." Although she was not part of the established civil rights structure and national leaders distanced themselves from her because she condoned violence, Richardson brought attention to unemployment and economic empowerment as civil rights issues.

## Fannie Lou Hamer

Fannie Lou Hamer became a crucial civil rights leader by refusing to compromise her attempts to eliminate Jim Crow laws. Born in Mississippi to sharecroppers, Hamer was the youngest of 20 children. She had a sixth-grade education and also became a sharecropper, eventually getting married

In the summer of 1962, Hamer went to a meeting sponsored by the Student Nonviolent Coordinating Committee (SNCC), which had recently begun a voter registration campaign in the Mississippi Delta. Hamer took the appeal seriously, and although blacks faced economic retaliation and physical violence whenever they tried to register to vote, Hamer volunteered to join a group of locals trying to do so. She was turned away, and when she refused to promise her plantation boss that she would never try to register again, he fired her and threw her out of the home she had lived in for 18 years.

Hamer joined SNCC as a field secretary and became one of its most important speakers and organizers. In 1963, she was jailed and severely beaten by police. After recovering from the assault, which left her permanently damaged, Hamer returned to the Delta to organize a series of voter registration drives. The following year she helped found the Mississippi Freedom Democratic Party (MFDP), which attempted to get the state's segregated Democratic Party to integrate. When the MFDP attended the Democratic National Convention that summer, Hamer was vital to the organization's articulation of its case to national party leaders.

Although the MFDP's 1964 campaign to be seated failed, long-term gains resulted from its efforts. In 1965, Congress passed the Voting Rights Act, which gave federal protection to blacks who tried to register to vote. By 1968, the state Democratic Party was no longer segregated. From 1969 to 1974, Hamer ran Freedom Farm, a cooperative that provided food and jobs to poor blacks. Fannie Lou Hamer died in 1977.

and working the land alongside her husband. For 18 years, they lived in Sunflower County, picking, planting, and preparing cotton fields.

When civil rights workers came to Mississippi in 1962 to run voter registration drives, Hamer was among the first locals to volunteer. When James Forman of SNCC and James Bevel of SCLC asked people to consider registering, Hamer agreed to. She later recalled her willingness: "The only thing they [whites] could do to me was kill me and it seemed like they'd been trying to do that a little bit at a time ever since I could remember" (Mills 1993, 13–14).

In total, 17 blacks turned out to register to vote. They rented a bus and drove to the courthouse. They were frightened about how they would be treated and what the consequences of their actions would be. When they arrived, Hamer announced that they had come to register. They were required to take a difficult literacy test, fill out a long questionnaire, and interpret sections of the Mississippi State Constitution. They also had to tell the county clerk their employment status. Hamer and the others flunked the test and no one registered that day. Hamer informed the registrar that she would return every 30 days until she passed the test, which she finally did in January 1963. When Hamer returned home, her boss told her that if she did not remove her name from the registration list she would lose her job. Hamer refused and was ordered off the plantation, forced to live with friends.

Hamer was vital to SNCC's Mississippi voting-rights efforts because she was familiar with the local people. She began traveling with SNCC, encouraging her fellow sharecroppers to register, organizing food and clothing drives, and teaching literacy. These acts alone were dangerous for anybody in rural Mississippi, but especially for a black woman. While attending a series of training workshops, Hamer and others were jailed when they tried to eat at a lunch counter at a bus station. Officers then directed two inmates to beat Hamer, which left her with permanent kidney injuries and a blood clot in the artery of her left eye (Mills 1993, 58–60; Levy 1998, 180–181).

In spite of everything she had been through, Hamer continued to fight for the principles of the movement by serving as an SNCC field secretary. As a part of SNCC's historic 1964 Freedom Summer campaign, Hamer cofounded the MFDP, which planned to demonstrate at the DNC to dramatize the exclusion of African Americans from the voting process in Mississippi. The MFDP attended the DNC with 68 members ready to be seated as Mississippi's only legal, all-inclusive, and democratically elected delegation. When the Democratic Party offered a compromise of two seats for MFDP members, Hamer responded in a now-famous speech, "We didn't come all this way for no two seats when all of us is tired" (Hamlet 1996, 570–571). With Hamer leading the charge, the MFDP eventually seated an integrated delegation at the 1968 DNC. Fueled by the belief that blacks were not treated properly, Hamer continued to fight for their fundamental rights. Hamer played a significant, though informal, role in the civil rights movement. Her efforts helped sustain the movement by encouraging others to participate in the efforts to fight racism and injustice.

## Anne Moody

Anne Moody's involvement with the civil rights movement began when she was a teenager and was similar to that of hundreds of other student activists across the South. Moody grew up in a small, rural Mississippi town. Her parents were sharecroppers, and Moody supplemented the family's finances by cleaning white people's homes. But it was not until she heard about the 1955 lynching of Emmett Till that she began to realize the difficulties of being black in the South.

A good student and hard worker, Moody earned a college basketball scholarship. While in school, she joined the NAACP and SNCC, becoming a dedicated member especially committed to voter registration drives. Moody was constantly involved with sit-ins, lunch counter demonstrations, and rallies. Jail also became a common occurrence in her life. Fearful of white retaliation, she was always scared for her family's safety.

Following her college graduation, in addition to conducting self-defense workshops for high school and college civil rights workers, Moody participated in a CORE voter registration campaign in the Mississippi town of Canton. Moody organized groups of teenagers so they could canvass the area to help register black voters. Canton's whites retaliated by shooting five CORE workers. As the violence escalated, so did Moody's involvement. Threats and violence continued against the student activists, and, at age 23, Moody found herself on the Ku Klux Klan's blacklist. Fearing for her life, she moved to New Orleans to hide out, but she eventually returned to Canton to continue her civil rights work. Moody had already sacrificed at least a quarter of her life to the movement. Along with hundreds of other female students, she risked everything on a daily basis hoping that blacks would someday be treated like first-class citizens of the United States. Female student activists organized, developed, and sustained the civil rights movement in the South at the local level. Without their help, the mobilization of rural citizens would have been much more difficult.

## The Treatment and Impact of Women in the Movement

The civil rights movement offered opportunities for many female students in both support and leadership roles. SNCC was at the forefront of apportioning leadership responsibilities and positions to females. Women in SNCC organized protests, ran meetings, taught nonviolence workshops, directed voter registration drives, and secured housing for new volunteers. Yet in spite of all of their accomplishments, many felt that they were treated unfairly. Often women in SNCC and other civil rights organizations were expected to cook and clean for male volunteers, manage secretarial duties, and handle behind-the-scenes work while being restrained from more public leadership roles. These feelings and actions culminated during a 1964 SNCC staff meeting when soon-to-be executive secretary Ruby Doris Smith presented her views on the treatment of female civil rights workers in a paper titled, "The Position of Women in SNCC." In response, future SNCC chairman Stokely Carmichael declared, "The only position for women in SNCC is prone." Such attitudes were pervasive throughout the student movement (Evans 1979, 83–95).

Despite relegation to specific gender roles, local women across the United States sustained the civil rights movement in thousands of different ways. In Mississippi, local women sent incarcerated Freedom Riders clothes, toiletries, magazines, and candy. They also supplied Freedom Riders with transportation, food, housing, clean clothes, and beauty services. Many of these Freedom Riders later attributed their endurance to these local women. During the Freedom Summer campaign of 1964, hundreds of nurses from across the United States provided health care to impoverished Mississippi black communities. Local black women also served as important role models for the younger activists, who often lived with black families. These older women knew that white retaliation was possible when housing civil rights volunteers, yet most continued despite the consequences. The civil rights movement gave women of all economic levels the opportunity to participate, usually for the first time, in politics and the public arena. As a result, local women entered the movement in large numbers and participated in all phases of activity. They usually constituted the majority at mass meetings, led marches, conducted voter registration

Civil rights protesters faced the constant threat of arrest or violent attack. This 1963 photograph shows a Birmingham, Alabama, demonstrator in a paddy wagon. (*Bob Adelman/Corbis*)

drives, served time in prison, taught nonviolent methods, and offered support. The efforts of the local women across the United States sustained the movement and contributed to its great successes (Dittmer 1994, 126–127, 264, 331; Theoharis and Woodard 2005, 17–37).

Women's contributions to the black freedom struggle were not limited to the South, as scores of northern women also bolstered the movement. One of the sites where their presence was strongest was in the fight for equal education. In 1958, one group, dubbed the Harlem Nine, decided to keep their children out of school because they were receiving a substandard education in New York's segregated public schools. A judge agreed, ruling that the schools were separate and unequal, marking the first northern decision against de facto segregation in public schools.

Another such example during this period was Ruth Batson's fight to integrate Boston's public school system. Her struggle began when she realized that her daughters and other African American students in Boston attended the oldest, most underfunded schools. In addition, few black teachers and no black principals were employed in the system, which not only left most blacks out of the running for well-paying jobs but also deprived black schoolchildren of role models. To reform the system, Batson worked with the NAACP, becoming the first female president of the New England region. For nearly 20 years, Batson and other activists organized, demonstrated, and attended hearings on desegregation. Their efforts finally paid off in 1974 when a federal judge ruled that city public schools were intentionally segregated. Despite an intense white backlash over court-ordered busing to remedy the problem, Batson stayed focused in her efforts to help the newly integrated students. She developed a program to train local leaders how to ride the buses, deal with white harassment, and work with children after school. Two years later, the judge acknowledged Batson's good work "for helping the Boston Public school system to pass their severest test in history" (Theoharis and Woodard 2005, 37). Northern women, through their school desegregation efforts and political activism, were vital in making the civil rights movement a national one (Theoharis and Woodard 2005, 17–37; Theoharis and Woodard 2003, 65–91).

## Conclusion

Based on these histories, it is obvious that women played an important and significant role in the civil rights movement. Women worked toward movement goals on all levels and achieved success. They formed the backbone of the civil rights movement. However, as they helped push forward equality for African Americans, they found their efforts being overshadowed by nationally recognized male civil rights leaders. The important contributions of women activists during the civil rights era have, until recently, been excluded from the general history of the movement. But a complete history of the movement must include the contributions of both men and women.

## References and Further Reading

Bates, Daisy. 1962. *The Long Shadow of Little Rock*. New York: David McKay.

Branch, Taylor. 1988. *Parting the Waters: America in the King Years, 1954–63*. New York: Touchstone.

Collier-Thomas, Bettye, and V. P. Franklin. 2001. *Sisters in the Struggle: African American Women in the Civil Rights–Black Power Movement*. New York: New York University Press.

Crawford, Vicki L., Jacqueline Anne Rouse, and Barbara Woods, eds. 1990. *Women in the Civil Rights Movement: Trailblazers and Torchbearers, 1941–1965*. New York: Carlson.

Curry, Constance, Joan C. Browning, Dorothy Dawson Burlage, Penny Patch, Theresa Del Pozzo, Sue Thrasher, Elaine DeLott Baker, Emmie Schrader Adams, and Casey Hayden. 2000. *Deep in Our Hearts: Nine White Women in the Freedom Movement*. Athens: University of Georgia Press.

Davis, Jack E., ed. 2001. *The Civil Rights Movement*. Malden, MA: Blackwell.

Dittmer, John. 1994. *Local People: The Struggle for Civil Rights in Mississippi*. Urbana: University of Illinois Press.

Evans, Sara. 1979. *Personal Politics: The Roots of Women's Liberation in the Civil Rights Movement and the New Left*. New York: Alfred A. Knopf.

Hamlet, Janice D. 1996. "Fannie Lou Hamer: The Unquenchable Spirit of the Civil Rights Movement." *Journal of Black Studies* 26:560–576.

Levy, Peter B. 1998. *The Civil Rights Movement*. Westport, CT: Greenwood Press.

Levy, Peter B. 2003. *Civil War on Race Street: The Civil Rights Movement in Cambridge, Maryland*. Gainesville: University Press of Florida.

Mills, Kay. 1993. *This Little Light of Mine: The Life of Fannie Lou Hamer*. New York: Dutton.

Moody, Anne. 1968. *Coming of Age in Mississippi*. New York: Laurel.

Nance, Teresa A. 1996. "Hearing the Missing Voice." *Journal of Black Studies* 26:543–559.

Olson, Lynne. 2001. *Freedom's Daughters: The Unsung Heroines of the Civil Rights Movement from 1830 to 1970*. New York: Scribner.

Ransby, Barbara. 2003. *Ella Baker and the Black Freedom Movement*. Chapel Hill: University of North Carolina Press.

Robnett, Belinda. 1997. *How Long? How Long? African American Women in the Struggle for Civil Rights*. New York: Oxford University Press.

Schultz, Debra L. 2001. *Going South: Jewish Women in the Civil Rights Movement*. New York: New York University Press.

Theoharis, Jeanne, and Komozi Woodard, eds. 2003. *Freedom North: Black Freedom Struggles outside the South, 1940–1980*. New York: Palgrave Macmillan.

Theoharis, Jeanne, and Komozi Woodard, eds. 2005. *Groundwork: Local Black Freedom Movements in America*. New York: New York University Press.

Williams, Juan. 1997. *Eyes on the Prize: America's Civil Rights Years, 1954–1965*. New York: Viking.

# *Primary Documents*

## *McLaurin v. Oklahoma State Regents for Higher Education et al.*

Argued: April 3–4, 1950
Decided: June 5, 1950

In 1948, George McLaurin won a case allowing him to enroll as a doctoral student at the University of Oklahoma. However, the university would only let him do so under segregated conditions. A desk was set up for him in the library apart from the regular reading room. Not allowed to sit with his peers during class, he was forced to listen to lectures and take notes from an anteroom adjacent to the regular classroom. The cafeteria was also off-limits to McLaurin while white students were eating; he was forced to take his meals at special times. McLaurin sued because such conditions violated the principle of separate but equal by imposing unfair handicaps on his pursuit of education that white students did not have to deal with. In 1950, the U.S. Supreme Court ruled unanimously that the University of Oklahoma had violated the Fourteenth Amendment and McLaurin's right to equal educational opportunity. The case became an important building block in the National Association for the Advancement of Colored People's (NAACP) battle to desegregate public education. In this excerpt, Supreme Court Chief Justice Fred Vinson delivers the Court's unanimous opinion that legitimated McLaurin's claim.

Appellant is a Negro citizen of Oklahoma. Possessing a Master's Degree, he applied for admission to the University of Oklahoma in order to pursue studies and courses leading to a Doctorate in Education. At that time, his application was denied, solely because of his race. The school authorities were required to exclude him by the Oklahoma statutes . . . which made it a misdemeanor to maintain or operate, teach or attend a school at which both whites and Negroes are enrolled or taught. Appellant filed a complaint requesting injunctive relief . . . a statutory three-judge District Court held that the State had a Constitutional duty to provide him with the education he sought as soon as it provided that education for applicants of any other group. It further held that to the extent the Oklahoma statutes denied him admission they were unconstitutional and void. . . .

Following this decision, the Oklahoma legislature amended these statutes to permit the admission of Negroes to institutions of higher learning attended by white students, in cases where such institutions offered courses not available in the Negro schools. . . . [McLaurin] was thereupon admitted to the University of Oklahoma Graduate School. In apparent conformity with the amendment, his admission was made subject to "such rules and regulations as to segregation as the President of the University shall consider to afford to Mr. G. W. McLaurin substantially equal educational opportunities as are afforded to other persons seeking the same education in the Graduate College," a condition which does not appear to have been withdrawn. Thus he was required to sit apart at a designated desk in an anteroom adjoining the classroom; to sit at a designated desk on the mezzanine floor of the library, but not to use the desks in the regular reading room; and to sit at a designated table and to eat at a different time from the other students in the school cafeteria.

. . .

These restrictions were obviously imposed in order to comply, as nearly as could be, with the statutory requirements of Oklahoma. But they signify that the State, in administering the facilities it affords for professional and graduate study, sets McLaurin apart from the other students. The result is that appellant is handicapped in his pursuit of effective graduate instruction. Such restrictions impair and inhibit his ability to study, to engage in discussions and exchange views with other students, and, in general, to learn his profession.

Our society grows increasingly complex, and our need for trained leaders increases correspondingly. Appellant's case represents, perhaps, the epitome of that need, for he is attempting to obtain an advanced degree in education, to become, by definition, a leader and trainer of others. Those who will come under his guidance and influence must be directly affected by the education he receives. Their own education and development will necessarily suffer to the extent that his training is unequal to that of his classmates. State-imposed restrictions which produce such inequalities cannot be sustained.

. . .

We conclude that the conditions under which this appellant is required to receive his education deprive him of his personal and present right to the equal protection of the laws. See *Sweatt v. Painter*, ante, p. 629. We hold that under these circumstances the Fourteenth Amendment precludes differences in treatment by the state based upon race. Appellant, having been admitted to a state-supported graduate school, must receive the same treatment at the hands of the state as students of other races.

*Source:* McLaurin v. Oklahoma State Regents, *339 U.S. 637 (1950).*

# Sweatt v. Painter et al.

Argued: April 4, 1950

Decided: June 5, 1950

Heman Sweatt was a postal worker who was denied admission to the University of Texas Law School on the grounds of race. He refused the state's offer of attending a separate and newly established law school for blacks because the already exist-ing whites-only school was richer in resources. Whereas the University of Texas Law School had 16 full-time professors, the school for blacks would have only 5. Further, whereas the University of Texas Law School had a library of 65,000 vol-umes, the school for blacks would have 16,500. Sweatt maintained in his case that the separate law school would provide him with an inferior education to what he would receive at the University of Texas. In 1950, the Supreme Court ruled that the State of Texas had violated Sweatt's right to equal educational opportunity. The case became a key component of the NAACP's campaign to desegregate public education. In this excerpt, Supreme Court Chief Justice Fred Vinson delivers the Court's opinion that legitimated Sweatt's claim.

This case and *McLaurin v. Oklahoma State Regents*, post, p. 637, present differ-ent aspects of this general question: To what extent does the Equal Protec-tion Clause of the Fourteenth Amendment limit the power of a state to distinguish between students of different races in professional and graduate education in a state university?

. . .

The state trial court recognized that the action of the State in denying petitioner the opportunity to gain . . . a legal education while granting it to others deprived him of the equal protection of the laws guaranteed by the Fourteenth Amendment. The court did not grant the relief requested, how-ever, but continued the case for six months to allow the State to supply sub-stantially equal facilities. At the expiration of the six months, in December, 1946, the court denied the writ on the showing that the authorized univer-sity officials had adopted an order calling for the opening of a law school for Negroes the following February. While petitioner's appeal was pending, such a school was made available, but petitioner refused to register therein.

. . .

The University of Texas Law School, from which petitioner was excluded, was staffed by a faculty of sixteen full-time and three part-time professors, some of whom are nationally recognized authorities in their field. Its student body numbered 850. The library contained over 65,000 vol-umes. Among the other facilities available to the students were a law review, moot court facilities . . . scholarship funds, and Order of the Coif affiliation. The school's alumni occupy the most distinguished positions in the private practice of the law and in the public life of the State. It may properly be con-sidered one of the nation's ranking law schools.

The law school for Negroes, which was to have opened in February 1947, would have had no independent faculty or library. The teaching was to be carried on by four members of the University of Texas Law School fac-ulty, who were to maintain their offices at the University of Texas while teaching at both institutions. Few of the 10,000 volumes ordered for the library had arrived; nor was there any full-time librarian. The school lacked accreditation.

Since the trial of this case, respondents report the opening of a law school at the Texas State University for Negroes. It is apparently on the road to full accreditation. It has a faculty of five full-time professors; a student body of 23; a library of some 16,500 volumes serviced by a full-time staff; a practice court and legal aid association; and one alumnus who has become a member of the Texas Bar.

Whether the University of Texas Law School is compared with the original or the new law school for Negroes, we cannot find substantial equality in the educational opportunities offered white and Negro law students by the State. In terms of number of the faculty, variety of courses and opportunity for specialization, size of the student body, scope of the library, availability of law review and similar activities, the University of Texas Law School is superior. What is more important, the University of Texas Law School possesses to a far greater degree those qualities which are incapable of objective measurement but which make for greatness in a law school. Such qualities, to name but a few, include reputation of the faculty, experience of the administration, position and influence of the alumni, standing in the community, traditions and prestige. It is difficult to believe that one who had a free choice between these law schools would consider the question close.

. . . [P]etitioner may claim his full constitutional right: legal education equivalent to that offered by the State to students of other races. Such education is not available to him in a separate law school as offered by the State. . . .

We hold that the Equal Protection Clause of the Fourteenth Amendment requires that petitioner be admitted to the University of Texas Law School. The judgment is reversed and the cause is remanded for proceedings not inconsistent with this opinion.

*Source:* Sweatt v. Painter, *339 U.S. 629 (1950).*

## Brown v. Board of Education of Topeka

Argued: December 9, 1952
Reargued: December 8, 1953
Decided: May 17, 1954

The *Brown* case was the culmination of the NAACP's long fight against segregated public accommodations and educational institutions. It was an umbrella case that aggregated five separate NAACP-led cases against segregated schools. In addition to Oliver Brown's suit against the Board of Education of Topeka, Kansas, it included *Briggs v. Elliott*, a suit brought by 20 residents of Clarendon County, South Carolina; *Bolling v. Sharpe*, which challenged segregated schools in Washington, D.C.; *Davis v. Prince Edward County School Board*, in Prince Edward County, Virginia; and *Belton v. Gebhart*, a Delaware case. All of the cases argued that segregated schools disadvantaged African Americans educationally. In the *Brown* case, Oliver Brown argued that his daughter had to travel a mile to attend the nearest segregated school, despite living seven blocks from an all-white school. *Briggs* focused on the overall inequalities between the county's white schools, which were clean, safe, and well equipped, and the county's black schools, which were inadequate and unhealthy. *Bolling* came about in response to the building of a new, all-white junior high school that refused to admit black students who tried to enroll in it as a way out of their overcrowded and outdated school. *Davis* addressed the lack of secondary school options available to black students in a Virginia county. *Bolton*, like *Brown*, addressed the logistic hardships that segregation forced upon black students who lived far from the high schools they were eligible to attend. In total, the cases made clear that educational segregation was a nationwide problem that severely compromised the chances for black equality. The successful litigation of *Brown v. Board of Education of Topeka* jumpstarted the civil rights movement by demolishing the legal basis upon which segregation was based. In this excerpt, Supreme Court Chief Justice Earl Warren delivers the majority opinion in favor of the plaintiffs.

Chief Justice Warren delivered the opinion of the Court.

These cases come to us from the States of Kansas, South Carolina, Virginia, and Delaware. In each of the cases, minors of the Negro race seek the aid of the courts in obtaining admission to the public schools of their community on a nonsegregated basis. In each instance, they had been denied admission to schools attended by white children under laws requiring or permitting segregation according to race. This segregation was alleged to deprive the plaintiffs of the equal protection of the laws under the Fourteenth Amendment. . . . The plaintiffs contend that segregated public schools are not "equal" and cannot be made "equal," and that hence they are deprived of the equal protection of the laws. . . .

. . .

. . . Here, unlike *Sweatt v. Painter*, there are findings below that the Negro and white schools involved have been equalized or are being equalized, with respect to buildings, curricula, qualifications and salaries of teachers, and other "tangible" factors. Our decision, therefore, cannot turn on merely a comparison of these tangible factors in the Negro and white schools involved in each of the cases. We must look instead to the effect of segregation itself on public education.

In approaching this problem, we cannot turn the clock back to 1868 when the Amendment was adopted, or even to 1896 when Plessy was written. We must consider public education in the light of its full development and its present place in American life throughout the Nation. Only in this way can it be determined if segregation in public schools deprives these plaintiffs of the equal protection of the laws.

Today, education is perhaps the most important function of state and local governments. Compulsory school attendance laws and the great expenditures for education both demonstrate our recognition of the importance of education to our democratic society. It is required in the performance of our most basic public responsibilities, even service in the armed forces. It is the very foundation of good citizenship. Today it is a principle instrument in awakening the child to cultural values, in preparing him for later professional training, and in helping him to adjust normally to his environment. In these days, it is doubtful that any child may reasonably be expected to succeed in life if he is denied the opportunity of an education. Such an opportunity, where the state has undertaken to provide it, is a right which must be made available to all on equal terms.

We come then to the question presented: Does segregation of children in public schools solely on the basis of race, even though the physical facilities and other "tangible" factors may be equal, deprive the children of the minority group of equal educational opportunities? We believe that it does. In *Sweatt* . . . in finding that a segregated law school for Negroes could not provide them equal educational opportunities, this Court relied in large part on "those qualities which are incapable of objective measurement but which make for greatness in a law school." In *McLaurin*, the Court, in requiring that a Negro admitted to a white graduate school be treated like all other students, again resorted to intangible considerations: "[his] ability to study, to engage in discussions and exchange views with other students, and, in general, to learn his profession." Such considerations apply with added force to children in grade and high schools. To separate them from others of similar age and qualifications solely because of their race generates a feeling of inferiority as to their status in the community that may affect their heart and minds in a way unlikely ever to be undone. The effect of this separation on their educational opportunities was well stated by a finding in the Kansas case by a court which nevertheless felt compelled to rule against the Negro plaintiffs: "Segregation of white and colored children in public schools has a detrimental effect upon the colored children. The impact is greater when it has the sanction of the law; for the policy of separating the races is usually interpreted as denoting the inferiority of the negro group. A sense of inferiority affects the motivation of a child to learn. Segregation with the sanction of law, therefore, has a tendency to [retard] the educational and mental development of Negro children and to deprive them of some of the benefits they would receive in a [racially] integrated school system." Whatever may have been the extent of psychological knowledge at the time of *Plessy v. Ferguson*, this finding is amply supported by modern authority. Any language in *Plessy v. Ferguson* contrary to this finding is rejected.

We conclude that in the field of public education the doctrine of "separate but equal" has no place. Separate educational facilities are inherently unequal. Therefore, we hold that the plaintiffs and others similarly situated for whom the actions have been brought are by reason of the segregation complained of, deprived of the equal protection of the laws guaranteed by the Fourteenth Amendment. This disposition makes unnecessary any discussion whether such segregation also violates the Due Process Clause of the Fourteenth Amendment.

Because these are class actions, because of the wide applicability of this decision, and because of the great variety of local conditions, the formulation of decrees in these cases presents problems of considerable complexity. On reargument, the consideration of appropriate relief was necessarily subordinated to the primary question—the constitutionality of segregation in public education. We have now announced that such segregation is a denial of the equal protection of the laws. In order that we may have the full assistance of the parties in formulating decrees, the cases will be restored to the docket, and the parties are requested to present further argument. . . .

It is so ordered.

*Source:* Brown v. Board of Education, *347 U.S. 483 (1954).*

## Founding Statement of the Student Nonviolent Coordinating Committee (1960)

In 1960, the Student Nonviolent Coordinating Committee (SNCC) was founded by college students who had been participating in sit-ins throughout the United States during the early part of the year. SNCC was dedicated to nonviolent, integrated, direct-action protest as a means of gaining equality for African Americans. The organization was among the civil rights movement's most pivotal groups between 1960 and 1967 before it was weakened by internal dissent. Among its leaders were John Lewis, Stokely Carmichael, H. Rap Brown, and Bob Moses. In its founding statement, SNCC emphasizes the key principles upon which it operated for the first six years of its existence, including interracial cooperation and a religious orientation.

We affirm the philosophical or religious ideal of nonviolence as the foundation of our purpose, the presupposition of our belief, and the manner of our action. Nonviolence, as it grows from the Judeo-Christian tradition, seeks a social order of justice permeated by love. Integration of human endeavor represents the crucial first step towards such a society.

Through nonviolence, courage displaces fear. Love transcends hate. Acceptance dissipates prejudice; hope ends despair. Faith reconciles doubt. Peace dominates war.

Mutual regards cancel enmity. Justice for all overthrows injustice. The redemptive community supersedes immoral social systems.

By appealing to conscience and standing on the moral nature of human existence, nonviolence nurtures the atmosphere in which reconciliation and justice become actual possibilities.

Although each local group in this movement must diligently work out the clear meaning of this statement of purpose, each act or phase of our corporate effort must reflect a genuine spirit of love and good-will.

*Source: The Sixties Project. http://www3.iath.virginia.edu/sixties/HTML_docs/Resources/Primary/Manifestos/SNCC_founding.html.*

## *"God's Judgment of White America"*

Speaker: Malcolm X
Date: December 4, 1963

This speech was delivered by Malcolm X following the assassination of President John F. Kennedy two weeks earlier. In his address, Malcolm X tried to explain that Kennedy's reputation as an ally to blacks was undeserved. Such comments angered people who were still mourning the loss of Kennedy. They also infuriated Nation of Islam leader Elijah Muhammad, who had instructed his ministers not to talk to the press about Kennedy. As a result of the speech and other comments Malcolm had made, Muhammad suspended him from the Nation of Islam and from speaking to the press for 90 days. Although Malcolm agreed to the sanction, it marked the disintegration of his relationship with Elijah Muhammad and his subsequent decision to leave the Nation of Islam. Once his 90-day suspension expired, rather than return to the Nation of Islam, Malcolm formed his own organization, Muslim Mosque, Inc.

. . .

So we of this present generation are also witnessing how the enslavement of millions of black people in this country is now bringing White America to her hour of judgment, to her downfall as a respected nation. And even those Americans who are blinded by childlike patriotism can see that it is only a matter of time before White America too will be utterly destroyed by her own sins, and all traces of her former glory will be removed from this planet forever.

The Honorable Elijah Muhammad teaches us that as it was divine will in the case of the destruction of the slave empires of the ancient and modern past, America's judgment and destruction will also be brought about by divine will and divine power. Just as ancient nations paid for their sins against humanity, White America must now pay for her sins against twenty-two million "Negroes." White America's worst crime is her hypocrisy and her deceit. White America pretends to ask herself: "What do these Negroes want?" White America knows that four hundred years of cruel bondage has made these twenty-two million ex-slaves too (mentally) blind to see what they really want.

White America should be asking herself: "What does God want for these twenty-two million ex-slaves?" Who will make White America know what God wants? Who will present God's plan to White America?

What is God's solution to the problem caused by the presence of twenty-two million unwanted slaves here in America? And who will present God's solution?

We, the Muslims who follow the Honorable Elijah Muhammad, believe whole-heartedly in the God of justice. We believe in the Creator, whose divine power and laws of justice created and sustain the universe.

. . .

Why is the American white man so set against the twenty-two million "Negroes" learning about the religion of Islam? Islam is the religion that elevates the morals of the people who want to do right. Just by teaching us the religion of Islam, and by showing us how to live the life of a Muslim, the Honorable Elijah Muhammad is turning hundreds of thousands of American "Negroes" away from drunkenness, drug addiction, nicotine, stealing, lying, cheating, gambling, profanity, filth, fornication, adultery, and the many other acts of immorality that are almost inseparable from this indecent Western society.

The Honorable Elijah Muhammad has restored our cultural roots, our racial identity, our racial pride, and our racial confidence. He has given us the incentive and energy to stand on our own feet and walk for ourselves.

Just as we believe in one God, whose proper name is Allah, we believe also that this one God has only one religion, the religion of Islam. We believe that we are living in the time of "prophecy fulfillment," the time predicted by the ancient prophets of God, when this one God would use his one religion to establish one world here on earth—the world of Islam, or Muslim world . . . which only means: a world of universal brotherhood that will be based upon the principles of truth, freedom, justice, equality, righteousness, and peace.

But before God can set up his new world, the Muslim world, or world of Islam, which will be established on the principles to truth, peace, and brotherhood, God himself must first destroy this evil Western world, the white world . . . a wicked world, ruled by a race of devils, that preaches falsehood, practices slavery, and thrives on indecency and immorality.

You and I are living in that great Doomsday, the final hour, when the ancient prophets predicted that God himself would appear in person, in the flesh, and with divine power He would bring about the judgment and destruction of this present evil world.

. . .

The Honorable Elijah Muhammad's mission as messenger is to remind America that God has not forgotten America's crimes against his long-lost people, who have spent four hundred miserable years in this land of bondage. His mission is to warn America of the divine destruction that will soon rain down upon her from the very skies above her.

His mission is to warn America to repent, and to atone for her sins against God's people . . . or face complete destruction and permanent removal from the face of this earth . . . and removal not only as a nation but removal even as a race!

. . .

The time is past when the white world can exercise unilateral authority and control over the dark world. The independence and power of the dark world is on the increase; the dark world is rising in wealth, power, prestige, and influence. It is the rise of the dark world that is causing the fall of the white world.

As the white man loses his power to oppress and exploit the dark world, the white man's own wealth (power or "world") decreases. His world is on its way down; it is on its way out . . . and it is the will and power of God himself that is bringing an end to the white world.

You and I were born at this turning point in history; we are witnessing the fulfillment of prophecy. Our present generation is witnessing the end of colonialism, Europeanism, Westernism, or "White-ism" . . . the end of white supremacy, the end of the evil white man's unjust rule.

I must repeat: The end of the world only means the end of a certain "power." The end of colonialism ends the world (or power) of the colonizer. The end of Europeanism ends the world (or power) of the European . . . and the end of "White-ism" ends the world (or power) of the white man.

. . .

White America is doomed! Death and devastating destruction hang at this very moment in the skies over America. But why must her divine execution take place? Is it too late for her to avoid this catastrophe?

All the prophets of the past listed America as number one among the guilty that would be too proud, and too blind, to repent and atone when God's last Messenger is raised in her midst to warn her. America's last chance, her last warning, is coming from the lips of the Honorable Elijah Muhammad today. Accept him and be saved; reject him and be damned!

It is written that White America will reject him; it is also written that White America will be damned and doomed . . . and the prophets who make these prophecies are never wrong in their divine predictions.

White America refuses to study, reflect, and learn a lesson from history; ancient Egypt didn't have to be destroyed. It was her corrupt government, the crooked politicians, who caused her destruction. Pharaoh hired Hebrew magicians to try and fool their own people into thinking they would soon be integrated into the mainstream of that country's life. Pharaoh didn't want the Hebrews to listen to Moses' message of separation. Even in that day separation was God's solution to the "slave's problem." By opposing Moses, the magicians were actually choosing sides against the God of their own people.

In like manner, modern Negro magicians are hired by the American government to oppose the Honorable Elijah Muhammad today. They pose as Negro "leaders." They have been hired by this white government (white so-called liberals) to make our people here think that integration into this doomed white society will soon solve our problem.

The Honorable Elijah Muhammad warns us daily: The only permanent solution to America's race problem is the complete separation of these twenty-two million ex-slaves from our white slave master, and the return of these ex-slaves to our own land, where we can then live in peace and security among our people.

The Honorable Elijah Muhammad warns us daily: The American government is trying to trick her twenty-two million ex-slaves with promises that she never intends to keep. The crooked politicians in the government are working with the Negro civil rights leaders, but not to solve the race problem. The greedy politicians who run this government give lip service to the civil rights struggle only to further their own selfish interests. And their main interest as politicians is to stay in power.

In this deceitful American game of power politics, the Negroes (i.e., the race problem, the integration and civil rights issues) are nothing but tools, used by one group of whites called liberals against another group of whites called conservatives, either to get into power or to remain in power.

Among whites here in America, the political teams are no longer divided into Democrats and Republicans. The whites who are now struggling for control of the American political throne are divided into "liberal" and "conservative" camps. The white liberals from both parties cross party lines to work together toward the same goal, and white conservatives from both parties do likewise.

The white liberal differs from the white conservative only in one way: the liberal is more deceitful than the conservative. The liberal is more hypocritical than the conservative.

Both want power, but the white liberal is the one who has perfected the art of posing as the Negro's friend and benefactor; and by winning the friendship, allegiance, and support of the Negro, the white liberal is able to use the Negro as a pawn or tool in this political "football game" that is constantly raging between the white liberals and white conservatives.

Politically the American Negro is nothing but a football and the white liberals control this mentally dead ball through tricks of tokenism: false promises of integration and civil rights. In this profitable game of deceiving and exploiting the political politician of the American Negro, those white liberals have the willing cooperation of the Negro civil rights leaders. These "leaders" sell out our people for just a few crumbs of token recognition and token gains. These "leaders" are satisfied with token victories and token progress because they themselves are nothing but token leaders.

. . .

These Uncle Tom leaders do not speak for the Negro majority; they don't speak for the black masses. They speak for the "black bourgeoisie," the brainwashed, white-minded, middle-class minority who are ashamed of black, and don't want to be identified with the black masses, and are therefore seeking to lose their "black identity" by mixing, mingling, intermarrying, and integrating with the white man.

The race problem can never be solved by listening to this white-minded minority. The white man should try to learn what the black masses want, and the only way to learn what the black masses wants is by listening to the man who speaks for the black masses of America. The one man here in America who speaks for the downtrodden, dissatisfied black masses is this same man so many of our people are flocking to see and hear. This same Mr. Muhammad who is labeled by the white man as a black supremacist and as a racist.

If the three million white-minded Negroes are casting their ballots for integration and intermarriage, what do the nonvoting black masses want? Find out what the black masses want, and then perhaps America's grave race problem can be solved.

. . .

Let us examine briefly some of the tricky strategy used by white liberals to harness and exploit the political energies of the Negro.

The crooked politicians in Washington, D.C., purposely make a big noise over the proposed civil rights legislation. By blowing up the civil rights issue they skillfully add false importance to the Negro civil rights "leaders." Once the image of these Negro civil rights "leaders" has been blown up way beyond its proper proportion, these same Negro civil rights "leaders" are then used by white liberals to influence and control the Negro voters, all for the benefit of the white politicians who pose as liberals, who pose as friends of the Negro.

The white conservatives aren't friends of the Negro either, but they at least don't try to hide it. They are like wolves; they show their teeth in a snarl that keeps the Negro always aware of where he stands with them. But the white liberals are foxes, who also show their teeth to the Negro but pretend that they are smiling. The white liberals are more dangerous than the conservatives; they lure the Negro, and as the Negro runs from the growling wolf, he flees into the open jaws of the "smiling" fox.

The job of the Negro civil rights leader is to make the Negro forget that the wolf and the fox both belong to the [same] family. Both are canines; and no matter which one of them the Negro places his trust in, he never ends up in the White House, but always in the doghouse.

The white liberals control the Negro and the Negro vote by controlling the Negro civil rights leaders. As long as they control the Negro civil rights leaders, they can also control and contain the Negro's struggle, and they can control the Negro's so-called revolt.

The Negro "revolution" is controlled by these foxy white liberals, by the government itself. But the black revolution is controlled only by God.

The black revolution is the struggle of the nonwhites of this earth against their white oppressors. The black revolution has swept white supremacy out of Africa, out of Asia, and is getting ready to sweep it out of Latin America. Revolutions are based upon land. Revolutionaries are the landless against the landlord. Revolutions are never peaceful, never loving, never nonviolent. Nor are they ever compromising. Revolutions are destructive and bloody. Revolutionaries don't compromise with the enemy; they don't even negotiate. Like the flood in Noah's day, revolution drowns all opposition, or like the fire in Lot's day, the black revolution burns everything that gets in its path.

America is the last stronghold of white supremacy. The black revolution, which is international in nature and scope, is sweeping down upon America like a raging forest fire. It is only a matter of time before America herself will be engulfed by the black flames, these black firebrands.

. . .

The Negro "revolt" is controlled by the white man, the white fox. The Negro "revolution" is controlled by this white government. The leaders of the Negro "revolution" (the civil rights leaders) are all subsidized, influenced and controlled by the white liberals; and all of the demonstrations that are taking place in this country to desegregate lunch counters, theaters, public toilets, etc., are just artificial fires that have been ignited and fanned by the white liberals in the desperate hope that they can use this artificial revolution to fight off the real black revolution that has already swept white supremacy out of Africa, Asia, and is sweeping it out of Latin America . . . and is even now manifesting itself also right here among the black masses in this country.

Can we prove that the Negro revolution is controlled by white liberals? Certainly! Right after the Birmingham demonstrations, when the entire world had seen on television screens the police dogs, police clubs, and fire hoses brutalizing defenseless black women, children, and even babies, it was reported on page twenty-six in the May 15 issue of *The New York Times*, that the late President Kennedy and his brother, Attorney General Robert Kennedy, during a luncheon conference with several newspaper editors from the State of Alabama, had warned these editors that they must give at least some token gains to the moderate Negro leaders in order to enhance the image of these moderate Negro leaders in the eyesight of the black masses; otherwise the masses of Negroes might turn in the direction of Negro extremists. And the late President named the Black Muslims as being foremost among the Negro extremist groups that he did not want Negroes to turn toward.

In essence, the late President told these southern editors that he was trying to build up the weak image of the Negro civil rights leaders, in order to offset the strong religious image of the Muslim leader, the Honorable Elijah Muhammad. He wasn't giving these Negro leaders anything they deserved; but he was confessing the necessity of building them up, and propping them up, in order to hold the black masses in check, keep them in his grasp, and under his control.

The late President knew that once Negroes hear the Honorable Elijah Muhammad the white liberals will never influence or control or misuse those Negroes for the benefit of the white liberals any more. So the late President was faced with a desperate situation.

Martin Luther King's image had been shattered the previous year when he failed to bring about desegregation in Albany, Georgia. The other civil rights leaders had also become fallen idols. The black masses across the country at the grassroots level had already begun to take their cases to the streets on their own. The government in Washington knew that something had to be done to get the rampaging Negroes back into the corral, back under the control of the white liberals.

The government propaganda machine began encouraging Negroes to follow only what it called "responsible" Negro leaders. The government actually meant, Negro leaders who were responsible to the government, and who could therefore by controlled by the government, and be used by that same government to control their impatient people.

The government knows that the Honorable Elijah Muhammad is responsible only to God and can be controlled only by God. But this white government of America doesn't believe in God!

. . .

History must repeat itself! Because of America's evil deeds against these twenty-two million "Negroes," like Egypt and Babylon before her, America herself now stands before the "bar of justice." White America is now facing her Day of Judgment, and she can't escape because today God himself is the judge. God himself is now the administrator of justice, and God himself is to be her divine executor!

Is it possible for America to escape this divine disaster? If America can't atone for the crimes she has committed against the twenty-two million "Negroes," if she can't undo the evils she has brutally and mercilessly heaped upon our people these past four hundred years, then America has signed her own doom . . . and our own people would be foolish to accept her deceitful offers of integration into her doomed society at this late date!

How can America atone for her crimes? The Honorable Elijah Muhammad teaches us that a desegregated theater or lunch counter won't solve our problems. Better jobs won't even solve our problems. An integrated cup of coffee isn't sufficient pay for four hundred years of slave labor, and a better job in the white man's factory or position in his business is, at best, only a temporary solution. The only lasting or permanent solution is complete separation on some land that we can call our own.

The Honorable Elijah Muhammad teaches us that the race problem can easily be solved, just by sending these twenty-two million ex-slaves back to our own homeland where we can live in peace and harmony with our own kind. But this government should provide the transportation, plus everything else we need to get started again in our own country. This government should provide everything we need in machinery, materials, and finance; enough to last us for from twenty to twenty-five years, until we can become an independent people in our own country.

If this white government is afraid to let her twenty-two million ex-slaves go back to our country and to our own people, then America must set aside some separate territory here in the Western Hemisphere, where the two races can live apart from each other, since we certainly don't get along peacefully while we are here together.

The size of the territory can be judged according to our own population. If our people number one-seventh of America's total population, then give us one-seventh of this land. We don't want any land in the desert, but where there is rain and much mineral wealth.

We want fertile, productive land on which we can farm and provide our own people with sufficient food, clothing, and shelter. This government must supply us with the machinery and other tools needed to dig into the earth. Give us everything we need for them for from twenty to twenty-five years, until we can produce and supply our own needs.

If we are a part of America, then part of what she is worth belongs to us. We will take our share and depart, then this white country can have peace. What is her net worth? Give us our share in gold and silver and let us depart and go back to our homeland in peace.

We want no integration with this wicked race that enslaved us. We want complete separation from this race of devils. But we should not be expected to leave America and go back to our homeland empty-handed. After four hundred years of slave labor, we have some back pay coming, a bill owed to us that must be collected.

If the government of White America truly repents of its sins against our people, and atones by giving us our true share, only then can America save herself!

But if America waits for Almighty God himself to step in and force her into a just settlement, God will take this entire continent away from her; and she will cease to exist as a nation. Her own Christian Scriptures warn her that when God comes He can give the "entire Kingdom to whomsoever He will" . . . which only means that the God of Justice on Judgment Day can give this entire continent to whomsoever He wills!

White America, wake up and take heed, before it is too late!

*Source: Imam Benjamin Karim, ed. 1971.* The End of White World Supremacy: Four Speeches by Malcolm X, *121–148. New York: Arcade.*

## *Black Panther Party Platform and Program:*
## *"What We Want, What We Believe"*

In October 1966, Huey P. Newton and Bobby Seale formed the Black Panther Party for Self-Defense (BPP) in Oakland, California. Although the BPP was best known for its militant rhetoric, brandishing of rifles, and colorful attire, the organization was deeply involved in day-to-day programs that delivered services to ghetto residents that the government did not provide. For example, when police brutality ran unchecked in Oakland and the police department was unwilling to open itself up to citizen reviews, members of the BPP began following police around the city, making sure that residents were not brutalized and that proper procedures were followed. Additionally, the BPP provided free breakfasts for poor schoolchildren. Other services initiated by the BPP over the years around the United States included a housing advocacy program, a community drug program, liberation schools, free medical clinics, free clothing, free bus rides to prisons, senior citizen advocacy programs, sickle cell anemia research, housing cooperatives, free shoe programs, pest control initiatives, plumbing and maintenance services, free food, and free ambulance services. It is important to recognize that although militant rhetoric and the association of the organization with violence receives a disproportionate amount of attention, it was the day-to-day programs that delivered services to ghetto residents that constituted the most significant element of the BPP's efforts.

1. **We want freedom. We want power to determine the destiny of our Black Community.**

We believe that black people will not be free until we are able to determine our destiny.

2. **We want full employment for our people.**

We believe that the federal government is responsible and obligated to give every man employment or a guaranteed income. We believe that if the white American businessmen will not give full employment, then the means of production should be taken from the businessmen and placed in the community so that the people of the community can organize and employ all of its people and give a high standard of living.

3. **We want an end to the robbery by the CAPITALIST of our Black Community.**

We believe that this racist government has robbed us and now we are demanding the overdue debt of forty acres and two mules. Forty acres and two mules was promised 100 years ago as restitution for slave labor and mass murder of black people. We will accept the payment in currency which will be distributed to our many communities. The Germans are now aiding the Jews in Israel for the genocide of the Jewish people. The Germans murdered six million Jews. The American racist has taken part in the slaughter of over fifty million black people; therefore, we feel that this is a modest demand that we make.

**4. We want decent housing, fit for shelter of human beings.**

We believe that if the white landlords will not give decent housing to our black community, then the housing and the land should be made into cooperatives so that our community, with government aid, can build and make decent housing for its people.

**5. We want education for our people that exposes the true nature of this decadent American society. We want education that teaches us our true history and our role in the present-day society.**

We believe in an educational system that will give to our people a knowledge of self. If a man does not have knowledge of himself and his position in society and the world, then he has little chance to relate to anything else.

**6. We want all black men to be exempt from military service.**

We believe that Black people should not be forced to fight in the military service to defend a racist government that does not protect us. We will not fight and kill other people of color in the world who, like black people, are being victimized by the white racist government of America. We will protect ourselves from the force and violence of the racist police and the racist military, by whatever means necessary.

**7. We want an immediate end to POLICE BRUTALITY and MURDER of black people.**

We believe we can end police brutality in our black community by organizing black self-defense groups that are dedicated to defending our black community from racist police oppression and brutality. The Second Amendment to the Constitution of the United States gives a right to bear arms. We therefore believe that all black people should arm themselves for self-defense.

**8. We want freedom for all black men held in federal, state, county and city prisons and jails.**

We believe that all black people should be released from the many jails and prisons because they have not received a fair and impartial trial.

**9. We want all black people when brought to trial to be tried in court by a jury of their peer group or people from their black communities, as defined by the Constitution of the United States.**

We believe that the courts should follow the United States Constitution so that black people will receive fair trials. The Fourteenth Amendment of the U.S. Constitution gives a man a right to be tried by his peer group. A peer is a person from a similar economic, social, religious, geographical, environmental, historical and racial background. To do this the court will be forced to select a jury from the black community from which the black defendant came. We have been, and are being, tried by all-white juries that have no understanding of the "average reasoning man" of the black community.

10. We want land, bread, housing, education, clothing, justice and peace. And as our major political objective, a United Nations–supervised plebiscite to be held throughout the black colony in which only black colonial subjects will be allowed to participate, for the purpose of determining the will of black people as to their national destiny.

When, in the course of human events, it becomes necessary for one people to dissolve the political bands which have connected them with another, and to assume, among the powers of the earth, the separate and equal station to which the laws of nature and nature's God entitle them, a decent respect to the opinions of mankind requires that they should declare the causes which impel them to the separation.

We hold these truths to be self-evident, that all men are created equal; that they are endowed by their Creator with certain unalienable rights; that among these are life, liberty, and the pursuit of happiness. **That, to secure these rights, governments are instituted among men, deriving their just powers from the consent of the governed; that, whenever any form of government becomes destructive of these ends, it is the right of the people to alter or to abolish it, and to institute a new government, laying its foundation on such principles, and organizing its powers in such form, as to them shall seem most likely to effect their safety and happiness.** Prudence, indeed, will dictate that governments long established should not be changed for light and transient causes; and accordingly, all experience hath shown, that mankind are more disposed to suffer, while evils are sufferable, than to right themselves by abolishing the forms to which they are accustomed. **But, when a long train of abuses and usurpations, pursuing invariably the same object, evinces a design to reduce them under absolute despotism, it is their right, it is their duty, to throw off such government, and to provide new guards for their future security.**

*Source: Philip S. Foner, ed. 1970. The Black Panthers Speak, 2–4. Reprint, New York: Da Capo Press, 1995.*

# Reference

**Abernathy, Ralph (1926–1990)** Pastor of the First Baptist Church in Montgomery, Alabama, and a key organizer of the Montgomery Improvement Association (MIA). Abernathy helped found the Southern Christian Leadership Conference (SCLC) and served as SCLC president from 1968 to 1977.

**Affirmative action** Policies first implemented by President Lyndon Johnson's Executive Order 11246, signed in 1965, which, in an effort to combat employment discrimination, required employers who contracted with the federal government to take "affirmative action" to hire without regard to race, religion, color, or national origin.

**Alabama Christian Movement for Human Rights (ACMHR)** Organized in 1956 by Birmingham pastors Fred Shuttlesworth, R. L. Alford, Edward Gardner, and Nelson Smith, the ACMHR led the Birmingham campaign.

**Albany Movement** Campaign to desegregate the city of Albany, Georgia. Although the most renowned phase of the movement took place from December 1961 to August 1962, when SCLC intervened, local people carried it further in the form of a voter registration campaign.

**Ali, Muhammad (1942–)** World heavyweight boxing champion who joined the Nation of Islam and refused to be drafted for military service during the Vietnam War. Ali was stripped of his title and sentenced to five years in prison in 1967, but the U.S. Supreme Court overturned his conviction in 1971.

*Autobiography of Malcolm X, The* Based on interviews with Malcolm X and written by Alex Haley, *The Autobiography of Malcolm X* was published in 1965.

**Baker, Ella (1903–1986)** Helped organize SCLC, was its first full-time staff member, and served as its acting director and associate director between 1958 and 1960. In 1960, Baker mentored the students affiliated with the sit-in movement who would form the Student Nonviolent Coordinating Committee (SNCC). Prior to her work with SCLC, she was national director of branches for the National Association for the Advancement of Colored People (NAACP) from 1943 to 1946 and president of its New York chapter from 1954 to 1958.

**Baldwin, James (1924–1987)** Writer whose work during the civil rights years articulated what it meant to be black in America.

**Barry, Marion (1936–)** First national chairman of SNCC, Barry later became mayor of Washington, D.C.

**Bates, Daisy (1920–1999)** President of the NAACP Arkansas State Conference and a member of the NAACP board of directors. Bates was a key figure in organizing the desegregation of Little Rock's public schools during the late 1950s.

**Belafonte, Harry (1927–)** Popular entertainer who gave key financial support and publicity to the civil rights movement.

**Bevel, James (1936–)** Minister and activist who was an important strategist for SCLC, helping organize key campaigns including the March on Washington and the Chicago Freedom Movement. Bevel was also a pivotal force during the Nashville student movement of 1960.

**Birmingham campaign** SCLC's 1963 push to desegregate the city of Birmingham, Alabama. The campaign helped the civil rights movement gain national attention, as observers could not help but sympathize with the nonviolent protesters who faced brutality from the city's police and fire departments who turned high-pressure water hoses on school-age demonstrators.

**Birmingham church bombing** Took place on September 15, 1963, when the Ku Klux Klan (KKK) dynamited the Sixteenth Street Baptist Church, resulting in the deaths of four children: Denise McNair, Carole Robertson, Addie Mae Collins, and Cynthia Wesley.

**Black Muslims** Term used by outsiders to refer to the Nation of Islam or its members.

**Black nationalism** Philosophy that positions African Americans as a nation with identities, goals, and needs that often diverge from those of other Americans. Black nationalism urges African Americans to organize politically, economically, and culturally along racial lines.

**Black Panther Party for Self-Defense (BPP)** Founded by Huey Newton and Bobby Seale in 1966 near Oakland, California, the BPP was a community organization that offered assistance to the poor. It administered programs and services from breakfasts for children to health care to police review monitors that its leaders perceived were not being provided by government agencies. The BPP advocated self-defense and incorporated both black nationalism and socialism into its rhetoric and programs. At its peak during the late 1960s, the BPP had 25 chapters and nearly 2,000 members.

**Black power** Political slogan that entered national consciousness during a 1966 march led by SNCC. The slogan quickly caught on among civil rights workers and reflected their growing impatience and frustration with the slow pace of change and the sustained white resistance the movement faced. For a large segment of the black freedom struggle during the late 1960s and early 1970s, black power became a key organizing principle.

**Blackwell, Unita (1933–)** SNCC field worker and a delegate of the Mississippi Freedom Democratic Party (MFDP). Blackwell later became the first African American woman to become a mayor in the state of Mississippi.

**Bloody Sunday** Took place on March 7, 1965, when Alabama state troopers brutally assaulted a group of civil rights activists who had planned to march from Selma to Montgomery, Alabama, to protest for voting rights.

**Bond, Julian (1940–)** Early member of SNCC who became the organization's director of public relations. Bond later became a politician, serving in both houses of the Georgia state legislature from 1966 to 1986. In 1998, he became chair of the NAACP.

**Boynton, Amelia (1911–)** Civil rights leader in Selma, Alabama.

**Branton, Wiley (1923–1988)** Named executive director of the Voter Education Project (VEP) in 1962, Branton had a distinguished legal career before taking this post.

*Briggs v. Elliot* School desegregation case that began in South Carolina. Grouped with *Brown v. Board of Education* and several other cases, it became the basis for the Supreme Court finding that racial segregation in public schools was unconstitutional.

*Browder v. Gayle* 1956 legal challenge by Montgomery activists to the Alabama statute requiring segregation on public buses.

**Brown, Elaine (1943–)** Deputy minister of information of the BPP who later became its chair. Brown ran unsuccessfully for the Oakland City Council in 1973.

**Brown, H. Rap (1943–)** Became national director of SNCC in 1967 and was known for rhetoric that expressed his commitment to armed self-defense.

*Brown v. Board of Education* 1954 court case that began in Topeka, Kansas. Grouped with four other cases, *Brown* was the centerpiece of the NAACP Legal Defense and Educational Fund, Inc.'s (LDF) successful Supreme Court argument that racial segregation in public schools was unconstitutional. The case sparked the civil rights movement by destroying the legal basis for segregation set by the 1896 *Plessy v. Ferguson* decision.

**Bunche, Ralph (1904–1971)** United Nations (UN) staff member who won the Nobel Peace Prize in 1950 for negotiating the treaty that ended the first Arab-Israeli War. During the civil rights years, Bunche served as a UN undersecretary general. He was also a member of the NAACP board of directors.

**Busing** Means of integrating racially imbalanced schools by transporting students via bus to schools outside their neighborhood. Court-ordered busing became a source of controversy in the early 1970s.

**Carmichael, Stokely (1941–1998)** Birth name of Kwame Ture, the organizer who introduced the slogan "black power" to the public. As a Howard University student, Carmichael was involved in demonstrations led by the Congress of Racial Equality (CORE) and SNCC. He helped organize the

Lowndes County Freedom Organization (LCFO) and became SNCC chair in 1966, leading the organization's turn toward black nationalism. In 1968, he joined the Black Panther Party.

**Chaney, James (1943–1964)** CORE field worker in Mississippi who was murdered by the KKK.

**Chavis, Benjamin (1948–)** Civil rights activist in North Carolina who as a teenager joined SCLC and later became its coordinator in that state. Chavis served as executive director of the NAACP from 1993 to 1994 and later became a minister for the Nation of Islam, helping to organize its 1995 Million Man March.

**Chicago Freedom Movement** Joint effort during the summer of 1966 by the Coordinating Committee of Community Organizations and SCLC to desegregate Chicago's public schools, open its housing market, and increase black employment.

**Chisholm, Shirley (1924–2005)** First black woman elected to the U.S. House of Representatives, serving as a New York Democrat from 1969 to 1983.

**Citizens' Council** Organization of white segregationists formed in 1954 to resist the *Brown v. Board of Education* decision. The council controlled the state government of Mississippi and had well over 50,000 members across the South by the late 1950s.

**Civil Rights Act of 1957** Strengthened the federal government's oversight of voting rights and established the Civil Rights Division of the U.S. Department of Justice.

**Civil Rights Act of 1960** Strengthened the federal government's oversight of civil rights by giving it the authority to prosecute those who interfered with court-ordered desegregation mandates.

**Civil Rights Act of 1964** Outlawed discrimination based on race, color, religion, sex, or national origin. The law gave the federal government the power to enforce the constitutional right to vote and provide injunctive relief against discrimination in public accommodations.

**Civil Rights Act of 1968** Prohibited discrimination according to race, religion, national origin, or sex in the sale, rental, or financing of housing.

**Civil rights movement** Name given by contemporaries and historians to the black struggle for freedom and equality during the period 1955–1975.

**Clark, Kenneth (1914–2005), and Clark, Mamie (1917–1983)** Psychologists whose studies of children correlating race and self-esteem became important evidence in the *Brown v. Board of Education* case.

**Clark, Septima (1898–1987)** NAACP member who became director of the Highlander Folk School and SCLC director of education.

**Cleage, Albert (1911–2000)** Religious leader who embraced black nationalism and developed a following in Detroit.

**Cleaver, Eldridge (1935–1998)** BPP minister of information and author of the book *Soul on Ice*. He was the husband of Kathleen Cleaver.

**Cleaver, Kathleen (1945–)** Member of SNCC who became communications secretary of the BPP. Now a legal scholar and writer, she is the former wife of Eldridge Cleaver.

**COINTELPRO** Counterintelligence program launched by Federal Bureau of Investigation director J. Edgar Hoover on August 25, 1967, that targeted black militants and resulted in a campaign of violent repression against members of the BPP, ultimately leading to the organization's demise.

**Cone, James (1938–)** Theologian who in 1969 published *Black Theology and Black Power*, which recast Christianity in terms of black liberation.

**Congress of Racial Equality (CORE)** Organization founded in 1942 that applied nonviolent protest techniques to challenge racial injustice. CORE was instrumental to the sit-in movement of 1960 and led the 1961 Freedom Rides, which catapulted public awareness of the civil rights movement upward. In later years, CORE shifted its focus toward employment and led a series of direct-action protests against corporations and businesses that had unfavorable minority hiring records. At its peak during the mid-1960s, it had more than 100 chapters and about 6,000 members.

**Connor, Theophilus "Bull" (1897–1973)** Public safety commissioner of Birmingham whose mistreatment of nonviolent civil rights demonstrators became an important symbol of white resistance to black equality.

**Conyers, John (1929–)** Democratic member of the U.S. House of Representatives since 1965, representing Michigan's black-majority 14th Congressional District, located north of downtown Detroit.

**Coordinating Council of Community Organizations (CCCO)** Chicago civil rights umbrella group founded in 1962 that joined forces with SCLC and Martin Luther King Jr. in 1966 to become the Chicago Freedom Movement and spearhead a series of demonstrations.

**Cotton, Dorothy (1931–)** Director of SCLC's Citizenship Education Program and a close confidante of Martin Luther King Jr.

**Council for United Civil Rights Leadership (CUCRL)** Formed in 1963 by philanthropist Stephen Currier, members included Martin Luther King Jr., James Farmer, Roy Wilkins, Whitney Young, Jack Greenberg, and Dorothy Height. CUCRL was an umbrella organization that allowed civil rights leaders to fund-raise and consider policy as a group rather than in competition with one another.

**Council of Federated Organizations (COFO)** Umbrella organization designed to coordinate the efforts of various civil rights groups working in Mississippi. It was created by local activists in 1962 and included representatives from SNCC, NAACP, SCLC, and CORE.

**Davis, Angela (1944–)** Marxist intellectual and college professor who was affiliated with the BPP and SNCC. For more than 30 years, Davis has been an advocate for prisoners' rights.

**Davis, Ossie (1917–2005)** Actor who supported the civil rights movement and delivered the eulogy at the funeral of Malcolm X.

*Davis v. County School Board of Prince Edward County, Virginia* 1954 case that was grouped with *Brown v. Board of Education* as part of the argument that racial segregation in public schools was unconstitutional.

**Deacons for Defense and Justice** Group formed in 1964 to provide armed protection from KKK violence for civil rights workers in Louisiana. The organization also protected SNCC demonstrators during a 1966 march in Mississippi.

**Delta Ministry** National Council of Churches civil rights program affiliated with the Mississippi Freedom Summer of 1964.

**Detroit race riot** The gravest uprising of 1967, lasting five days. Forty-three people were killed.

**Durr, Clifford (1899–1975), and Durr, Virginia Foster (1903–1999)** White liberals who supported the Montgomery bus boycott.

**Edelman, Marian Wright (1939–)** The first African American woman admitted to the Mississippi state bar. She served as counsel to the Poor People's Campaign and established the Children's Defense Fund, a lobbying group that works to benefit poor children.

**Equal Employment Opportunity Act of 1972** Authorized the federal government to file suit against employers with discriminatory hiring practices.

**Equal Employment Opportunity Commission (EEOC)** Federal commission empowered to enforce the Equal Employment Opportunity Act of 1972.

**Evers, Charles (1922–)** Became the NAACP Mississippi field secretary following his brother Medgar's assassination. Throughout the late 1960s, Evers was an important civil rights leader in rural Mississippi, leading economic boycotts and organizing black voting blocs.

**Evers, Medgar (1925–1963)** First NAACP field secretary in Mississippi. Evers was assassinated for organizing voting rights campaigns, boycotts, and legal battles against segregation.

*Eyes on the Prize* Influential documentary about the civil rights movement. The first part was released in 1987 and consisted of six one-hour television programs that covered the civil rights movement between 1954 and 1966. The second half of the series was released in 1990 and covered the movement from 1965 to 1985. Countless people have learned about the civil rights era through these films.

**Farmer, James (1920–1999)** Founding member of CORE and the organization's first national director, a position he held from 1961 to 1966. Dedicated to nonviolent direct-action protest, Farmer left CORE and became involved in politics when the organization drifted from its integrationist roots. He was President Richard Nixon's assistant secretary of health, education, and welfare.

**Farrakhan, Louis (1933–)** Nightclub singer who was influenced by Malcolm X to join the Nation of Islam in 1955 and led the organization's mosque in Boston. When Elijah Muhammad died in 1975, Farrakhan carried on his militant black nationalist message, becoming the organization's leader in 1978. Throughout the 1980s, Farrakhan received attention for the stridency of his rhetoric. He organized the 1995 Million Man March.

**Fellowship of Reconciliation (FOR)** was a pacifist organization that practiced civil disobedience. In 1942, a number of FOR members in Chicago decided to apply nonviolent civil disobedience to challenge racial discrimination. This group of activists became CORE.

**Forman, James (1928–2005)** Reporter for the *Chicago Defender* who participated in the Freedom Rides. He later joined SNCC and served as the organization's executive secretary from 1964 to 1966. In 1972, Forman published a memoir of the civil rights movement entitled *The Making of Black Revolutionaries: A Personal Account.*

**Freedom Rides** Held in 1961 by an interracial group of CORE activists who took a bus ride through the South to test the Supreme Court ruling banning segregation in interstate commerce and transportation. They met terrible violence, and many were beaten severely.

**Freedom Summer** Took place in 1964 in Mississippi when northern college students joined forces with civil rights activists in efforts to desegregate the state. Freedom Summer officials and volunteers worked on several fronts. They organized voter registration campaigns, established 30 freedom schools whose curriculum countered the white supremacy of the Mississippi public schools, and created community centers that provided key services to the state's black residents.

**Gaston, A. G. (1892–1996)** Birmingham businessman who supported campaigns to desegregate the city.

**Goodman, Andrew (1943–1964)** Was working with CORE in Mississippi when he was murdered by the KKK.

**Granger, Lester (1896–1976)** Executive secretary of the National Urban League (UL) from 1941 to 1961.

**Gray, Fred (1930–)** Founding member of the MIA, Gray filed *Browder v. Gayle* as a lawyer for the Alabama NAACP.

**Greenberg, Jack (1924–)** Legal counselor for the LDF, Greenberg was involved in some of the era's most important civil rights cases. His memoirs, entitled *Crusaders in the Courts: How a Dedicated Band of Lawyers Fought for the Civil Rights Movement,* was released in 1994.

**Greensboro sit-in movement** Series of sit-ins by students in Greensboro, North Carolina, February 1–5, 1960, that launched similar campaigns in 31 cities throughout eight southern states by the end of that month.

**Gregory, Dick (1932–)** Comedian who supported the civil rights movement both financially and as an activist. As a write-in candidate for U.S. president in 1968, Gregory received 1.5 million votes.

*Griffin v. Prince Edward School Board* 1964 case in which the Supreme Court ordered the county school board to reopen its schools after it had closed them to counter federal desegregation orders.

**Groppi, James (1930–1985)** Civil rights leader in Milwaukee.

**Guyot, Lawrence (1939–)** SNCC field secretary who helped organize COFO and then became chairman of the MFDP.

**Haley, Alex (1921–1992)** Author who collaborated with Malcolm X to write *The Autobiography of Malcolm X*. He later wrote *Roots: The Saga of An American Family*, which was published in 1976.

**Hamer, Fannie Lou (1917–1977)** Lost her job as a timekeeper on a cotton plantation after attempting to register to vote and became an important part of SNCC's Mississippi projects and the MFDP political campaigns. Hamer became a national figure in 1964 when she testified at the Democratic National Convention (DNC) about the violence she and other black Mississippians faced for exercising their citizenship rights. She was a founding member of the National Women's Political Caucus, which was formed in 1971.

**Hampton, Fred (1948–1969)** Was deputy chairman of the Illinois BPP when he was killed by Chicago police officers. A subsequent investigation revealed that the killing had been carried out as part of the COINTELPRO program.

**Height, Dorothy (1912–)** President of the National Council of Negro Women (NCNW) for 40 years, beginning in 1957. Height spoke at the March on Washington and helped desegregate the Young Women's Christian Association. She also participated in the 1966 White House conference To Fulfill These Rights.

**Henry, Aaron (1922–1997)** State president of the Mississippi NAACP, he led the formation of COFO in February 1962. Henry also helped direct Freedom Summer and was the founding chair of the MFDP. Later he became a member of the Mississippi state legislature.

**Highlander Folk School** Training center for the civil rights movement located in Tennessee and directed by Septima Clark. Some of the most well-known movement figures, including Martin Luther King Jr., Rosa Parks, Stokely Carmichael, Fannie Lou Hamer, and Andrew Young studied there.

**Hill, Herbert (1924–2004)** NAACP labor secretary who challenged racial discrimination within trade unions.

**Hooks, Benjamin (1925–)** Lawyer, activist, and Baptist minister who sat on the SCLC board of directors from 1957 to 1977. In 1977, Hooks replaced Roy Wilkins as NAACP executive director and also became chair of the Leadership Council on Civil Rights (LCCR). He was the first African American to address both the Democratic and Republican national conventions. He left the NAACP in 1992 to resume his duties as a minister.

**Houston, Charles Hamilton (1895–1950)** Lawyer who taught at Howard University Law School, where he recruited and trained students to battle for equality through the courts. Houston was responsible for mentoring many of the lawyers who worked for the LDF.

**Hurley, Ruby (1909–1980)** NAACP national youth secretary from 1943 to 1951. In 1951, Hurley became the NAACP southeast regional director, the first full-time NAACP officer in the Deep South.

**"I Have a Dream"** Martin Luther King Jr.'s famous address at the March on Washington, representing one of the signature moments in U.S. history.

**Innis, Roy (1934–)** Longtime CORE member who became the organization's associate national director in 1968.

**Jackson, George (1941–1971).** While incarcerated in San Quentin prison, his 1970 book *Soledad Brother: The Prison Letters of George Jackson* became a national best seller. Prison guards killed Jackson the following year, and many people remain convinced that his death was a political assassination.

**Jackson, Jesse (1941–)** Was a seminary student when he began working with SCLC in 1965. In 1967, Jackson became director of SCLC's Operation Breadbasket. He helped lead the Poor People's Campaign in 1968. Three years later, he formed Operation PUSH, a black advocacy group, which he led until 1989. In 1984 and 1988 Jackson was a serious contender in the Democratic primary elections for U.S. president.

**Jackson, Jimmie Lee (1938–1965)** Alabama civil rights activist who was shot to death by state troopers during a demonstration.

**Jackson, Joseph (1900–1990)** President of the National Baptist Convention U.S.A. from 1953 to 1982. Jackson opposed Martin Luther King Jr. and the civil rights movement and instead favored black economic development as a liberation strategy.

**Jackson, Lillie Mae (1889–1975)** Longtime NAACP member who headed the organization's Baltimore branch.

**Jackson, Maynard (1938–2003)** First African American to become mayor of a major southern city; Jackson was elected to the post in Atlanta in 1973. He served two terms and was later reelected to a third term in 1990.

**Jackson State College** Site of an antiwar protest on May 13, 1970, that became a race riot when members of the Jackson police department and Mississippi highway patrol fired on demonstrators, killing 2 black students and wounding 12.

**Jim Crow** Broad term that refers to the myriad types of racial discrimination, both legal and illegal, aimed at African Americans prior to the *Brown v. Board of Education* decision.

**Johnson, Frank (1918–1999)** Federal district judge in Alabama who made several important rulings in favor of civil rights that angered white segregationists.

**Jones, Leroi (1934–)** Birth name of Amiri Baraka, the black nationalist writer who became politically active in Newark, New Jersey, and chaired the National Black Political Convention in 1972.

**Jordan, Vernon (1935–)** NAACP field director who later worked for the VEP. He was also a key adviser to the Albany Movement. Jordan later became executive director of the United Negro College Fund and president of the UL. He was an adviser to President Bill Clinton.

**Karenga, Ron "Maulana" (1941–)** Black cultural nationalist who founded the organization United Slaves and created the holiday Kwanzaa.

**Kerner Commission,** or National Advisory Commission on Civil Disorders A federal commission appointed by President Lyndon Johnson in 1967 to investigate the race riots that took place between 1965 and 1968. It was headed by Illinois governor Otto Kerner. It found that the United States was "moving toward two societies, one black, one white—separate and unequal." Its recommendations, however, were largely ignored, as a conservative backlash to the civil rights movement engulfed federal politics.

**King, C. B. (1923–1988)** Lead attorney for and a key organizer of the Albany Movement. In 1970, King became the first African American to run for governor of Georgia.

**King, Coretta Scott (1927–2006)** Advocate for nonviolent change and the wife of Martin Luther King Jr. In 1969, King founded the Martin Luther King Jr. Center for Nonviolent Social Change in Atlanta. Throughout the 1980s, she advocated for the creation of a federal holiday honoring her husband, succeeding in 1986.

**King, Ed (1936–)** Pastor who became involved in the civil rights struggle in Mississippi. King was one of the few white delegates who traveled to the 1964 DNC with the MFDP.

**King, Martin Luther, Jr. (1929–1968)** Pastor of the Dexter Avenue Baptist Church in Montgomery who became one of the civil rights movement's most important leaders. King led the Montgomery bus boycott and later was elected president of the SCLC, which he helped found. As SCLC president, King led a series of high-profile movements to desegregate several cities, including Albany, Georgia; Selma, Alabama; Birmingham; St. Augustine, Florida; and Chicago. In 1963, he gave the "I Have a Dream" speech to climax the March on Washington. In 1964, King won the Nobel Peace Prize for his dedication to nonviolent change. In 1967, he publicly opposed the Vietnam War. King was organizing the interracial Poor People's Campaign when he was assassinated in 1968. By all accounts, he is one of the most significant figures in the history of the United States. Even today, he is an important symbol of both America's promise and its shortcomings.

**Ku Klux Klan (KKK)** Organization dedicated to white supremacy and the oppression of African Americans. It was responsible for much of the violence faced by civil rights workers in the South.

**Kwanzaa** Holiday created in 1966 and celebrated by African Americans during the last week of December. An alternative to Christmas, it commemorates the African roots of black American life.

**Lawson, James (1928–)** Influential among students in the sit-in movement and an important associate of Martin Luther King Jr. Dedicated to nonviolence, Lawson served prison time for refusing to fight in the Korean War. After his release, he traveled to India to study the tactics of Mohandas Gandhi. Lawson was associated with both SCLC and SNCC and led training workshops that helped civil rights volunteers practice nonviolent methods. He also participated in the Freedom Rides.

**Leadership Council for Civil Rights (LCCR)** Cofounded by the NAACP in 1950. LCCR was a lobbying group that represented more than 150 organizations and pressured politicians to produce more comprehensive federal civil rights legislation. It played an important role in the passage of almost all major civil rights legislation of the era, including the Civil Rights Acts of 1957, 1960, 1964, and 1968 and the Voting Rights Act of 1965.

**Lee, Herbert (1912–1961)** Was murdered for participating in an SNCC voter registration drive in Mississippi.

**Lester, Julius (1939–)** Freedom Summer volunteer and writer who later became a professor of Afro-American studies.

**"Letter from Birmingham Jail"** Martin Luther King Jr.'s 1963 response to criticism of the demonstrations he had led in that city.

**Lewis, Chester, Jr. (1929–1990)** President of the Wichita, Kansas, chapter of the NAACP, Lewis spearheaded several key desegregation campaigns in the Midwest.

**Lewis, John (1940–)** Helped organize the student sit-in movement, was a founding member of SNCC, and later became the organization's chair. Disillusioned with the organization's turn toward black nationalism, Lewis resigned from SNCC in 1966 after losing the chairmanship to Stokely Carmichael and became director of the VEP. He has been a member of the U.S. House of Representatives since 1986.

**Little Rock crisis** Began in 1957 when whites rioted in response to the proposed integration of Central High School. When Arkansas governor Orval Faubus defied a federal order to desegregate city schools, President Dwight Eisenhower sent in troops to enforce it.

**Liuzzo, Viola (1925–1965)** Was murdered by the KKK while transporting civil rights demonstrators from Montgomery to Selma.

*Loving v. Virginia* 1967 Supreme Court case that found state laws against interracial marriage to be unconstitutional.

**Lowery, Joseph (1921–)** Helped found SCLC and was the organization's president from 1977 to 1997.

**Lowndes County Freedom Organization (LCFO)** Independent, black-led political party formed in 1966 by residents of Lowndes County, Alabama, with the help of SNCC organizers. The LCFO was designed to challenge the segregated Alabama Democratic Party for local representation.

**Lucy, Autherine (1929–)** Successfully sued the University of Alabama when it denied her admission application on racial grounds. She was the first African American to attend the school.

**Maddox, Lester (1915–2003)** Segregationist governor of Georgia elected in 1967. He ardently opposed integration, making him a hero to white supremacists.

**Malcolm X (1925–1965)** National spokesperson of the Nation of Islam before a falling out with Elijah Muhammad led him to form the Organization of Afro-American Unity in 1964. One of the most important black nationalist figures of the era, Malcolm X offered tactical and rhetorical alternatives to the nonviolent and interracial integrationism that had dominated the public face of the civil rights movement. He was assassinated in February 1965 but remains a powerful and controversial symbol of the era.

**March on Washington for Jobs and Freedom** Took place on August 28, 1963. The brainchild of A. Philip Randolph and planned by Bayard Rustin, the March on Washington was a powerful display of support for the civil rights movement. An estimated 250,000 people attended.

**Marshall, Thurgood (1908–1993)** NAACP chief counsel for critical civil rights cases including *Shelley v. Kraemer, Sweatt v. Painter, McLaurin v. Oklahoma State Regents,* and *Brown v. Board of Education.*

**Mays, Benjamin (1894–1984)** President of Morehouse College in Atlanta from 1950 to 1967. Mays developed a close relationship with student Martin Luther King Jr., who later called Mays his spiritual mentor and intellectual father.

**McKissick, Floyd (1922–1991)** Longtime member of CORE who became its national director in 1966. The next year, he resigned to direct a Ford Foundation program designed to train young African Americans for leadership positions.

*McLaurin v. Oklahoma State Regents* 1950 Supreme Court case that found racial segregation within public institutions to be unconstitutional. It was a key building block of the *Brown v. Board of Education* case.

**Meredith, James (1933–)** First African American to attend the University of Mississippi. In 1966, he led a "march against fear" from Memphis to Jackson but was shot by a sniper shortly into his journey. Civil rights organizations rallied to his support and continued the march without him. Later, however, Meredith earned the enmity of the civil rights community when he became a conservative.

**Mississippi Freedom Democratic Party** (MFDP) A black-led party, it challenged the leadership of the all-white Mississippi Democratic Party. Assisted by SNCC, the MFDP demonstrated at the 1964 DNC for representation.

**Mitchell, Clarence (1911–1984)** Headed the Washington, D.C., branch of the NAACP. Mitchell's influence in Washington was so strong that he was commonly referred to as the "101st Senator."

**Montgomery bus boycott** Eleven-month mass protest in Alabama that began in December 1955 and ended when the Supreme Court, in *Browder v. Gayle*, upheld a lower court ruling that found public bus segregation unconstitutional. The Montgomery bus boycott is given credit for being the first campaign of the historical era known as the civil rights movement.

**Montgomery Improvement Association (MIA)** Formed in 1955 by ministers and community leaders in Montgomery to organize the 11-month bus boycott against segregation by the city's black residents.

**Moody, Anne (1940–)** CORE organizer in Mississippi from 1961 to 1963 who wrote an important autobiography about life in the movement called *Coming of Age in Mississippi*, which was published in 1968.

**Moore, Amzie (1911–1982)** Mississippi NAACP worker who mentored SNCC members who had joined voter registration campaigns in that state.

**Moses, Bob (1935–)** Director of the SNCC Mississippi Project and codirector of COFO. Moses also was influential in founding the MFDP. Today he heads the Algebra Project, an organization that links math literacy and civil rights.

**Motley, Constance Baker (1921–2005)** First African American woman to serve as a federal court judge. Prior to that, Motley was the LDF lead trial attorney. She argued nine LDF cases before the Supreme Court, including those that won Autherine Lucy the right to go to the University of Alabama and James Meredith admission into the University of Mississippi.

**Muhammad, Elijah (1897–1975)** Led the Nation of Islam from the 1930s until his death. Muhammad believed in racial separatism and felt that economic development was pivotal for black liberation. Under his leadership, the Nation of Islam built an impressive economic empire that included real estate, a newspaper, farmland, grocery stores, bakeries, and bookstores.

**NAACP Legal Defense and Educational Fund, Inc. (LDF)** Founded in 1940 as a tax-exempt organization designed to provide free representation to African Americans who suffered legal injustices or were denied educational opportunity by reason of race or color. It was the organization that pursued the successful *Brown v. Board of Education* Supreme Court challenge, as well as a host of other important civil rights cases.

*NAACP v. Alabama* 1964 Supreme Court case that overturned the decision by an Alabama court to bar the NAACP from the state.

**Nash, Diane (1938–)** One of the founders of SNCC and a leader of the student sit-in movement.

**Nashville Student Movement** Began with a sit-in on February 13, 1960. Demonstrations around the city during that year produced some of the civil rights movement's most important leaders, including James Bevel, John Lewis, and Diane Nash.

**Nation of Islam** Religious organization founded in the 1930s that came into prominence during the late 1950s under the leadership of Elijah Muhammad. The Nation of Islam derived its theology by adapting various tenets of traditional Islam to an African American context. The Nation of Islam's focus on economic self-reliance, its uncompromising stance toward whites, and the rhetorical abilities of national spokesperson Malcolm X made it attractive to those seeking alternatives to mainstream civil rights leadership.

**National Association for the Advancement of Colored People (NAACP)** The oldest active civil rights organization in the United States, founded in 1909. During the civil rights movement, the NAACP program was organized into three areas: political lobbying, court cases, and direct-action campaigns. NAACP Executive Secretary Roy Wilkins was an adviser to President Lyndon Johnson. During the 1960s, the NAACP boasted more than 500,000 members, making it the largest civil rights organization in the United States.

**National Council of Churches (NCC)** Religious umbrella organization that lent support to a number of civil rights campaigns and on occasion organized its own projects.

**National Council of Negro Women (NCNW)** Founded in 1935 by Mary McLeod Bethune. During the civil rights era it became a nonprofit organization, which allowed it to receive grants from the Ford Foundation and the federal government.

**National Urban League (UL)** Commonly known as the Urban League, it was a social welfare organization founded in 1910 that became more involved in the civil rights struggle under the leadership of Whitney Young. The UL devoted most of its resources to issues of employment. During the early part of the civil rights movement, it focused almost exclusively on integrating unions, but as the era progressed, the organization became dedicated to a wider range of activities.

**National Welfare Rights Organization (NWRO)** Formed in 1967, it held marches, protests, and rallies to publicize the rights and needs of welfare recipients. The NWRO was partly responsible for the Johnson administration's antipoverty initiatives.

**Newark race riot** Taking place in 1967, it lasted six days and resulted in 23 deaths.

**Newton, Huey (1942–1989)** Cofounder of the BPP, Newton advocated armed self-defense and helped steer the BPP toward socialism.

**Nixon, E. D. (1899–1987)** Organized the Montgomery Voter's League in 1940, was president of the Montgomery NAACP from 1939 to 1951, and was a key organizer of the Montgomery bus boycott and the MIA.

**Nonviolence** Philosophy that urges its adherents to refrain from using violence of any kind, even in self-defense when attacked.

*North Carolina State Board of Education v. Swann* 1971 case in which the Supreme Court ruled that a state law banning the busing of students to create racially balanced schools was unconstitutional.

**Norton, Eleanor Holmes (1937–)** Founded the New Haven, Connecticut, chapter of CORE and was assistant legal director of the American Civil Liberties Union. In 1977, President Jimmy Carter appointed Norton to the EEOC.

**Operation Breadbasket** Economic arm of SCLC established in 1962 and designed to create employment and business opportunities for African Americans.

**Organization of Afro-American Unity (OAAU)** Formed by Malcolm X in 1964 following his split with Elijah Muhammad and the Nation of Islam.

**Parks, Rosa (1913–2005)** Refused to give up her seat to a white man on an Alabama bus, sparking the Montgomery bus boycott. Prior to that act, Parks had been a member of the Montgomery NAACP.

*Plessy v. Ferguson* 1896 Supreme Court case that legalized segregation by ruling "separate but equal" public accommodations for blacks and whites to be constitutional. It was overturned by the 1954 *Brown v. Board of Education* case.

**poll tax** Method used to bar qualified voters by charging them money to vote. The practice was banned by the 1964 Civil Rights Act.

**Poor People's Campaign of 1968** Martin Luther King Jr. and SCLC's response to the growing need of the civil rights movement to address poverty outside the rural South. The Poor People's Campaign was envisioned as a massive civil disobedience initiative that would take place in Washington, D.C., and disrupt business there. King's assassination and other problems prevented the Poor People's Campaign from reaching this scale.

**Powell, Adam Clayton, Jr. (1908–1972)** Pastor of Abyssinian Baptist Church in New York, Powell served in the U. S. House of Representatives from 1944 to 1971.

**Pritchett, Laurie (1926–2000)** Police chief of Albany, Georgia, when SCLC conducted a desegregation campaign there during 1961–1962.

**Progress Plaza** Black-owned and -operated shopping center that opened in 1968 in Philadelphia under the leadership of Leon Sullivan.

**Raby, Al (1933–1988)** Teacher who battled school segregation and helped organize the Chicago Freedom Movement.

**Randolph, A. Philip (1889–1979)** Prior to the civil rights movement, Randolph advised some of the struggle's most important figures. He was the leader of the Brotherhood of Sleeping Car Porters, the first African American labor union, and was instrumental in convincing President Harry Truman to desegregate the armed forces and defense industries that contracted with the federal government. Alongside Bayard Rustin and Martin Luther King Jr., Randolph organized the 1963 March on Washington.

**Rauh, Joseph (1911–1992)** Civil rights attorney who counseled the LCCR and the MFDP.

**Reeb, James (1927–1965)** Minister who was beaten to death in Selma following a voting rights march.

**Revolutionary Action Movement (RAM)** Founded in 1962 by radical black college students in Ohio. Inspired by Robert F. Williams and Malcolm X, its members vowed to wage armed guerrilla warfare in U.S. cities.

**Richardson, Gloria (1922–)** Civil rights leader in Cambridge, Maryland.

**Robinson, Jo Ann Gibson (1912–)** Key figure in the Montgomery bus boycott and president of the Women's Political Council.

**Robinson, Ruby Doris (1942–1967)** Founding member of SNCC. In 1966, Robinson became the organization's only female executive secretary.

**Rush, Bobby (1946–)** Member of SNCC who later cofounded the Illinois BPP. Rush has been a member of the U.S. House of Representatives since 1993.

**Rustin, Bayard (1912–1987)** One of the most important behind-the-scenes figures in the civil rights movement, providing strategic advice and counsel to some of the movement's most important leaders, including Martin Luther King Jr. Rustin was one of the principal organizers of the March on Washington.

**Schwerner, Michael (1939–1964)** CORE field worker in Mississippi who was murdered by the KKK.

**Seale, Bobby (1936–)** Cofounded the BPP. In 1973, Seale unsuccessfully ran for election to be mayor of Oakland, California.

*Shelley v. Kraemer* 1948 Supreme Court case that found racially restrictive real estate covenants to be illegal.

**Sherrod, Charles (1937–)** Field secretary for SNCC who became an important figure in the Albany Movement.

**Shuttlesworth, Fred (1922–)** Pastor of Bethel Baptist Church in Birmingham and a founder of both the ACMHR and SCLC.

**sit-in movement** Began on February 1, 1960, when black students in Greensboro, North Carolina, sat down at a Woolworth's lunch counter and asked to be served. The demonstrations spread throughout the state and then the region, leading to a student conference in April that culminated in the founding of SNCC.

**Smitherman, Joseph (1929–2005)** Mayor of Selma, Alabama, from 1964 to 2000.

**Southern Christian Leadership Conference (SCLC)** Founded in 1957 by a group of ministers and headed by Martin Luther King Jr. SCLC was a nonviolent protest organization. During the 1960s, SCLC led a series of single-city desegregation campaigns: Albany, Georgia, in 1962; Birmingham, Alabama, in 1963; St. Augustine, Florida, in 1964; Selma, Alabama, in 1965; and Chicago in 1966. SCLC was also pivotal to the organization of the interracial Poor People's Campaign of 1968.

**Student Nonviolent Coordinating Committee (SNCC)** Created in 1960 to organize the student sit-in movement that had taken place during the early part of the year. SNCC played a key role in important civil rights campaigns including the Freedom Rides, the March on Washington, Freedom Summer, and the MFDP.

**Sullivan, Leon (1922–2001)** Pastor of Zion Baptist Church in Philadelphia who developed a series of business enterprises for African Americans.

*Sweatt v. Painter* 1950 case in which the Supreme Court required the University of Texas Law School to admit an African American student.

**Till, Emmett (1941–1955)** Lynched for allegedly flirting with a white woman in Mississippi. Till's murder, and the trial that exonerated his killers, sparked nationwide outrage.

**To Fulfill These Rights** Conference on civil rights called by President Lyndon Johnson in 1966.

**US Organization** Cultural nationalist organization founded by Maulana Karenga in 1965.

**Vivian, C. T. (1924–)** Member of SCLC and an important spokesperson for the civil rights movement.

**Voter Education Project (VEP)** Encouraged African Americans in the South to register to vote. It was organized by the Southern Regional Council.

**Voting Rights Act of 1965** Gave the federal government the right to register voters in areas where minority registration was underrepresented. It also gave the U.S. Department of Justice the power to oversee elections and to supervise changes in election law.

**Walker, Wyatt Tee (1929–)** Founding member of SCLC who served as the organization's executive director from 1960 to 1964.

**Wallace, George (1919–1998)** Segregationist governor of Alabama who opposed the civil rights movement.

**Watts race riot of 1965** One of the first urban uprisings of the 1960s. It lasted five days, during which time 34 people were killed.

**Weaver, Robert (1907–1997)** First African American to serve as a presidential cabinet member. Weaver was President Lyndon Johnson's secretary of housing and urban development from 1966 to 1968, overseeing many of the administration's antipoverty efforts. Prior to that, he had served as chair of the NAACP board of directors.

**Wilkins, Roy (1901–1981)** Executive director of the NAACP from 1955 to 1977. Prior to that, Wilkins had served from 1934 to 1949 as editor of the NAACP journal *Crisis*.

**Williams, Hosea (1926–2000)** Civil rights activist who sat on the SCLC board of directors.

**Williams, Robert (1925–1996)** President of the Monroe, North Carolina, branch of the NAACP, Williams urged African Americans to practice armed self-defense against violent oppression. He organized RAM in 1963.

**Women's Political Council (WPC)** Organization in Montgomery dedicated to increasing black participation in city life. It was a key driving force behind the MIA. Its president was Jo Ann Gibson Robinson.

**Young, Andrew (1932–)** SCLC member who became its executive director in 1964. Young later was elected to the U.S. House of Representatives, was mayor of Atlanta, and served as U.S. ambassador to the UN.

**Young, Whitney (1921–1971)** Executive director of the UL from 1960 until his death. Young revived the organization by expanding its involvement in the civil rights movement and increasing its budget through corporate donations and federal antipoverty monies.

**Younge, Sammy, Jr. (1944–1966)** A college student and SNCC organizer, Younge was killed for using a whites-only public bathroom in Alabama.

# Bibliography

Abernathy, Donzaleigh. *Partners to History: Martin Luther King Jr., Ralph David Abernathy, and the Civil Rights Movement.* New York: Crown, 2003.

Abernathy, Ralph David. *And the Walls Came Tumbling Down: An Autobiography.* New York: Harper and Row, 1989.

Abram, Morris. *The Day Is Short: An Autobiography.* New York: Harcourt Brace Jovanovich, 1982.

Abubadika, Mwlina Imiri (Sonny Carson). *The Education of Sonny Carson.* New York: W. W. Norton, 1972.

Abu-Jamal, Mumia. *We Want Freedom: A Life in the Black Panther Party.* Cambridge, MA: South End Press, 2004.

Adams, Frank, and Myles Horton. *Unearthing Seeds of Fire: The Idea of Highlander.* Winston-Salem, NC: John F. Blair, 1975.

Adickes, Sandra. *Legacy of a Freedom School.* New York: Palgrave Macmillan, 2005.

Ahmed, Muhammad. *We Will Return in the Whirlwind: Black Radical Organizations, 1965–1975.* Chicago: Charles H. Kerr, 2007.

Albert, Peter J., and Ronald Hoffman, eds. *We Shall Overcome: Martin Luther King, Jr. and the Black Freedom Struggle.* New York: Pantheon, 1990.

Alkebulan, Paul. *Survival Pending Revolution: The History of the Black Panther Party.* Tuscaloosa: University of Alabama Press, 2007.

Allen, Ivan, Jr., with Paul Hemphill. *Mayor: Notes on the Sixties.* New York: Simon and Schuster, 1971.

Allen, Robert L. *Black Awakening in Capitalist America: An Analytic History.* Garden City, NY: Doubleday, 1969.

Alvis, Joel L., Jr. *Religion and Race: Southern Presbyterians, 1946–1983.* Tuscaloosa: University of Alabama Press, 1994.

Anderson, Alan B., and George W. Pickering. *Confronting the Color Line: The Broken Promise of the Civil Rights Movement in Chicago.* Athens: University of Georgia Press, 1986.

Anderson, Carol. *Eyes Off the Prize: African Americans, the United Nations, and the Struggle for Human Rights, 1944–1955.* New York: Cambridge University Press, 2003.

Anderson, J. W. *Eisenhower, Brownell and the Congress: The Tangled Origins of the Civil Rights Bill of 1956–1957.* Tuscaloosa: University of Alabama Press, 1964.

Anderson, Jervis. *A. Philip Randolph: A Biographical Portrait.* New York: Harcourt Brace Jovanovich, 1973.

Anderson, Jervis. *Bayard Rustin: Troubles I've Seen, A Biography.* New York: HarperCollins, 1997.

Anderson, Martin. *The Federal Bulldozer: A Critical Analysis of Urban Renewal, 1949–1962.* Cambridge, MA: MIT Press, 1964.

Anderson, Terry H. *The Movement and the Sixties: Protest in America from Greensboro to Wounded Knee.* New York: Oxford University Press, 1995.

Andrew, John A., III. *The Other Side of the Sixties: Young Americans for Freedom and the Rise of Conservative Politics.* New Brunswick, NJ: Rutgers University Press, 1997.

Andrews, Kenneth T. *Freedom Is a Constant Struggle: The Mississippi Civil Rights Movement and Its Legacy.* Chicago: University of Chicago Press, 2004.

Andrews, Lori B. *Black Power, White Blood: The Life and Times of Johnny Spain.* New York: Pantheon, 1996.

Ansbro, John. *Martin Luther King, Jr.: The Making of a Mind.* Maryknoll, NY: Orbis, 1982.

Anthony, Earl. *Picking Up the Gun: A Report on the Black Panthers.* New York: Dial Press, 1970.

Anthony, Earl. *Spitting in the Wind: The True Story behind the Violent Legacy of the Black Panther Party.* Malibu, CA: Roundtable, 1990.

Appiah, Kwame Anthony, and Henry Louis Gates Jr. *Africana: Civil Rights; An A-to-Z Reference of the Movement that Changed America.* Philadelphia: Running Press, 2005.

Aptheker, Bettina. *The Morning Breaks: The Trial of Angela Davis.* Ithaca, NY: Cornell University Press, 1997.

Armstrong, Gregory. *The Dragon Has Come Home.* New York: Harper and Row, 1974.

Armstrong, Julie Buckner, ed. *Teaching the American Civil Rights Movement: Freedom's Bittersweet Song.* New York: Routledge, 2002.

Arnesen, Eric, ed. *The Black Worker: Race, Labor, and Civil Rights since Emancipation.* Urbana: University of Illinois Press, 2007.

Arnesen, Eric, and David Howard-Pitney. *Black Protest and the Great Migration: Martin Luther King, Jr., Malcolm X, and the Civil Rights Struggle of the 1950s.* New York: Bedford/St. Martin's, 2006.

Arsenault, Raymond. *Freedom Riders: 1961 and the Struggle for Racial Justice.* New York: Oxford University Press, 2006.

Asch, Chris Myers. *The Senator and the Sharecropper: The Freedom Struggles of James O. Eastland and Fannie Lou Hamer.* New York: New Press, 2008.

Ashmore, Harry. *An Epitaph for Dixie.* New York: Norton, 1958.

Ashmore, Harry. *The Negro and the Schools.* Chapel Hill: University of North Carolina Press, 1954.

Ashmore, Susan Youngblood. *Carry It On: The War on Poverty and the Civil Rights Movement in Alabama, 1964–1972.* Athens: University of Georgia Press, 2008.

Austin, Curtis J. *Up against the Wall: Violence in the Making and Unmaking of the Black Panther Party.* Fayetteville: University of Arkansas Press, 2006.

Baldwin, James. *The Fire Next Time.* New York: Dial Press, 1963.

Baldwin, Lewis V. *There Is a Balm in Gilead: The Cultural Roots of Martin Luther King, Jr.* Minneapolis: Fortress Press, 1991.

Baldwin, Lewis V. *To Make the Wounded Whole: The Cultural Legacy of Martin Luther King, Jr.* Minneapolis: Fortress Press, 1992.

Baldwin, Lewis V., and Aprille V. Woodson. *Freedom Is Never Free: A Biographical Portrait of Edgar Daniel Nixon.* Atlanta: A. Woodson, 1992.

Ball, Howard. *The Bakke Case: Race, Education, and Affirmative Action.* Lawrence: University Press of Kansas, 2000.

Ball, Howard. *Justice in Mississippi: The Murder Trial of Edgar Ray Killen.* Lawrence: University Press of Kansas, 2006.

Ball, Howard. *Murder in Mississippi:* United States v. Price *and the Struggle for Civil Rights.* Lawrence: University Press of Kansas, 2004.

Ball, Howard, Dale Krane, and Thomas P. Laut. *Compromised Compliance: Implementation of the 1965 Voting Rights Act.* Westport, CT: Greenwood Press, 1982.

Baraka, Amiri. *African Congress: A Documentary of the First Modern Pan-African Conference.* New York: William Morrow, 1972.

Baraka, Amiri. *The Autobiography of Leroi Jones.* New York: Freundlich, 1984.

Barber, David. *A Hard Rain Fell: SDS and Why It Failed.* Jackson: University Press of Mississippi, 2008.

Barber, Lucy. *Marching on Washington: The Forging of an American Political Tradition.* Berkeley: University of California Press, 2002.

Barbour, Floyd, ed. *The Black Power Revolt: A Collection of Essays.* Boston: P. Sargent, 1968.

Barbour, Floyd, ed. *The Black Seventies*. Boston: P. Sargent, 1970.

Bardolph, Richard A., ed. *The Civil Rights Record: Black Americans and the Law, 1849–1970*. New York: Crowell, 1970.

Barlow, William, and Peter Shapiro. *An End to Silence: The San Francisco State College Student Movement in the '60s*. New York: Pegasus, 1971.

Barnes, Catherine A. *Journey from Jim Crow: The Desegregation of Southern Transit*. New York: Columbia University Press, 1983.

Barrett, Russell H. *Integration at Ole Miss*. Chicago: Quadrangle, 1965.

Bartley, Numan V. *The Rise of Massive Resistance: Race and Politics in the South during the 1950s*. Baton Rouge: Louisiana State University Press, 1969.

Bartley, Numan V., and Hugh D. Graham. *Southern Politics and the Second Reconstruction*. Baltimore: Johns Hopkins University Press, 1975.

Baruch, Ruth-Marion, and Pirkle Jones. *The Vanguard: A Photographic Essay on the Black Panthers*. Boston: Beacon Press, 1970.

Bass, Jack. *Taming the Storm: The Life and Times of Judge Frank M. Johnson, Jr., and the South's Fight over Civil Rights*. Garden City, NY: Doubleday, 1993.

Bass, Jack. *Unlikely Heroes*. Tuscaloosa: University of Alabama Press, 1990.

Bass, Jack, and Jack Nelson. *The Orangeburg Massacre*. Macon, GA: Mercer University Press, 2004.

Bass, Patrik Henry. *Like a Mighty Stream: The March on Washington, August 28, 1963*. Philadelphia: Running Press, 2002.

Bass, Paul, and Douglas W. Rae. *Murder in the Model City: The Black Panthers, Yale, and the Redemption of a Killer*. New York: Basic, 2006.

Bass, S. Jonathan. *Blessed Are the Peacemakers: Martin Luther King Jr., Eight White Religious Leaders, and the "Letter from Birmingham Jail."* Baton Rouge: Louisiana State University Press, 2001.

Bates, Daisy. *The Long Shadow of Little Rock: A Memoir*. New York: David McKay, 1962.

Bauman, Mark K., and Berkley Kalin, eds. *The Quiet Voices: Southern Rabbis and Black Civil Rights, 1880s to 1990s*. Tuscaloosa: University of Alabama Press, 1997.

Bayor, Ronald H. *Race and the Shaping of Twentieth-Century Atlanta*. Chapel Hill: University of North Carolina Press, 1996.

Beals, Melba Pattillo. *Warriors Don't Cry: A Searing Memoir of the Battle to Integrate Little Rock's Central High*. New York: Pocket, 1994.

Becker, Natalie, and Marjorie Myhill. *Power and Participation in the San Francisco Community Action Program, 1964–1967*. Berkeley, CA: Institute of Urban and Regional Development, 1967.

Beifuss, Joan Turner. *At the River I Stand: Memphis, the 1968 Strike, and Martin Luther King.* Memphis: B&W, 1985.

Belfrage, Sally. *Freedom Summer.* New York: Viking Press, 1965.

Belknap, Michal R., ed. *Civil Rights, the White House, and the Justice Department, 1945–1968.* New York: Garland, 1991.

Belknap, Michal R. *Federal Law and Southern Order: Racial Violence and Constitutional Conflict in the Post-*Brown *South.* Athens: University of Georgia Press, 1987.

Bell, Derrick. *Silent Covenants:* Brown v. Board of Education *and the Unfulfilled Hopes for Racial Reform.* New York: Oxford University Press, 2004.

Bell, Inge Powell. *CORE and the Strategy of Nonviolence.* New York: Random House, 1968.

Bennett, Lerone, Jr. *Confrontation: Black and White.* Chicago: Johnson, 1965.

Bennett, Lerone, Jr. *The Negro Mood, and Other Essays.* Chicago: Johnson, 1964.

Bennett, Lerone, Jr. *What Manner of Man: A Biography of Martin Luther King, Jr.* Chicago: Johnson, 1968.

Berg, Manfred. *The Ticket to Freedom: The NAACP and the Struggle for Black Political Integration.* Gainesville: University Press of Florida, 2005.

Berman, Daniel M. *A Bill Becomes a Law: The Civil Rights Act of 1960.* New York: Macmillan, 1962.

Berman, Daniel M. *It Is So Ordered: The Supreme Court Rules on School Segregation.* New York: Norton, 1966.

Berman, William C. *The Politics of Civil Rights in the Truman Administration.* Columbus: Ohio State University Press, 1970.

Bernstein, Barton J., and Allen Matusow, eds. *Twentieth Century America: Recent Interpretations.* New York: Harcourt, Brace and World, 1969.

Berry, Brian J. L. *The Open Housing Question: Race and Housing in Chicago, 1966–1976.* Cambridge, MA: Ballinger, 1979.

Berson, Lenora. *Case Study of a Riot: The Philadelphia Story.* New York: Institute of Human Relations Press, 1966.

Biondi, Martha. *To Stand and Fight: The Struggle for Civil Rights in Postwar New York City.* Cambridge, MA: Harvard University Press, 2003.

Black, Earl. *Southern Governors and Civil Rights: Racial Segregation as a Campaign Issue in the Second Reconstruction.* Cambridge, MA: Harvard University Press, 1976.

Blackstock, Nelson. *COINTELPRO: The FBI's Secret War on Political Freedom.* New York: Vintage, 1975.

Blair, Thomas L. *Retreat to the Ghetto: The End of a Dream?* New York: Hill and Wang, 1977.

Blake, John. *Children of the Movement.* Chicago: Lawrence Hill, 2004.

Bland, Randall W. *Private Pressure on Public Law: The Legal Career of Justice Thurgood Marshall.* Port Washington, NY: Kennikat Press, 1973.

Blaustein, Albert P., and Clarence Clyde Ferguson Jr. *Desegregation and the Law: The Meaning and Effect of the School Segregation Cases.* New Brunswick, NJ: Rutgers University Press, 1957.

Blaustein, Albert P., and Richard Zangrando, eds. *Civil Rights and the American Negro: A Documentary History.* New York: Washington Square Press, 1968.

Bloom, Jack M. *Class, Race, and the Civil Rights Movement: The Political Economy of Southern Racism.* Bloomington: Indiana University Press, 1987.

Blossom, Virgil T. *It Has Happened Here.* New York: Harper and Brothers, 1959.

Blumberg, Rhoda. *Civil Rights: The 1960s Freedom Struggle.* Boston: Twayne, 1984.

Boesak, Allan A. *Farewell to Innocence: A Socio-Ethical Study on Black Theology and Black Power.* Maryknoll, NY: Orbis, 1977.

Boesal, David, and Peter H. Rossi, eds. *Cities under Siege: An Anatomy of the Ghetto Riots, 1964–1968.* New York: Basic, 1971.

Boggs, Grace Lee. *Living for Change: An Autobiography.* Minneapolis: University of Minnesota Press, 1998.

Boggs, James. *Racism and the Class Struggle: Further Pages from a Worker's Notebook.* New York: Monthly Review Press, 1970.

Bolton, Charles C. *The Hardest Deal of All: The Battle over School Integration in Mississippi, 1870–1980.* Jackson: University Press of Mississippi, 2005.

Bond, Julian. *A Time to Speak, A Time to Act: The Movement in Politics.* New York: Simon and Schuster, 1972.

Borstelmann, Thomas. *The Cold War and the Color Line: American Race Relations in the Global Arena.* Cambridge, MA: Harvard University Press, 2002.

Boyle, Kay. *The Long Walk at San Francisco State, and Other Essays.* New York: Grove Press, 1970.

Boyle, Kevin. *Arc of Justice: A Saga of Race, Civil Rights, and Murder in the Jazz Age.* New York: Henry Holt, 2004.

Boyle, Sarah Patton. *The Desegregated Heart: A Virginian's Stand in Time of Transition.* New York: William Morrow, 1962.

Bracey, John H., Jr., with August Meier and Elliott Rudwick, eds. *Conflict and Competition: Studies in the Recent Black Protest Movement.* Belmont, CA: Wadsworth, 1971.

Braden, Anne. *The Wall Between*, 2nd ed. Knoxville: University of Tennessee Press, 1999.

Branch, Taylor. *At Canaan's Edge: America in the King Years, 1965–68*. New York: Simon and Schuster, 2006.

Branch, Taylor. *Parting the Waters: America in the King Years, 1954–63*. New York: Simon and Schuster, 1988.

Branch, Taylor. *Pillar of Fire: America in the King Years, 1963–65*. New York: Simon and Schuster, 1998.

Brauer, Carl. *John F. Kennedy and the Second Revolution*. New York: Columbia University Press, 1977.

Breines, Wini. *Community and Organization in the New Left, 1962–1968: The Great Refusal*. New York: Praeger, 1982.

Breitman, George. *The Assassination of Malcolm X*. New York: Pathfinder Press, 1988.

Breitman, George. *The Last Year of Malcolm X: The Evolution of a Revolutionary*. New York: Merit, 1967.

Brent, William Lee. *Long Time Gone: A Black Panther's True-Life Story of His Hijacking and Twenty-Five Years in Cuba*. New York: Crown, 1996.

Brink, William, and Louis Harris. *Black and White: A Study of U.S. Racial Attitudes Today*. New York: Simon and Schuster, 1967.

Brink, William, and Louis Harris. *The Negro Revolution in America*. New York: Simon and Schuster, 1964.

Brinkley, Douglas. *Rosa Parks*. New York: Penguin, 2000.

Brisbane, Robert H. *Black Activism: Racial Revolution in the United States, 1954–1970*. Valley Forge, PA: Judson Press, 1974.

Brooks, Thomas. *Walls Come Tumbling Down: A History of the Civil Rights Movement, 1940–1970*. Englewood Cliffs, NJ: Prentice Hall, 1974.

Brown, Bernard. *Ideology and Community Action: The West Side Organization of Chicago, 1964–1967*. Chicago: Center for the Scientific Study of Religion, 1978.

Brown, Cynthia S., ed. *Ready from Within: Septima Clark and the Civil Rights Movement*. Trenton, NJ: Africa World Press, 1990.

Brown, Elaine. *A Taste of Power: A Black Woman's Story*. New York: Pantheon, 1992.

Brown, H. Rap. *Die, Nigger, Die! A Political Autobiography of Jamil Abdullah al-Amin*. New York: Dial Press, 1969.

Brown, Scot. *Fighting for US: Maulana Karenga, the US Organization, and Black Cultural Nationalism*. New York: New York University Press, 2003.

Bruner, Richard. *Whitney M. Young, Jr.: The Story of a Pragmatic Humanist*. New York: D. McKay, 1972.

Bryant, Nick. *The Bystander: John F. Kennedy and the Struggle for Black Equality.* New York: Basic, 2006.

Burghardt, Steven. *Tenants and the Urban Housing Crisis.* Dexter, MI: New Press, 1972.

Burk, Robert F. *The Eisenhower Administration and Black Civil Rights.* Knoxville: University of Tennessee Press, 1984.

Burner, David. *Making Peace with the 60s.* Princeton, NJ: Princeton University Press, 1996.

Burner, Eric R. *And Gently He Shall Lead Them: Robert Parris Moses and Civil Rights in Mississippi.* New York: New York University Press, 1994.

Burns, Stewart, ed. *Daybreak of Freedom: The Montgomery Bus Boycott.* Chapel Hill: University of North Carolina Press, 1997.

Burns, Stewart. *Social Movements of the 1960s: Searching for Democracy.* Boston: Twayne, 1990.

Burns, Stewart. *To the Mountaintop: Martin Luther King Jr.'s Sacred Mission to Save America, 1955–1968.* San Francisco: HarperSanFrancisco, 2004.

Burns, W. Heywood. *The Voices of Negro Protest in America.* New York: Oxford University Press, 1963.

Bush, Rod. *We Are Not What We Seem: Black Nationalism and Class Struggle in the American Century.* New York: New York University Press, 1999.

Button, James. *Black Violence: Political Impact of the 1960s Race Riots.* Princeton, NJ: Princeton University Press, 1978.

Button, James. *Blacks and Social Change: Impact of the Civil Rights Movement in Southern Communities.* Princeton, NJ: Princeton University Press, 1989.

Cagin, Seth, and Philip Dray. *We Are Not Afraid: The Story of Goodman, Schwerner, and Chaney and the Civil Rights Campaign for Mississippi.* New York: Macmillan, 1988.

Callahan, Nancy. *The Freedom Quilting Bee: Folk Art and the Civil Rights Movement in Alabama.* Tuscaloosa: University of Alabama Press, 2005.

Campbell, Angus. *White Attitudes toward Black People.* Ann Arbor, MI: Institute for Social Research, 1971.

Campbell, Clarice. *Civil Rights Chronicle: Letters from the South.* Jackson: University Press of Mississippi, 1997.

Campbell, Will. *A Life Is More Than a Moment: The Desegregation of Little Rock's Central High.* Bloomington: Indiana University Press, 2007.

Caplan, Marvin. *Farther Along: A Civil Rights Memoir.* Baton Rouge: Louisiana State University Press, 1999.

Carbado, Devon W., and Donald Wiese. *Time on Two Crosses: The Collected Writings of Bayard Rustin.* San Francisco: Cleis Press, 2003.

Carew, Jan. *Ghosts in Our Blood: With Malcolm X in Africa, England, and the Caribbean*. Chicago: Lawrence Hill, 1994.

Carmichael, Stokely. *Stokely Speaks: Black Power Back to Pan-Africanism*. New York: Random House, 1971.

Carmichael, Stokely, and Charles V. Hamilton. *Black Power: The Politics of Liberation in America*. New York: Random House, 1967.

Carmichael, Stokely, and Ekwueme M. Thelwell. *Ready for Revolution: The Life and Struggles of Stokely Carmichael (Kwame Ture)*. New York: Scribner, 2003.

Carrier, Jim. *A Traveler's Guide to the Civil Rights Movement*. Orlando, FL: Harcourt, 2004.

Carson, Clayborne, ed. *The Autobiography of Martin Luther King, Jr.* New York: Warner, 1998.

Carson, Clayborne. *In Struggle: SNCC and the Black Awakening of the 1960s*. Cambridge, MA: Harvard University Press, 1981.

Carson, Clayborne. *Malcolm X: The FBI File*. New York: Carroll and Graf, 1991.

Carson, Clayborne, ed. *Reporting Civil Rights, Part Two: American Journalism, 1963–1973*. New York: Library of America, 2003.

Carson, Clayborne, et al., eds. *The Papers of Martin Luther King, Jr.,* multiple vols. Berkeley: University of California Press, 1992–2007.

Carson, Clayborne, David J. Garrow, Bill Kovach, and Carol Polsgrove, eds. *Reporting Civil Rights, Part One: American Journalism, 1941–1963*. New York: Library of America, 2003.

Carter, Dan T. *The Politics of Rage: George Wallace, the Origins of the New Conservatism, and the Transformation of American Politics*. New York: Simon and Schuster, 1995.

Carter, Robert L. *A Matter of Law: A Memoir of Struggle in the Cause of Equal Rights*. New York: New Press, 2004.

Catsam, Derek Charles. *Freedom's Main Line: The Journey of Reconciliation and the Freedom Rides*. Lexington: University Press of Kentucky, 2008.

Caute, David. *The Year of the Barricades: A Journey through 1968*. New York: Harper and Row, 1988.

Cecelski, David. *Along Freedom Road: Hyde County, North Carolina, and the Fate of Black Schools in the South*. Chapel Hill: University of North Carolina Press, 1994.

Chafe, William H. *Civilities and Civil Rights: Greensboro, North Carolina, and the Black Struggle for Freedom*. New York: Oxford University Press, 1980.

Chafe, William H. *Never Stop Running: Allard Lowenstein and the Struggle to Save American Liberalism*. New York: Basic, 1993.

Cha-Jua, Sundiata Keita, and Clarence Lang. "The 'Long Movement' as Vampire: Temporal and Spatial Fallacies in Recent Black Freedom Studies." *Journal of African American History* 92 (2007): 265–288.

Chalfen, Michael. "'The Way Out May Lead In': The Albany Movement beyond Martin Luther King, Jr." *Georgia Historical Quarterly* 89 (1995): 560–598.

Chalmers, David. *Backfire: How the Ku Klux Klan Helped the Civil Rights Movement*. Lanham, MD: Rowman and Littlefield, 2003.

Chancey, Andrew S. "'A Demonstration Plot for the Kingdom of God': The Establishment and Early Years of Koinonia Farm." *Georgia Historical Quarterly* 75 (1991): 321–353.

Chappell, David L. *Inside Agitators: White Southerners in the Civil Rights Movement*. Baltimore: Johns Hopkins University Press, 1994.

Chappell, David L. *A Stone of Hope: Prophetic Religion and the Death of Jim Crow*. Chapel Hill: University of North Carolina Press, 2004.

Chestnut, J. L., Jr., and Julia Cass. *Black in Selma: The Uncommon Life of J.L. Chestnut, Jr.* New York: Farrar, Straus and Giroux, 1990.

Chevigny, Paul. *Cops and Rebels: A Study of Provocation*. New York: Pantheon, 1972.

Churchill, Ward, and Jim Vander Wall. *Agents of Repression: The FBI's Secret Wars against the Black Panther Party and the American Indian Movement*. Boston: South End Press, 1988.

Churchill, Ward, and Jim Vander Wall. *The COINTELPRO Papers: Documents from the FBI's Secret Wars against Domestic Dissent*. Boston: South End Press, 1990.

Clar, D., David J. Garrow, Gerald Gill, Vincent Harding, Clayborne Carson, eds. *The Eyes on the Prize Civil Rights Reader: Documents, Speeches, and Firsthand Accounts from the Black Freedom Struggle, 1954–1990*. New York: Penguin, 1991.

Clark, E. Culpepper. *The Schoolhouse Door: Segregation's Last Stand at the University of Alabama*. Tuscaloosa: University of Alabama Press, 1993.

Clark, James G. *The Jim Clark Story: I Saw Selma Raped*. Birmingham: Sizemore, 1966.

Clark, Kenneth. *The Negro Protest: James Baldwin, Malcolm X, and Martin Luther King Talk with Kenneth B. Clark*. Boston: Beacon Press, 1963.

Clark, Roy Peter, and Raymond Arsenault, eds. *The Changing South of Gene Patterson: Journalism and Civil Rights, 1960–1968*. Gainesville: University Press of Florida, 2002.

Clark, Septima Poinsette, and LeGette Blythe. *Echo in My Soul*. New York: Dutton, 1962.

Clark, Septima Poinsette, and Cynthia Stokes Brown, eds. *Ready from Within: Septima Clark and the Civil Rights Movement*. Navarro, CA: Wild Trees Press, 1986.

Clarke, John Henrik, ed. *Malcolm X: The Man and His Times*. New York: Macmillan, 1969.

Classen, Steven D. *Watching Jim Crow: The Struggles over Mississippi TV, 1955–1969*. Durham, NC: Duke University Press, 2004.

Cleage, Albert B. *Black Christian Nationalism: New Directions for the Black Church*. New York: William Morrow, 1972.

Cleaver, Eldridge. *Soul on Ice*. New York: McGraw-Hill, 1967.

Cleaver, Eldridge. *Target Zero: A Life in Writing*. New York: Palgrave Macmillan, 2007.

Cleaver, Eldridge, and Robert Scheer, eds. *Eldridge Cleaver: Post-Prison Writings and Speeches*. New York: Random House, 1969.

Cleaver, Kathleen, and George Katsiaficas, eds. *Liberation, Imagination, and the Black Panther Party: A New Look at the Panthers and Their Legacy*. New York: Routledge, 2001.

Clegg, Claude Andrew, III. *An Original Man: The Life and Times of Elijah Muhammad*. New York: St. Martin's Press, 1997.

Cluster, Dick, ed. *They Should Have Served That Cup of Coffee*. Boston: South End Press, 1979.

Cobb, Charles E., Jr. *On the Road to Freedom: A Guided Tour of the Civil Rights Trail*. Chapel Hill, NC: Algonquin, 2007.

Cobb, James C. *The* Brown *Decision, Jim Crow, and Southern Identity*. Athens: University of Georgia Press, 2005.

Cobbs, Elizabeth, and Petric Smith. *Long Time Coming: An Insider's Story of the Birmingham Church Bombing that Rocked the World*. Birmingham, AL: Crane Hill, 1994.

Cohen, Robert Carl. *Black Crusader: Robert Franklin Williams*. New York: Lyle Stuart, 1972.

Colburn, David. *Racial Change and Community Crisis: St. Augustine, Florida, 1877–1980*. New York: Columbia University Press, 1985.

Collier-Thomas, Bettye, and V. P. Franklin. *My Soul Is a Witness: A Chronology of the Civil Rights Era, 1954–1965*. New York: Henry Holt, 1999.

Collier-Thomas, Bettye, and V. P. Franklin, eds. *Sisters in the Struggle: African-American Women in the Civil Rights–Black Power Movement*. New York: New York University Press, 2001.

Collins, Donald. *When the Church Bell Rang Racist: The Methodist Church and the Civil Rights Movement in Alabama*. Macon, GA: Mercer University Press, 1998.

Collins, Lisa Gail, and Margo Crawford. *New Thoughts on the Black Arts Movement*. New Brunswick, NJ: Rutgers University Press, 2006.

Cone, James H. *Black Theology and Black Power*. New York: Seabury Press, 1969.

Cone, James H. *Martin & Malcolm & America: A Dream or a Nightmare*. Maryknoll, NY: Orbis, 1991.

Connery, Robert H., ed. *Urban Riots: Violence and Social Change*. New York: Columbia University Press, 1968.

Conot, Robert E. *Rivers of Blood, Years of Darkness*. New York: Bantam, 1967.

Cook, Robert. *Sweet Land of Liberty? The African-American Struggle for Civil Rights in the Twentieth Century*. New York: Longman, 1998.

Cottrol, Robert J., Raymond T. Diamond, and Leland B. Ware. Brown v. Board of Education: *Caste, Culture, and the Constitution*. Lawrence: University Press of Kansas, 2003.

Countryman, Matthew J. *Up South: Civil Rights and Black Power in Philadelphia*. Philadelphia: University of Pennsylvania Press, 2006.

Counts, Will. *A Life Is Worth More Than a Moment: The Desegregation of Little Rock's Central High*. Bloomington: Indiana University Press, 1999.

Cousens, Frances R. *Public Civil Rights Agencies and Fair Employment: Promise vs. Performance*. New York: Praeger, 1969.

Couto, Richard A. *Ain't Gonna Let Nobody Turn Me Round: The Pursuit of Racial Justice in the Rural South*. Philadelphia: Temple University Press, 1991.

Cox, Julian. *Road to Freedom: Photographs of the Civil Rights Movement, 1956–1968*. Atlanta: High Museum of Art, 2008.

Crawford, Vicki, Jacqueline Anne Rouse, and Barbara Woods, eds. *Women in the Civil Rights Movement: Trailblazers and Torchbearers, 1941–1965*. Brooklyn: Carlson, 1990.

Crespino, Joseph. *In Search of Another Country: Mississippi and the Conservative Counterrevolution*. Princeton, NJ: Princeton University Press, 2007.

Crosby, Emilye. *A Little Taste of Freedom: The Black Freedom Struggle in Claiborne County, Mississippi*. Chapel Hill: University of North Carolina Press, 2005.

Cross, Theodore. *The Black Power Imperative: Racial Inequality and the Politics of Nonviolence*. New York: Faulkner, 1984.

Crowe, Daniel. *Prophets of Rage: The Black Freedom Struggle in San Francisco, 1945–1969*. New York: Garland, 2000.

Cruse, Harold. *The Crisis of the Negro Intellectual*. New York: William Morrow, 1967.

Cruse, Harold. *Rebellion or Revolution?* New York: Morrow, 1968.

Cummins, Eric. *The Rise and Fall of California's Radical Prison Movement*. Palo Alto, CA: Stanford University Press, 1994.

Curry, Constance. *Silver Rights*. Chapel Hill, NC: Algonquin, 1995.

Curry, Constance, et al. *Deep in Our Hearts: Nine White Women in the Freedom Movement*. Athens: University of Georgia Press, 2000.

Curtis, Edward E., IV. *Black Muslim Religion in the Nation of Islam, 1960–1975.* Chapel Hill: University of North Carolina Press, 2006.

Dailey, Jane, Glenda Gilmore, and Bryant Simon, eds. *Jumpin' Jim Crow: Southern Politics from Civil War to Civil Rights.* Princeton, NJ: Princeton University Press, 2000.

Dalfiume, Richard M. *Desegregation of the U.S. Armed Forces: Fighting on Two Fronts, 1939–1953.* Columbia: University of Missouri Press, 1969.

Dalfiume, Richard M. "The 'Forgotten Years' of the Negro Revolution." *Journal of American History* 55 (1968): 90–106.

D'Angelo, Raymond. *The American Civil Rights Movement: Readings and Interpretations.* Guilford, CT: McGraw-Hill, 2001.

Daugherity, Brian J., and Charles C. Bolton. *With All Deliberate Speed: Implementing* Brown v. Board of Education. Fayetteville: University of Arkansas Press, 2008.

Davey, Elizabeth, and Rodney Clark, eds. *Remember My Sacrifice: The Autobiography of Clinton Clark, Tenant Farm Organizer and Early Civil Rights Activist.* Baton Rouge: Louisiana State University Press, 2007.

Davidson, Chandler, and Bernard Grofman, eds. *Quiet Revolution in the South: The Impact of the Voting Rights Act, 1965–1990.* Princeton, NJ: Princeton University Press, 1994.

Davies, David R., ed. *The Press and Race: Mississippi Journalists Confront the Movement.* Jackson: University Press of Mississippi, 2001.

Davies, Garieth. *From Opportunity to Entitlement: The Transformation and Decline of Great Society Liberalism.* Lawrence: University Press of Kansas, 1996.

Davis, Allison. *Leadership, Love, and Aggression.* New York: Harcourt Brace Jovanovich, 1983.

Davis, Angela. *Angela Davis: An Autobiography.* New York: Random House, 1974.

Davis, Jack, ed. *The Civil Rights Movement.* Malden, MA: Blackwell, 2001.

Davis, Jack. *Race against Time: Culture and Separation in Natchez since 1930.* Baton Rouge: Louisiana State University Press, 2001.

Davis, Townsend. *Weary Feet, Rested Souls: A Guided History of the Civil Rights Movement.* New York: W. W. Norton, 1998.

Dawson, Michael C. *Black Visions: The Roots of Contemporary African-American Political Ideologies.* Chicago: University of Chicago Press, 2001.

De Caro, Louis A., Jr. *Malcolm and the Cross: The Nation of Islam, Malcolm X and Christianity.* New York: New York University Press, 1998.

De Jong, Greta. *A Different Day: African American Struggles for Justice in Rural Louisiana, 1900–1970.* Chapel Hill: University of North Carolina Press, 2002.

Demerath, Nicholas J., Gerald Marwell, and Michael Aiken. *Dynamics of Idealism: White Activists in a Black Movement*. San Francisco: Jossey-Bass, 1971.

D'Emilio, John. *Lost Prophet: The Life and Times of Bayard Rustin*. New York: Free Press, 2003.

Dent, Thomas C. *Southern Journey: A Return to the Civil Rights Movement*. New York: William Morrow, 1997.

Dickerson, Dennis C. *Militant Mediator: Whitney M. Young, Jr.* Lexington: University Press of Kentucky, 1998.

Dickerson, James. *Dixie's Dirty Secret: The True Story of How the Government, the Media, and the Mob Conspired to Combat Integration and the Vietnam Antiwar Movement*. Armonk, NY: M. E. Sharpe, 1998.

Dierenfield, Bruce J. *The Civil Rights Movement*. Harlow, UK: Pearson, 2004.

Dierenfield, Bruce J. *Keeper of the Rules: Congressman Howard W. Smith of Virginia*. Charlottesville: University Press of Virginia, 1987.

Dillard, Angela. *Faith in the City: Preaching Radical Social Change: An Autobiography*. Ann Arbor: University of Michigan Press, 2007.

Dittmer, John. *Local People: The Struggle for Civil Rights in Mississippi*. Urbana: University of Illinois Press, 1994.

Dorman, Michael. *We Shall Overcome: A Reporter's Eyewitness Account of the Year of Racial Strife and Triumph*. New York: Dell, 1964.

Dougherty, Jack. *More Than One Struggle: The Evolution of Black School Reform in Milwaukee*. Chapel Hill: University of North Carolina Press, 2004.

Douglas, Davison M. *Reading, Writing, and Race: The Desegregation of the Charlotte Schools*. Chapel Hill: University of North Carolina Press, 1995.

Doyle, William. *An American Insurrection: The Battle of Oxford, Mississippi, 1962*. Garden City, NY: Doubleday, 2001.

Draper, Alan. *Conflict of Interests: Organized Labor and the Civil Rights Movement in the South, 1954–1968*. Ithaca, NY: ILR Press, 1994.

Draper, Theodore. *The Rediscovery of Black Nationalism*. New York: Viking Press, 1970.

Dudziak, Mary L. *Cold War Civil Rights: Race and the Image of American Democracy*. Princeton, NJ: Princeton University Press, 2000.

Dudziak, Mary L. "Desegregation as a Cold War Imperative." *Stanford Law Review* 41 (1988): 61–120.

Due, Tananarive, and Patricia Stephens Due. *Freedom in the Family: A Mother-Daughter Memoir of the Fight for Civil Rights*. New York: Ballantine, 2003.

Dulany, Marvin, and Kathleen Underwood, eds. *Essays on the American Civil Rights Movement*. College Station: Texas A&M University Press, 1993.

Dulles, Foster Rhea. *The Civil Rights Commission, 1957–1965.* East Lansing: Michigan State University Press, 1968.

Duram, James. *A Moderate among Extremists: Dwight D. Eisenhower and the School Desegregation Crisis.* Chicago: Nelson-Hall, 1981.

Durden-Smith, Jo. *Who Killed George Jackson?* New York: Knopf, 1976.

Durham, Michael S. *Powerful Days: The Civil Rights Photography of Charles Moore.* Tuscaloosa: University of Alabama Press, 2005.

Durr, Virginia Foster. *Outside the Magic Circle: The Autobiography of Virginia Foster Durr.* Tuscaloosa: University of Alabama Press, 1985.

Dwyer, Owen J., and Derek H. Alderman. *Civil Rights Memorials and the Geography of Memory.* Athens: University of Georgia Press, 2008.

Dyson, Michael Eric. *April 4, 1968: Martin Luther King Jr.'s Death and the Transformation of America.* New York: Basic Civitas, 2008.

Dyson, Michael Eric. *I May Not Get There With You: The True Martin Luther King, Jr.* New York: Free Press, 2000.

Dyson, Michael Eric. *Making Malcolm: The Myth and Meaning of Malcolm X.* New York: Oxford University Press, 1995.

Eagles, Charles, ed. *The Civil Rights Movement in America: Essays.* Jackson: University Press of Mississippi, 1986.

Eagles, Charles. *Jonathan Daniels and Race Relations: The Evolution of a Southern Liberal.* Knoxville: University of Tennessee Press, 1982.

Eagles, Charles. *Outside Agitator: Jon Daniels and the Civil Rights Movement in Alabama.* Chapel Hill: University of North Carolina Press, 1993.

Eagles, Charles. "Toward New Histories of the Civil Rights Era." *Journal of Southern History* 66 (2000): 815–848.

Edelman, Marion Wright. *Lanterns: A Memoir of Mentors.* Boston: Beacon Press, 1999.

Edwards, Harry. *The Revolt of the Black Athlete.* New York: Macmillan, 1969.

Edwards, Harry. *The Struggle that Must Be: An Autobiography.* New York: Macmillan, 1980.

Edwards, Thomas Bentley, and Frederick Wirt, eds. *School Desegregation in the North: The Challenge and the Experience.* San Francisco: Chandler, 1967.

Egerton, John. *Speak Now against the Day: The Generation before the Civil Rights Movement in the South.* New York: Knopf, 1994.

Ehle, John. *The Free Men.* New York: Harper and Row, 1965.

Eick, Gretchen Cassel. *Dissent in Wichita: The Civil Rights Movement in the Midwest, 1954–72.* Urbana: University of Illinois Press, 2001.

Eley, Lynn W., and Thomas W. Casstevens. *The Politics of Fair Housing Legislation: State and Local Case Studies*. San Francisco: Chandler, 1968.

Ely, James W., Jr. *The Crisis of Conservative Virginia: The Byrd Organization and the Politics of Massive Resistance*. Knoxville: University of Tennessee Press, 1976.

Epps, Archie, ed. *The Speeches of Malcolm X: Malcolm X and the American Negro Revolution*. London: P. Owen, 1996.

Erenrich, Susie, ed. *Freedom Is a Constant Struggle: An Anthology of the Mississippi Civil Rights Movement*. Montgomery, AL: Black Belt Press, 1999.

Eskew, Glenn T. *But for Birmingham: The Local and National Movements in the Civil Rights Struggle*. Chapel Hill: University of North Carolina Press, 1997.

Essien-Udom, E. U. *Black Nationalism: A Search for an Identity in America*. Chicago: University of Chicago Press, 1962.

Estes, Steve. *I Am a Man! Race, Manhood, and the Civil Rights Movement*. Chapel Hill: University of North Carolina Press, 2005.

Eubanks, W. Ralph. *Ever Is a Long Time: A Journey into Mississippi's Dark Past. A Memoir*. New York: Basic, 2003.

Evans, Sara. *Personal Politics: The Roots of Women's Liberation in the Civil Rights Movement and the New Left*. New York: Knopf, 1979.

Evanzz, Karl. *The Messenger: The Rise and Fall of Elijah Muhammad*. New York: Pantheon, 1999.

Evers, Charles. *Evers*. New York: World, 1971.

Evers, Charles, and Andrew Szanton. *Have No Fear: The Charles Evers Story*. New York: J. Wiley and Sons, 1997.

Evers, Myrlie, and William Peters. *For Us, the Living*. Garden City, NY: Doubleday, 1967.

Evers-Williams, Myrlie, and Manning Marable, eds. *The Autobiography of Medgar Evers: A Hero's Life and Legacy Revealed through His Writings, Letters, and Speeches*. New York: Basic Civitas, 2005.

Fager, Charles E. *Selma, 1965*. New York: Scribner, 1974.

Fager, Charles E. *Uncertain Resurrection: The Poor People's Washington Campaign*. Grand Rapids, MI: W. B. Eerdmans, 1969.

Fager, Charles E. *White Reflections on Black Power*. Grand Rapids, MI: W. B. Eerdmans, 1967.

Fairclough, Adam. *Better Day Coming: Blacks and Equality, 1890–2000*. New York: Penguin, 2002.

Fairclough, Adam. *Martin Luther King, Jr.* Athens: University of Georgia Press, 1995.

Fairclough, Adam. *Race and Democracy: The Civil Rights Struggle in Louisiana, 1915–1972.* Athens: University of Georgia Press, 1995.

Fairclough, Adam. *To Redeem the Soul of America: The Southern Christian Leadership Conference and Martin Luther King, Jr.* Athens: University of Georgia Press, 1987.

Fanon, Frantz. *The Wretched of the Earth.* New York: Grove Press, 1965.

Farber, David. *The Age of Great Dreams: America in the 1960s.* New York: Hill and Wang, 1994.

Farmer, James. *Freedom—When?* New York: Random House, 1965.

Farmer, James. *Lay Bare the Heart: An Autobiography of the Civil Rights Movement.* New York: Plume, 1985.

Farrell, James J. *The Spirit of the Sixties: The Making of Postwar Radicalism.* New York: Routledge, 1997.

Feagin, Joe, and Harlan Hahn. *Ghetto Revolts: The Politics of Violence in American Cities.* New York: Macmillan, 1973.

Ferber, Michael, and Staughton Lynd. *The Resistance.* Boston: Beacon Press, 1971.

Finch, Minnie. *The NAACP: Its Fight for Justice.* Metuchen, NJ: Scarecrow Press, 1981.

Findlay, James F., Jr. *Church People in the Struggle: The National Council of Churches and the Black Freedom Movement, 1950–1970.* New York: Oxford University Press, 1997.

Fine, Sidney. *Expanding the Frontiers of Civil Rights: Michigan, 1948–1968.* Detroit: Wayne State University Press, 2000.

Fine, Sidney. *Violence in the Model City: The Cavanaugh Administration, Race Relations, and the Detroit Race Riot of 1967.* Ann Arbor: University of Michigan Press, 1989.

Fish, John Hall. *Black Power/White Control: The Struggle of the Woodlawn Organization in Chicago.* Princeton, NJ: Princeton University Press, 1973.

Fisher, Robert. *Let the People Decide: Neighborhood Organizing in America.* Boston: Twayne, 1984.

Fleming, Cynthia Griggs. *In the Shadow of Selma: The Continuing Struggle for Civil Rights in the Rural South.* Lanham, MD: Rowman and Littlefield, 2004.

Fleming, Cynthia Griggs. *Soon We Will Not Cry: The Liberation of Ruby Doris Smith Robinson.* Lanham, MD: Rowman and Littlefield, 1998.

Fleming, Karl. *Son of the Rough South: An Uncivil Memoir.* New York: PublicAffairs, 2006.

Fogelson, Robert. *Violence as Protest: A Study of Riots and Ghettos.* Garden City, NY: Doubleday, 1971.

Foner, Philip S., ed. *The Black Panthers Speak*. Philadelphia: J. B. Lippincott, 1970.

Forbes, Flores Alexander. *Will You Die With Me? My Life and the Black Panther Party*. New York: Atria, 2006.

Forman, James. *The Making of Black Revolutionaries: A Personal Account*. New York: Macmillan, 1972.

Forman, James. *Sammy Younge, Jr.: The First Black College Student to Die in the Black Liberation Movement*. New York: Grove Press, 1968.

Formisano, Ronald. *Boston against Busing: Race, Class, and Ethnicity in the 1960s and 1970s*. Chapel Hill: University of North Carolina Press, 1991.

Fosl, Catherine. *Subversive Southerner: Anne Braden and the Struggle for Racial Justice in the Cold War South*. New York: Palgrave Macmillan, 2002.

Foster, Lorn S., ed. *The Voting Rights Act: Consequences and Implications*. New York: Praeger, 1985.

Frady, Marshall. *Martin Luther King, Jr.: A Life*. New York: Penguin, 2006.

Frady, Marshall. *Wallace*. New York: World, 1968.

Franklin, John Hope, and Isidore Starr, eds. *The Negro in Twentieth Century America: A Reader on the Struggle for Civil Rights*. New York: Vintage, 1967.

Freed, Donald. *Agony in New Haven: The Trial of Bobby Seale, Ericka Huggins, and the Black Panther Party*. New York: Simon and Schuster, 1973.

Freund, David. *Colored Property: State Policy and White Racial Politics in Suburban America*. Chicago: University of Chicago Press, 2007.

Freyer, Tony A. *The Little Rock Crisis: A Constitutional Interpretation*. Westport, CT: Greenwood Press, 1984.

Freyer, Tony A. *Little Rock on Trial:* Cooper v. Aaron *and School Desegregation*. Lawrence: University Press of Kansas, 2007.

Friedland, Michael B. *Lift Up Your Voice Like a Trumpet: White Clergy and the Civil Rights and Antiwar Movements, 1954–1973*. Chapel Hill: University of North Carolina Press, 1998.

Friedman, Leon, ed. Brown v. Board*: The Landmark Oral Argument before the Supreme Court*. New York: New Press, 2004.

Friedman, Leon, ed. *The Civil Rights Reader: Basic Documents of the Civil Rights Movement*. New York: Walker, 1967.

Fujino, Diane Carol. *Heartbeat of Struggle: The Revolutionary Life of Yuri Kochiyama*. Minneapolis: University of Minnesota Press, 2005.

Gaillard, Frye. *Cradle of Freedom: Alabama and the Movement that Changed America*. Tuscaloosa: University of Alabama Press, 2004.

Gaines, Kevin K. *American Africans in Ghana: Black Expatriates and the Civil Rights Era*. Chapel Hill: University of North Carolina Press, 2006.

Gaines, Kevin K. *Uplifting the Race: Black Leadership, Politics, and Culture in the Twentieth Century*. Chapel Hill: University of North Carolina Press, 1996.

Gallen, David, ed. *Malcolm X: As They Knew Him*. New York: Carroll and Graf, 1992.

Gardner, Michael R. *Harry Truman and Civil Rights: Moral Courage and Political Risks*. Carbondale: Southern Illinois University Press, 2002.

Garrow, David J., ed. *At the River I Stand: Memphis, the 1968 Strike, and Martin Luther King*. Brooklyn, NY: Carlson, 1989.

Garrow, David J., ed. *Atlanta, Georgia, 1960–1961: Sit-Ins and Student Activism*. Brooklyn, NY: Carlson, 1989.

Garrow, David J. *Bearing the Cross: Martin Luther King, Jr., and the Southern Christian Leadership Conference*. New York: William Morrow, 1986.

Garrow, David J., ed. *Birmingham, Alabama, 1956–1963: The Black Struggle for Civil Rights*. Brooklyn, NY: Carlson, 1989.

Garrow, David J., ed. *Chicago 1966: Open Housing Marches, Summit Negotiations, and Operation Breadbasket*. Brooklyn, NY: Carlson, 1989.

Garrow, David J., ed. *Conscience of a Troubled South: The Southern Conference Educational Fund*. Brooklyn, NY: Carlson, 1989.

Garrow, David J., ed. *Direct Action and Desegregation, 1960–1962: Toward a Theory of the Rationalization of Protest*. Brooklyn, NY: Carlson, 1989.

Garrow, David J. *The FBI and Martin Luther King, Jr.: From "Solo" to Memphis*. New York: W. W. Norton, 1981.

Garrow, David J., ed. *The Highland Folk School: A History of Its Major Programs, 1932–1961*. Brooklyn, NY: Carlson, 1989.

Garrow, David J. *Protest at Selma: Martin Luther King, Jr. and the Voting Rights Act of 1965*. New Haven, CT: Yale University Press, 1978.

Garrow, David J., ed. *The Sit-In Movement of 1960*. Brooklyn, NY: Carlson, 1989.

Garrow, David J., ed. *St. Augustine, Florida, 1963–1964: Mass Protest and Racial Violence*. Brooklyn, NY: Carlson, 1989.

Garrow, David J., ed. *The Walking City: The Montgomery Bus Boycott, 1955–1956*. Brooklyn, NY: Carlson, 1989.

Garry, Charles, and Art Goldberg. *Streetfighter in the Courtroom: The People's Advocate*. New York: Dutton, 1977.

Gates, Robbins L. *The Making of Massive Resistance: Virginia's Politics of Public School Desegregation, 1954–1956*. Chapel Hill: University of North Carolina Press, 1962.

Gentile, Thomas. *March on Washington: August 28, 1963*. Denver: Dawn of a New Day, 1983.

Georgakas, Dan, and Marvin Surkin. *Detroit: I Do Mind Dying*. Boston: South End Press, 1998.

Germany, Kent. *New Orleans after the Promises: Poverty, Citizenship, and the Search for the Great Society*. Athens: University of Georgia Press, 2007.

Geschwinder, James. *Class, Race, and Worker Insurgency: The League of Revolutionary Workers*. Cambridge, UK: Cambridge University Press, 1977.

Giddings, Paula. *When and Where I Enter: The Impact of Black Women on Race and Sex in America*. New York: W. Morrow, 1984.

Gilbert, Ben W. *Ten Blocks from the White House: Anatomy of the Washington Riots of 1968*. New York: F. A. Praeger, 1968.

Gilmore, Glenda. *Defying Dixie: The Radical Roots of Civil Rights, 1919–1950*. New York: Norton, 2008.

Gitlin, Todd. *The Sixties: Years of Hope, Days of Rage*. Toronto: Bantam, 1987.

Gitlin, Todd. *The Whole World is Watching: Mass Media in the Making and Unmaking of the New Left*. Berkeley: University of California Press, 1980.

Glasker, Wayne. *Black Students in the Ivory Tower: African American Student Activism at the University of Pennsylvania, 1967–1990*. Amherst: University of Massachusetts Press, 2002.

Glaude, Eddie, Jr., ed. *Is It Nation Time? Contemporary Essays on Black Power and Black Nationalism*. Chicago: University of Chicago Press, 2002.

Gleijeses, Piero. *Conflicting Missions: Havana, Washington, and Africa, 1959–1975*. Chapel Hill: University of North Carolina Press, 2002.

Glen, John M. *Highlander: No Ordinary School, 1932–1962*. Lexington: University Press of Kentucky, 1988.

Glisson, Susan M. *The Human Tradition in the Civil Rights Movement*. Lanham, MD: Rowman and Littlefield, 2006.

Goldfield, David R. *Black, White, and Southern: Race Relations and Southern Culture, 1940 to the Present*. Baton Rouge: Louisiana State University Press, 1990.

Goldman, Peter. *The Death and Life of Malcolm X*. New York: Harper and Row, 1973.

Goldman, Peter. *Report from Black America*. New York: Simon and Schuster, 1970.

Goluboff, Risa. *The Lost Promise of Civil Rights*. Cambridge, MA: Harvard University Press, 2007.

Good, Paul. *The Trouble I've Seen: White Journalist/Black Movement*. Washington, DC: Howard University Press, 1975.

Gordon, Jane Anna. *Why They Couldn't Wait: A Critique of the Black-Jewish Conflict in Ocean Hill–Brownsville, 1967–1971*. New York: RoutledgeFalmer, 2001.

Grady-Willis, Winston. *Challenging U.S. Apartheid: Atlanta and Black Struggles for Human Rights, 1960–1977*. Chapel Hill: University of North Carolina Press, 2006.

Graetz, Robert S. *Montgomery: A White Preacher's Memoir*. Minneapolis: Fortress Press, 1991.

Graglia, Lino S. *Disaster by Decree: The Supreme Court Decision on Race and the Schools*. Ithaca, NY: Cornell University Press, 1976.

Graham, Alison. *Framing the South: Hollywood, Television, and Race during the Civil Rights Struggle*. Baltimore: Johns Hopkins University Press, 2001.

Graham, Hugh Davis. *The Civil Rights Era: Origins and Development of National Policy, 1960–1972*. New York: Oxford University Press, 1990.

Graham, Hugh Davis. *Crisis in Print: Desegregation and the Press in Tennessee*. Nashville: Vanderbilt University Press, 1967.

Grant, Joanne, ed. *Black Protest: History, Documents and Analyses, 1619 to the Present*. New York: Fawcett World Library, 1968.

Grant, Joanne. *Ella Baker: Freedom Bound*. New York: John Wiley and Sons, 1998.

Gray, Fred D. *Bus Ride to Justice: Changing the System by the System. The Life and Works of Fred D. Gray, Preacher, Attorney, Politician*. Montgomery, AL: Black Belt Press, 1995.

Green, Ben. *Before His Time: The Untold Story of Harry T. Moore, America's First Civil Rights Martyr*. New York: Free Press, 1999.

Green, Laurie B. *Battling the Plantation Mentality: Memphis and the Black Freedom Struggle*. Chapel Hill: University of North Carolina Press, 2007.

Greenberg, Cheryl Lynn, ed. *A Circle of Trust: Remembering SNCC*. New Brunswick, NJ: Rutgers University Press, 1998.

Greenberg, Jack. *Crusaders in the Courts: How a Dedicated Band of Lawyers Fought for the Civil Rights Revolution*. New York: Basic, 1994.

Greenberg, Jack. *Race Relations and American Law*. New York: Columbia University Press, 1959.

Greene, Christina. *Our Separate Ways: Women and the Black Freedom Movement in Durham, North Carolina*. Chapel Hill: University of North Carolina Press, 2005.

Hadden, Jeffrey K. *The Gathering Storm in the Churches*. Garden City, NY: Doubleday, 1969.

Haines, Herbert H. *Black Radicals and the Civil Rights Mainstream, 1954–1970*. Knoxville: University of Tennessee Press, 1988.

Halberstam, David. *The Children*. New York: Random House, 1998.

Hall, Jacquelyn Dowd. "The Long Civil Rights Movement and the Political Uses of the Past." *Journal of American History* 91 (2005): 1233–1263.

Hall, Simon. *Peace and Freedom: The Civil Rights and Antiwar Movements of the 1960s*. Philadelphia: University of Pennsylvania Press, 2005.

Hamby, Alonzo. *Liberalism and Its Challengers: From FDR to Bush*. New York: Oxford University Press, 1992.

Hamer, Fannie Lou. *To Praise My Bridges: An Autobiography*. Jackson, MS: KIPCO, 1967.

Hamilton, Charles V. *Adam Clayton Powell, Jr.: The Political Biography of an American Dilemma*. New York: Macmillan, 1991.

Hamilton, Charles V. *The Bench and the Ballot: Southern Federal Judges and Black Voters*. New York: Oxford University Press, 1973.

Hamilton, Dona Cooper, and Charles V. Hamilton. *The Dual Agenda: The African American Struggle for Civil and Economic Equality*. New York: Columbia University Press, 1997.

Hampton, Henry, and Steve Fayer. *Voices of Freedom: An Oral History of the Civil Rights Movement from the 1950s through the 1980s*. New York: Bantam, 1990.

Hanks, Lawrence J. *The Struggle for Black Political Empowerment in Three Georgia Counties*. Knoxville: University of Tennessee Press, 1987.

Hannerz, Ulf. *Soulside: Inquiries into Ghetto Culture and Community*. New York: Columbia University Press, 1969.

Hansen, Drew. *The Dream: Martin Luther King, Jr., and the Speech that Inspired a Nation*. New York: Ecco Press, 2003.

Harding, Vincent. *Hope and History: Why We Must Share the Story of the Movement*. Maryknoll, NY: Orbis, 1990.

Harding, Vincent. *Martin Luther King: The Inconvenient Hero*. Maryknoll, NY: Orbis, 1996.

Harding, Vincent. *There Is a River: The Black Struggle for Freedom in America*. New York: Harcourt Brace Jovanovich, 1981.

Harding, Vincent. *We Changed the World: African Americans 1945–1970*. New York: Oxford University Press, 1997.

Harmon, David A. *Beneath the Image of the Civil Rights Movement and Race Relations: Atlanta, Georgia, 1946–1981*. New York: Garland, 1996.

Harris, J. William. *The New South: New Histories*. New York: Routledge, 2007.

Harris, Robert V. *The Quest for Equality: The Constitution, Congress and the Supreme Court*. Baton Rouge: Louisiana State University Press, 1960.

Harvey, James. *Black Civil Rights during the Johnson Administration*. Jackson: University and College Press of Mississippi, 1973.

Harvey, James. *Civil Rights during the Kennedy Administration*. Jackson: University and College Press of Mississippi, 1971.

Haskins, James. *Profiles in Black Power*. Garden City, NY: Doubleday, 1972.

Hayden, Tom. *Rebellion in Newark: Official Violence and Ghetto Response*. New York: Random House, 1967.

Haygood, Wil. *King of the Cats: The Life and Times of Adam Clayton Powell, Jr.* New York: Houghton Mifflin, 1993.

Hays, Brooks. *A Southern Moderate Speaks*. Chapel Hill: University of North Carolina Press, 1959.

Heath, G. Louis. *The Black Panther Leaders Speak: Huey P. Newton, Bobby Seale, Eldridge Cleaver and Company Speak Out through the Black Panther Party's Official Newspaper*. Metuchen, NJ: Scarecrow Press, 1976.

Hedgeman, Anna Arnold. *The Trumpet Sounds: A Memoir of Negro Leadership*. New York: Holt, Rinehart and Winston, 1964.

Height, Dorothy. *Open Wide the Freedom Gates: A Memoir*. New York: PublicAffairs, 2003.

Helfer, Andrew, and Randy DuBurke. *Malcolm X: A Graphic Biography*. New York: Hill and Wang, 2006.

Hendrickson, Paul. *Sons of Mississippi: A Story of Race and Its Legacy*. New York: Knopf, 2003.

Henry, Aaron, and Constance Curry. *Aaron Henry: The Fire Ever Burning*. Jackson: University Press of Mississippi, 2000.

Hentoff, Nat. *The New Equality*. New York: Viking Press, 1964.

Herbers, John. *The Lost Priority: What Happened to the Civil Rights Movement in America*. New York: Funk and Wagnalls, 1970.

Hersey, John. *The Algiers Motel Incident*. New York: Knopf, 1968.

Higham, John, ed. *Civil Rights and Social Wrongs: Black-White Relations since World War II*. University Park, PA: Penn State University Press, 1997.

Hill, Herbert. *Black Labor and the American Legal System: Race, Work, and the Law*. Washington, DC: Bureau of International Affairs, 1977.

Hill, Lance E. *The Deacons for Defense: Armed Resistance and the Civil Rights Movement*. Chapel Hill: University of North Carolina Press, 2004.

Hilliard, David, ed. *The Black Panther: Intercommunal News Service*. New York: Atria, 2007.

Hilliard, David, and Lewis Cole. *This Side of Glory: The Autobiography of David Hilliard and the Story of the Black Panther Party*. Boston: Little, Brown, 1993.

Hilliard, David, and Don Weise, eds. *The Huey P. Newton Reader*. New York: Seven Stories Press, 2002.

Hilliard, David, with Keith Zimmerman and Kent Zimmerman. *Huey: Spirit of the Panther*. New York: Thunder's Mouth Press, 2006.

Himes, Joseph S. *Racial Conflict in American Society*. Columbus, OH: Merrill, 1973.

Hine, Darlene Clark. "Black Professionals and Race Consciousness: Origins of the Civil Rights Movement, 1890–1950." *Journal of American History* 89 (2003): 1279–1294.

Hine, Darlene Clark. *Black Victory: The Rise and Fall of the White Primary in Texas*. Millwood, NY: KTO Press, 1979.

Hippler, Arthur E. *Hunter's Point: A Black Ghetto*. New York: Basic, 1974.

Hirsch, Arnold R. *Making the Second Ghetto: Race and Housing in Chicago, 1940–1960*. New York: Cambridge University Press, 1983.

Hogan, Wesley C. *Many Minds, One Heart: SNCC's Dream for a New America*. Chapel Hill: University of North Carolina Press, 2007.

Holt, Len. *The Summer that Didn't End*. New York: William Morrow, 1965.

Honey, Michael K. *Black Workers Remember: An Oral History of Segregation, Unionism, and the Freedom Struggle*. Berkeley: University of California Press, 1999.

Honey, Michael K. *Going Down Jericho Road: The Memphis Strike, Martin Luther King's Last Campaign*. New York: Norton, 2007.

Honey, Michael K. *Southern Labor and Black Civil Rights: Organizing Memphis Workers*. Urbana: University of Illinois Press, 1993.

Honigsberg, Peter Jan. *Crossing Border Street: A Civil Rights Memoir*. Berkeley: University of California Press, 2000.

Horne, Gerald. *Black and Red: W. E. B. Du Bois and the Afro-American Response to the Cold War, 1944–1963*. Albany: State University of New York Press, 1986.

Horne, Gerald. *Communist Front? The Civil Rights Congress, 1946–1956*. Rutherford, NJ: Associated University Presses, 1988.

Horne, Gerald. *Fire This Time: The Watts Uprising and the 1960s*. Charlottesville: University Press of Virginia, 1995.

Horwitt, Sanford D. *Let Them Call Me Rebel: Saul Alinsky, His Life and Legacy*. New York: Knopf, 1989.

Houck, Davis, and Matthew A. Grindy. *Emmett Till and the Mississippi Press*. Jackson: University Press of Mississippi, 2008.

Hough, Joseph C., Jr. *Black Power and White Protestants: A Christian Response to the New Negro Pluralism*. New York: Oxford University Press, 1968.

Howard-Pitney, David, ed. *Martin Luther King, Jr., Malcolm X, and the Civil Rights Struggle of the 1950s and 1960s: A Brief History with Documents*. Boston: Bedford/St. Martin's, 2004.

Howlett, Duncan. *No Greater Love: The James Reeb Story*. New York: Harper and Row, 1966.

Huckaby, Elizabeth. *Crisis at Central High, Little Rock, 1957–58*. Baton Rouge: Louisiana State University Press, 1980.

Hudson, David. *Along Racial Lines: Consequences of the 1965 Voting Rights Act*. New York: Peter Lang, 1998.

Hudson, Winson, and Constance Curry. *Mississippi Harmony: Memoirs of a Freedom Fighter*. New York: Palgrave Macmillan, 2002.

Huey, Gary. *Rebel with a Cause: P. D. East, Southern Liberalism, and the Civil Rights Movement, 1953–1971*. Wilmington, DE: Scholarly Resources, 1985.

Hughes, Langston. *Fight for Freedom: The Story of the NAACP*. New York: W. W. Norton, 1962.

Huie, William Bradford. *He Slew the Dreamer: My Search, with James Earl Ray, for the Truth about the Murder of Martin Luther King*. New York: Delacorte Press, 1970.

Huie, William Bradford. *Three Lives for Mississippi*. New York: WCC, 1965.

Hunter-Gault, Charlayne. *In My Place*. New York: Farrar, Straus and Giroux, 1992.

Huntley, Horace, and David Montgomery, eds. *Black Workers' Struggle for Equality in Birmingham*. Urbana: University of Illinois Press, 2004.

Isserman, Maurice, and Michael Kazin. *America Divided: The Civil War of the 1960s*. New York: Oxford University Press, 2000.

Jackson, George. *Soledad Brother: The Prison Letters of George Jackson*. New York: Coward-McCann, 1970.

Jackson, Mandi Isaacs. *Model City Blues: Urban Space and Organized Resistance in New Haven*. Philadelphia: Temple University Press, 2008.

Jackson, Miles M., ed. "They Followed the Trade Winds: African Americans in Hawai'i." Special issue, *Social Process in Hawai'i* 43 (2004).

Jackson, Thomas F. *From Civil Rights to Human Rights: Martin Luther King, Jr., and the Struggle for Economic Justice*. Philadelphia: University of Pennsylvania Press, 2006.

Jackson, Troy. *Becoming King: Martin Luther King Jr. and the Making of a National Leader*. Lexington: University Press of Kentucky, 2008.

Jacoway, Elizabeth. *Turn Away Thy Son: Little Rock, the Crisis That Shocked the Nation*. New York: Free Press, 2007.

Jacoway, Elizabeth, and David Colburn, eds. *Southern Businessmen and Desegregation*. Baton Rouge: Louisiana State University Press, 1982.

Jacoway, Elizabeth, and C. Fred Williams, eds. *Understanding the Little Rock Crisis: An Exercise in Remembrance and Reconciliation*. Fayetteville: University of Arkansas Press, 1999.

Jamal, Hakim A. *From the Dead Level: Malcolm X and Me*. New York: Warner, 1973.

James, Michael E. *The Conspiracy of the Good: Civil Rights and the Struggle for Community in Two American Cities, 1875–2000*. New York: Peter Lang, 2005.

Jeffries, Judson L., ed. *Black Power in the Belly of the Beast*. Urbana: University of Illinois Press, 2006.

Jeffries, Judson L., ed., *Comrades: A Local History of the Black Panther Party*. Bloomington: Indiana University Press, 2008.

Jeffries, Judson L. *Huey P. Newton: The Radical Theorist*. Jackson: University Press of Mississippi, 2002.

Johnson, Cedric. *Revolutionaries to Race Leaders: Black Power and the Making of African American Politics*. Minneapolis: University of Minnesota Press, 2007.

Johnson, Lubertha, with R. T. King and Jamie Coughtry. *Civil Rights Efforts in Las Vegas: 1940s–1960s*. Reno: University of Nevada Oral History Program, 1988.

Johnson, Lyndon B. *The Vantage Point: Perspectives of the Presidency, 1963–1969*. New York: Holt, Rinehart and Winston, 1971.

Johnston, Erle. *I Rolled with Ross: A Political Portrait*. Baton Rouge, LA: Moran, 1980.

Jolly, Kenneth. *Black Liberation in the Midwest: The Struggle in St. Louis, Missouri, 1964–1970*. New York: Routledge, 2006.

Jonas, Gilbert. *Freedom's Sword: The NAACP and the Struggle against Racism in America, 1909–1969*. New York: Routledge, 2005.

Jones, Charles, ed. *The Black Panther Party [Reconsidered]*. Baltimore: Black Classic Press, 1998.

Jordan, Vernon E., Jr. *Vernon Can Read! A Memoir*. New York: PublicAffairs, 2001.

Joseph, Peniel E. "Black Liberation without Apology: Reconceptualizing the Black Power Movement." *Black Scholar* 31 (2001): 2–19.

Joseph, Peniel E., ed. *The Black Power Movement: Rethinking the Civil Rights–Black Power Era*. New York: Routledge, 2006.

Joseph, Peniel E. *Waiting 'Til the Midnight Hour: A Narrative History of Black Power in America*. New York: Henry Holt, 2006.

Kadalie, Mobido. *Internationalism, Pan-Africanism, and the Struggle of Social Classes*. Savannah, GA: One Quest Press, 2000.

Kasher, Steven. *The Civil Rights Movement: A Photographic History, 1954–1968*. New York: Abbeville Press, 1996.

Katagiri, Yasuhiro. *The Mississippi State Sovereignty Commission: Civil Rights and States' Rights*. Jackson: University Press of Mississippi, 2001.

Keating, Edward M. *Free Huey!* Berkeley, CA: Ramparts, 1971.

Keech, William. *The Impact of Negro Voting: The Role of the Vote in the Quest for Equality*. Chicago: Rand McNally, 1968.

Kellar, William Henry. *Make Haste Slowly: Moderates, Conservatives, and School Desegregation in Houston*. College Station: Texas A&M University Press, 1999.

Kelley, Robin D. G. *Freedom Dreams: The Black Radical Imagination*. Boston: Beacon Press, 2002.

Kellogg, Peter J. "Civil Rights Consciousness in the 1940s." *Historian* 42 (1979): 18–41.

Kempton, Murray. *The Briar Patch:* The People of the State of New York v. Lumumba Shakur et al. New York: Dutton, 1973.

Killian, Lewis. *The Impossible Revolution: Black Power and the American Dream*. New York: Random House, 1968.

Killian, Lewis, and Charles Grigg. *Racial Crisis in America: Leadership in Conflict*. Englewood Cliffs. NJ: Prentice Hall, 1964.

Kilpatrick, James J. *The Southern Case for School Segregation*. New York: Collier-Crowell Press, 1962.

Kilpatrick, Judith. *There When We Needed Him: Wiley Austin Branton, Civil Rights Warrior*. Fayetteville: University of Arkansas Press, 2007.

King, Coretta Scott, ed. *The Martin Luther King, Jr., Companion: Quotations from the Speeches, Essays, and Books of Martin Luther King, Jr.* New York: St. Martin's Press, 1993.

King, Coretta Scott. *My Life with Martin Luther King, Jr.* New York: Holt, Reinhart and Winston, 1969.

King, Martin Luther, Jr. *The Measure of a Man*. Philadelphia: Christian Education Press, 1959.

King, Martin Luther, Jr. *Strength to Love*. New York: Harper and Row, 1963.

King, Martin Luther, Jr. *Stride toward Freedom: The Montgomery Story*. New York: Harper, 1958.

King, Martin Luther, Jr. *The Trumpet of Conscience*. New York: Harper and Row, 1967.

King, Martin Luther, Jr. *Where Do We Go From Here: Chaos or Community?* New York: Harper and Row, 1967.

King, Martin Luther, Jr. *Why We Can't Wait*. New York: Harper and Row, 1964.

King, Mary. *Freedom Song: A Personal Story of the 1960s Civil Rights Movement*. New York: William Morrow, 1987.

King, Richard H. *Civil Rights and the Idea of Freedom*. New York: Oxford University Press, 1992.

Kirk, John A. *Beyond Little Rock: The Origins and Legacies of the Central High Crisis*. Fayetteville: University of Arkansas Press, 2007.

Kirk, John A. *An Epitaph for Little Rock: A Fiftieth Anniversary Retrospective on the Central High Crisis*. Fayetteville: University of Arkansas Press, 2008.

Kirk, John A., ed. *Martin Luther King, Jr. and the Civil Rights Movement: Controversies and Debates*. New York: Palgrave Macmillan, 2007.

Klarman, Michael J. Brown v. Board of Education *and the Civil Rights Movement*. New York: Oxford University Press, 2007.

Klarman, Michael J. *From Jim Crow to Civil Rights: The Supreme Court and the Struggle for Racial Equality*. New York: Oxford University Press, 2004.

Klarman, Michael J. "How *Brown* Changed Race Relations: The Backlash Thesis." *Journal of American History* 81 (1994): 81–118.

Kluger, Richard. *Simple Justice: The History of* Brown v. Board of Education *and Black America's Struggle for Equality*. New York: Random House, 1975.

K'Meyer, Tracy Elaine. *Interracialism and Christian Community in the Postwar South: The Story of Koinonia Farm*. Charlottesville: University Press of Virginia, 1997.

Koehlinger, Amy L. *The New Nuns: Racial Justice and Religious Reform in the 1960s*. Cambridge, MA: Harvard University Press, 2007.

Kohl, Herbert. *She Would Not Be Moved: How We Tell the Story of Rosa Parks and the Montgomery Bus Boycott*. New York: New Press, 2005.

Kornbluh, Felicia. *The Battle for Welfare Rights: Politics and Poverty in Modern America*. Philadelphia: University of Pennsylvania Press, 2007.

Korstad, Robert R. *Civil Rights Unionism: Tobacco Workers and the Struggle for Democracy in the Mid-Twentieth-Century South*. Chapel Hill: University of North Carolina Press, 2003.

Korstad, Robert R., and Nelson Lichtenstein. "Opportunities Found and Lost: Labor, Radicals, and the Early Civil Rights Movement." *Journal of American History* 75 (1988): 786–811.

Kosof, Anna. *The Civil Rights Movement and Its Legacy*. New York: Franklin Watts, 1989.

Kotlowski, Dean J. *Nixon's Civil Rights: Politics, Principle, and Policy*. Cambridge, MA: Harvard University Press, 2002.

Kotz, Nick. *Judgment Days: Lyndon Baines Johnson, Martin Luther King, Jr., and the Laws that Changed America*. Boston: Houghton Mifflin, 2005.

Kotz, Nick, and Mary Lynn Kotz. *A Passion for Equality: George A. Wiley and the Movement*. New York: W. W. Norton, 1977.

Kousser, J. Morgan. *Colorblind Injustice: Minority Voting Rights and the Undoing of the Second Reconstruction*. Chapel Hill: University of North Carolina Press, 1999.

Kramer, Ralph M. *Participation of the Poor: Comparative Community Case Studies in the War on Poverty.* Englewood Cliffs, NJ: Prentice Hall, 1969.

Krenn, Michael L., ed. *The African-American Voice in U.S. Foreign Policy since World War II.* New York: Routledge, 1998.

Krenn, Michael L. *Black Diplomacy: African Americans and the State Department, 1945–1969.* Armonk, NY: M. E. Sharpe, 1999.

Kruse, Kevin M. *White Flight: Atlanta and the Making of Modern Conservatism.* Princeton, NJ: Princeton University Press, 2005.

Kuettner, Al. *March to a Promised Land: The Civil Rights Files of a White Reporter, 1952–1968.* Sterling, VA: Capital, 2006.

Ladino, Robyn Duff. *Desegregating Texas Schools: Eisenhower, Shivers, and the Crisis at Mansfield High.* Austin: University of Texas Press, 1986.

Landsberg, Brian K. *Enforcing Civil Rights: Race Discrimination and the Department of Justice.* Lawrence: University Press of Kansas, 1997.

Landsberg, Brian K. *Free at Last to Vote: The Alabama Origins of the 1965 Voting Rights Act.* Lawrence: University Press of Kansas, 2007.

Lane, Mark, and Dick Gregory. *Code Name "Zorro": The Murder of Martin Luther King, Jr.* Englewood Cliffs, NJ: Prentice Hall, 1977.

Lasch, Christopher. *The Agony of the American Left.* New York: Knopf, 1969.

Lassiter, Matthew D., and Andrew B. Lewis, eds. *The Moderates' Dilemma: Massive Resistance to School Desegregation in Virginia.* Charlottesville: University Press of Virginia, 1998.

Lau, Peter F. *Democracy Rising: South Carolina and the Fight for Black Equality since 1865.* Lexington: University Press of Kentucky, 2006.

Lau, Peter F., ed. *From the Grassroots to the Supreme Court:* Brown v. Board of Education *and American Democracy.* Durham, NC: Duke University Press, 2004.

Lawson, Steven F. *Black Ballots: Voting Rights in the South, 1944–1969.* New York: Columbia University Press, 1976.

Lawson, Steven F. *Civil Rights Crossroads: Nation, Community, and the Black Freedom Struggle.* Lexington: University Press of Kentucky, 2003.

Lawson, Steven F. "Freedom Then, Freedom Now: The Historiography of the Civil Rights Movement." *American Historical Review* 96 (1991): 456–471.

Lawson, Steven F. *In Pursuit of Power: Southern Blacks and Electoral Politics, 1965–1982.* New York: Columbia University Press, 1985.

Lawson, Steven F. *Running for Freedom: Civil Rights and Black Politics in America since 1941.* Philadelphia: Temple University Press, 1991.

Lawson, Steven F., and Charles Payne. *Debating the Civil Rights Movement, 1945–1968.* Lanham, MD: Rowman and Littlefield, 1998.

Layton, Azza Salama. *International Politics and Civil Rights Politics in the United States, 1941–1960*. Cambridge, UK: Cambridge University Press, 2000.

Lazerow, Jama, and Yohuru Williams, eds. *In Search of the Black Panther Party: New Perspectives on a Revolutionary Movement*. Durham, NC: Duke University Press, 2006.

Lee, Chana Kai. *For Freedom's Sake: The Life of Fannie Lou Hamer*. Urbana: University of Illinois Press, 1999.

Lefever, Harry G. *Undaunted by the Fight: Spelman College and the Civil Rights Movement, 1957–1967*. Macon, GA: Mercer University Press, 2005.

Leidholdt, Alexander. *Standing before the Shouting Mob: Lenoir Chambers and Virginia's Massive Resistance to Public School Integration*. Tuscaloosa: University of Alabama Press, 1997.

Lemann, Nicholas. *The Promised Land: The Great Black Migration and How It Changed America*. New York: Knopf, 1991.

Lemon, Richard. *The Troubled American*. New York: Simon and Schuster, 1970.

Lentz, Richard. *Symbols, the News Magazines, and Martin Luther King*. Baton Rouge: Louisiana State University Press, 1990.

Lerner, Gilda, ed. *Black Women in White America: A Documentary History*. New York: Pantheon, 1973.

Lesher, Stephan. *George Wallace: American Populist*. Reading, MA: Addison-Wesley, 1994.

Lester, Julius. *Look Out, Whitey! Black Power's Gon' Get Your Mama!* New York: Dial Press, 1968.

Lester, Julius. *Revolutionary Notes*. New York: Grove Press, 1969.

Levine, Daniel. *Bayard Rustin and the Civil Rights Movement*. New Brunswick, NJ: Rutgers University Press, 2000.

Levy, Charles. *Voluntary Servitude: Whites in the Negro Movement*. New York: Appleton-Century-Crofts, 1968.

Levy, Peter. *Civil War on Race Street: The Civil Rights Movement in Cambridge, Maryland*. Gainesville: University Press of Florida, 2003.

Levy, Peter, ed. *Let Freedom Ring: A Documentary History of the Modern Civil Rights Movement*. Westport, CT: Greenwood Press, 1998.

Lewis, Anthony. *Portrait of a Decade: The Second American Revolution*. New York: Random House, 1964.

Lewis, Catherine M., and J. Richard Lewis. *Race, Politics, and Memory: A Documentary History of the Little Rock School Crisis*. Fayetteville: University of Arkansas Press, 2007.

Lewis, David L. *King: A Critical Biography*. New York: Praeger, 1970.

Lewis, John, with Michael D'Orso. *Walking with the Wind: A Memoir of the Movement.* New York: Simon and Schuster, 1998.

Lincoln, C. Eric. *The Black Muslims in America.* Boston: Beacon Press, 1961.

Lincoln, C. Eric, ed. *Is Anyone Listening to Black America?* New York: Seabury Press, 1968.

Ling, Peter J. "Local Leadership in the Early Civil Rights Movement: The South Carolina Citizenship Education Program of the Highlander Folk School." *Journal of American Studies* 29 (1995): 399–422.

Ling, Peter J. *Martin Luther King, Jr.* New York: Routledge, 2002.

Ling, Peter J., and Sharon Monteith, eds. *Gender in the Civil Rights Movement.* New York: Garland, 1999.

Lipsitz, George. *A Life in the Struggle: Ivory Perry and the Culture of Opposition.* Philadelphia: Temple University Press, 1988.

Lipsky, Michael. *Protest in City Politics: Rent Strikes, Housing, and the Power of the Poor.* Chicago: Rand McNally, 1969.

Lischer, Richard. *The Preacher King: Martin Luther King, Jr. and the Word That Moved America.* New York: Oxford University Press, 1995.

Lockwood, Lee. *Conversations with Eldridge Cleaver: Algiers.* New York: McGraw-Hill, 1970.

Lomax, Louis E. *The Negro Revolt.* New York: Harper, 1962.

Lomax, Louis E. *To Kill a Black Man.* Los Angeles: Holloway House, 1968.

Lomax, Louis E. *When the Word is Given: A Report on Elijah Muhammad, Malcolm X, and the Black Muslim World.* Cleveland: World, 1963.

Long, Michael G., ed. *First Class Citizenship: The Civil Rights Letters of Jackie Robinson.* New York: Henry Holt, 2007.

Longenecker, Stephen L. *Selma's Peacemaker: Ralph Smeltzer and Civil Rights Mediation.* Philadelphia: Temple University Press, 1987.

Lord, Walter. *The Past That Would Not Die.* New York: Harper and Row, 1965.

Louis, Debbie. *And We Are Not Saved: A History of the Movement as People.* Garden City, NY: Doubleday, 1970.

Lowery, Charles D., and John S. Marzolek, eds. *Encyclopedia of African-American Civil Rights: From Emancipation to the Present.* Westport, CT: Greenwood Press, 1992.

Lowndes, Joseph E. *From the New Deal to the New Right: Race and the Southern Origins of Modern Conservatism.* New Haven, CT: Yale University Press, 2008.

Lubell, Samuel. *White and Black: Test of a Nation.* New York: Harper and Row, 1964.

Lubiano, Wahneema, ed. *The House That Race Built: Black Americans, U.S. Terrain*. New York: Pantheon, 1997.

Luker, Ralph E. *Historical Dictionary of the Civil Rights Movement*. Lanham, MD: Scarecrow Press, 1997.

Lynd, Staughton. *Living Inside Our Hope: A Steadfast Radical's Thoughts on Rebuilding the Movement*. Ithaca, NY: Cornell University Press, 1997.

Lynn, Conrad. *There Is a Fountain: The Autobiography of a Civil Rights Lawyer*. Westport, CT: Lawrence Hill, 1979.

Lyon, Danny. *Memories of the Southern Civil Rights Movement*. Chapel Hill: University of North Carolina Press, 1992.

Lytle, Mark Hamilton. *America's Uncivil Wars: The Sixties Era from Elvis to the Fall of Richard Nixon*. New York: Oxford University Press, 2006.

Madhubuti, Haki. *YellowBlack: The First Twenty-One Years of a Poet's Life*. Chicago: Third World Press, 2005.

Major, Reginald. *A Panther Is a Black Cat*. New York: William Morrow, 1971.

Manis, Andrew M. *A Fire You Can't Put Out: The Civil Rights Life of Birmingham's Reverend Fred Shuttlesworth*. Tuscaloosa: University of Alabama Press, 1999.

Manis, Andrew M. *Southern Civil Religions in Conflict: Black and White Baptists and Civil Rights, 1947–1957*. Athens: University of Georgia Press, 1987.

Mann, Robert. *The Walls of Jericho: Lyndon Johnson, Hubert Humphrey, Richard Russell, and the Struggle for Civil Rights*. Fort Washington, PA: Harvest, 1997.

Mann, Robert. *When Freedom Would Triumph: The Civil Rights Struggle in Congress, 1954–1968*. Baton Rouge: Louisiana State University Press, 2007.

Marable, Manning. *Race, Reform, and Rebellion: The Second Reconstruction in Black America, 1945–2006*, 3rd ed. Jackson: University Press of Mississippi, 2007.

Marine, Gene. *The Black Panthers*. New York: New American Library, 1969.

Marsh, Charles. *The Beloved Community: How Faith Shapes Social Justice from the Civil Rights Movement to Today*. New York: Basic, 2006.

Marsh, Charles. *God's Long Summer: Stories of Faith and Civil Rights*. Princeton, NJ: Princeton University Press, 1997.

Martin, John B. *The Deep South Says "Never."* New York: Ballantine, 1957.

Martin, Waldo E. Brown v. Board of Education: *A Brief History with Documents*. Boston: Bedford/St. Martin's, 1998.

Martin, Waldo E., and Patricia A. Sullivan, eds. *Civil Rights in the United States: An Encyclopedia*. New York: Macmillan, 2000.

Marx, Gary T. *Protest and Prejudice: A Study of Belief in the Black Community*. New York: Harper and Row, 1967.

Mason, Gilbert, with James Patterson Smith. *Beaches, Blood, and Ballots: A Black Doctor's Civil Rights Struggle*. Jackson: University Press of Mississippi, 2000.

Masotti, Louis, and Don Bowen, eds. *Riots and Rebellion: Civil Violence in the Urban Community*. Beverly Hills, CA: Sage, 1968.

Massengill, Reed. *Portrait of a Racist*. New York: St. Martin's Press, 1997.

Massey, Douglas, and Nancy Denton. *American Apartheid: Segregation and the Making of the Underclass*. Cambridge, MA: Harvard University Press, 1993.

Matthews, Donald R., and James W. Prothro. *Negroes and the New Southern Politics*. New York: Harcourt, Brace and World, 1966.

Matusow, Allen J. *The Unraveling of America: A History of Liberalism in the 1960s*. New York: Harper and Row, 1984.

May, Gary. *The Informant: The FBI, the Ku Klux Klan, and the Murder of Viola Liuzzo*. New Haven, CT: Yale University Press, 2005.

Mayer, Michael. "With Much Deliberation and Some Speed: Eisenhower and the *Brown* Decision." *Journal of Southern History* 52 (1986): 43–76.

McAdam, Doug. *Freedom Summer*. New York: Oxford University Press, 1998.

McAdam, Doug. *Political Process and the Development of Black Insurgency, 1930–1970*. Chicago: University of Chicago Press, 1982.

McCartney, John T. *Black Power Ideologies: An Essay in African-American Political Thought*. Philadelphia: Temple University Press, 1992.

McCord, William. *Mississippi: The Long Hot Summer*. New York: W. W. Norton, 1965.

McCormick, Richard P. *The Black Student Protest Movement at Rutgers*. New Brunswick, NJ: Rutgers University Press, 1990.

McCoy, Donald R., and Richard T. Reutten. *Quest and Response: Minority Rights and the Truman Administration*. Lawrence: University Press of Kansas, 1973.

McDonald, Dora E. *Sharing the Dream: Martin Luther King Jr., the Movement, and Me*. Athens, GA: Hill Street Press, 2002.

McDonald, Laughlin. *A Voting Rights Odyssey: Black Enfranchisement in Georgia*. Cambridge, UK: Cambridge University Press, 2003.

McGreevy, John T. *Parish Boundaries: The Catholic Encounter with Race in the Twentieth-Century Urban North*. Chicago: University of Chicago Press, 1996.

McKissick, Floyd B. *Three-Fifths of a Man*. New York: Macmillan, 1969.

McKnight, Gerald D. *The Last Crusade: Martin Luther King, Jr., the FBI, and the Poor People's Campaign*. Boulder, CO: Westview Press, 1998.

McMillan, James B., with R. T. King and Gary E. Elliott. *Fighting Back: A Life in the Struggle for Civil Rights*. Reno: University of Nevada Oral History Program, 1997.

McMillen, Neil R. *The Citizens' Council: Organized Resistance to the Second Reconstruction, 1954–1964.* Urbana: University of Illinois Press, 1971.

McMillen, Neil R., ed. *Remaking Dixie: The Impact of World War II on the American South.* Jackson: University Press of Mississippi, 1997.

McNeil, Genna Rae. *Groundwork: Charles Hamilton Houston and the Struggle for Civil Rights.* Philadelphia: University of Pennsylvania Press, 1983.

McWhorter, Diane. *Carry Me Home: Birmingham, Alabama: The Climactic Battle of the Civil Rights Revolution.* New York: Simon and Schuster, 2001.

Meacham, Jon, ed. *Voices in Our Blood: America's Best on the Civil Rights Movement.* New York: Random House, 2001.

Mealy, Rosemari. *Fidel and Malcolm X: Memories of a Meeting.* Melbourne, Australia: Ocean Press, 1993.

Meier, August, and John H. Bracey Jr. "The NAACP as a Reform Movement, 1909–1965: 'To Reach the Conscience of America.'" *Journal of Southern History* 59 (1993): 3–30.

Meier, August, and Elliott Rudwick, eds. *Black Protest in the Sixties.* Chicago: Quadrangle, 1970.

Meier, August, and Elliott Rudwick. *CORE: A Study in the Civil Rights Movement, 1942–1968.* New York: Oxford University Press, 1973.

Meier, August, Elliott Rudwick, and Francis Broderick, eds. *Black Protest Thought in the Twentieth Century.* Indianapolis: Bobbs-Merrill, 1971.

Melanson, Philip H. *The MURKIN Conspiracy: An Investigation into the Assassination of Dr. Martin Luther King, Jr.* New York: Praeger, 1989.

Melcher, Mary. "Blacks and Whites Together: Interracial Leadership in the Phoenix Civil Rights Movement." *Journal of Arizona History* 32 (1991): 195–216.

Mendelsohn, Jack. *The Martyrs: Sixteen Who Gave Their Lives for Racial Justice.* New York: Harper and Row, 1966.

Menkart, Deborah, Alana D. Murray, and Jenice L. View, eds. *Putting the Movement Back into Civil Rights Teaching.* Washington, DC: Teaching for Change, 2004.

Meredith, James. *James Meredith vs. Ole Miss.* Jackson, MS: Meredith, 1995.

Meredith, James. *Me and My Kind: An Oral History.* Jackson, MS: Meredith, 1995.

Meredith, James. *Three Years in Mississippi.* Bloomington: Indiana University Press, 1966.

Meriwether, James H. *Proudly We Can Be Africans: Black Americans and Africa, 1935–1961.* Chapel Hill: University of North Carolina Press, 2002.

Metress, Christopher, ed. *The Lynching of Emmett Till: A Documentary Narrative.* Charlottesville: University Press of Virginia, 2002.

Michel, Gregg L. *Struggle for a Better South: The Southern Student Organizing Committee, 1964–1969*. New York: Palgrave Macmillan, 2004.

Miller, Keith D. *Voice of Deliverance: The Language of Martin Luther King, Jr. and Its Sources*. New York: Free Press, 1992.

Miller, William Robert. *Martin Luther King, Jr.* New York: Avon, 1969.

Mills, J. Thornton. *Dividing Lines: Municipal Politics and the Struggle for Civil Rights in Montgomery, Birmingham, and Selma*. Tuscaloosa: University of Alabama Press, 2002.

Mills, Kay. *Changing Channels: The Civil Rights Case That Transformed Television*. Jackson: University Press of Mississippi, 2004.

Mills, Kay. *This Little Light of Mine: The Life of Fannie Lou Hamer*. New York: Dutton, 1993.

Mills, Nicolaus. *Like a Holy Crusade: Mississippi 1964: The Turning Point of the Civil Rights Movement in America*. Chicago: Ivan R. Dee, 1992.

Minchin, Timothy J. *The Color of Work: The Struggle for Civil Rights in the Southern Paper Industry, 1945–1980*. Chapel Hill: University of North Carolina Press, 2001.

Minchin, Timothy J. *From Rights to Economics: The Ongoing Struggle for Black Equality in the U.S. South*. Gainesville: University Press of Florida, 2007.

Minchin, Timothy J. *Hiring the Black Worker: The Racial Integration of the Southern Textile Industry, 1960–1980*. Chapel Hill: University of North Carolina Press, 1999.

Mitchell, Dennis J. *Mississippi Liberal: A Biography of Frank E. Smith*. Jackson: University Press of Mississippi, 2001.

Mollenkopf, John. *The Contested City*. Princeton, NJ: Princeton University Press, 1983.

Mollin, Marian. *Radical Pacifism in Modern America: Egalitarianism and Protest*. Philadelphia: University of Pennsylvania Press, 2006.

Monhollon, Rusty L. *This Is America? The Sixties in Lawrence, Kansas*. New York: Palgrave, 2002.

Moody, Anne. *Coming of Age in Mississippi*. New York: Dial Press, 1968.

Moore, Gilbert. *A Special Rage*. New York: Harper and Row, 1971.

Moore, Jesse Thomas, Jr. *A Search for Equality: The National Urban League, 1910–1961*. University Park, PA: Penn State University Press, 1981.

Moore, Leonard N. *Carl B. Stokes and the Rise of Black Political Power*. Urbana: University of Illinois Press, 2003.

Moore, Winfred B., Jr., and Orville Vernon Burton, eds. *Toward the Meeting of the Waters: Currents in the Civil Rights Movement of South Carolina during the Twentieth Century*. Charleston: University of South Carolina Press, 2008.

Moreno, Paul D. *From Direct Action to Affirmative Action: Fair Employment Law and Policy in America, 1933–1972*. Baton Rouge: Louisiana State University Press, 1997.

Morgan, Charles, Jr. *A Time to Speak*. New York: Harper and Row, 1964.

Morgan, Edward. *The 60s Experience: Hard Lessons about Modern America*. Philadelphia: Temple University Press, 1991.

Morgan, Ruth P. *The President and Civil Rights: Policy Making by Executive Order*. New York: St. Martin's Press, 1970.

Morris, Aldon. *The Origins of the Civil Rights Movement: Black Communities Organizing for Change*. New York: Free Press, 1984.

Morris, Milton D. *The Politics of Black America*. New York: Harper and Row, 1975.

Morris, Willie. *The Ghosts of Medgar Evers: A Tale of Race, Murder, Mississippi, and Hollywood*. New York: Random House, 1998.

Morrison, Minion. *Black Political Mobilization: Leadership, Power, and Mass Behavior*. Albany: State University of New York Press, 1987.

Morrow, E. Frederic. *Black Man in the White House: A Diary of the Eisenhower Years by the Administrative Officer for Special Projects, the White House, 1955–1961*. New York: Coward-McCann, 1963.

Moses, Robert P., and Charles E. Cobb Jr. *Radical Equations: Math Literacy and Civil Rights*. Boston: Beacon Press, 2001.

Motley, Constance Baker. *Equal Justice under Law: An Autobiography*. New York: Farrar, Straus and Giroux, 1998.

Moye, J. Todd. *Let the People Decide: Black Freedom and White Resistance Movements in Sunflower County, Mississippi, 1945–1986*. Chapel Hill: University of North Carolina Press, 2004.

Moynihan, Daniel P. *Maximum Feasible Misunderstanding: Community Action in the War on Poverty*. New York: Free Press, 1969.

Mumford, Kevin. *Newark: A History of Race, Rights, and Riots in America*. New York: NYU Press, 2007.

Murphree, Vanessa. *The Selling of Civil Rights: The Student Nonviolent Coordinating Committee and the Use of Public Relations*. New York: Routledge, 2006.

Murray, Paul T., ed. *The Civil Rights Movement: References and Resources*. New York: G. K. Hall, 1993.

Muse, Benjamin. *The American Negro Revolution: From Nonviolence to Black Power, 1963–1967*. Bloomington: Indiana University Press, 1968.

Muse, Benjamin. *Ten Years of Prelude: The Story of Integration since the Supreme Court's 1954 Decision*. New York: Viking Press, 1964.

Muse, Benjamin. *Virginia's Massive Resistance*. Bloomington: Indiana University Press, 1961.

Namorato, Michael V., ed. *Have We Overcome? Race Relations since* Brown: *Essays*. Jackson: University Press of Mississippi, 1979.

Nasstrom, Kathryn L. *Everybody's Grandmother and Nobody's Fool: Frances Freeborn Pauley and the Struggle for Social Justice*. Ithaca, NY: Cornell University Press, 2000.

National Archives and Records Administration. *Federal Records Relating to Civil Rights in the Post–World War II Era*. Reference Information Paper 113, compiled by Walter B. Hill Jr. Washington, DC: U.S. Government Printing Office, 2007.

Navasky, Victor S. *Kennedy Justice*. New York: Atheneum, 1971.

Neary, John. *Julian Bond: Black Rebel*. New York: William Morrow, 1971.

Nelson, Bruce. *Divided We Stand: American Workers and the Struggle for Black Equality*. Princeton, NJ: Princeton University Press, 2001.

Newby, I. A. *Challenge to the Court: Social Scientists and the Defense of Segregation, 1954–1966*. Baton Rouge: Louisiana State University Press, 1967.

Newfield, Jack. *Prophetic Minority*. New York: Dutton, 1966.

Newman, Mark. *Divine Agitators: The Delta Ministry and Civil Rights in Mississippi*. Athens: University of Georgia Press, 2004.

Newton, Huey P. *Revolutionary Suicide*. New York: Harcourt Brace Jovanovich, 1973.

Newton, Huey P. *To Die for the People: The Writings of Huey P. Newton*. New York: Random House, 1972.

Newton, Huey P., and Erik H. Erikson. *In Search of Common Ground*. New York: Norton, 1973.

Newton, Michael. *Bitter Grain*. Los Angeles: Holloway House, 1980.

Nichols, David A. *A Matter of Justice: Eisenhower and the Beginning of the Civil Rights Revolution*. New York: Simon and Schuster, 2007.

Niven, David. *The Politics of Injustice: The Kennedys, the Freedom Rides, and the Electoral Consequences of a Moral Compromise*. Knoxville: University of Tennessee Press, 2003.

Noble, Phil. *Beyond the Burning Bus: The Civil Rights Revolution in a Southern Town*. Montgomery, AL: NewSouth Books, 2003.

Norrell, Robert J. *Reaping the Whirlwind: The Civil Rights Movement in Tuskegee*. New York: Knopf, 1985.

Nossiter, Adam. *Of Long Memory: Mississippi and the Murder of Medgar Evers*. Reading, MA: Addison-Wesley, 1994.

Oates, Stephen B. *Let the Trumpet Sound: The Life of Martin Luther King, Jr.* New York: Harper and Row, 1982.

Ogbar, Jeffrey O. G. *Black Power: Radical Politics and African American Identity.* Baltimore: Johns Hopkins University Press, 2004.

Olsen, Jack. *Last Man Standing: The Tragedy and Triumph of Geronimo Pratt.* Garden City, NY: Doubleday, 2000.

Olson, Lynne. *Freedom's Daughters: The Unsung Heroines of the Civil Rights Movement from 1830 to 1970.* New York: Scribner, 2001.

O'Neill, Timothy. *Bakke & the Politics of Equality: Friends and Foes in the Classroom of Litigation.* Middletown, CT: Wesleyan University Press, 1984.

O'Neill, William. *Coming Apart: An Informal History of America in the 1960s.* Chicago: Quadrangle, 1971.

Oppenheimer, Martin. *The Sit-In Movement of 1960.* Brooklyn, NY: Carlson, 1989.

O'Reilly, Kenneth. *Racial Matters: The FBI's Secret File on Black America, 1960–1972.* New York: Free Press, 1989.

Orfield, Gary. *The Reconstruction of Southern Education: The Schools and the 1964 Civil Rights Act.* New York: Wiley-Interscience, 1969.

Ownby, Ted, ed. *The Role of Ideas in the Civil Rights South.* Jackson: University Press of Mississippi, 2002.

Panetta, Leon, and Peter Gall. *Bring Us Together: The Nixon Team and Civil Rights Retreat.* Philadelphia: J. B. Lippincott, 1971.

Paris, Peter. *Black Leaders in Conflict: Joseph H. Jackson, Martin Luther King, Jr., Malcolm X, Adam Clayton Powell, Jr.* New York: Pilgrim Press, 1978.

Parker, Frank R. *Black Votes Count: Political Empowerment in Mississippi after 1965.* Chapel Hill: University of North Carolina Press, 1990.

Parks, Rosa, with Jim Haskins. *Rosa Parks: My Story.* New York: Dial, 1992.

Parris, Guichard, and Lester Brooks. *Blacks in the City: A History of the National Urban League.* Boston: Little, Brown, 1971.

Parsons, Sarah Mitchell. *From Southern Wrongs to Civil Rights: The Memoir of a White Civil Rights Activist.* Tuscaloosa: University of Alabama Press, 2000.

Patterson, James T. *America's Struggle against Poverty, 1900–1980.* Cambridge, MA: Harvard University Press, 1981.

Patterson, James T. Brown v. Board of Education: *A Civil Rights Milestone and Its Troubled Legacy.* New York: Oxford University Press, 2001.

Pauley, Garth. *LBJ's American Promise: The 1965 Voting Rights Address.* College Station: Texas A&M University Press, 2007.

Payne, Charles M. *I've Got the Light of Freedom: The Organizing Tradition and the Mississippi Freedom Struggle.* Berkeley: University of California Press, 1995.

Peake, Thomas R. *Keeping the Dream Alive: A History of the Southern Christian Leadership Conference from King to the 1980s*. New York: Peter Lang, 1987.

Pearson, Hugh. *The Shadow of the Panther: Huey Newton and the Price of Black Power in America*. Reading, MA: Addison-Wesley, 1994.

Pearson, Hugh. *When Harlem Nearly Killed King: The 1958 Stabbing of Dr. Martin Luther King, Jr.* New York: Seven Stories Press, 2002.

Peck, James. *Freedom Ride*. New York: Simon and Schuster, 1962.

Peeks, Edward. *The Long Struggle for Black Power*. New York: Scribner's Sons, 1971.

Pekar, Harvey, Paul Buhle, and Gary Dumm. *Students for a Democratic Society: A Graphic History*. New York: Hill and Wang, 2008.

Pepper, William. *An Act of State: The Execution of Martin Luther King*. London: Verso, 2003.

Perkins, Margo V. *Autobiography as Activism: Three Black Women of the Sixties*. Jackson: University Press of Mississippi, 2000.

Perry, Bruce. *Malcolm: The Life of a Man Who Changed Black America*. Barrytown, NY: Station Hill, 1991.

Petalson, J. W. *Fifty-Eight Lonely Men: Southern Federal Judges and School Desegregation*. Urbana: University of Illinois Press, 1971.

Pettigrew, Thomas. *A Profile of the Negro American*. Princeton, NJ: Van Nostrand, 1964.

Pfeffer, Paula F. *A. Philip Randolph, Pioneer of the Civil Rights Movement*. Baton Rouge: Louisiana State University Press, 1996.

Pierce, Richard B. *Polite Protest: The Political Economy of Race in Indianapolis, 1920–1970*. Bloomington: Indiana University Press, 2005.

Pinkney, Alphonso. *The Committed: White Activists in the Civil Rights Movement*. New Haven, CT: College and University Press, 1968.

Piven, Frances Fox, and Richard Cloward. *Poor People's Movements: Why They Succeed, How They Fail*. New York: Pantheon, 1977.

Plummer, Brenda Gayle. *Rising Wind: Black Americans and U.S. Foreign Affairs, 1935–1960*. Chapel Hill: University of North Carolina Press, 1996.

Plummer, Brenda Gayle, ed. *Window on Freedom: Race, Civil Rights, and Foreign Affairs, 1945–1988*. Chapel Hill: University of North Carolina Press, 2003.

Podair, Jerald. *Bayard Rustin: American Dreamer*. Lanham, MD: Rowman and Littlefield, 2008.

Polsgrove, Carol. *Divided Minds: Intellectuals and the Civil Rights Movement*. New York: W. W. Norton, 2001.

Posner, Gerald L. *Killing the Dream: James Earl Ray and the Assassination of Martin Luther King, Jr.* New York: Random House, 1998.

Powledge, Fred. *Black Power, White Resistance: Notes on the New Civil War.* Cleveland: World, 1967.

Powledge, Fred. *Free at Last? The Civil Rights Movement and the People Who Made It.* Boston: Little, Brown, 1991.

Pratt, Robert A. *The Color of Their Skin: Education and Race in Richmond, Virginia, 1954–1989.* Charlottesville: University Press of Virginia, 1992.

Price, Steven, ed. *Civil Rights, Volume 2, 1967–68,* New York: Facts on File, 1973.

Pritchett, Wendell. *Brownsville, Brooklyn: Blacks, Jews and the Changing Face of the Ghetto.* Chicago: University of Chicago Press, 2002.

Proudfoot, Merrill. *Diary of a Sit-In.* Chapel Hill: University of North Carolina Press, 1962.

Quadagno, Jill. *The Color of Welfare: How Racism Undermined the War on Poverty.* New York: Oxford University Press, 1994.

Queen, Edward L. *In the South the Baptists Are the Center of Gravity: Southern Baptists and Social Change, 1930–1980.* Brooklyn, NY: Carlson, 1991.

Rabby, Glenda Alice. *Pain and the Promise: The Struggle for Civil Rights in Tallahassee, Florida.* Athens: University of Georgia Press, 1999.

Rae, Douglas W., and Paul Bass. *Murder in the Model City: The Black Panthers, Yale, and the Redemption of a Killer.* New York: Basic, 2006.

Raines, Howell. *My Soul is Rested: Movement Days in the Deep South Remembered.* New York: G. P. Putnam, 1977.

Rainwater, Lee, and William L. Yancey. *The Moynihan Report and the Politics of Controversy: A Trans-Action Social Science and Public Policy Report.* Cambridge, MA: MIT Press, 1967.

Ralph, James R. *Northern Protest: Martin Luther King, Jr., Chicago, and the Civil Rights Movement.* Cambridge, MA: Harvard University Press, 1993.

Ransby, Barbara. *Ella Baker & the Black Freedom Movement: A Radical Democratic Vision.* Chapel Hill: University of North Carolina Press, 2003.

Reavis, Dick J. *If White Kids Die: Memories of a Civil Rights Movement Volunteer.* Denton: University of North Texas Press, 2001.

Record, Wilson, and Jane C. Record, eds. *Little Rock, U.S.A.: Materials for Analysis.* San Francisco: Chandler, 1960.

Reddick, Lawrence D., Jr. *Crusader without Violence: A Biography of Martin Luther King, Jr.* New York: Harper, 1959.

Reed, Adolph. *Stirrings in the Jug: Black Politics in the Post-Segregation Era.* Minneapolis: University of Minnesota Press, 1999.

Reed, Christopher Robert. *The Chicago NAACP and the Rise of Black Professional Leadership, 1910–1966.* Bloomington: Indiana University Press, 1997.

Reed, Merl E. *Seedtime for the Modern Civil Rights Movement: The President's Committee on Fair Employment Practice, 1941–1946.* Baton Rouge: Louisiana State University Press, 1991.

Reed, Roy. *Faubus: The Life and Times of an American Prodigal.* Fayetteville: University of Arkansas Press, 1997.

Reynolds, Barbara. *Jesse Jackson: The Man, the Movement, the Myth.* Chicago: Nelson-Hall, 1975.

Rhodes, Jane. *Framing the Panthers: The Spectacular Rise of a Black Power Icon.* New York: New Press, 2006.

Richardson, James. *Willie Brown: A Biography.* Berkeley: University of California Press, 1996.

Riches, William T. Martin. *The Civil Rights Movement: Struggle and Resistance.* New York: St. Martin's Press, 1997.

Rieder, Jonathan. *The Word of the Lord Is Upon Me: The Righteous Performance of Martin Luther King, Jr.* Cambridge, MA: Belknap Press, 2008.

Roberts, Gene, and Hank Klibanoff. *The Race Beat: The Press, the Civil Rights Struggle, and the Awakening of a Nation.* New York: Knopf, 2006.

Robinson, Amelia Boynton. *Bridge across Jordan.* Washington, DC: Schiller Institute, 1991.

Robinson, Armstead L., and Patricia Sullivan, eds. *New Directions in Civil Rights Studies.* Charlottesville: University Press of Virginia, 1991.

Robinson, Dean. *Black Nationalism in American Politics and Thought.* Cambridge, UK: Cambridge University Press, 2001.

Robinson, Jo Ann Gibson. *The Montgomery Bus Boycott and the Women Who Started It: The Memoir of Jo Ann Gibson Robinson.* Knoxville: University of Tennessee Press, 1987.

Robinson, Lewis G. *The Making of a Man: An Autobiography.* Cleveland: Green, 1970.

Robnett, Belinda. *How Long? How Long? African-American Women in the Struggle for Civil Rights.* New York: Oxford University Press, 1997.

Roche, Jeff. *Restructured Resistance: The Silbey Commission and the Politics of Desegregation in Georgia.* Athens: University of Georgia Press, 1998.

Rodgers, Harrell R., and Charles S. Bullock III. *Law and Social Change: Civil Rights Laws and Their Consequences.* New York: McGraw-Hill, 1972.

Rogers, Kim Lacy. "Oral History and the History of the Civil Rights Movement." *Journal of American History* 75 (1988): 567–576.

Rogers, Kim Lacy. *Righteous Lives: Narratives of the New Orleans Civil Rights Movement.* New York: New York University Press, 1993.

Rojas, Fabio. *From Black Power to Black Studies: How a Radical Social Movement Became an Academic Discipline*. Baltimore: Johns Hopkins University Press, 2007.

Romano, Renee C. *Race Mixing: Black-White Marriage in Postwar America*. Cambridge, MA: Harvard University Press, 2003.

Romano, Renee C., and Leigh Raiford, eds. *The Civil Rights Movement in American Memory*. Athens: University of Georgia Press, 2006.

Rorabaugh, W. J. *Berkeley at War: The 1960s*. New York: Oxford University Press, 1989.

Rosenberg, Jonathan. *How Far the Promised Land? World Affairs and the American Civil Rights Movement from the First World War to Vietnam*. Princeton, NJ: Princeton University Press, 2006.

Rosenberg, Jonathan. *Kennedy, Johnson, and the Quest for Justice: The Civil Rights Tapes*. New York: Norton, 2003.

Ross, James Robert. *The War Within: Violence or Nonviolence in the Black Revolution*. New York: Sheed and Ward, 1971.

Rossinow, Doug. *Visions of Progress: The Left-Liberal Tradition in America*. Philadelphia: University of Pennsylvania Press, 2008.

Rothschild, Mary Aickin. *A Case of Black and White: Northern Volunteers and the Southern Freedom Summers, 1964–1965*. Westport, CT: Greenwood Press, 1982.

Rubel, David. *The Coming Free*. New York: DK, 2005.

Rustin, Bayard. *Down the Line: The Collected Writings of Bayard Rustin*. Chicago: Quadrangle, 1971.

Rustin, Bayard. *Strategies for Freedom: The Changing Patterns of Black Protest*. New York: Columbia University Press, 1976.

Sales, William W., Jr. *From Civil Rights to Black Liberation: Malcolm X and the Organization of Afro-American Unity*. Boston: South End Press, 1994.

Salmond, John A. *"My Mind Set on Freedom": A History of the Civil Rights Movement, 1954–1968*. Chicago: Ivan R. Dee, 1997.

Salter, John R., Jr. *Jackson, Mississippi: An American Chronicle of Struggle and Schism*. Hicksville, NY: Exposition Press, 1979.

Sanchez, Sonia. *Homecoming*. Detroit: Broadside Press, 1971.

Sanders-Cassell, Katrina M. *Intelligent and Effective Direction: The Fisk University Race Relations Institute and the Struggle for Civil Rights, 1944–1969*. New York: Peter Lang, 2005.

Sarratt, Reed. *The Ordeal of Desegregation: The First Decade*. New York: Harper and Row, 1966.

Saunders, Doris E. *The Day They Marched*. Chicago: Johnson, 1963.

Saunders, Doris E., ed. *The Kennedy Years and the Negro*. Chicago: Johnson, 1964.

Savage, Barbara Dianne. *Broadcasting Freedom: Radio, War, and the Politics of Race, 1938–1948*. Chapel Hill: University of North Carolina Press, 1999.

Sawyer, Grant, with R. T. King and Gary E. Elliott. *Hang Tough! Grant Sawyer: An Activist in the Governor's Mansion*. Reno: University of Nevada Oral History Program, 1993.

Schneider, Mark Robert. *We Return Fighting: The Civil Rights Movement in the Jazz Age*. Boston: Northeastern University Press, 2002.

Schneier, Marc. *Shared Dreams: Martin Luther King, Jr. and the Jewish Community*. Woodstock, VT: Jewish Lights, 1999.

Schulke, Flip. *He Had a Dream: Martin Luther King, Jr., and the Civil Rights Movement*. New York: Norton, 1995.

Schultz, Debra L. *Going South: Jewish Women in the Civil Rights Movement*. New York: New York University Press, 2001.

Schwartz, Bernard. *Swann's Way: The School Busing Case and the Supreme Court*. New York: Oxford University Press, 1986.

Scott, John H., with Cleo Scott Brown. *Witness to the Truth: My Struggle for Human Rights in Louisiana*. Columbia: University of South Carolina Press, 2003.

Scott, Robert L., and Wayne Brockriede. *The Rhetoric of Black Power*. New York: Harper and Row, 1969.

Seale, Bobby. *A Lonely Rage: The Autobiography of Bobby Seale*. New York: Times, 1978.

Seale, Bobby. *Seize the Time: The Story of the Black Panther Party and Huey P. Newton*. New York: Random House, 1970.

Seeger, Pete, and Bob Reiser. *Everybody Says Freedom*. New York: W. W. Norton, 1989.

Selby, Gary S. *Martin Luther King and the Rhetoric of Freedom: The Exodus Narrative in America's Struggle for Civil Rights*. Waco, TX: Baylor University Press, 2008.

Self, Robert O. *American Babylon: Race and the Struggle for Postwar Oakland*. Princeton, NJ: Princeton University Press, 2003.

Self, Robert O. "'To Plan Our Liberation': Black Power and the Politics of Place in Oakland, California, 1965–1977." *Journal of Urban History* 26 (2000): 759–792.

Sellers, Cleveland, with Robert Terrell. *The River of No Return: The Autobiography of a Black Militant and the Life and Death of SNCC*. New York: William Morrow, 1973.

Senna, Carl. *The Black Press and the Struggle for Civil Rights*. New York: Franklin Watts, 1993.

Shakoor, Jordana Y. *Civil Rights Childhood*. Jackson: University Press of Mississippi, 1999.

Shakur, Assata. *Assata: An Autobiography*. Westport, CT: Lawrence Hill, 1987.

Shames, Stephen. *The Black Panthers*. New York: Aperture, 2006.

Shattuck, Gardiner H. *Episcopalians and Race: Civil War to Civil Rights*. Lexington: University Press of Kentucky, 2000.

Shultz, Debra. *Going South: Jewish Women in the Civil Rights Movement*. New York: New York University Press, 2001.

Sikora, Frank. *The Judge: The Life & Opinions of Alabama's Frank M. Johnson, Jr.* Montgomery, AL: NewSouth Books, 2007.

Sikora, Frank. *Until Justice Rolls Down: The Birmingham Church Bombing Case*. Tuscaloosa: University of Alabama Press, 2005.

Silberman, Charles E. *Crisis in Black and White*. New York: Random House, 1964.

Silver, James W. *Running Scared: Silver in Mississippi*. Jackson: University Press of Mississippi, 1984.

Singh, Nikhil Pal. *Black Is a Country: Race and the Unfinished Struggle for Democracy*. Cambridge, MA: Harvard University Press, 2004.

Sitkoff, Harvard. *King: Pilgrimage to the Mountaintop*. New York: Hill and Wang, 2007.

Sitkoff, Harvard. *A New Deal for Blacks: The Emergence of Civil Rights as a National Issue*. New York: Oxford University Press, 1978.

Sitkoff, Harvard. *The Struggle for Black Equality, 1954–1992*. New York: Hill and Wang, 1993.

Smead, Howard. *Blood Justice: The Lynching of Mack Charles Parker*. New York: Oxford University Press, 1986.

Smethurst, James Edward. *The Black Arts Movement: Literary Nationalism in the 1960s and 1970s*. Chapel Hill: University of North Carolina Press, 2005.

Smith, C. Fraser. *Here Lies Jim Crow: Civil Rights in Maryland*. Baltimore: Johns Hopkins University Press, 2008.

Smith, Frank. *Congressman from Mississippi*. New York: Pantheon, 1964.

Smith, Jennifer B. *An International History of the Black Panther Party*. New York: Garland, 1999.

Smith, Lillian. *Now Is the Time*. New York: Viking Press, 1955.

Smith, R. C. *They Closed Their Schools: Prince Edward County, Virginia, 1951–1964*. Chapel Hill: University of North Carolina Press, 1965.

Smith, Suzanne E. *Dancing in the Street: Motown and the Cultural Politics of Detroit*. Cambridge, MA: Harvard University Press, 1999.

Sobel, Lester, ed. *Civil Rights, 1960–66*, New York: Facts on File, 1967.

Sokol, Jason. *There Goes My Everything: White Southerners in the Age of Civil Rights, 1945–1975*. New York: Knopf, 2006.

Sosna, Morton. *In Search of the Silent South: Southern Liberals and the Race Issue*. New York: Columbia University Press, 1977.

Springer, Kimberly. *Living for the Revolution: Black Feminist Organizations, 1968–1980*. Durham, NC: Duke University Press, 2005.

Springer, Kimberly, ed. *Still Lifting, Still Climbing: Contemporary African American Women's Activism*. New York: New York University Press, 1999.

Stanley, Harold W. *Voter Mobilization and the Politics of Race*. New York: Praeger, 1987.

Stanton, Mary. *Freedom Walk: Mississippi or Bust*. Jackson: University Press of Mississippi, 2003.

Stanton, Mary. *From Selma to Sorrow: The Life and Death of Viola Liuzzo*. Athens: University of Georgia Press, 1998.

Stanton, Mary. *Journey toward Justice: Juliette Hampton Morgan and the Montgomery Bus Boycott*. Athens: University of Georgia Press, 2006.

Stern, Mark. *Kennedy, Johnson, and Civil Rights*. New Brunswick, NJ: Rutgers University Press, 1992.

Stockley, Grif. *Daisy Bates: Civil Rights Crusader from Arkansas*. Jackson: University Press of Mississippi, 2005.

Stone, Willie. *I Was a Black Panther, as Told to Chuck Moore*. Garden City, NY: Doubleday, 1970.

Stoper, Emily. *The Student Nonviolent Coordinating Committee: The Growth of Radicalism in a Civil Rights Organization*. Brooklyn, NY: Carlson, 1989.

Strain, Christopher B. *Pure Fire: Self-Defense as Activism in the Civil Rights Era*. Athens: University of Georgia Press, 2005.

Street, Joe. *The Culture War in the Civil Rights Movement*. Gainesville: University Press of Florida, 2007.

Strickland, Arvarh E. *History of the Chicago Urban League*. Urbana: University of Illinois Press, 1966.

Sugarman, Tracy. *Stranger at the Gates: A Summer in Mississippi*. New York: Hill and Wang, 1966.

Sugrue, Thomas J. "Affirmative Action from Below: Civil Rights, the Building Trades, and the Politics of Racial Equality in the Urban North, 1945–1969." *Journal of American History* 91 (2004): 145–173.

Sugrue, Thomas J. *The Origins of the Urban Crisis: Race and Inequality in Postwar Detroit*. Princeton, NJ: Princeton University Press, 1996.

Sullivan, Leon H. *Build, Brother, Build*. Philadelphia: Macrae Smith, 1969.

Sullivan, Patricia. *Days of Hope: Race and Democracy in the New Deal Era*. Chapel Hill: University of North Carolina Press, 1996.

Sullivan, Patricia, ed. *Freedom Writer: Virginia Foster Durr, Letters from the Civil Rights Years*. New York: Routledge, 2003.

Sunnemark, Fredrik. *Ring Out Freedom! The Voice of Martin Luther King, Jr. and the Making of the Civil Rights Movement*. Bloomington: Indiana University Press, 2004.

Sutherland, Elizabeth. *Letters from Mississippi*. New York: McGraw-Hill, 1965.

Sweeney, James R., ed. *Race, Reason, and Massive Resistance: The Diary of David J. Mays, 1954–1959*. Athens: University of Georgia Press, 2008.

Taylor, Clarence. *Knocking at Our Own Door: Milton A. Galamison and the Struggle to Integrate New York City Schools*. New York: Columbia University Press, 1997.

Taylor, Quintard. *The Forging of a Black Community: Seattle's Central District from 1870 through the Civil Rights Era*. Seattle: University of Washington Press, 1994.

Thelen, David. "Becoming Martin Luther King, Jr.: An Introduction," *Journal of American History* 78 (1991): 11–22.

Theoharis, Jeanne, and Komozi Woodard, eds. *Groundwork: Local Black Freedom Movements in America*. New York: New York University Press, 2005.

Theoharis, Jeanne, Komozi Woodard, and Matthew Countryman, eds. *Freedom North: Black Freedom Struggles Outside the South, 1940–1980*. New York: Palgrave Macmillan, 2003.

Thomas-Houston, Marilyn M. *"Stony the Road" to Change: Black Mississippians and the Culture of Social Relations*. Cambridge, UK: Cambridge University Press, 2004.

Thompson, Heather Ann. *Whose Detroit? Politics, Labor, and Race in a Modern American City*. Ithaca, NY: Cornell University Press, 2001.

Thornbrough, Emma Lou. *Indiana Blacks in the Twentieth Century*. Bloomington: Indiana University Press, 2000.

Thurber, Timothy. *The Politics of Equality: Hubert H. Humphrey and the African American Freedom Struggle*. New York: Columbia University Press, 1999.

Till-Mobley, Mamie, and Christopher Benson. *Death of Innocence: The Story of the Hate Crime that Changed America*. New York: Ballantine, 2003.

Torres, Sasha. *Black, White, and in Color: Television and Black Civil Rights*. Princeton, NJ: Princeton University Press, 2003.

Travis, Dempsey. *An Autobiography of Black Politics*. Chicago: Urban Research Institute, 1987.

Tsesis, Alexander. *We Shall Overcome: A History of Civil Rights and the Law*. New Haven, CT: Yale University Press, 2008.

Tuck, Stephen G. N. *Beyond Atlanta: The Struggle for Racial Equality in Georgia, 1940–1980*. Athens: University of Georgia Press, 2001.

Tushnet, Mark V. *Making Civil Rights Law: Thurgood Marshall and the Supreme Court, 1936–1961*. New York: Oxford University Press, 1994.

Tushnet, Mark V. *Making Constitutional Law: Thurgood Marshall and the Supreme Court, 1961–1991*. New York: Oxford University Press, 1997.

Tushnet, Mark V. *The NAACP's Legal Strategy against Segregated Education, 1925–1950*. Chapel Hill: University of North Carolina Press, 1987.

Tyson, Timothy B. *Blood Done Sign My Name*. New York: Crown, 2004.

Tyson, Timothy B. *Radio Free Dixie: Robert F. Williams and the Roots of Black Power*. Chapel Hill: University of North Carolina Press, 1999.

Tyson, Timothy B. "Robert F. Williams, 'Black Power,' and the Roots of the African American Freedom Struggle." *Journal of American History* 85 (1998): 540–570.

Umoja, Akinyele O. "Ballots and Bullets: A Comparative Analysis of Armed Resistance in the Civil Rights Movement." *Journal of Black Studies* 32 (2002): 558–578.

Valk, Anne M. *Radical Sisters: Second-Wave Feminism and Black Liberation in Washington, D.C.* Urbana: University of Illinois Press, 2008.

Van Deburg, William. *New Day in Babylon: The Black Power Movement and American Culture, 1965–1975*. Chicago: University of Chicago Press, 1992.

Vander Zanden, James W. *Race Relations in Transition: The Segregation Crisis in the South*. New York: Random House, 1965.

Verney, Kevern. *Black Civil Rights in America*. New York: Routledge, 2000.

Viorst, Milton. *Fire in the Streets: America in the 1960s*. Simon and Schuster, 1980.

Vivian, C. T. *Black Power and the American Myth*. Philadelphia: Fortress Press, 1970.

Vollers, Maryanne. *Ghosts of Mississippi: The Murder of Medgar Evers, the Trials of Byron de la Beckwith, and the Haunting of the New South*. Boston: Little, Brown, 1995.

Von Eschen, Penny. *Race against Empire: Black Americans and Anticolonialism, 1937–1957*. Ithaca, NY: Cornell University Press, 1997.

Von Hoffman, Nicholas. *Mississippi Notebook*. New York: David White, 1964.

Walker, Jack L. *Sit-Ins in Atlanta*. New York: McGraw-Hill, 1964.

Walker, Melissa. *Down from the Mountaintop: Black Women's Novels in the Wake of the Civil Rights Movement, 1966–1989*. New Haven, CT: Yale University Press, 1991.

Wall, Wendy L. *Inventing the American Way: The Politics of Consensus from the New Deal to the Civil Rights Movement*. New York: Oxford University Press, 2008.

Wallenstein, Peter, ed. *Higher Education and the Civil Rights Movement: White Supremacy, Black Southerners, and College Campuses*. Gainesville: University Press of Florida, 2008.

Walters, Ron. *Pan-Africanism in the African Diaspora: An Analysis of Modern Afrocentric Political Movements*. Detroit: Wayne State University Press, 1993.

Walton, Hanes, Jr. *The Political Philosophy of Martin Luther King, Jr.* Westport, CT: Greenwood Press, 1971.

Walton, Hanes, Jr. *When the Marching Stopped: The Politics of Civil Rights Regulatory Agencies*. Albany: State University of New York Press, 1988.

Ward, Brian. *Just My Soul Responding: Rhythm and Blues, Black Consciousness, and Race Relations*. Berkeley: University of California Press, 1998.

Ward, Brian, ed. *Media, Culture, and the Modern African American Freedom Struggle*. Gainesville: University Press of Florida, 2001.

Ward, Brian. *Radio and the Struggle for Civil Rights in the South*. Gainesville: University Press of Florida, 2006.

Ward, Brian, and Tony Badger, eds. *The Making of Martin Luther King and the Civil Rights Movement*. New York: New York University Press, 1996.

Ward, Hiley H. *Prophet of the Black Nation*. Philadelphia: Pilgrim Press, 1969.

Warren, Dan R. *If It Takes All Summer: Martin Luther King, the KKK, and States' Rights in St. Augustine, 1964*. Tuscaloosa: University of Alabama Press, 2008.

Warren, Robert Penn. *Who Speaks for the Negro?* New York: Random House, 1965.

Washington, James M., ed. *I Have a Dream: Writings and Speeches that Changed the World*. San Francisco: HarperSanFrancisco, 2003.

Washington, James M., ed. *A Testament of Hope: The Essential Writings of Martin Luther King, Jr.* San Francisco: Harper and Row, 1986.

Washington, Paul M., with David McI. Gracie. *Other Sheep I Have: The Autobiography of Father Paul M. Washington*. Philadelphia: Temple University Press, 1994.

Waskow, Arthur I. *From Race Riot to Sit-In, 1919 and the 1960s: A Study in the Connections between Conflict and Violence*. Garden City, NY: Doubleday, 1966.

Watson, Denton L. "Assessing the Role of the NAACP in the Civil Rights Movement." *Historian* 55 (1993): 453–469.

Watson, Denton L. *Lion in the Lobby: Clarence Mitchell Jr.'s Struggle for the Passage of Civil Rights Laws.* New York: William Morrow, 1990.

Watters, Pat. *Down to Now: Reflections on the Southern Civil Rights Movement.* New York: Pantheon, 1971.

Watters, Pat, and Reese Cleghorn. *Climbing Jacob's Ladder: The Arrival of Negroes in Southern Politics.* New York: Harcourt, Brace and World, 1967.

Watts, Jerry Gafio. *Amiri Baraka: The Politics and Art of a Black Intellectual.* New York: New York University Press, 2001.

Webb, Clive. *Fight against Fear: Southern Jews and Black Civil Rights.* Athens: University of Georgia Press, 2001.

Webb, Sheyann, and Rachel West Nelson, as told to Frank Sikora. *Selma, Lord, Selma: Girlhood Memories of the Civil-Rights Days.* Tuscaloosa: University of Alabama Press, 1980.

Weill, Susan. *In a Madhouse's Din: Civil Rights Coverage by Mississippi's Daily Press, 1948–1968.* Westport, CT: Praeger, 2002.

Weisbrot, Robert. *Freedom Bound: A History of America's Civil Rights Movement.* New York: W. W. Norton, 1990.

Weiss, Nancy J. *Whitney M. Young, Jr., and the Struggle for Civil Rights.* Princeton, NJ: Princeton University Press, 1989.

Wendt, Simon. *The Spirit and the Shotgun: Armed Resistance and the Struggle for Civil Rights.* Gainesville: University Press of Florida, 2007.

Wendt, Simon. "'Urge People Not to Carry Guns': Armed Self Defense in the Louisiana Civil Rights Movement and the Radicalization of the Congress of Racial Equality." *Louisiana History* 45 (2004): 261–286.

West, Thomas, and James Mooney. *To Redeem a Nation: A History and Anthology of the Civil Rights Movement.* Malden, MA: Wiley-Blackwell, 1993.

Westin, Alan F. *Freedom Now! The Civil Rights Struggle in America.* New York: Basic, 1964.

Wexler, Sanford. *An Eyewitness History of the Civil Rights Movement.* New York: Checkmark, 1999.

Whalen, Charles, and Barbara Whalen. *The Longest Debate: A Legislative History of the 1964 Civil Rights Act.* Cabin John, MD: Seven Locks Press, 1985.

Whitaker, Matthew C. *Race Work: The Rise of Civil Rights in the Urban West.* Lincoln: University of Nebraska Press, 2005.

White, Deborah Gray. *Too Heavy a Load: Black Women in Defense of Themselves, 1894–1994.* New York: Norton, 1999.

White, E. Francis. "Africa on My Mind: Gender, Counter Discourse and African American Nationalism." *Journal of Women's History* 2 (1990): 73–97.

White, George, Jr. *Holding the Line: Race, Racism, and American Foreign Policy toward Africa, 1953–1961*. Lanham, MD: Rowman and Littlefield, 2005.

White, Marjorie L., and Andrew M. Manis, eds. *Birmingham's Revolutionaries: Fred Shuttlesworth and the Alabama Christian Movement for Civil Rights*. Macon, GA: Mercer University Press, 2000.

Whitfield, Stephen J. *A Death in the Delta: The Story of Emmett Till*. New York: Free Press, 1988.

Whitt, Margaret Earley, ed. *Short Stories of the Civil Rights Movement, an Anthology*. Athens: University of Georgia Press, 2006.

Wilhoit, Francis M. *The Politics of Massive Resistance*. New York: G. Braziller, 1973.

Wilkins, Roy, with Tom Mathews. *Standing Fast: The Autobiography of Roy Wilkins*. New York: Viking Press, 1982.

Wilkinson, J. Harvie, III. *From Brown to Bakke: The Supreme Court and School Integration, 1954–1978*. New York: Oxford University Press, 1981.

Williams, Cecil J. *Freedom & Justice: Four Decades of the Civil Rights Struggle as Seen by a Black Photographer of the Deep South*. Macon, GA: Mercer University Press, 1995.

Williams, Donnie, with Wayne Greenhaw. *The Thunder of Angels: The Montgomery Bus Boycott and the People Who Broke the Back of Jim Crow*. Chicago: Lawrence Hill, 2006.

Williams, Johnny E. *African American Religion and the Civil Rights Movement in Arkansas*. Jackson: University Press of Mississippi, 2003.

Williams, Juan. *Eyes on the Prize: America's Civil Rights Years, 1954–1965*. New York: Viking Press, 1987.

Williams, Juan, ed. *My Soul Looks Back in Wonder: Voices of the Civil Rights Experience*. New York: AARP/Sterling, 2004.

Williams, Rhonda Y. *The Politics of Public Housing: Black Women's Struggles against Urban Inequality*. New York: Oxford University Press, 2004.

Williams, Robert F. *Negroes with Guns*. New York: Marzani and Munsell, 1962.

Williams, Yohurhu. *Black Politics/White Power: Civil Rights, Black Power, and the Black Panthers in New Haven*. St. James, NY: Brandywine Press, 2000.

Williamson, Joy Ann. *Black Power on Campus, the University of Illinois, 1965–1975*. Urbana: University of Illinois Press, 2003.

Williamson, Joy Ann. *Radicalizing the Ebony Tower: Black Colleges and the Black Freedom Struggle in Mississippi*. New York: Teachers College Press, 2008.

Wirt, Frederick M. *Politics of Southern Equality: Law and Social Change in a Mississippi County*. Chicago: Aldine, 1970.

Wirt, Frederick M. *"We Ain't What We Was": Civil Rights in the New South.* Durham, NC: Duke University Press, 1997.

Witherspoon, William R. *Martin Luther King, Jr.: To the Mountaintop.* Garden City, NY: Doubleday, 1985.

Witt, Andrew R. *The Black Panthers in the Midwest: The Community Programs and Services of the Black Panther Party, 1966–1977.* New York: Routledge, 2007.

Wolfenstein, Eugene. *The Victims of Democracy: Malcolm X and the Black Revolutionaries.* Berkeley: University of California Press, 1981.

Wolff, Miles. *Lunch at the Five and Ten: The Greensboro Sit-Ins, a Contemporary History.* New York: Stein and Day, 1970.

Wolk, Allan. *The Presidency and Black Civil Rights: Eisenhower to Nixon.* Rutherford, NJ: Fairleigh Dickinson University Press, 1971.

Wolters, Raymond. *The Burden of* Brown*: Thirty Years of School Desegregation.* Knoxville: University of Tennessee Press, 1984.

Wood, Joe, ed. *Malcolm X: In Our Own Image.* New York: St. Martin's Press, 1992.

Woodard, Komozi. *A Nation within a Nation: Amiri Baraka (LeRoi Jones) & Black Power Politics.* Chapel Hill: University of North Carolina Press, 1999.

Woods, Jeff. *Black Struggle, Red Scare: Segregation and Anti-Communism in the South, 1948–1968.* Baton Rouge: Louisiana State University Press, 2004.

Workman, William D. *The Case for the South.* New York: Devin-Adair, 1960.

Wright, Gavin. "The Civil Rights Revolution as Economic History." *Journal of Economic History* 59 (1999): 267–289.

Wright, Nathan, Jr. *Black Power and Urban Unrest: Creative Possibilities.* New York: Hawthorn, 1967.

Wright, Richard. *Black Power: A Record of Reaction in a Land of Pathos.* New York: Harpers and Brother, 1954.

Wrinn, Stephen M. *Civil Rights in the Whitest State: Vermont's Perceptions of Civil Rights, 1945–1968.* Lanham, MD: University Press of America, 1998.

Wynn, Linda T. "The Dawning of a New Day: The Nashville Sit-Ins, Feb.13–May 10, 1960." *Tennessee Historical Quarterly* 50 (1991): 42–54.

X, Malcolm. *The End of White World Supremacy: Four Speeches.* New York: Merlin House, 1971.

X, Malcolm. *Malcolm X on Afro-American History.* New York: Merit, 1967.

X, Malcolm. *Malcolm X Speaks: Selected Speeches and Statements.* New York: Merit, 1965.

X, Malcolm, with Alex Haley. *The Autobiography of Malcolm X.* New York: Ballantine, 1964.

Yarbrough, Tinsley E. *Judge Frank Johnson and Human Rights in Alabama*. Tuscaloosa: University of Alabama Press, 1981.

Yarbrough, Tinsley E. *A Passion for Justice: J. Waties Waring and Civil Rights*. New York: Oxford University Press, 2001.

Young, Albert, ed. *Dissent: Explorations in the History of American Radicalism*. De Kalb: Northern Illinois University Press, 1968.

Young, Andrew. *An Easy Burden: The Civil Rights Movement and the Transformation of America*. New York: HarperCollins, 1996.

Young, Cynthia A. *Soul Power: Culture, Radicalism, and the Making of a U.S. Third World Left*. Durham, NC: Duke University Press, 2006.

Young, Richard P., ed. *Roots of Rebellion: The Evolution of Black Politics and Protest since World War II*. New York: Harper and Row, 1970.

Young, Whitney M., Jr. *Beyond Racism: Building an Open Society*. New York: McGraw-Hill, 1969.

Young, Whitney M., Jr. *To Be Equal*. New York: McGraw-Hill, 1964.

Zepp, Ira G., Jr. *The Social Vision of Martin Luther King, Jr.* Brooklyn, NY: Carlson, 1989.

Zimroth, Peter L. *Perversions of Justice: The Prosecution and Acquittal of the Panther 21*. New York: Viking Press, 1974.

Zinn, Howard. *SNCC: The New Abolitionists*. Boston: Beacon Press, 1964.

Zinn, Howard. *The Southern Mystique*. New York: Knopf, 1964.

# Index